Getting to War

Predicting International Conflict with Mass Media Indicators

W. BEN HUNT

Ann Arbor

THE UNIVERSITY OF MICHIGAN PRESS

Copyright © by the University of Michigan 1997
All rights reserved
Published in the United States of America by
The University of Michigan Press
Manufactured in the United States of America
♾ Printed on acid-free paper

2000   1999   1998   1997   4   3   2   1

A CIP catalog record for this book is available from the British Library

Library of Congress Cataloging-in-Publication Data

Hunt, W. Ben (William Ben)
    Getting to war : predicting international conflict with mass media
  indicators / W. Ben Hunt.
        p.   cm.
    Includes bibliographical references and index.
    ISBN 0-472-10751-8 (cloth)
    1. War—Forecasting.   2. Mass media and war.   3. War in mass
  media.   4. Political indicators.   I. Title.
  U21.2.H83   1997
  355. 02—dc21   96-39405
                                                          CIP

To Jennifer

Contents

Preface

My father is a Winston Churchill fanatic, and he enjoys reminding me of Churchill's politically incorrect dictum regarding authorship. To paraphrase, a book begins as a mistress and gradually becomes a cruel shrew. I shudder to think what Churchill would have said had he ever attempted a dissertation. This book has a dissertation as its seed, although I doubt that my advisors—Robert Keohane, Gary King, and James Alt—will recognize more than a glimmer of what they read so long ago. A special thanks to these three scholars, who provided standards of rigorous thinking and intellectual curiosity that are quite impossible to live up to. They are, of course, absolved from all mistakes that still lurk in the book.

Two anonymous reviewers at the University of Michigan Press were extremely helpful throughout this process, but the lion's share of credit (or blame) for seeing this project through to completion belongs to Colin Day and Malcolm Litchfield. Despite a ridiculously slow author, they never lost faith in this project (or at least never told me so to my face), making them the most wonderful of prescient and steadfast editors.

A variety of people, in no particular order, gave sound counsel and advice on the arguments herein. Warmest thanks, then, to Jacek Kugler, Steven Brams, Youssef Cohen, David Denoon, Alexander Schuessler, Michael Gilligan, Lea Brilmayer, Aaron Friedberg, Bruce Russett, Karl Deutsch, James Rosenau, Robert Powell, Robert Jervis, Joshua Lerner, and Marc Levy. Financial support during the dissertation writing phase was provided by the MacArthur Foundation and the Center for Science and International Affairs at Harvard University. More recently, a Research Challenge Grant and a Goddard Junior Faculty Sabbatical at New York University gave me the necessary time to make necessary revisions.

Finally, despite the Churchill quotes, thanks to my father and mother for their unstinting support and love. As for my wife, Jennifer—well, I would have given up on far more than this book were it not for her.

## CHAPTER 1

The Dilemma of Getting to War

Introduction and Assumptions

This book is concerned with why war occurs when it occurs. My focus, however, is on neither the immediate tactical decision of timing nor the slow changes in relative capabilities that may set the stage for conflict. I do not examine why war breaks out at noon rather than midnight, nor why war breaks out this decade rather than the last, because neither of these issues is particularly helpful in preventing the wars they foretell. The prospects of conflict are too inevitable in the former and too inchoate in the latter to design feasible policies to avoid conflict altogether.

Instead, I want to know when a decision to initiate conflict has been made by the national command structure of the country in question. The length of time between that decision and actual conflict is potentially as short as the seconds it takes to press a button or as long as the years it takes to expand a military-industrial complex. But I find that the political constraints of building domestic support for war prevent initiation from following decision so rapidly as to preclude domestic support or so slowly as to lose that support once created. Certain predictive indicators, based on the existence of these domestic constraints, allow us to anticipate in a meaningful fashion the initiation of war—meaningful in the sense that these measures occur soon enough before conflict to identify the particular issues under dispute and long enough before conflict to perhaps resolve those issues.

The goal here is the identification of *leading indicators* of war. We commonly speak of economic leading indicators—housing starts, factory orders, etc.—and their implications for future economic performance. Fortunes are made and lost on the basis of these indicators; they are analyzed and reported ad nauseam by the news media. But we have no such discussion (or vocabulary) of political leading indicators, even though the events foretold by such indicators are potentially far more momentous than an impending quarter percentage point change in interest rates.

Public opinion polls, when used to predict the outcome of elections, are the closest equivalent in political science to economic leading indicators. The difference, however, is critical. Preelection polls ask people to say how they will actually behave in the future. But, as pollsters are reminded every election day, there is often a significant gap between word and deed. Not only do people frequently fail to vote at all (even if they fit some profile of a "likely voter") in patterns that systematically skew election results, but virtually any incentive to give false information to a pollster will outweigh the nominal social norm to volunteer the truth. Michigan primary voters in 1972 did not admit that they intended to vote for George Wallace for fear of being perceived as racists; Nicaraguan voters in 1990 did not admit that they intended to vote for Chamorro for fear of government retribution; the list is endless. Polls are a valuable predictive tool under certain conditions, but not when talk is cheap or (more to the point in the examples given) when truthful talk is potentially costly. Economists do not construct their leading indicators by asking people how much they intend to consume and produce in the upcoming months for the very good reason that such polls are not particularly accurate. Instead, economists use actual behavior right now to predict actual behavior in the future.

Polls are a doubly problematic predictor of international events because there is no clear population of people to question. Who should pollsters ask if a war is brewing? Why would anyone who knew the answer tell the truth? Like domestic leading economic indicators, our international leading political indicators must be based on behavior rather than stated intentions. But what behavior? If China is shelling the Vietnamese border today, odds are good that they will be shelling the border tomorrow. Artillery fire is obviously an excellent predictor of future interstate conflict, but it is just as obviously a circular indicator with no independent predictive power.

The economic indicators used by the Federal Reserve avoid this behavioral identification problem by simply defining the phenomenon to be predicted in terms of the indicators. That is, if concurrent economic indicators are in the negative range for three months in a row, then the economy is, by definition, in a recession. Conversely, no matter how many people are laid off or how high interest rates climb, the economy is not in an official recession until the magic three-in-a-row condition is met. And since there is a virtual one-to-one correlation between leading economic indicators and concurrent indicators (in fact, they are constructed precisely so that this correlation exists), three negative economic summary leading indicators in succession are, by definition, an excellent predictor of an upcoming recession.

Defining war on the basis of its indicators is not a problem for this project. Although all social phenomena are contentiously defined, and most have that "I know it when I see it" quality used by Potter Stewart to define pornography, war is more sui generis (and recognizable as such) than most. But as the Vietnamese border shelling example suggests, it is just as important that we not define our indicators in terms of the events to be predicted. The behavior noted by the indicators must be highly correlated with war, but it must not be the behavior *of* war, either immediately or precipitantly. For example, troop mobilizations are both nonviolent and an excellent leading indicator of war, yet they have as little independent predictive power as artillery fire.

Inevitably, any leading political indicators found here will overidentify the phenomenon of war. War is (thankfully) as rare as it is catastrophic, and no indicator, not even artillery fire, is a perfect predictor. This is a characteristic of economic indicators as well as political. As Wall Street savants are fond of saying, sharp declines in the stock market have predicted 11 of the past 7 recessions. Both recessions and wars have a distinct class of mediating events—crises—that limit their occurrence and push indicators into overprediction.[1] Crises are generally distinguishable from the calm that precedes them and the conflict that (sometimes) follows them in both scope and type. That is, not only will there be fewer instances of interstate conflict during a crisis than a war, but the type of conflict will differ as well.

Crises, as a class of events, pose difficulties for this research. Since most wars are mediated by crisis, how can we distinguish between leading indicators of crisis and leading indicators of war? In fact, if crisis behavior *determines* whether a given set of conditions will escalate into war or return to peace, then crisis prediction is really the most we can hope to accomplish. To return to the earlier examples of troop mobilization and artillery fire as excellent (although flawed) leading indicators of war, they are even better predictors of international crisis. If one instance of troop mobilization sets off a crisis that escalates into war and another mobilization, under otherwise similar initial circumstances, sets off a crisis that does not escalate, then the troop mobilization per se has no predictive value once the crisis stage is reached.

In many circumstances the leading indicators identified here *are* more accurately described as predictors of crisis, not war, and we should look to the crisis bargaining and negotiation literature to tell us what will happen next. But it is often misleading to compartmentalize events into discrete stages such as "precipitant," "crisis," "resolution," and so on. In truth, the distinction between armed peace, crisis, militarized dispute, and war is rarely neat and clean. What each of these terms has in common is interstate conflict expressed through force, where *war* is just the name we give to the most violent and forceful cases. One would hope that a predictor of war would vary according to type and frequency of the force employed at each stage on the road to war, revealing the participants' preferences and positions along the way. The dynamics of crisis negotiation and bargaining clearly play a crucial role in determining how or if nations get to war, but we should not ignore the parameters in which these dynamics exist or how these parameters change over time. Bargaining and negotiation theories have strong practical applications, *if* one has accurate information concerning each party's preferences. There is nothing in these theories that gives us this information—preferences are taken as given, as exogenous to the issue at hand. I argue that a good leading indicator provides precisely this information, that it can reveal to us how the parties value the issues and options under contention. As such, this work is a necessary complement to crisis behavior research, not a substitute.

And, too, not all wars are preceded by crises, however defined. Surprise attacks still happen in the world, if not on a Pearl Harbor scale at least on a Falklands scale. The hard cases, economic or political, for any leading indicator are those that take professional observers by surprise. In fact, since it is hardly a breakthrough in political science research to find a new way to anticipate what everyone knew would happen anyway, the primary added value of this research must apply to precisely these cases. This is not as small a set of cases at it might first appear. Even if one sees conflict as ultimately inevitable between two countries, the timing of that conflict is not written in stone. In retrospect, it may have surprised no one that Israel finally invaded southern Lebanon, but why invade in 1982 rather than 1980? If we can agree that there is value in identifying the short- to medium-term indicators of a decision for war, or even a decision to escalate interstate conflict, then this is an enterprise worth undertaking.

This is not the first work to attempt to predict wars, and it builds on the foundation of previous efforts.[2] Key to all of these works, as well as my own, is a reliance on decision-making models assuming procedural rationality. Yet most other attempts to predict war rely at least in part on a substantive assumption that rational national leaders seek to maximize security given their propensity for risk,[3] that security is a priori a higher rational good than others. This is one hallmark of "structural neorealism"[4]—the theoretical vantage point of the vast majority of these authors—that national interests (and by extension the interests of national leaders) are substantively defined in terms of national security. My conception is entirely procedural because its operationalization does not limit the determination of utilities to issues of national security. So long as preferences are transitively ordered, my models hold regardless of the substantive rationality or even sanity of the preferences; they hold regardless of the misperceptions that may very well be built into those preferences, and they do not require that all possible preferences or outcomes be identified or evaluated. It is immaterial to this study whether national leaders seek to maximize security, power, prestige, wealth, territory, the spread of some revolutionary ideal, or any other goal; all I assume is that they evaluate some outcomes more highly than others and that they act on the basis of that evaluation.

It is in the construction of a predictive calculus that I part company radically from previous research efforts. By relying almost exclusively on the systemic variables of power distribution and alliances, structural neorealist calculations are constrained by the ponderous nature of these inputs. That is, the distribution of power in the international system changes very slowly, almost imperceptibly. The same can be said for alliances; although we see some major changes occur rapidly, the time between those changes is often measured in decades. The effect of this lack of variation is twofold. First, observation periods shorter than a calendar year are, by and large, either impossible or redundant—impossible if the data is aggregated on a yearly basis (as is usually the case), redundant if the data from one observation period to another is identical. Second, even using observation periods of calendar years, predictions change very little from one observation to another, "locking in" erroneous predictions.

The lack of change in such calculations points out the limited relevance of these systemic variables. Power distribution and alliance portfolios, because they are such broad and general measures, simply do not capture the appropriate variation in international tension. For example, relations between Britain and Argentina in 1982 demonstrate peace, growing tension, war, de-escalation, and peace, all in the same year, all with essentially no changes in power distribution or alliance portfolios. Even if a systemically based calculus predicted that Argentina would initiate war with Britain in 1982, such an operationalization would be incapable of distinguishing between January 1982 and March 1982 and would necessarily generate a similar prediction of war in 1981, 1980, 1979, etc. Operationalizing on the basis of systemic variables alone predicts so much as to end up predicting very little, and such overidentification of the necessary conditions for conflict is of limited practical use.

To be fair, the questions asked by most structural neorealist investigations of international relations are different from my questions. If one is looking for the broad constraints on international behavior that explain, say, changes in systemic polarity over the past 200 years, then annual power distribution data is the most appropriate source of information—likewise if one is looking for the long-term indicators of war. But if one's interests are the short- to medium-term indicators of conflict, other sources of data must be tapped.

The solution is to cut open the systemic shell and extract information from the domestic level.[5] It is here that we find the sources of variation in international conflict that allow for timely predictions. I will examine the theoretical dangers and rewards of this plunge into the domestic level in the concluding chapter. For now I am simply claiming that for a predictive model to be of any practical use, in order to avoid predicting so much as to predict nothing, we must find, in Robert North's words, "a valuational/affective indicator—*hostility, negative leverage, level of threat/violence, or merely the record of past interactions conceived in these terms.*"[6] Such an affective indicator is inherently a unit-level, or nonsystemic, attribute; in fact, the source of the observed hostility might have no relation to the distribution of power or the arrangement of states in the system at all. Such an indicator should be able to take advantage of any number of domestic sources of conflict, including provocative actions by foreign nations, and it should provide short- to medium-term information on future regime policies.

Building on the insights of Karl Deutsch and Alexander George,[7] I begin by specifying the domestic-level phenomenon that drives the predictive calculus. The underlying dilemma modern governments face when they wish to initiate war—how to maintain international secrecy vis-à-vis some target state while at the same time generating domestic support for such a risky future action—provides a window of opportunity for the analyst. By systematically looking at the domestic mass media, we can identify North's affective measure despite contrary statements and actions on the international stage. Furthermore, this equilibrium between maintaining surprise and maintaining support has hypothetical implications for issues other than the timing of war, such as the observed reluctance of democratic states to fight one another.

Having established the formal foundations of a predictive model of interstate conflict, I test it on a variety of data sets and find that the hypothesized mass media indicator is a significant and influential leading indicator of conflictual events, regardless of data set and largely independent of prior conflict. Not only are the predictive results robust, but, since the data are aggregated on a monthly rather than yearly basis, they are extremely timely as well. Including such systemic attributes as the distribution of national capabilities improves the model's specification only slightly, suggesting that this domestic-level indicator accounts for the lion's share of variation.

Next, I attempt to go beyond the prediction of general interstate conflict to identify what form that conflict will likely take. By taking a second cut at the mass media variable, by getting inside the black box of the general indicator, I try to identify the nature of the affective complaint as well as its existence. Such complaints fall into two categories, one that tends to precede diplomatic or economic conflict and one that tends to precede violent military conflict. Furthermore, the two types of affective complaints suggest two different bargaining structures leading to conflict as well as ways in which those structures change over time, generating implications for crisis negotiations and our understanding of the security dilemma.

The final substantive chapter of this book provides an analysis of six cases from U.S. diplomatic history in terms of this predictive framework. The cases were chosen in an attempt to pair examples of military intervention and nonintervention against similar or identical targets in the same general period of time. In particular, I look at events surrounding the forceful response to Iraq in 1991 and the diplomatic response to Iran in 1980; the 1950 military intervention in Korea and the 1948 airlift to Berlin; and the entry into World War I in 1917 rather than 1915, despite the recurrent issue of unrestricted German submarine warfare. The analysis here is not intended as a rigorous test of the models developed previously but, instead, provides historical confirmation of these principles in action.

In conclusion, I explore the theoretical implications of this research. Even if I have been successful in identifying an accurate tool for the prediction of interstate conflict, the question remains whether we have learned anything new about the underlying process of conflict between nations. I argue that these methods identify a heretofore largely untapped link between domestic politics and international behavior and that this approach combines the generality of systemic factors with the explanatory power of unit-level attributes to create both a powerful and specific account of when nations fight.

By no means, however, is this work intended as a comprehensive theory of why nations go to war. Identifying the entire causal process of international conflict is too great a task for these efforts or perhaps any efforts. Like a Grand Unification Theory in physics, a satisfactory comprehensive theory of why nations go to war is currently out of our grasp; like physics, we need to have some idea of how the general and specific forces of international relations work before building an overarching explanatory theory. The intention here is simply to provide a new way of looking at the timing of conflict. Not only do these new tools help us understand particular facets of the causal process better, but they also suggest a methodological approach by which future research might well seek to understand other such facets. I hope that this work will be ultimately judged not on its identification of a particular indicator of conflict but, rather, on its contribution to the development of a comprehensive understanding of how to prevent war.

Foreign Policy Information Management

Two vital facets of modern foreign policy-making—maintaining international secrecy and generating domestic support for foreign policy decisions—have been analyzed individually by the existing literature in some depth, but the relationship between the two has yet to be looked at systematically. That relationship, in a nutshell, is that, while secrecy and public support are each a sine qua non for today's national leaders, efforts to build one have the inexorable effect of reducing the other.

Attempts to maintain international secrecy depend upon hiding intentions from foreign audiences; attempts to build public support depend upon showing intentions to the domestic audience and encouraging a positive response. There is an obvious contradiction in incentives here, and, unless governments can separate the two audiences completely, something must give. No matter how much governments would prefer there to be no overlap between foreign and domestic information flows, however, such spillage exists. In the past governments could attempt to separate the two simply by strictly managing direct personal contacts, whether through trade or immigration. For example, Japan before the arrival of Commodore Perry, with its policy of extreme isolation from the West, insulated itself rather effectively from this tension between maintaining international secrecy and building public support. Today, however, the ubiquitous presence of telecommunications equipment, not to mention the widespread dissemination of domestic media on a timely basis throughout the world, conspire to thwart the most aggressively autarchic policy. Even Hoxha's Albania or Kim's North Korea could not turn the clock back in this regard. Just as governments find it more difficult to control currency smuggling now that the medium has changed from heavy gold bullion to ephemeral wire transfers, so do governments find it more difficult to control information smuggling now that the medium has changed from face-to-face conversations to fax transmissions.

It simply is not possible today to hide intentions from a foreign audience and reveal those intentions to a domestic audience without risk of one or both audiences becoming aware of the conflicting information being transferred to the other. Just as a private corporation cannot distribute internal memos detailing plans for a hostile takeover without fear of leaking the plans to the outside world, so does a nation find it impossible to communicate intentions through the domestic media without fear of tipping its hand to other nations. Yet, because building that support is so important to regime survival or success, governments are forced to run this risk every day.

I am certainly not arguing that this dilemma exists in every foreign policy decision. In fact, while domestic support has some value for virtually all regime decisions, hiding true intentions from other nations can be valueless (as when a regime has overwhelmingly superior forces and has no need of a force multiplier through strategic surprise) or even counterproductive (as when a regime is in a purely cooperative relationship with another country).[8] But in any adversarial relationship where military action is considered and effective resistance is anticipated, both international secrecy and domestic support must be maximized through effective information management, despite their cross-purposes.

The relationship between international secrecy and domestic support, while interesting in itself, provides the key for understanding a still greater puzzle. *By recognizing the trade-off between a government's twin desires of maintaining international secrecy and building domestic support, we can accurately predict international conflict.* If a government uses the domestic media to prepare its populace for conflict, then we should rely on that activity as a clear sign of impending conflict initiation, regardless of other signals or communications made by that government.

This is not an entirely original idea. In a 1957 article Karl Deutsch suggested essentially this same point:

> In order to be able to choose among several acceptable foreign-policy alternatives, any government must be able to command some significant portion of the income and manpower of its population. Dictatorships can compel a limited amount of such sacrifices in the face of public apathy; democracies will find it necessary, and even dictatorships find it expedient, to reduce or dispel this apathy by confronting their populations with the image of a single, sharply defined enemy and a single, clear-cut conflict. . . .
>
> Governments, of course, may find it expedient to encourage this process in its early stage; they may even consider it essential, up to some unspecified point, in order to marshal public support for any effective but costly foreign policy.
>
> *It should be possible to say whether the amount of attention given to a specific conflict area or to the image of a particular "enemy" country is reaching the danger point, . . . it should be possible to construct an "early warning system," in regard to the mass-communication aspects of inter-state conflicts.*[9]

The thrust of Deutsch's article is to call for a research program to investigate the hypothesized role of mass media in preceding war, not to provide any supporting evidence that such an "early warning system" is possible. Still, Deutsch thought that this research program could provide the practical information necessary for international organizations to supervise or intervene in domestic mass media communications, including embargo of newsprint and jamming of radio frequencies. At the very least he saw these efforts leading to "arrangements that would notify governments of any dangerously high level of conflict news in the media of mass communication in their countries," apparently under the assumption that governments would want to reverse this buildup.

Evidence broadly supportive of Deutsch's observations was supplied by Alexander George in his examination of German propaganda efforts during World War II.[10] George found that some strategic German decisions during the course of the war, such as the initiation of hostilities with Brazil in 1942, were anticipated by American and British intelligence agencies through a rigorous analysis of German propaganda.[11] Unfortunately, while there have been more recent attempts to link foreign behavior with public rhetoric, such as the "integrative complexity" research program of Philip Tetlock and others,[12] there has been very little success in extending Deutsch's research program of predicting war. Bhaskara Rao reached similar conclusions to Deutsch concerning the relationship between domestic media and preparations for war in his study of the

1965 Second Kashmir War between India and Pakistan,[13] but Rao did not seek to construct or analyze a Deutsch-like early warning system. Like Deutsch, Rao takes a very optimistic view of the prospects for actually mitigating conflict through the control of newspaper editorials, suggesting that merely printing more "two-sided" editorial messages would create a significant measure of peace in the region. More recently, Keith Spicer, chair of the Canadian government's broadcast regulation commission, has made precisely the same suggestion to prevent future ethnic conflict.[14]

I am less sanguine about the prospects of turning media opinion into a direct tool for promoting peace. Opinions expressed by certain media outlets are indicative of and heavily influenced by regime intentions; if some outlets are not successful in communicating those intentions, either from lack of public attention or (as Deutsch and Rao hoped) some imposition of an alternative opinion, then the regime will find another outlet. The regime's future course of action may well be constrained by the imposition of alternative opinions, as they will be forced to spend more resources on getting their message out, but the regime's intentions are not themselves changed.

In fact, the strong ties between a regime and at least some media outlets should not be seen as guaranteeing pernicious propaganda but, rather, as providing a beneficial window onto decision makers' intentions. If such ties did not exist, then domestic mass media might well lose its ability to provide this early warning of conflict initiation. Fortunately for the prospects of this research program, not only does such media influence continue unabated, but the forces that drive a government to devote resources to maintain that influence continue as well. Both horns of the dilemma—the desire to maintain international secrecy and the desire to generate domestic support—are extremely strong and powerful.

Sources of Dilemma Strength—the Advantage of Secrecy

The first of these governmental objectives, hiding true intentions from rival nations, is the international equivalent of maintaining a poker face. The point of hiding intentions is to preserve the potential for strategic surprise,[15] in which an adversary is ambushed by a political decision to initiate conflict. Surprise is a force multiplier regardless of its form, but strategic surprise provides a geometric advantage. Compare, for example, the virtues of tactical surprise in the U.S. launching of an air campaign against Iraq, in which coalition forces were able to suppress primary Iraqi air defense radar, with the virtues of strategic surprise in the Iraqi invasion of Kuwait, in which Iraqi forces overran the entire country with hardly any losses. Both forms of surprise help initiators; strategic surprise simply gives a larger boost.[16]

The focus here is on intentions rather than capabilities, not because relative capabilities are less important but because they are rather impervious to strategic management. That is, determining capabilities is more and more a matter of technology, and the management of this information flow hinges on confusing other states' national means of verification. For most countries this effectively removes the ability to manage that flow. No matter how much Libya or Egypt would like to prevent U.S. and Russian satellites from noticing a new tank division, they can do very little about it.[17] Even for the great powers attempts to control this information are possible only at the margins.

Information concerning intentions, on the other hand, can still be effectively managed by the most technologically deprived country in the world. Intentions live in the minds of national decision makers and are not physically visible or palpable in and of themselves. We can see and measure reflections of these intentions,[18] but our inability to develop a mind-reading technology (so far, anyway) allows a window of opportunity for governments to manage this aspect of information. For example, U.S. intelligence agencies picked up the massive redeployment of Iraqi forces along the Kuwaiti border well before the August 1990 invasion but utterly missed the intentions behind that deployment, concluding that the tanks were there as a bargaining tool for OPEC (Organization of Petroleum Exporting Countries) talks rather than as an invasion force.

Given the advantages stemming from strategic surprise, it should come as no shock that nations devote tremendous efforts toward hiding their aggressive intentions as much as possible. The means of seeking such an edge are legion, ranging from protestations of friendship, such as Hitler's nonaggression pact with the Soviet Union, to proclaiming hatred so much as to be perceived as crying wolf, such as Sadat's "year of decision." All of these strategies share the same logic. Expectations of peaceful behavior are built through actions and words, until the adversary discounts the potential of aggressive behavior and signals. In Hitler's case enough truthful statements were made to establish credibility with Stalin, allowing German troop movements up to and across the Russian border with almost no resistance. In Sadat's case enough lies were made to lose all credibility with Israel, so that a truthful threat of war and subsequent troop movements to the Bar-Lev line were discounted as just another lie.

Intentions can be transferred to foreign consumers directly, as when Ambassador Dobrynin told President Carter what the Soviet designs on Afghanistan are, or they can be communicated indirectly, as when Iraq ordered hundreds of thousands of burial shrouds from foreign textile firms before initiating hostilities with Iran. There are certainly good reasons to concentrate limited information-gathering resources on direct communications rather than indirect communications, as the former are much more readily available.[19] In fact, it is this factor—that most information flows to foreign consumers move through direct communications from a government ministry—that is the salient and pervasive aspect of the structure of attempts to control that flow. The danger, however, is that direct communications are much more susceptible to deliberate lies and misinformation than indirect communications.[20]

Three primary routes of direct communication concerning intentions exist: bilateral talks between two governments, multilateral talks via international organizations, and announcements or leaks to the foreign press.[21] It does not require a great deal of digging to find examples of misinformation supplied through these avenues; in fact, the Gulf War alone can supply examples of all three.[22] And, even though each of these routes is a minefield of misinformation, foreign consumers persist in giving these sources more emphasis than indirect communications concerning intentions. As we shall see later in this chapter, it is precisely one of these methods of indirect communication to foreign consumers, editorial comment in domestic newspapers, that provides a much more accurate picture of the true intentions of government leaders.

Direct communications create insurmountable difficulties for foreign consumers (or, on the flip side, tremendous opportunities for suppliers) because of their underlying logic. Direct communications with potential adversaries are driven by a desire to reap the rewards of strategic surprise at some point in the future. Such surprise requires a foreign consumer's expectations to diverge from reality. This divergence may be self-imposed through some cognitive or organizational failure, or it may be manufactured by a credible lie provided by an adversary. Since information suppliers can only work on this latter method, attempts to create strategic surprise have two components. First, enough truthful statements must be made to build credibility; second, a lie must be told to create the divergence in expectations and reality. The key factor is that there are no intrinsic incentives to tell the truth here, only instrumental ones. The only incentive to tell the truth to a foreign audience is to maintain a reputation as truthful, and the primary advantage of having such a reputation is to take advantage of some future lie.[23]

Hiding intentions is perhaps the international equivalent of maintaining a poker face, but the analogy of betting strategy better illustrates the logic at work. The whole point of strategic betting in poker is to manage the flow of information concerning your hidden cards to the adversaries sitting around the table. A truthful bet is a cash wager commensurate to the relative strength of the hand; untruthful bets are not commensurate. If rational, untruthful bets are either small wagers accompanying strong hands (sandbagging) or large wagers accompanying weak hands (bluffing). Like strategic surprise, successful sandbags or bluffs in poker are very rare and very effective.

Truthful bets are not made because a player wishes to represent her hand accurately; they are made in order to make a future bluff or sandbag possible. If a player is known as a frequent bluffer, the chances of bluffing successfully are almost nil. If a player has a reputation of never bluffing, however, then a bluff has a good chance of success.[24] Likewise, providing intentions truthfully to foreign consumers provides no immediate advantage, but it does make possible the ability to hide true intentions in the future, creating the potential for strategic surprise.

In short, then, the world of foreign information flows hypothesized here is a fairly simple one. Governments have instrumental rather than intrinsic incentives to tell the truth to adversarial foreign consumers concerning their intentions, and the ultimate goal is to put across a lie that makes strategic surprise possible. Most foreign consumers persist in accepting their information through direct channels of communication, even though certain indirect channels may not have the same incentive structure that makes direct communications potentially so treacherous.

Sources of Dilemma Strength—the Necessity of Public Support

Mobilizing domestic public opinion to support foreign policy, especially the waging of war, is no less important to governments than maximizing international secrecy. Unlike strategic surprise, however, the importance of which has been recognized since Cain ambushed Abel, public opinion management has become a necessity comparatively recently.[25] That is, so long as feudal bonds of personal loyalty held sway, rulers needed to convince or command a relatively small number of immediate vassals in order to wage war, not the population at large. Two related trends, in addition to the dissolution of feudal society with the advent of the modern nation-state, helped create this transformation in the role of domestic opinion. First, the Napoleonic Wars made mass conscription the norm rather than the exception, leading to a diffusion of the state's monopoly of force. Rulers have always been concerned about the support of their troops—even Alexander the Great couldn't get past that roadblock—and, to the degree the general population becomes the troops, rulers are forced to pay attention to what the general population wants or believes. Second, the development of governments based on some notion of popular consent demanded that rulers pay attention to public opinion if they wished to remain in power or if they believed their proper role to be that of an agent.[26]

Despite its comparatively recent relevance, public opinion has become perhaps the single most pertinent factor in foreign policy decision making. Governments have gradually learned that to ignore such opinion is to court military disaster or, perhaps worse, electoral defeat. Although the failed U.S. venture in Vietnam was not the first time a government paid the price for lack of support at home, that experience at least crystallized the need for such support into accepted knowledge, to the point that it is now an official axiom of Defense Department policy.[27]

Like maintaining strategic surprise, maintaining domestic support generally requires the control of information flows. Domestic support might well spring unbidden into a government's lap, just as strategic surprise can at times result from an adversary's self-imposed failings, but the risks involved with not having this support suggest that the wise or self-interested government will go to great lengths to guide opinion actively. In fact, looking solely at the United States, not only are there several smoking guns admitting just such a policy,[28] but there is also an overwhelming abundance of circumstantial evidence that such a policy exists.[29]

The number of individuals a government must deal with in managing its foreign information flows is quite small relative to its domestic population. Face-to-face meetings, so effective for intergovernmental communications, are laughably ineffective for domestic information transfers. If it takes a presidential candidate over a year to achieve a nominal level of name recognition in Iowa via speeches and handshakes, one can imagine the logistical difficulties inherent in extending that mechanism to the nation as a whole. Fortunately for government leaders, domestic communications, unlike foreign information transfers, are particularly well suited to a powerful and manageable tool: mass media.

This is not to say that foreign information transfers have no role for the mass media or that manipulating foreign popular opinion through the foreign mass media is not a goal of governments.[30] The important distinction is that governments generally have neither the direct or indirect control over foreign mass media that they possess over domestic mass media. Governments may seek to control the information supplied to foreign media sources in the same manner they seek to control information flows to foreign governments (i.e., via direct, face-to-face or small group communications such as meetings or conferences), but they rarely possess the broad sources of influence found at home. If *Pravda* were the primary mass circulation newspaper in the United States or if NBC had replaced state-owned network television in the Soviet Union, a different logic would apply, as the distinction between foreign and domestic mass media would be severely blurred. Some nations, generally poorer countries whose broadcast programming is dominated by foreign sources, face precisely this problem.[31] For example, during the Gulf War Iraq successfully molded public opinion in the indigent Arab population of Jordan (as well as Syria and Egypt, to a lesser degree), precisely because some facets of the mass media in Jordan have greater ties to Iraqi leaders than the domestic Hashemite regime. Fortunately for this research program's attempt to uncover government intentions via domestic mass media, such foreign-controlled domestic media sources are never the exclusive (and very rarely a prominent) media outlet.

The sources of government influence over domestic mass media can be direct or indirect. Where the domestic media is itself an organ of the government, leaders may maintain direct control over the transfer of information to the public. In nations with a more open system, in which media outlets are not owned by the government, leaders do not have this luxury. Yet, even in such an open system, indirect control over certain media outlets creates a powerful influence over the flow of information to the general public.

Media influence in an open system does not require a conspiratorial theory in which media tycoons meet with government leaders in a smoke-filled room to form an unholy cabal (although there are scattered anecdotes of this behavior).[32] Instead, the organizational structure of the modern media, combined with the incentives of an open system, give government leaders some leverage over virtually all media outlets.[33] Edward Herman and Noam Chomsky present this argument clearly:

> The media need a steady, reliable flow of the raw material of news. . . . Economics dictates that they concentrate their resources where significant news often occurs, where important rumors and leaks abound, and where regular press conferences are held. The White House, the Pentagon, and the State Department, in Washington, D.C., are central nodes of such news activity at the national level . . . taking information from sources that may be presumed credible [government sources] reduces investigative expense, whereas material from sources that are not *prima facie* credible, or that will draw criticism and threats, requires careful checking and costly research.[34]

Richard Barnet makes a similar argument:

> Although he neither pays the press for what it writes nor can he throw reporters and editors into jail, the President has other levers of power over the fourth estate. The gift of access—the hint of exclusive interviews, invitations to White House dinners, and leaks—encourages respectful treatment. . . . Nor should the role of indolence be underestimated. . . . Reporting official truth or reinterpreting it in a column after a pleasant lunch at the Metropolitan Club or a dinner party with old friends is easier and for most of the press more congenial than probing mendacity or nonsense in high places.[35]

This broad-based, structural influence combines with specific influence particular to a few select media outlets to complete the mechanism of indirect government control over information flows to a domestic audience, even in an open media system. This specific influence takes the form of shared personnel and preferential access and is generally limited to one or two mass circulation newspapers. For example, in the United States there are only two prestige newspapers with nationwide subscriber bases, the *New York Times* and the *Wall*

Street Journal. With a Republican president in office the *Wall Street Journal* maintains very close relations with the administration, through the shared mind-sets of editorial board members and administration officials as well as shared information and preferential access, while the *New York Times* is not privy to such contacts and does not share the same worldview. With a Democratic president the relationship is reversed.[36]

Television, like the newspaper, is a vital source of public information, but the restrictions on broadcast media, even in the most open systems, permit little advantage from preferential access policies.[37] We rarely see one television station in the loop and another station out of the loop, as we do with print media. This is not to say that governments do not go to great lengths to attempt to influence television reportage. In fact, by all accounts of recent presidencies, television gets the lion's share of attention.[38] The difference is that influencing television requires taking advantage of broad organizational constraints rather than sharing information or personnel preferentially with one network over another. For example, political candidates attempt to present campaign ideas as sound bites instead of detailed speeches because television stations can more easily fit such snippets into a 22-minute nightly news broadcast. Candidates gain little benefit, however, by attempting to give preferential access to one station over another, because regulations governing equal time in broadcast media, but not print, allow little advantage for such extra attention.

Radio stations are very rarely included in this set of highly influenced media outlets, although some evidence exists for a nascent shift in this structure. Nations in which radio plays a large role as a source of information are generally poorer countries more likely to have closed media systems, where the government directly controls the stations and has no need of indirect means of influence. Nations with open media systems are almost always relatively wealthy countries, in which radio has had little importance as a source of public information for the past 40 years. Judging from the recent spurt in popularity of talk radio programs, however, this pattern of information flow may be changing. By portraying themselves as entertainers first and political figures second, talk radio hosts avoid the equal time regulations of editorial broadcasts and can maintain a highly partisan content to their programs. Time will tell whether this sidestepping of broadcast regulations can be extended to the potentially far greater audience of television.

Perhaps the most important reason, however, why some newspapers maintain a special role as media confidant is historical. Newspapers, unlike television or radio, developed as an explicitly political and partisan media outlet. The *New York Times* and the *Wall Street Journal* are both captives and beneficiaries of their historical baggage. When a sympathetic administration is in office, they enjoy preferential access and information; when an opposing administration takes office, they pay the penalty. It should come as no surprise that more recent national newspapers, such as *USA Today,* not only place a more television-like emphasis on visual information but also present a more nonpartisan appearance.

Just as the form of domestic communications is markedly different from that of foreign communications, so too is the underlying logic. The incentive structure of domestic communications suggests that intrinsic reasons to relate intentions truthfully exist in this arena, while they are conspicuously absent in foreign communications. That is, truthful statements concerning policy intentions are not simply instrumental attempts to make some future lie to the domestic audience possible. On the contrary, in order to prepare the public for future actions, governments need to relate intentions truthfully as well as make the argument for these intentions as compelling as possible.

I am not claiming that governments lack incentives to lie to the public; what they lack are incentives to lie to the public concerning their basic intentions. A government seeking to build public support for an aggressive military move might well lie to the public concerning the rationale for such a move, but it will not lie to the public about the intention to make this move. For example, the Gulf of Tonkin Resolution lied about both the supposed North Vietnamese provocation and the goals of U.S. intervention; however, the intention to intervene militarily on a large scale was clear. The incentive structure for governments when dealing with the domestic audience resembles that in place for advertising agencies. Advertisers do not try to convince the public to buy cornflakes because they really want to sell wheat flakes; they might very well lie or stretch the truth about the relative virtues of cornflakes, but their intentions are clearly demonstrated.

The assumption here is neither that government decision makers have completely independent foreign policy beliefs that they then seek to impose on the general population nor that they are unwitting sponges of public sentiment.[39] Most recent analysts of public opinion development suggest that external events influence the opinion of a rather broad band of politically cognizant citizens. Through a variety of means, including opinions expressed in the mass media, these views are made known to decision makers at the top level of government. If these top decision makers consider the opinions percolating upwards to represent some sort of consensus of popular opinion, then those decision makers, concerned about maintaining popular support, will incorporate these opinions with their own. At the same time, national leaders are constantly trying to channel or mold public opinion in ways that support their independent policy objectives.[40] To further complicate any simple vision of public opinion, one can easily imagine that different nations might have different institutional constraints on this circular process, even if the broad outlines of their polities are similar.[41]

I am assuming neither a pure top-down model, in which leaders attempt to convince the public to support their position, nor a pure bottom-up model, in which leaders decide what to do on the basis of popular opinion. The true decision-making process is better understood as a spectrum, with these two models on opposite ends, than as a binary phenomenon specified wholly by one or the other. Relative to domestic policy, however, foreign policy decisions veer more to the top-down pole. Decisions for war are certainly constrained by existing public opinion (President Bush did not have an iota of a chance of convincing the public to support an invasion of Canada, so he would not rationally suggest such a policy, no matter how fervently he might have believed such an invasion to be the right thing to do), but no war has been forced on leaders by public opinion.[42]

Bismarck's Germany is a severe example of a government reserving autocratic control over foreign policy-making while instituting a measure of popular representation on domestic policy, but even in the United States foreign policy is driven more by the relatively independent executive than the relatively responsive legislative branch.[43] While domestic politics no longer stop at the water's edge, in the ubiquitous (and historically misleading) words of Senator Vandenberg and others, the aura of bipartisanship that to a large degree still surrounds foreign policy-making gives government leaders some leeway to follow their beliefs and massage public opinion, rather than the other way around. Furthermore, the willingness of the public to be led on matters of foreign policy appears to be greater than its willingness to be led on domestic policy, allowing policy makers the luxury of taking positions more in line with their personal vision of the public good. Recent scholarship cautions against viewing the U.S. electorate as a tabula rasa on foreign policy concerns or as ignoring foreign policy when voting, but the overwhelming consensus is still consistent with the conclusions Gabriel Almond drew in 1950—that domestic policy is a more contentious and salient arena of electoral politics than foreign policy.[44] Or, in the now ubiquitous phrase attributed to James Carville in the 1992 presidential election, "It's the economy, stupid."

It will certainly affect certain aspects of getting to war whether the decision-making process is more accurately described as top-down or bottom-up,[45] and that description will change from country to country, from time to time. Fortunately for this project, any of these decision-making model variations is ultimately consistent with the dilemma of support versus secrecy. Regardless of where intentions originate, at some point top decision makers must decide to act on those intentions; at that time, we could well imagine a concerted attempt by the regime to use the media both to convince the uninformed citizens of the wisdom of this future action and to reassure the informed citizens that the regime was acting on their desires. Regardless of the degree to which the decision by a national command structure for war fundamentally comes from within or from below, it is extremely valuable to know at what point that decision is made. It is that decision that I am trying to reveal, and the subsequent domestic media signals hypothesized here are the means to that discovery.

The Dilemma at Work

So far, then, I am hypothesizing a world in which governments are faced with a problem. How to balance the demands of international secrecy and domestic support, when the former requires hiding intentions and the latter requires revealing them? In Argentina's attempt to reclaim the Falklands by force in 1982—described by the novelist Jorge Luis Borges as a fight between two bald men for a comb[46]—we see every aspect of the hypothesized relationship, including an intriguing attempt to manipulate the equilibrium function.

Claimed as a colony and administered as such by the United Kingdom since 1832, the Falklands have been one of the primary foci of Argentine foreign policy for more than 160 years. Argentine governments were routinely rebuffed by British negotiators for the first 128 years of their efforts to reclaim the islands. With the 1960 passage of United Nations Resolution A/1514, a declaration on the granting of independence to colonial countries and peoples,[47] Argentina moved its arguments for sovereignty to the United Nations.[48] In September 1964 the Argentine representative presented his country's case to the subcommittee set up to implement Resolution A/1514, and in January 1966 UN Resolution A/2065 invited Britain and Argentina to begin negotiations to solve their dispute peacefully.[49] The talks accomplished little and soon broke off, and in January 1974 the General Assembly again requested that the United Kingdom and Argentina meet under its auspices in order to come to a peaceful solution,[50] again resulting in much intransigence and little progress.

Tensions rose in 1976, as first the Organization of American States (OAS) declared "that the Republic of Argentina has an undeniable right of sovereignty over the Malvinas Islands,"[51] and then several weeks later an Argentine destroyer fired on an unarmed British research ship 400 miles off the Argentine coast but only 78 miles from the Falklands, under the pretext that the British ship was in Argentine territorial waters.[52] No further violence came out of this incident, however. In fact, the Falklands controversy submerged again for several years, as secret talks in Rome and open talks in New York finally took place regarding the islands' future.[53]

In 1982, following the bloodless December 11, 1981, coup by the military junta of Adm. Jorge Anaya, Air Force Gen. Basilio Lami Dozo, and Army Lt. Gen. Leopoldo Galtieri, the Falklands issue finally came to a head. The junta sparked an inflammatory incident on March 19, 1982, by landing several dozen construction workers under the Argentine flag on South Georgia Island without obtaining the necessary work permits and visas.[54] Following a reprisal looting of Argentine State Airline offices in Port Stanley by Falkland Islanders, Argentine troops seized the Falklands and related islands on April 2. British marines recaptured South Georgia on April 25 and accepted the surrender of Argentine forces in Port Stanley on June 14, effectively ending the war (although Argentina did not declare a formal end to hostilities). Galtieri resigned his posts of president, commander in chief of the army, and member of the ruling junta on June 17, to be replaced on June 22 by Maj. Gen. Reynaldo Bignone.

According to the Argentine navy's account of the decisions leading up to the Falklands attack,[55] the ruling junta set up a Joint Armed Forces study group on January 5, 1982, to begin making plans for an invasion should the negotiations fail as expected. Eddy and Linklater make an even stronger claim, that the Argentine junta, driven by Adm. Anaya, made the decision in December 1981, just days after assuming power from President Viola, to take the Falklands by force if necessary.[56] On the basis of interviews with Gen. Juan Guglialmelli, then editor of *Estrategia,* Guillermo Makin confirms this analysis.[57]

Whatever the precise source of military planning, the junta approved National Strategy Directive 1/82 by the end of January. It stated in part:

> The Military Committee, faced with the evident and repeated lack of progress in the negotiations with Great Britain to obtain recognition of our sovereignty over the Malvinas, Georgias and South Sandwich Islands; convinced that the prolongation of this situation affects national honor, the full exercise of sovereignty and the exploration of resources; has resolved to analyze the possibility of the use of military power to obtain the political objective. This resolution must be kept in strict secrecy and should be circulated only to the heads of the respective military departments.[58]

In addition to the purposes stated in the National Strategy Directive, the invasion appears to have been intended to quiet the opposition parties in general and to strengthen the junta's hand against calls for early elections in particular.[59] In many ways the junta's decision for war is one of the clearest examples we have of a regime actively pursuing a rally-round-the-flag effect.[60]

Having made a decision for war, the junta was faced with the paradox of foreign policy information management—how to manufacture the necessary strategic surprise to seize and hold territory from a militarily superior nation, while at the same time mobilizing the public for such a war?

Attempts to manage foreign information flows throughout 1982 followed the process hypothesized in this chapter. Information regarding Argentine intentions came to British decision makers not through indirect signals provided by Argentine behavior but via direct communications with Argentine Foreign Ministry officials or intelligence reports based on direct communications with Argentine government officials.[61] As Lippencott and Treverton conclude: "British intelligence and the Foreign Office agreed that while threats of Argentine military action were in the air, such action was unlikely to occur before both a formal breakdown of negotiations and graduated economic pressures against the islanders."[62] The British were not the only nation caught unawares by Argentine actions. As Richard Haass, then director of the U.S. State Department's Office of Regional Security Affairs, said:

> The Falklands was not even a back-burner issue; it wasn't even on the stove. I would expect that the only people who could have located the islands on a map were the few folks who worked in ARA's [Bureau of Inter-American Affairs] Office of Southern Cone Affairs. A few people around the intelligence community might also have kept a corner of one eye turned in their direction, but again, the Falklands was not a full-time job even for those at the bottom of the bureaucratic ladder.[63]

The negotiations pursued in good faith by Argentina from 1960 on paid dividends here, as the repetitive truthfulness to their past claims to be willing to solve the issue peacefully created a tremendous divergence in British expectations and reality. In fact, the British were so trusting that the only British warship regularly stationed in the area, the *Endurance,* had been withdrawn in June 1981.[64] Equally indicative of waning British interest in the Falklands, at least to Argentine eyes, Parliament voted in 1981 to deprive third- and fourth-generation Falkland Islanders (almost half of the population) of Commonwealth citizenship while maintaining it for Gibraltar residents.[65] As late as March 31, two days before the attack, an opinion piece ran in the *Times,* entitled "These paltry islands which separate us."[66]

The Argentine government's success in achieving the goal of this foreign information management—strategic surprise—was accomplished by two separate lies. First, the waters vis-à-vis the Falklands were muddied by indications that Argentina was preparing to move against Chile, rather than the United Kingdom, over essentially the same issue: disputed territorial claims to certain islands. For many months the Vatican had been mediating negotiations between Argentina and Chile on islands surrounding the Beagle Channel. On January 13 reports began to surface that the junta was considering a change in attitude toward the talks, including, but not limited to, a change in negotiators.[67] On January 21 the junta took the alarming step of announcing its decision to terminate the existing general treaty for solutions of controversies with Chile, originally signed in 1972, as it proved ineffective "in overcoming that most acute crisis which, for that reason, had to be instead submitted to mediation by the Holy See."[68] The Rome negotiations were to continue unaffected, although a new negotiator was announced, Carlos Ortiz de Rosas, then (and continuing as) ambassador to London.[69]

Although Ortiz de Rosas denied that there was any link between the Chilean negotiations and prospects of settlement on the Falklands, a small note in the Argentine press reveals that he flew for several days to London after picking up his negotiation instructions from Galtieri (in itself a strong signal—according to Makin, the ambassador would ordinarily receive instructions from the foreign minister)[70] and before flying to Rome to continue the Chilean meetings.[71] When asked about the contents of those negotiation instructions, Galtieri responded only that it "served to reassert the national position in the mediation in defense of the sovereignty over the Atlantic,"[72] words that could apply as easily to the Falklands as to the Beagle zone. In fact, it was widely reported in the domestic Argentine press that the primary concern in these discussions for both Galtieri and Ortiz de Rosas were the Falklands rather than the Beagles.[73]

On February 19 an incident occurred that could have sparked a full-fledged war between Chile and Argentina had that been the junta's goal. An Argentine patrol boat was anchored at Deceit Island inside the Beagle zone under mediation in Rome, ostensibly providing support for sport boats participating in the Rio de Janeiro–Sydney boat race. A Chilean torpedo boat approached and ordered the Argentine ship to leave the area. The torpedo boat then fired several warning shots when the Argentine craft refused to move, as other Chilean ships converged on the scene. Although originally ordered not to leave the area and to wait for Argentine warships to arrive, the patrol boat received new orders to proceed to port as it became obvious that the Chilean navy had no intentions of backing down.[74] By February 25 Argentine foreign minister Costa Mendes said that the issue had been completely resolved.[75] In fact, aside from a brief disagreement over public statements made by the Chilean representative to the Rome negotiations, the Beagle issue did not spark up again; instead, negotiations continued smoothly in Rome until the Falklands War began in earnest.

It would seem that the Argentine government was trying to accomplish two goals by making an issue of the Chilean negotiations before launching their push for the Falklands. First, by making such a public issue over the Beagle zone and by bringing in their British ambassador to lead the negotiations, government leaders sent a clear message to London that they were more concerned about the Beagles than the Falklands.[76] Second, by linking the Falkland negotiations to the Beagle negotiations, they sent an equally clear message that they intended to handle the Falklands like the Beagle zone—nonviolently, even if provoked by overly aggressive torpedo boats.

There is no smoking gun to support these claims, either that the Argentines used the Chilean crisis to further the goal of secrecy vis-à-vis Britain or that the British were influenced by the supposed Chilean subterfuge. Nor am I claiming that the Argentines manufactured the Beagle incident; rather, it seems much more likely that the Beagle incident was entirely genuine and that deceiving the British was making the best out of a bad situation. We know, however, that American diplomats were far more concerned about Argentine-Chilean relations than Argentine-British relations as late as mid-March and that they communicated this perception to British leaders. When Thomas Enders, U.S. undersecretary for Latin American affairs, visited Buenos Aires on March 6, his conversation with Costa Mendes was dominated by discussion of possible conflict with Chile; Enders met with the British ambassador to Argentina later that week and informed him that not only was Argentina not going to attack Chile but also that he could detect no signal that Argentina was planning military force against the Falklands.[77] After Enders reported back to Washington, U.S. secretary of state Alexander Haig communicated these sentiments directly to British Foreign Secretary Carrington.[78]

The second lie that created the strategic surprise necessary to initiate conflict was simply the continuation of the long-running direct assurance to the world in general and the British government in particular that Argentina intended to settle the Falklands dispute by peaceful means. In fact, through the first week of February the only public foreign communication to Britain concerning the Falklands was a note of protest concerning the British government's intention to issue stamps marked with the inscription "Falkland Islands" to commemorate the 21st birthday of Princess Di.[79]

On February 16 the Argentine Foreign Ministry announced that negotiations with Britain concerning the Falklands would resume in New York on February 26 and 27. Notably, although headed by the undersecretary for foreign affairs, Enrique J. Ros, the delegation also included the ambassador to London and negotiator with Chile, Carlos Ortiz de Rosas.[80] Apparently, the British negotiators approached these talks under the assumption that, as in all previous negotiations, simply dragging out the discussions would be sufficient to hold onto the Falklands, since Argentina had no recourse but to talk.[81] After the conclusion of the talks—unsuccessful talks, to no one's surprise—Costa Mendes answered questions regarding the Falklands on March 5 at a press conference in Brasilia, following a two-day visit to Brazil. To these foreign reporters he stated that he was very unhappy with the results of the negotiation and that Argentina would "try, through all the means which the UN Charter makes available, to recover its sovereignty over the islands."[82] When asked specifically whether Argentina would resort to military means to accomplish that goal, he replied, "Those means are not included in the UN Charter."[83] Moreover, Costa Mendes directly told the British ambassador to Argentina that his country did not wish "in any way to threaten" Britain over the Falklands.[84]

The controversy over the landing of Argentine workers on South Georgia Island erupted on March 20, leading to a flurry of diplomatic activity. Throughout this activity Costa Mendes resolutely maintained through direct meetings with the British ambassador that a diplomatic solution was possible and that Argentina would not attack. As late as March 31, the Argentine Foreign Ministry was suggesting to the United Kingdom that, if restrictions on visiting workers were relaxed and negotiations on sovereignty were entered into in a serious manner, then the whole controversy would conclude.[85] Britain apparently believed that a peaceful resolution was still possible, as demonstrated by Margaret Thatcher's cable to Ronald Reagan, asking him to dissuade Galtieri from his belligerent stance.[86] On April 1 the Argentine ambassador to the United Nations, Eduardo Roca, claimed that "his country has formulated its demands in a peaceful manner because it is convinced that a solution can be achieved through dialogue."[87] Of course, by this time preparations for the Argentine invasion on April 2 were in high gear; the die was cast for war.

The junta was as successful in mobilizing public opinion through its management of domestic information flows as it was in creating strategic surprise through its management of foreign information flows. Eddy and Linklater claim that "the task of preparing the Argentine people for an invasion had begun in late December 1981, when Costa Mendes began briefing a close circle of senior journalists about the government's intentions."[88] Even before Galtieri came to power the future junta leader spoke in favor of action to return sovereignty over the Falklands to Argentina in a highly publicized Armed Forces Day speech in May 1981.[89]

From January on, articles, reports, and commentaries in the Argentine mass media spoke directly on the need to take military action against Britain to seize the Falklands. For example, in a January 24 *La Prensa* commentary, "The Foreign Offensive," J. Iglesias Rouco wrote that "it is believed that if the next Argentine attempt to 'clarify' the negotiations with London fails, Buenos Aires will take over the island by force this year."[90] *Conviccion,* a newspaper linked closely with the navy, argued in mid-February that, if negotiations did not improve immediately, "other forms of action, including recovery of the islands by military means, would be considered."[91] According to a February report in the *Latin American Weekly Report,* Galtieri visited Uruguay to receive assurances from his counterpart, General Alvarez, that Uruguay would be neutral in any war over the Falklands.[92] Just prior to the landing of construction workers on South Georgia Island, reports began circulating in the Argentine press that projects aimed at cutting off supplies to the Falklands were about to be implemented by the regime.[93] Throughout this period editorial after editorial referred to the horrible affront to Argentina's sovereignty posed by continued British rule over the Falklands.[94]

In sharp contrast to Costa Mendes's press conference in Brasilia following the breakdown of the New York talks, in which he explicitly stated that military means would not be used to extend Argentine sovereignty over the Falklands, the regime's press conference at home allowed for precisely that possibility. According to the announcement read by Gustavo Figueroa, chief of the Foreign Ministry Cabinet, "if a solution should not be reached, Argentina maintains the right to end the system [of negotiations] and freely choose the procedure which it may deem most convenient to its interests."[95] As the Argentine newspaper *Clarin* reported the next day, the announcement "obviously does not exclude the possibility of military occupation of the islands."[96] Interestingly, Costa Mendes was originally scheduled to make this announcement but gave the assignment to Figueroa at the last second.[97] One possible explanation for this switch is an attempt by Costa Mendes to preserve as much credibility as possible for his upcoming direct talks with British ambassador Anthony Williams.

To Williams's credit, not only did he alert London about the seriousness of the hostile unilateral communiqué, accounting for most of what limited notice Britain did take of the danger of an Argentine attack,[98] but he was also quite cognizant of the junta's efforts to use the domestic press to build public support for an invasion. Based on his interviews, Freedman wrote:

> Sir Anthony Williams, the British Ambassador to Buenos Aires, had taken to reporting articles such as these [Rouco's January piece in *La Prensa*] back to London. . . . He was also convinced, despite denials, that Sr. Rouco was an instrument in a campaign of diplomatic pressure on Britain.[99]

Just as playing the Chile card perhaps allowed the junta to disguise their intentions in foreign communications, so did it perhaps allow the Argentine regime to mobilize public opinion more effectively for the Falklands attack. It is at least possible that the Argentine regime used the Chilean negotiations to begin its attempts to gear up the public for a military action based on assertions of territorial sovereignty. Once territorial sovereignty was clearly on the public's agenda, it was a simple matter to switch the focus of these complaints from Chile to the United Kingdom.[100] The strength of this strategy is that the final target of these complaints regarding sovereignty, Britain, was not at all alarmed by Argentine complaints directed against Chile; thus, Argentina ran no risk of tipping its hand to Britain that it planned to initiate conflict in the near future. As with the possible use of the Beagle incident to deceive international observers, I am not claiming that the Argentine junta purposefully initiated a media campaign against Chile, all the while planning to turn that campaign eventually against Britain; rather, given that tensions with Chile unexpectedly flared up, I am suggesting that slowly altering editorial positions from anti–Chilean sovereignty threats to anti–general sovereignty threats to anti–British sovereignty threats is a competent strategy to make the most out of an unforeseen event.[101] By complaining about Chile for the same reasons it would later use against Britain, the Argentine regime was able to sidestep temporarily, by luck or design, the dilemma of strategic surprise versus public support. Fortunately for this research project, however, the switch to complaints about Britain per se was made well over a month before the April 2 invasion.

In conclusion, then, through active control over both foreign and domestic information flows, the Argentine regime was able to achieve a balance of strategic surprise and domestic support that made for a successful initiation of conflict. Unfortunately for the junta, its success in building surprise and rallying support at home was not mirrored by accuracy in predicting British resolve when faced with such a fait accompli. Indicative of the rose-colored lenses through which Argentina viewed a possible military conflict over the islands, J. Iglesias Rouco wrote:

> It is believed that the operation [seizing the Falklands by force] would be relatively easy, in view of the islands' scarce military forces (there are a little more than 80 armed men today), and even of the advantages that islanders could gain from the seizure, since it is believed that Argentina is determined to avoid any bloodshed and to generously compensate the islanders for the economic difficulties which may be raised by the change of the administration. As for England, diplomatic relations are likely to "freeze" for a time, but such a situation is not likely to last too long within the context of the Western strategic schemes. The Malvinas and the Beagle, perhaps housing joint bases under a south Atlantic treaty, would in this way turn into two of the main pillars of the region's defensive structure.[102]

Like the sleeping giant Adm. Yamamoto feared he had awakened with the attack on Pearl Harbor, the British regime marshaled its forces and thrashed Argentina, albeit at great financial and diplomatic expense. Of course, had the British paid better attention to the dilemma of foreign policy information management, their costs might have been greatly reduced. Still, even in retrospect this dilemma provides the researcher a window to understand this particular road to war a little better. Future chapters will show in a more systematic fashion how domestic mass media can be used as a leading indicator of conflict as well as the light it sheds on theories of war initiation.

CHAPTER 2

Predicting War in Theory

An Equilibrium Model

The tension between international secrecy and domestic support is best understood as an equilibrium situation, in which competing goals must be balanced. Like the age-old question of guns versus butter, in which finite resources must be divided between military and domestic spending, this question of secrecy versus public support cannot be answered by ignoring one or the other. Instead, some balance between the two must be found, depending on the particular characteristics of the state in question.

By expressing this equilibrium formally, we can generate specific and falsifiable hypotheses that can be evaluated empirically across a large set of cases. This is not to denigrate the importance of detailed case analysis; in fact, subsequent chapters will look closely at a few instances of going to war (and not going to war), just as Argentine behavior vis-à-vis the Falklands was examined in chapter 1. But historical analysis must be informed by theory, by a lens that brings certain events into sharp focus. I want to establish confidence in my particular set of lenses by clearly setting out how the constraints of secrecy and support should affect each other and the process of getting to war, and then showing that the world actually behaves in this manner.

Often a rigorously deductive approach simply confirms our intuition or common sense about how a phenomenon works. It is precisely the empirical substantiation of a counterintuitive deduction, however, that inspires the greatest confidence in a theory. To claim that the speed of light is a constant or that time slows down as speed increases seems ridiculous on the face of it. But empirical evidence has borne out these claims to the point where the general and special theories of relativity are virtually taken as articles of faith, just as the failure of the Michelson-Morley experiments led to an utter lack of confidence in the equally elegant (and much more intuitive) theory of ether. Even if such surprising findings are not forthcoming (and I am certainly not claiming any Einsteinian breakthroughs here), there is still inherent value in a consciously scientific approach, as it forces us to reveal our assumptions and make consistent claims about the phenomenon in question.

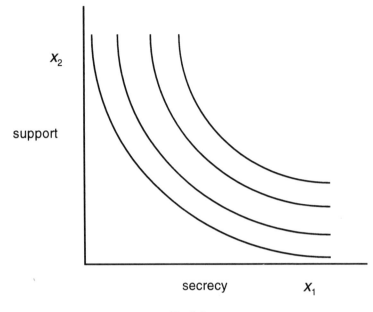

Fig. 2.1

As a first step in this formal analysis, let us think in terms of convex utility curves between secrecy and support, where the regime is indifferent to the bundle of secrecy and support at any point on a given curve. Graphically, such a relationship is usually expressed as in figure 2.1. The regime is not indifferent to points on separate curves, as any point on a curve to the right of a given curve has greater total utility associated with it.

Indifference curves are simply expressions of preferences—a curve can be assumed to exist regardless of whether the mix of utilities commensurate with that curve is really possible to attain. To include reality in our equilibrium we must assume a budget line that demarcates the space containing all bundles of these two goods that can actually be achieved (see fig. 2.2 for a hypothetical example). The budget line can be thought of as the horizon beyond which it is impossible to muster some requisite blend of secrecy and support. Every possible initiation target will require its own particular mix of support and secrecy. For some nations this blend is to the right of the budget line, and conflict initiation is impossible; for others this blend is well within the capabilities of the regime in question (the shaded area in the given hypothetical case) and awaits only the political decision to start the ball rolling.

With these two theoretical concepts—indifference curves and a budget line—we can now determine the blend of secrecy and support that maximizes

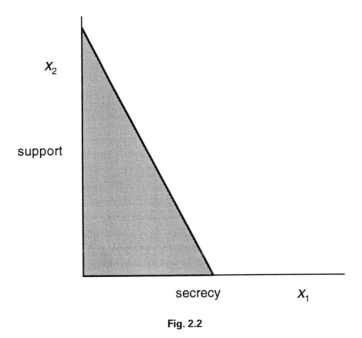

Fig. 2.2

utility for the regime. Intuitively, it would seem that the point where the budget line serves as a tangent for a utility curve (point A in fig. 2.3) should be the point where a regime maximizes both secrecy and security given its preferences (the utility curves) and its abilities (the budget line).[1] Such a point is the unique intersection of the set of attainable outcomes and the farthest rightward, and thus highest utility, indifference curve. Expressed differently, utility is maximized at the point where the slope of the budget line equals the slope of an indifference curve.

We can go beyond intuition and demonstrate this basic equilibrium property mathematically rather than graphically. The general utility function U linking two goods x_1 and x_2 (international secrecy and domestic support in the figures shown) is customarily written as:

$$U = U(x_1, x_2)$$

and an indifference curve is given by the equation:

$$U(x_1, x_2) = a$$

where a is a constant.

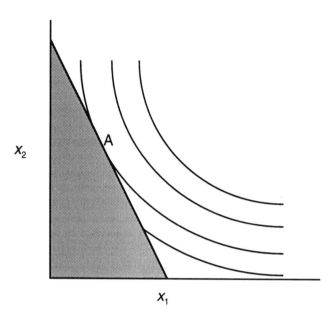

Fig. 2.3

To establish the budget line, let b be the fixed amount of resources available to the regime with which it can maintain international secrecy or generate domestic support, and let p_1 and p_2 be the respective unit resource costs of x_1 and x_2. This relationship can be expressed as:

$$p_1 x_1 + p_2 x_2 = b$$

or as:

$$x_2 = b/p_2 - (p_1/p_2)x_1$$

where the slope of the line is $-(p_1/p_2)$ and the vertical intercept is b/p_2.

To maximize U with respect to the constraints of the budget line, we construct the function:

$$L = U(x_1, x_2) - \lambda(p_1 x_1 + p_2 x_2 - b)$$

where λ is a Lagrangian multiplier (a term included solely to facilitate derivation). Taking the derivatives of this function with respect to x_1, x_2, and λ in order to generate the first-order conditions for a maximum, we see that:

$$\frac{\partial L}{\partial x_1} = \frac{\partial U}{\partial x_1} - \lambda p_1 = 0$$

$$\frac{\partial L}{\partial x_2} = \frac{\partial U}{\partial x_2} - \lambda p_2 = 0$$

$$\frac{\partial L}{\partial \lambda} = b - p_1 x_1 - p_2 x_2 = 0$$

Setting the first two of these equations equal to each other, we have:

$$\frac{\frac{\partial U}{\partial x_1}}{p_1} = \frac{\frac{\partial U}{\partial x_2}}{p_2}$$

which can be restated as:

$$\frac{\partial U}{\partial x_1} \bigg/ \frac{\partial U}{\partial x_2} = p_1/p_2$$

The left side of this equation can be thought of as the marginal rate of sub-stitution between x_1 and x_2, or as the negative of the slope of the indifference curve U (since we assume convex indifference curves, the slope itself must be negative). Recalling that p_1/p_2 is the negative of the slope of the budget line, we see that L is maximized when the slope of the budget line equals the slope of the indifference curve.

Given such a standard equilibrium model, we must now ask what general factors influence the budget lines and utility curves for international secrecy and domestic support. First, I will hypothesize systematically different prefer-ence functions for different regime types and suggest how these differences may affect behavior. Second, I will argue that two facets of managing informa-tion flows—the marketing problem and the signaling problem—are centrally important to the determination of the set of attainable outcomes below the budget line.

Preference Functions across Regime Types

No one would assume that all regimes share identical indifference curves for the utility associated with bundles of secrecy and support. But it is conceivable that different types of regimes have systematic differences in their preference functions and that these systematic differences can have a measurable effect on international behavior.

Let us assume that all regimes, regardless of how authoritarian, must maintain at least a minimal level of popular acceptance. It seems reasonable to postulate, however, that the more a regime can rely on police powers to stay in office, the less concerned it must be with popular opinion. The less a regime can rely on force or intimidation to stay in power, the more concerned it must be with domestic opinion. In other words, for any given total sum of resources a regime possesses, liberal states will "spend" more of those resources on domestic support than an illiberal state.[2] In terms of the budget function set up here, out of the total resources b, the support term p_2/x_2 for a democratic regime will be greater than the support term p_2/x_2 for an authoritarian regime. Note that we cannot say that either regime, even the liberal one, will spend more on support than secrecy, only that the liberal regime values domestic support more than the illiberal regime values such support.

This higher value that a democratic regime places on support can be expressed in terms of the regime's preference function or utility curves for the two goods. Utility curves can be empirically measured by revealed preferences; if I spend 20 percent of my entertainment budget on opera tickets and 80 percent on movie tickets, my revealed substitution rate for opera and movies at this level of spending is four to one. Of course, there is no actual budget for government efforts to maintain secrecy and garner public support to reveal preferences in this case. I am assuming that, if such a budget existed, it would systematically reveal that democracies value domestic support more than authoritarian regimes, that they will sacrifice only a little public support even for substantial gains in international secrecy. The effect of such a difference is to reduce the slope of the utility curves of a democracy relative to a nondemocracy (as in previous examples, domestic support, x_2, is measured along the vertical axis and international secrecy, x_1, along the horizontal axis). Figure 2.4 shows the difference graphically, with the illustration on the right showing the flattened utility curves of a democracy relative to a nondemocracy.

Given identical budget lines, two regimes with differently sloped utility curves will have different bundles of secrecy and support that maximize utility. Intuitively, we would probably guess that the flatter utility curves will form a tangent with the budget line at a higher point on the line than that made by steeper utility curves. A cursory mathematical look at the problem confirms the intuition. Recall that utility is maximized at the point where the slope of the budget line equals the slope of the tangential utility curve, where

$$-\frac{\partial U}{\partial x_1}\bigg/\frac{\partial U}{\partial x_2}=-(p_1/p_2)$$

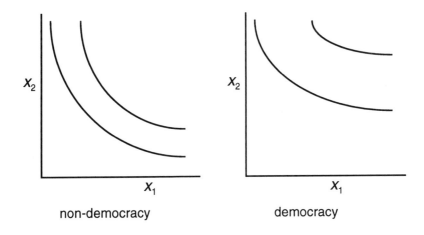

non-democracy   democracy

Fig. 2.4

Since the slope of the budget line is held constant for both cases, the maximal utility points for democratic and nondemocratic regimes must be those two points where their utility curve slopes are equal. Yet, for every coordinate x_1 the slope of the democratic utility curve is less than that of the nondemocratic utility curve. On both curves the slope increases as x_1 decreases (recall that we assume convex utility functions). Thus, the slope of the democratic curve can only equal the slope of the nondemocratic curve when the x_1 coordinate of the democratic curve is sufficiently less than the x_1 coordinate of the nondemocratic curve. Since x_2 is negatively related to x_1 according to the function $x_2 = b/p_2 - (p_1/p_2)x_1$, the x_2 coordinate corresponding to a lower x_1 coordinate (the democratic curve) must be greater than the corresponding x_2 coordinate of the nondemocratic curve. In other words, the equilibrium point for a democratic regime has coordinates (x_1^*, x_2^*), and the equilibrium point for a nondemocratic regime has coordinates (x_1, x_2), where $x_1^* < x_1$ and $x_2^* > x_2$.

The simple upshot of all this is that, all other factors held constant, nations that value domestic support more than international secrecy will maximize the utility of their support/secrecy equilibrium at a higher level of support (and a lower level of secrecy) than those nations that do not. This is a necessary first step in establishing the baseline of regime effects.

The Price of Support: Marketing and Signaling

We could not assume that all regimes share identical preference functions when it comes to valuing international secrecy and domestic support, nor can we assume that all regimes share the same constraints when it comes to achieving some mix of these goods. In particular, I argue that regimes face systematic differences in the unit resource cost of garnering public support, p_2.

I call the first of these factors creating differences in the cost of support across regime types the marketing problem. How difficult is it for a regime to "sell" its preferred opinion on future international actions when other domestic opinion leaders are promoting their vision of the future?[3] Regimes communicate their position on future actions by making their case in the mass media. To the degree their communications are the only positions being disseminated in the domestic arena, the marketing problem does not apply. To the degree a regime's domestic communications must compete with other opinions for airtime or newsprint, the marketing problem can significantly increase the cost of achieving a given level of opinion dissemination. The unit cost of public support for such a regime is increased because, as with any form of advertising (opinion advertising in this case), increased competition for a limited supply of media outlets inexorably drives up the price of communicating through any particular outlet. For example, television advertising rates for a particular broadcast depend not only on the projected number of viewers but also the number of advertisers seeking to market their products to those viewers.

A related phenomenon affecting mass media communications is the signaling problem. With the marketing problem, support is more costly because there are other opinion advertisers. With the signaling problem, support is more costly because, for some regimes, there is no media outlet through which they can express their preferences clearly. From the regime's point of view lack of a direct media outlet makes it more difficult to signal its preferences and communicate its opinions. That is, unless a regime publicly and directly controls a media outlet, it is not immediately apparent to the domestic audience which disseminated opinions are the regime's and which are, relatively speaking, the confounding white noise of other opinion leaders.

When the noise-to-signal ratio is high, greater efforts must be expended to achieve the same signal level possible with less effort if the ratio is low. And, assuming a limited supply of media messages available for purchase, this greater signaling effort should lead to an increase in the price of these outlets. For example, government regulation of radio broadcast wavelengths—the supply of which is inherently limited by the electromagnetic spectrum—keeps broadcast prices artificially low precisely by prohibiting radio stations from making greater signaling efforts.

Regardless of its source—either the marketing problem or the signaling problem—how does this increase in the price of support affect the budget line and its enclosed set of attainable policy bundles? Recall that the budget line can be expressed as:

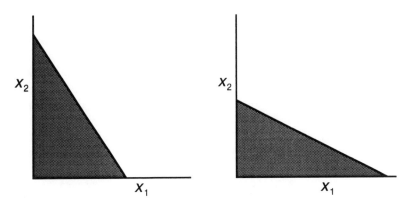

Fig. 2.5

$$x_2 = b/p_2 - (p_1/p_2)x_1$$

where the slope of the line is $-(p_1/p_2)$ and the vertical intercept is b/p_2. Assuming that all other factors are held constant, any increase in p_2 will generate a lower vertical intercept and a less steep slope. Figure 2.5 shows the difference graphically, with the line on the right possessing the higher p_2. Where a reduced slope for the utility curves generated an equilibrium point emphasizing x_2 over x_1 when budget lines were held constant, the equilibrium point corresponding to a reduced slope in the budget line emphasizes x_1 when utility curves are held constant.[4] Simply put, a regime that finds domestic support—x_2 as set up here— relatively expensive will maximize the utility of its bundle of the two goods at a higher level of international secrecy than a regime that does not.

Not only is the slope of the budget line on the right in figure 2.5 less steep, but the area under the budget line—the set of attainable bundles of domestic support and international secrecy—is reduced as well. The area under the budget line can be expressed as:

$$\frac{1}{2}\left(\frac{b}{p_1} \times \frac{b}{p_2}\right)$$

Since we are comparing budget lines where only p_2—the price of domestic support—varies, a budget line with a greater p_2 must have a smaller set of attainable bundles of support and secrecy.

We have yet to ask what types of regimes will be faced with a relatively high price for domestic support, either from marketing or signaling concerns. Both concerns are determined by the nature of a nation's mass media system. Media systems are often described in terms of "openness," of how easy it is for information to be transmitted to a mass audience, of how much direct government control exists over this transfer of information. Media system openness, as one might expect, is closely correlated with liberal democratic government, but the relationship is far from perfect. For example, Brazil under military rule had a much more open media system than Russia under communist rule, even though both regimes were far from liberal democracies. And, too, *openness* is a very broad term. It conflates the marketing and signaling problems by linking in one concept both the number of media providers and the degree to which the government directly controls one or more of these providers. These are separate, albeit related, issues (see fig. 2.6). One can imagine a country, say Peru, with relatively few national media outlets but a tradition of private media ownership. The regime here would not have much of a marketing problem, as few separate information sources exist, but it would face a substantial signaling problem, as there is no obvious way to communicate its preferred brand of information directly. On the other hand, one can imagine a country, say the former Soviet Union, with clearly defined media channels for the regime but a large number of such channels. Everyone knows where to find the Central Committee's opinion (the official editorial in *Pravda*), but that point of view must compete for the public's attention with the army's mass circulation newspaper, Party-owned television stations, radio stations controlled by the KGB, etc. These opinions may or may not be similar, depending on the degree to which conformity on a certain issue is enforced from above. But, regardless of whether this is more accurately described as a coordination or enforcement problem than as a marketing problem, the effect on the support/secrecy equilibrium is identical.

Other factors that may influence the shape of the budget line are the price of secrecy, p_1, and the absolute amount of resources a regime has to spend on these two goods, b. One could make the argument that democratic regimes, with less institutional support for international secrecy than nondemocratic regimes,[5] must expend more resources to achieve a given level of international secrecy, systematically increasing p_1 for democratic regimes. The effect of changes in p_1 on the secrecy/support equilibrium follow straightforwardly and in the same manner as the changes demonstrated for changes in p_2, although with an opposite effect on the slope of the budget line. That is, regimes faced with expensive secrecy will find an equilibrium point that corresponds to more domestic support than a regime that can acquire secrecy easily. Like regimes faced with expensive support, the total area under the budget line is reduced—in this case the x_1 intercept declines and the slope increases.

One could also argue that b is a rough measure of the total resources of the state, not just the resources that can be brought to bear to obtain secrecy and support, and thus should be a function of the nation's GNP and the ability of the

Number of media opinion providers

High   Low

High   Marketing problem

**Regime identification
with one or more
media outlets**

Low   Marketing problem

Signaling problem   Signaling problem

Fig. 2.6

regime to extract resources from the nation. All other factors held constant, then, larger nations and nations with higher tax extraction rates should have larger b. A larger b, again with all other factors held constant, increases the area under the budget line. In fact, by taking the derivative of the area function A with respect to b:

$$A = \frac{1}{2}\left(\frac{b}{p_1} \times \frac{b}{p_2}\right)$$

$$\frac{\partial A}{\partial b} = \frac{b}{p_1 p_2}$$

we see that every unit increase in b will enlarge the set of attainable outcomes proportionally to b.

I am less confident in these arguments regarding p_1 and b than I am in the arguments for systematic regime differences for the utility function U and the price of support p_2.[6] As noted earlier, while public support would seem to be a goal of all governments at all times, international secrecy is not so clearly a constant necessity. To the degree that regimes do not care if their intentions are hidden from potential adversaries—for example, when the United States makes plans to intervene militarily in Haiti—the price of international secrecy is zero. I would argue that the dictates of public support building established here apply even in these situations, but clearly the equilibrium relationship itself loses much relevance.[7] Fortunately for this analysis, no participant in conflicts meeting the Singer and Small criteria for interstate war[8] shows such a disdain for secrecy, largely because one of the criteria is effective resistance to the initiated conflict (i.e., many dead soldiers on both sides). Only initiators absolutely certain that resistance will be virtually nonexistent (like the U.S. vs. Haiti) can afford to ignore the advantages provided by strategic surprise, and these conflicts never become full-blown wars. Thus, while the systematic regime differences noted for p_2 apply to both military interventions and interstate wars, regime differences for p_1 (and the equilibrium relationship itself) apply only to the latter.

Implications for International Behavior

So far, then, I have made the following assumptions about systematic regime differences:

   A1. Democracies value domestic support more than nondemocracies.
   A2. Regimes dealing with open media systems (many media outlets and/or little direct regime control over one or more outlets) find support relatively expensive to acquire.
   A3. Democracies find secrecy relatively expensive to acquire.
   A4. Wealthy regimes (large GNP and/or high government extraction rates) have more resources to spend on public support and international secrecy.

And the comparative statics of the functions pertaining to the support/secrecy equilibrium can be summarized with the corresponding deductions:

   D1. Regimes that value domestic support more highly than other regimes will maximize their utility at a relatively higher level of support and lower level of secrecy.
   D2. Regimes that find support relatively expensive to acquire will maximize their utility at a higher level of secrecy; the set of attainable outcomes will be reduced.
   D3. Regimes that find secrecy relatively expensive to acquire will maximize their utility at a higher level of support; the set of attainable outcomes will be reduced.
   D4. Regimes that have more resources to spend on the support/secrecy trade-off will have a greater set of attainable outcomes.

   D1 and A1 deal solely with the preference function for secrecy and support—the utility indifference curves. The utility curves are assumed to be convex, meaning that the curve "flattens" as x_1 increases, but this is simply a property of this sort of analysis. My additional claim is that the curve is system-

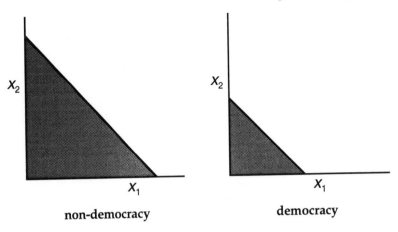

non-democracy   democracy

Fig. 2.7

atically more flattened for democracies than nondemocracies, that the slope becomes less negative more quickly for democracies than nondemocracies. The
end effect of this flattening is that democracies should find their utility for the
two goods of secrecy and support maximized at a relatively high level of support and low level of secrecy.

A2 and A3 (and their commensurate deductions D2 and D3) generate implications for both the utility function and the budget line. Figure 2.7 shows
how these assumptions and deduced attributes affect the set of attainable outcomes available to a hypothetical democracy and nondemocracy.[9] If domestic
support and international secrecy are both relatively expensive for democracies
to obtain, then both the x_2-intercept and the x_1-intercept will be reduced for the
democratic budget line. The resulting slope of the budget line is an empirical
question that depends on the relative influence of, respectively, a particular
media system and a particular institutional arrangement for international secrecy. If the former has more influence, through the marketing and/or signaling
problem, then the regime will maximize its utility by emphasizing international
secrecy. If the latter has more influence, then emphasizing domestic support
will be the utility-maximizing behavior of a rational government. Regardless of
whether the resulting slope of the reduced budget line is skewed either to favor
an equilibrium point of secrecy or support, the set of attainable bundles of support and secrecy will be smaller than the set of outcomes attainable by an
otherwise identical nondemocracy.

This reduced area is critical if we make two additional assumptions (see
fig. 2.8).

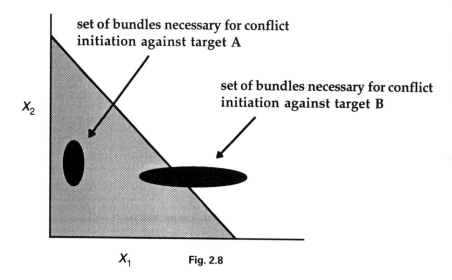

set of bundles necessary for conflict initiation against target A

set of bundles necessary for conflict initiation against target B

X_2

X_1 Fig. 2.8

A5. There exists a set of bundles of support/secrecy vis-à-vis any potential target that, in the minds of national decision makers, allows conflict initiation against that target.[10]

A6. If and only if a bundle of support/secrecy within that set is attained will conflict be initiated against that target.

One can easily imagine how an alteration in the set of attainable outcomes could leave the set of bundles necessary to initiate conflict with target B outside of the attainable set and yet still include all or part of the set corresponding to conflict initiation against target A. And, if we apply these assumptions to figure 2.7, we must conclude that a democracy will not have more possible initiation targets than an identical nondemocracy and will possibly have fewer.

If we assume that for any possible initiation target there exists an independent nonzero probability that conflict will indeed be initiated against that target within a given time frame, then a greater number of such potential targets leads to a higher probability that conflict will be initiated against some target within that time frame.[11] In other words:

A7. The more potential targets for conflict initiation, the more likely that conflict will be initiated against one of those targets.

Such an assumption, in light of figure 2.7, would suggest that democracies will initiate conflict less often than nondemocracies.

But, just as democratic rule is highly (but not perfectly) correlated with media system openness, so is democratic rule highly (but not perfectly) correlated with national wealth. If greater regime wealth leads to more resources to purchase secrecy and/or support, as per A4, then the relationship of figure 2.7 will be reversed: the area under the democracy's budget line will be greater than that of the nondemocracy. If we were to look just at regime wealth, then, we would conclude that a democracy will not have fewer initiation targets than an otherwise identical nondemocracy and may very well have more. Based on D4, we can draw the related conclusion that, as b increases, so does the total utility associated with the equilibrium point, wherever it might fall on the budget line, as the larger b pushes the budget line to form a tangent with a higher indifference curve.

Obviously enough, the hypothesized pressures on international behaviors created by this equilibrium do not all push in the same direction. In fact, the clearest implication of these observations is that these regime, media, and economic characteristics cannot just be lumped together in a single measure—"liberal democracy"—that is in turn used to make sweeping generalizations about the war proneness of different regime types. Instead, each separate factor must be carefully accounted for before we can compare how nations get to war. A rich democratic regime with strong ties to the media will have a very different set of constraints facing it than a poor democratic regime with few such connections.

This is not to say that connections between war proneness and regime type do not exist, only that they cannot be painted with too broad a brush. In fact, one of the most compelling issues in international relations today—democratic peace—points out a possible relationship between war proneness and regime type. A robust set of observations suggests that liberal democracies are just as likely to fight wars as nondemocracies but that, statistically speaking, they are much less likely to fight each other than one would otherwise expect.[12] Recent scholarship has attempted to separate factors such as geographic propinquity and economic strength in order to isolate the effect of the regime variable, and these efforts show that liberal democracies fight each other less often than we would otherwise expect even if you control for, among other factors, economic wealth.[13] In terms of the support/secrecy equilibrium model, this puts us back at figure 2.7, in which a democratic regime has a smaller area of attainable bundles of domestic support and international security than a nondemocracy, and eliminates the possibly confounding effect of a larger b (and hence a larger area) through increased economic resources.

Implications for Predicting War

There are a variety of possible hypotheses regarding international behavior that we can derive from the secrecy/support equilibrium model. For example, on the basis of assumptions A4, A5, A6, and A7 we could test:

H0. Wealthy regimes, with more resources to spend on secrecy and support, will have more potential initiation targets and a higher rate of
conflict initiation than poor regimes.

But the central research concern of this book remains the timing of a national
command structure's decision for conflict, not the war proneness of this regime
or that. Can we make similarly empirically falsifiable hypotheses regarding
how nations get to war? Can we predict, in a meaningful way, when and how a
government is moving toward war?

The two basic implications of this model that should apply to all regimes,
regardless of type, are the following hypotheses:

H1. Before initiating war with another nation, all regimes will attempt to
build domestic support for that action.
H2. Before initiating war with another nation, regimes expecting meaningful opposition will attempt to keep these intentions secret from
their target.

Of the two, hypothesis H1 will receive more attention in future chapters because it bears more directly on predicting war. That is, empirical evidence supporting H1 will take the form of a leading indicator of conflict, of a positive
action made publicly by a regime to garner support. Any evidence for H2 will
take the form of efforts to hide such indicators from international eyes, of
hidden actions that are only revealed indirectly or through error. Evidence
for H2 is inherently truncated; like covert actions in general, we see only failed
attempts to maintain secrecy or their effects after the fact. In any event such
evidence is not a reliable leading indicator for conflict. Not only is H1 a more
counterintuitive proposition (and thus a more influential claim if supported empirically), but it is more amenable to empirical investigation in the first place.

I am claiming that all wars will have demonstrable propaganda efforts preceding them, but I am not claiming that all propaganda efforts will have wars
following them. The latter is far too deterministic, as it assumes away any role
for international bargaining and negotiation. All the same, if domestic support–
building efforts are identical before both war and peace, the usefulness of such
efforts as a predictive indicator is clearly limited. To predict a phenomenon we
must go beyond simply identifying necessary conditions to find those that are
both necessary and at least somewhat sufficient.

As suggested in chapter 1, we can try to resolve this problem by thinking of
war initiation as a process rather than a single yes/no irrevocable decision. Getting to war takes time, and over that period of time a government's intentions
and goals may change as well, depending on both international and domestic
events. If Britain had unexpectedly acquiesced to Argentine demands in Febru-

ary 1982, I doubt that the junta would still have invaded in April. But during each chunk of time along that road to war (or perhaps peaceful resolution) there should be evidence of a direct relationship between efforts to generate support and subsequent behavior. Propaganda efforts should wax and wane as the likelihood of future episodes of conflict initiation waxes and wanes. Or, as stated by the following hypothesis:

> H3. The level of a regime's domestic support–building effort will be commensurate to the degree of conflictual behavior subsequently directed against a target.

Of course, this will be an imperfect relationship. An external shock may still make previous propaganda efforts unnecessary or insufficient, whether the observation period is by month, by year, or by crisis. But, by breaking down the road to war into smaller observation periods, I generate more cases over which the hypotheses should apply. Also, by hypothesizing a link between level of effort and level of conflict over a set of observation periods, I am setting a much more difficult goal for this model than H1 alone implies.

Although H1 is the linchpin to all other efforts in this work, we can make additional testable hypotheses that bear on predicting conflict by incorporating the assumptions regarding the influence of regime type (A1 and A3) and media system (A2). These supplemental hypotheses are valuable, not so much for their ability to provide a leading indicator of conflict on their own but for their refinement of the central claim.

> H4. Democratic regimes will make greater efforts to garner domestic support than nondemocratic regimes, both from their greater reliance on public support to remain in office and their reduced institutional resources for international secrecy (A1, A3).
>
> H5. Regimes constrained by marketing and/or signaling difficulties within their domestic mass media system must make greater efforts to achieve the same level of public support than a regime not so constrained (A2).

Including regime and media system characteristics in the general predictive function described by H1 and H3 should improve both the overall fit of the model and the accuracy of parameter estimates.

An International Signaling Model

The equilibrium function between support and secrecy described thus far is a one-sided, entirely domestic model. There is no allowance for strategic interaction between nations given these constraints. Clearly, this must be addressed before we can have confidence that efforts to secure public support through mass media are an effective leading indicator of war. If these efforts are such an effective indicator, why don't other nations pay more attention to them? If an adversary did pay attention to nation A's domestic media, why couldn't nation A influence its enemy's behavior by changing its domestic media activities? Some bureaucratic justifications for why governments pay more attention to direct information through diplomatic channels rather than indirect information sources (such as foreign media) were presented in chapter 1, but by modeling these conundrums more fully we can perhaps glean additional insights. Unfortunately, I conclude that the gains from such a foray into "signaling games" are limited at best.

Signaling games are models of strategic interaction with incomplete information. As in most formal games, the goal is to find equilibrium behavior, but the catch here is that one or more players have private and valuable information regarding their decision parameters. Not only is information incomplete in a signaling game, but the player with the private and valuable information moves first by taking some action that can "signal" the other players what her hidden decision parameters really are.[14]

The signal in this model is the media activity instigated by a regime in an attempt to build domestic political support for war. We want to know how much information this action gives to other governments and what sorts of strategic behavior it might spawn. Previous work on the subject provides valuable signposts but few direct applications. There is a substantial body of work on legislative signaling games involving political rhetoric and speeches but little on international games involving such wordy signals.[15] And, too, the legislative signaling research of Gilligan and Krehbiel, Austen-Smith, etc., usually assumes that rhetoric is a costless signal, that it plays an informational role but does not in and of itself impact any player's utility function. I am claiming just the opposite for these signals—that they have a cost, often a high one, separate from the potential effect of recipients' reactions to those signals.

Assume that regime A has been beating the war drums at home for months to build public support to invade the X territory, now held by regime B, if B will not hand it over. One morning, however, the president of A wakes up and decides that the X territory is not that vital after all, that A can achieve the same goals through better trade relations with B. Can President A simply change her mind without incurring significant domestic political risks? Many of A's citizens, both in and out of government, believe that the X territory is worth fighting for. I doubt that they will be too pleased with President A once they hear of her change of heart. By stating a preference for the takeover of X effectively enough to rally support, President A has also committed herself to following through with the takeover. Her actions helped create a constituency for annexing

X that now (perhaps) has the means to punish her for reneging on her commitment. In other words, I am arguing that governments pay a price for rousing the sleeping giant of public opinion and then failing to act. At the very least governments *anticipate* that they will pay such a price. In either event a regime's actions to mobilize public support, in and of themselves, have consequences for the regime's evaluation of whether to go to war or not. Once committed to such a course of action governments do not believe that they can back down without suffering serious domestic consequences. Certainly, regimes will differ about the political cost of mobilizing public support, but no regime will find these signals to be costless.[16]

The cost associated with such signals provides the first cut at an answer to why regimes do not use their domestic media in a strategic fashion to influence other governments' behavior. As Michael Spence puts it in an analysis of credit formulas used by lenders:

> Yet it is clear, on reflection, that many potentially alterable characteristics such as home ownership and marital status are not in fact the subject of active signaling in the loan market. Such characteristics, then, function in the market as though they were indices. . . . The reason that many potential signals turn into effective indices is that the costs of altering them swamp the gains. Thus even when banks and other credit institutions react to them, it is not worth investing in them. It is difficult, for example, to imagine someone marrying purely for the purpose of appearing to a bank to be a stable family type.[17]

The distinction between signals and indices as they apply to international politics is more clearly drawn by Robert Jervis.[18] To create the foundations for what he calls a "theory of deception," Jervis provides a wealth of historical examples to demonstrate the relative usefulness of indices ("statements or actions that carry some inherent evidence that the image projected is correct because they are believed to be inextricably linked to the actor's capabilities or intentions")[19] in predicting international behavior.

Jervis is clear that the difference between signal and index is rarely cut and dried, that there is a continuum of behavior with cheap talk on one end and nonmanipulatable index on the other. In fact, if an actor can manipulate an index by extricating himself from the supposedly inextricable link, with this manipulation kept secret from his adversary, this is precisely the most effective way to foster international deception. For example, Jervis points out that Hitler was adept at feigning extreme anger or even insanity in order to take advantage of the perceived link between such personal characteristics and actual beliefs.[20] And, too, just because I perceive that a stable indexed link exists does not necessarily make it so.[21] But even if a regime discovers both that one of its behaviors is perceived as a sure indicator of other behavior *and* that this supposed indexed behavior is in fact controllable, it is far from certain that the regime will actually seek to manipulate this index. Depending on the costs of such manipulation, the game may not be worth the candle.

> For example, the Chinese may have decided in the Fall of 1950 that the increased chance of convincing the United Nations forces to withdraw from North Korea, which might have been attained by manipulating indices of their intention of intervening (e.g., by not disguising their presence in North Korea), was outweighed by the military advantages of surprise.[22]

And in a passage that is extremely relevant for this particular analysis Jervis writes:

> In World War II a Swiss journalist was able to give "amazingly accurate" reports of the movement of German troops by keeping track of all mention in the German papers of the location of military personnel and units. While once the Germans discovered this they might have been able to withhold information (at a considerable cost to home morale), it would not be worth the huge expenditure of resources needed to manipulate this minutiae.[23]

This is the critical point—that, if the costs of manipulation are high enough, indices are useful tools in predicting behavior even if those indices are recognized by the source nation as providing useful information to potential adversaries.[24]

The vital role of indices in developing leading indicators of international events certainly does not diminish the role of signaling in international relations, especially in crisis bargaining. On the contrary, as pointed out earlier in this chapter, sometimes nations (U.S. relations toward Haiti are a good example) would prefer to sacrifice any tactical advantage from surprise in order to signal their intentions more clearly. My point is merely that the domestic media is a dangerous arena for regimes to engage in this sort of signaling, that such behavior is better understood as a nonmanipulated index rather than as a manipulated signal per se. Far better for governments to signal their resolve through means such as troop maneuvers and high-ranking envoys (precisely the primary U.S. strategy vis-à-vis Haiti), signals that are costless (in terms of the game) and still informative.

Precisely because the potential cost of bluffing with domestic media is high, precisely because it is a dangerous signal, such behavior is a good leading indicator. Why, then, don't nations pay more attention to their neighbors' media behavior? Let us return to regime A and its stated desire to seize the X territory. For months regime A has been telling its citizens that they should fight, if necessary, to get X. What is regime B, which currently controls X, to think about this?

Assume that, if regime B is certain that A is willing to fight to take X, then B would rather give X to A than fight a war over the territory. This does *not* necessarily mean that B expects to lose a war with A over X, only that the costs of even a successful war effort are greater than the costs of losing X. Think, for example, of Berlin during the Cold War. Even if the United States "won" a nuclear war with the USSR over the issue of Berlin, it would be less costly for the United States simply to hand the city over without a fight. But capitulation would be rational behavior only if the United States had complete information and was certain that the USSR would rather start and lose a full-scale war than back down from its demands. Otherwise, under either incomplete information or a different utility function for the Soviet Union, a stable crisis equilibrium exists (it may not last or be reached, but it exists) such that the status quo is preserved, regardless of the "resolve" of either side.[25] B prefers giving up X without a shot to fighting over X, but only if B is certain that A will attack. B does *not* prefer giving up X without a shot to fighting over X if there is uncertainty whether A will attack. Otherwise, B is practically begging A to take the X territory off its hands.

By definition, no signal or leading indicator can provide B with the complete information necessary to justify capitulation. A partial answer to the question of why nations don't pay more attention to leading indicators, then, would have to be that there is no indication they could receive that would change their essential plans—to fight if attacked. The only benefit provided by leading indicators is to minimize the danger of being taken unawares by A's attack, making it more difficult to fight back. But, since collecting and analyzing signals and leading indicators are themselves costly undertakings, it is often more cost effective to simply assume that an attack might take place at any time. For example, the readiness protocols of the U.S. Strategic Air Command (SAC) and the North American Air Defense Command (NORAD) were predicated on ignoring indicators of Soviet intent (under an assumption that Soviet intent was uniformly belligerent and opportunistic) in favor of identifying visible indicators of Soviet mobilization behavior.[26]

Regardless of whether B is even interested in receiving signals from A, the fundamental indeterminacy of signaling efforts undermine the transmission of this information to B. If we assume that governments prefer to receive concessions without sacrificing the blood and treasure of even a successful war, it is to the signaling regime's advantage to portray its signaling costs as quite high regardless of what they truly are. Only then—by convincing an accommodationist regime that they will definitely fight rather than withdraw their demands—do they have a chance of gaining at least some of their demands without firing a shot. Assuming a government even knows how costly its domestic signals are, it has a clear strategy to portray its costs to be as high as possible. In this environment, receiving governments should systematically downplay their perception

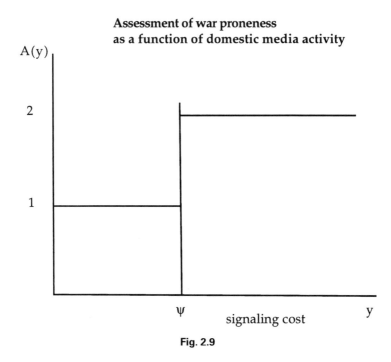

**Assessment of war proneness
as a function of domestic media activity**

Fig. 2.9

of the costliness of other nations' media signals, precisely because they expect that other nations will falsely magnify those costs. And, the more a receiving regime consistently underestimates the costliness of signaling efforts, the more it will tend to overlook the signal itself as a leading indicator of conflict.

A simple signaling model, adapted from Spence,[27] illustrates this indeterminacy problem nicely. Assume two groups of signaling regimes: those that are indeed likely to fight a war over a certain claim (W) and those that are not (P), with corresponding war assessments of 2 and 1. The signal receiver must assess whether a regime has a war proneness value of 2 or 1 on the basis of its signals (the domestic media activity). Such a decision depends on the conditional beliefs of the signal receiver. Let us assume a step function for this example, such that the receiver assesses value 2 with probability of 1 to any regime where $y \geq \psi$ and assesses value 1 with probability of 1 to any regime where $y < \psi$ (see fig. 2.9). We can ignore the rational response of the signaler for now given these conditional beliefs of the receiver. What is critical is the influence of systematic underestimation of y—the perceived cost of signaling. The more the receiver adjusts y downward, the less likely an assessment of 2. In fact, if the receiver believes that the real cost of signaling is 0, regardless of how much credence the receiver gives to the signal itself, then the signaling nation will be assessed a value of 1, in effect ignoring any information conveyed by the domestic media.[28] Moreover, if such a misperception were widespread, or came close to being so,[29] no regime would rationally use its domestic media as an international signal in the first place, although it would still have a strong incentive to use media for domestic support–building purposes.

The real world, of course, is not so absolute. Bumblebees fly; used cars are bought and sold between private individuals—just to name two systems that should not work in theory. Certainly, receiving governments pay some attention to other nations' domestic media; certainly, governments make some limited attempts to use their media as an international signal. The point here is simply that there are significant constraints on using domestic media for strategic purposes. Not only are there strong bureaucratic and cultural reasons for governments to favor information gathered through traditional diplomatic channels, but it is also quite rational for governments to have a relatively jaundiced view of foreign media activity. Between these factors, attempts to use domestic media as an international signal will be feeble at best.[30]

CHAPTER 3

Testing the Theory

In the simplest operationalization of hypothesis H1, I am proposing a world in which public opinion–building efforts precede a war initiated against any other nation. Graphically, we can think of this process as:

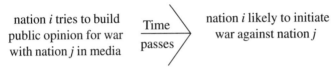

| nation i tries to build public opinion for war with nation j in media | Time passes | nation i likely to initiate war against nation j |

I must emphasize that this is not a causal model, in which media harangues cause a nation to start a war. Instead, the logic of building public support creates a situation in which domestic media provide an informative indicator that a government is likely to initiate hostilities at some point in the future, even though that government may be giving very different signals through diplomatic communications.

In order to test the idea that mass media can actually serve as a leading indicator of conflict initiation, as an "early warning network" in Deutsch's terms, we need to narrow our focus. The three components of this simple model—mass media, time, and war—are all sufficiently inchoate to require further definition and explication.

A First Cut at Operationalization

As described in chapter 1, newspapers hold a special position as both influential and competitively partisan molders of public opinion. Not only do newspapers possess general advantages over television and radio for the purposes of this research, but they also have a particular attribute designed specifically and openly to influence opinion: the editorial.

For being one of the most constant features of modern communications, editorials have been largely ignored by researchers, despite their advantages for systematic study. All newspapers have editorials of some sort, printed on a daily (or near daily) basis. Since all modern nations have newspapers of some sort, domestic editorials have been written on a highly regular basis in every country on Earth for the past century. What is more, editorials have had very roughly the same purpose and meaning across time and across nations, despite immense differences in the purpose and meaning of their respective media systems, making relevant international comparisons possible. That is, despite the differences in the largely open media system of Israel and the largely closed system of the Soviet Union, both the editorials of *Pravda* and the editorials of the *Jerusalem Post* are forthrightly trying to convince the reader to agree with some policy position. I am not claiming that these editorials are identical in scope or purpose; however, by looking solely at editorials, the propagandizing difference between the newspapers is largely minimized. As a final advantage for researchers, editorials from even the most autarchic or geographically distant nation are freely and easily available within weeks of publication, and they are usually transferred to microfilm for permanent storage.

This is not to suggest that newspaper editorials are especially effective in mobilizing public opinion. Only a limited proportion of a nation's population even reads a newspaper occasionally, much less the editorial page. Nor do I suggest that even an ideologically friendly newspaper will print only glowing pieces regarding government policy. But the goal here is to identify the facet of mass media that provides the best indicator of the true preferences of national decision makers, not to identify the most efficient (only regime opinions are presented) or effective (everyone reads the opinions) tool with which to sell those preferences to the public. I am not saying that editorials are a clear and unbroken mirror of leaders' intentions, but I will argue that they are the best available under difficult circumstances. So long as we can agree that editorials are one way in which opinion leaders attempt to lead opinion and that a newspaper more or less in sync with the government will exist for any country, editorials satisfy the minimal requirement of appropriateness for this study. It is editorials' other attributes—longevity, similarity in purpose, availability, and regularity—that make them the best choice for this research.

Even after identifying editorials as the most salient aspect of mass media for this research program, we are still left with the problem of how to operationalize them. Rather than implement a complicated content analysis such as finding affect-laden terms within some specified distance of a foreign nation's name, I ask one simple question. Does the editorial discuss a threat posed by a foreign nation? If yes, the editorial is coded as critical vis-à-vis that nation; if no, then not.[1] One complicating factor in this operationalization is deciding what to do with groups of nations. For example, if the Soviet Union writes an editorial critical of NATO, should that count as one critical editorial directed against all individual NATO members? The assumption here is that only focused editorials, directed against, at most, two nations, are reflective of tension with the potential for conflict. Egypt might start a war with Israel, for instance, but not against the "Western imperialist conspiracy." If more than two nations, or an organized group of more than two nations, are the subject of such an editorial, none of the nations are credited with any portion of a critical editorial. Since some newspapers print six or more editorials per day and others only one or two, I have analyzed the editorial data both in terms of a simple count and in terms of a percentage of all editorials written.

One last operationalization question remains here: the choice of newspaper in nations with more than one mass circulation daily. The choice is easy when an official newspaper, an organ of the ruling regime, exists. When there is no official government paper, I use the prestige daily closest in editorial opinion to the government. For example, the *Wall Street Journal* is more appropriate for my concerns than the *New York Times* for an analysis of the United States government during Republican administrations, at least since World War II. By "prestige daily" I mean a newspaper with national circulation and recognition by the international press as some sort of paper of record for the country in question. Various reference sources were consulted to link regime interests and editorial sympathies; where references were unclear, editorial opinions were correlated informally with government actions to determine which of two or more newspapers is closest to the government.[2]

The observation period used for this project is the calendar month, similar to the observation period of commonly reported economic leading indicators. A month is long enough to smooth out the wildest fluctuations in editorial and conflictual behavior while preserving the meaningful variation. In this test of H1, then, I will be counting the number and percentage of critical editorials vis-à-vis some foreign nation in the four weeks preceding a given date (such as a war initiation date). To be sure, a variety of statistical problems arise from any sort of temporal aggregation.[3] I will explore the robustness of this particular aggregation with the initial statistical tests.

Conflict can obviously come in a variety of forms, but I am concerned here with overt military conflict rather than trade wars or some other sort of nonviolent conflict (chap. 4 will try to differentiate between various types of conflict). Even so, there remain many of the same questions we had for operationalizing editorials. What level of violence should count as a case of interstate conflict, much less war? Should one case of conflict be considered as a collection of violent events, or should each event be counted separately? In this first cut at the model I will use a binary war/no war operationalization. Further tests will break each of these wars into discrete events, allowing us to broaden the study to include crises falling short of war as well as to examine the specific paths nations follow in getting to war.

Data Set 1: Preliminary Evidence

The best data set to use for an investigation of this model would be the universe of all cases—every pair of nations for every month (dyad/months) during some span of time. Barring that, we would want to take a random sample of cases from the universe of dyad/months. Unfortunately for this research program (but very fortunately for everyone else), war is an exceedingly rare event when considered in terms of such an operationalization. Just as an epidemiologist cannot take a random sample of 1,000 people and expect to discover the disease vectors of bubonic plague, a political scientist cannot take a random sample of dyad/months and expect to find sufficient variation on the dependent variable of war to make meaningful conclusions. For example, in a random sample of 1,000 dyad/months I might expect to find one or two cases of war. My theory of war prediction given such a sample would be both statistically sound and completely useless: I would never predict war to occur. The study of war is almost inherently a quasi-experiment, in which truly random assignation to experimental and control groups is either impossible or leads to trivial findings.[4]

On the other hand, if I were arbitrarily to select only cases of past wars to study, I would be making the classic statistical error of selection on the dependent variable. Without a comparison of cases in which wars did and did not occur, my analysis would be hopelessly biased, as I could not accurately separate meaningful independent variables from spurious ones. As Sherlock Holmes pointed out to Dr. Watson, the dogs that don't bark are as important in solving mysteries as the dogs that do.

Whenever we attempt to predict rare events, whether it be wars between nations or Earth's collisions with wayward asteroids, we must chart a difficult course between the Scylla of irrelevance and the Charybdis of case selection on the dependent variable. My path will be to take the universe of rare events over a given time span and compare it to a random sample of the far more numerous null cases over the same time span. This is precisely the method employed by Bruce Bueno de Mesquita and David Lalman in their study of the causes of war, although, as they point out, "the danger is that the disproportionate representation of the two subsets may distort the empirical findings."[5] I avoid this problem in the first cut at statistical tests as they do, by using a logit analysis. As Christopher Achen points out in an application of public health methodology to political science,[6] the different composition of the subsets is irrelevant when we compare their odds ratio (or its log, the logit). In subsequent event-count analyses simple logit tests are not as appropriate, and we must adjust the statistical tests accordingly.

As a preliminary data set, four nations (Argentina, India, Israel, and Pakistan) were evaluated vis-à-vis their neighbors immediately before six wars (Second Kashmir, Six Day, Bangladesh, Yom Kippur, Falklands, Lebanon). Not only was the to-be-warring nation evaluated for each of these dates, but the other nations—for example, Argentina before the Six Day War—were evaluated vis-à-vis their neighbors as well to provide a random no-war sample. That is, if we assume that each nation's conflict decision making is independent, the start of a war involving one of these countries is just like any other day to the other countries in the set. The exception here would be India and Pakistan, but their linked decision making poses a problem only if any of the wars examined involved one of these two but not the other. In effect, India and Pakistan are treated as one independent unit in this data set. I included both nations because it is unclear which nation should be considered the initiator of their wars, especially the Bangladesh War in 1971.

Figures 3.1–3.6 provide snapshots of the information in the data set for each date in question. For example, in figure 3.1 we see five nation pairs showing critical editorials written in the four weeks prior to the initiation of the Second Kashmir War between India and Pakistan,[7] out of a total of 20 nation pairs. Pakistan versus India generates the highest number of critical editorials during this period, with India versus Pakistan in fourth place. Compare these results to the other Indo-Pakistani war in this data set, the Bangladesh War (fig. 3.3). Here India versus Pakistan and Pakistan versus India are more clearly the leaders of their class, with 10 critical editorials written by Pakistan against India, and 9 written by India against Pakistan. No other nation pair comes close to these totals, and only six other nation pairs even generated a single critical editorial.

In figure 3.2 we see seven dyads with critical editorials written in the month prior to the Israeli initiation of the Six Day War. As expected, Israel versus Egypt and Israel versus Syria lead the list here, with 7 and 6 editorials, respectively. Israel versus Jordan is in fourth place, with 3 editorials during this period. Compare these results to the other Arab-Israeli war in this sample, the Yom Kippur War (fig. 3.4). Since this conflict was initiated by Egypt, we should not expect Israel to demonstrate any great number of critical editorials in the month preceding the initiation. This is precisely what we find, as nine nation pairs show minor editorial activity, but none show more than 3 hostile editorials. Israel's participation in another war in this sample, the Lebanon War of 1982, is clearly preceded by critical editorial activity far above the norm (fig. 3.6).

Support for the basic model and hypothesis H1 is fairly clear. In all 123 cases only nations about to initiate a war (or already involved in a war—Argentina was still fighting Britain when Israel invaded Lebanon) show 4 or more critical editorials during the month leading up to the outbreak of war. In all cases the most critical editorials written by a nation about to start a war are directed against that nation's actual target.

Logit models, in which the expected value of a dependent variable can be represented as $1/(1 + e^{-x_i \beta})$, are commonly employed to determine the measure of association between a binary dependent variable and an assortment of independent variables (x_i). In this case we have only one such independent variable: editorial count in the preceding month (table 3.1) or editorial count expressed as a percentage of all editorials written (table 3.2). Note that, since a decision to

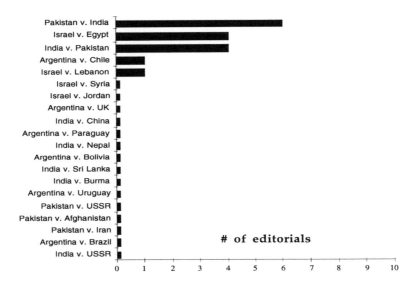

Fig. 3.1.   August 15, 1965: Pre–Second Kashmir War

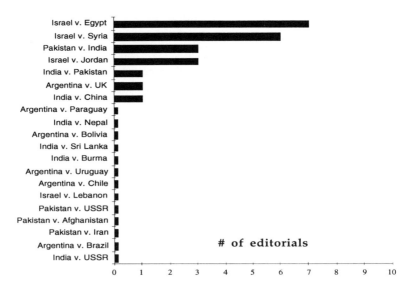

Fig. 3.2.   June 5, 1967: Pre–Six Day War

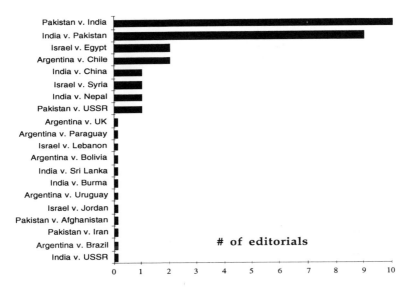

Fig. 3.3.   December 2, 1971: Pre–Bangladesh War

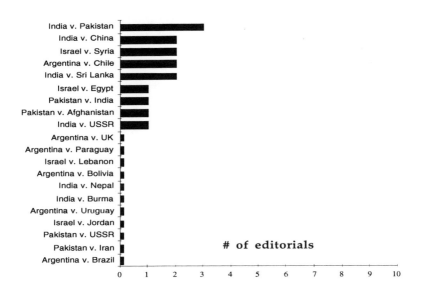

Fig. 3.4.   October 5, 1973: Pre–Yom Kippur War

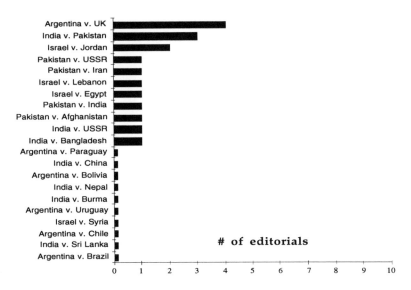

Fig. 3.5.   April 1, 1982: Pre–Falklands War

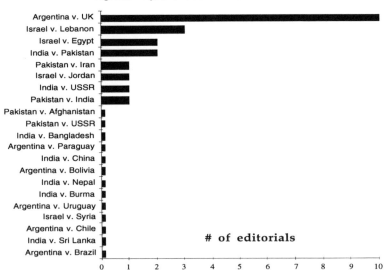

Fig. 3.6.   June 3, 1982: Pre–Lebanon War

fight one adversary is not independent of a decision to fight another adversary at any particular point in time, the 123 total cases shown in figures 3.1–6 must be reduced to 92 by eliminating the warring nation's nonconflictual dyads. For example, India versus Nepal prior to the Bangladesh War is not a legitimate no-war case; India versus Nepal prior to the Yom Kippur War is. (See app. 1.1 for a complete listing of data set 1).

For all statistical tests in this chapter, maximum likelihood estimators are generated for the proposed independent variables. They should be interpreted as parameter estimates with the greatest relative likelihood of accounting for the observed values of the dependent variable. For each estimate the standard error is reported as well. Roughly speaking, a standard error less than half of the estimate shows parameter significance below the .05 level. One additional test statistic is generated for each of these regressions: the log-likelihood value. Like the more well-known r-squared result, log-likelihood is a measure of the goodness of fit of one specification of the model relative to another specification. Like r-squared, log-likelihood has no independent meaning; it should only be used to compare two specifications of the model using the same data. In such a comparison the model with the larger log-likelihood accounts better for the observed values. For logit regressions I have also included the percentage of cases correctly predicted by an application of the specified model.

Parameter estimates here are clearly significant and in the right direction for both regressions. That is, we expected a positive relationship between the number or percentage of critical editorials written versus a potential target and the subsequent chances that conflict actually took place. Interestingly, using the simpler operationalization of critical editorial—count rather than percentage—provides a slightly better specification of the model. Also, incorporating various measures of national capabilities—power—into the model failed to improve its predictive strength or provide a significant variable along these lines.

TABLE 3.1.   Data Set 1
             Model: Logit
             Dependent variable: War$_t$

Parameter name	Estimate	S.E.
constant	7.957	2.865
Editorial Count$_{t-1}$	2.500	0.964

log-likelihood = −7.1336
$n = 92$
% correctly predicted = 95.65

TABLE 3.2.   Data Set 1
             Model: Logit
             Dependent variable: War$_t$

Parameter name	Estimate	S.E.
constant	− 4.643	0.972
% Editorial$_{t-1}$	0.441	0.112

log-likelihood = −12.132
$n = 92$
% correctly predicted = 94.57

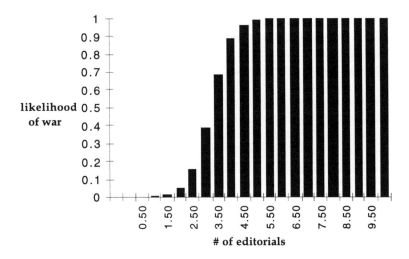

Fig. 3.7.   Data Set 1

With only one independent variable a two-dimensional graph can provide a substantive interpretation of the parameter estimates, showing the probability of war given different levels of editorial activity in the preceding month (fig. 3.7). Using the parameter estimates of table 3.1, such a graph is generated by substituting –7.957 and 2.500 for β in the function $1/(1 + e^{-x_i\beta})$:

Such an analysis would, on the face of it, suggest that three or more critical editorials in any given four-week span is an excellent predictor of subsequent war. But in reality such a deterministic claim would be suspect. The underlying distribution of data set 1 is such that 83/92 cases—90.22 percent—are nonwar cases (see table 3.3). In other words, a constant term could "predict" 90 percent of these cases correctly; for the model to improve on that by five or six percentage points is not saying that much. And, as we shall see with a more sophisticated data set, a high number of critical editorials rarely just materializes out of thin air. If many critical editorials are written in Time $t - 1$, it is a good bet that some critical editorials were also written in Time $t - 2$. But critical editorials in Time $t - 2$ are, by definition, written one to two months prior to the outbreak of war, meaning that three or more editorials written then, while indicative of war in two months, are not at all indicative of war in one month. The point here is to read figure 3.7 as circumstantial evidence for the importance of critical editorials in predicting war, not as a simple-minded causal threshold test.

One could more fundamentally criticize this preliminary data set on two grounds. First, the selection of wars is rather ad hoc, reflecting easily available data sources rather than a random sample of wars or the universe of wars over a set time period. Second, the no-war component of this data set is not really randomly determined. While the dates chosen are effectively random, the nations are not, unless one makes the questionable assumption that nations that have initiated wars are just as unlikely as other nations to initiate another war. On the contrary, it seems more reasonable to postulate that starting a war in 1965 is indeed correlated with the chances of starting a war in 1971. By including only nations with a history of conflict in this sample, the data set leaves out nations that (through luck or design) have a pacifist past.

In a sense such a truncated data set is actually more interesting than one with truly random no-war cases, as it provides a more difficult hurdle for this model. If starting a war in 1965 in and of itself increases the likelihood of starting a war in subsequent years, there is a correspondingly greater likelihood that subsequent initiations will fail to show the posited relationship between editorials and war. That is, to the extent that simply starting a war in the past determines starting a war today, the number of editorials written has nothing to do with the process. At the very least the parameter estimates for the effect of editorials on war initiation will be artificially reduced.[8] Since these estimates are still significant and influential in the logit analysis, data set 1, although flawed, actually offers impressive evidence in favor of hypothesis H1 when one considers its bias.

Data Set 2: All Wars, 1965 through 1984

Data set 2 attempts to remove the bias of data set 1 by improving the selection of both the war and no-war cases. The Wages of War data set, compiled by J. David Singer and Melvin Small as part of the larger Correlates of War project, provides a standard source for the universe of interstate war cases from 1816 to 1980.[9] Beginning with the Vietnam War in 1965, I included all of Singer and

TABLE 3.3. Data Set 1

	Editorial Count ≤ 3	Editorial Count > 3
War	3	6
No war	82	1

Small's wars through 1980. Since I wanted a minimum time period of 20 years for this study, I extended the Singer and Small criteria to international events through 1984, adding two conflicts not found in Wages of War, the Argentine attack on the Falklands and the Israeli invasion of Lebanon (see table 3.4).

Singer and Small include some non-interstate wars in their list, in which one nation fights another political entity that "does not qualify as a member of the interstate system because of serious limitations on its independence, a population that was not large enough to meet the interstate system membership criteria or a failure of other states to recognize it as a legitimate member."[10] In other words, some major civil wars ("colonial wars" in their parlance) are included in the interstate war section of the Wages of War data set. Singer and Small also include all major combatants for any given conflict, whether they were the attacker or the attacked. I am concerned with the initiation of interstate

TABLE 3.4. Interstate Wars, 1965–84

	Initiator	War	Initiation Date
1.	Israel	Lebanon	6/4/82
2.	Argentina	Falklands	4/2/82
3.	Iraq	Irani-Iraqi	9/22/80
4.	USSR	Russo-Afghan	12/22/79
5.	China	Sino-Vietnamese	2/1/79
6.	Vietnam	Vietnamese-Cambodian	12/1/78
7.	Uganda	Ugandan-Tanzanian	10/30/78
8.	Cuba	Ogaden	11/1/77
9.	Somalia	Ogaden	8/1/77
10.	Turkey	Turco-Cypriot	7/20/74
11.	Egypt	Yom Kippur	10/6/73
12.	Syria	Yom Kippur	10/6/73
13.	India	Bangladesh	12/3/71
14.	Pakistan	Bangladesh	12/3/71
15.	El Salvador	Football	7/14/69
16.	Israel	Israeli-Egyptian	3/6/69
17.	Israel	Six Day (Egypt)	6/5/67
18.	Israel	Six Day (Syria)	6/5/67
19.	Egypt	Six Day	6/5/67
20.	Pakistan	Second Kashmir	8/5/65
21.	U.S.	Vietnam	3/2/65[a]

[a]It is particularly difficult to pinpoint the start of the Vietnam War. Singer and Small code the initiation of the war with the February 7, 1965, Viet Cong attack on Pleiku and the limited U.S. military response. Other scholars point to the Gulf of Tonkin Resolution (August 7, 1964) as the war initiation date. I use the date of the first large-scale U.S. attack on North Vietnam. Prior to March 2, 1965, the United States was involved in a civil war in the South, albeit against a guerilla force openly supported by the North; U.S. forces were not authorized to attack North Vietnam directly (except in a very limited fashion after Pleiku) for fear of bringing China into the war. With the bombing attacks of Operation Rolling Thunder, however, the United States turned the Vietnam War into an acknowledged interstate war.

war in this test, so my data set is accordingly reduced. That is, I am not looking at nations that respond to a military attack with their own military means. I would not expect a self-defense response driven by external events to be preceded by the same media effort hypothesized for regimes planning such an effort regardless of external events. Likewise, since most revolutionary groups do not have an accessible media system that I can look at (although I will certainly argue that revolutionaries generally make tremendous efforts to win popular support), I cannot apply this operationalization of my model to civil wars.

Certainly, there can be considerable disagreement over the identity of the initiating nation in some wars. For example, is a preemptive strike against a nation about to launch its own attack an initiation or a response? When both nations are authorizing border crossings and small-scale assaults, who gets "credit" for being the initiator when the war begins in earnest? Such concerns are frequently expressed for two wars in this data set—the 1971 Bangladesh War between India and Pakistan and the 1967 Six Day War between Israel and Egypt/Syria. The identity of the initiator could be argued for the Vietnam War and the Ugandan-Tanzanian War as well, but in each case I will make an argument for excluding North Vietnam and Tanzania, respectively. Exclusion from this data set as a noninitiator does not mean that subsequent analysis will ignore the pattern of media opinion leading in these countries. In fact, a lack of editorial activity in nations that are eventually attacked (but are not initiators) is in itself evidence that the model works.

As for civil wars, not only can such conflicts escalate into interstate wars (either from another nation's intervention or the successful secession of the revolutionary group, e.g., Eritrea), but they are such an important part of the phenomenon of war in general that I would like to apply this model to them as well, even if this operationalization, with its focus on established media outlets, can only capture half of the action. Table 3.5 lists the civil/colonial wars from the Singer and Small database during this 20-year time period under scrutiny, and, while these cases are inappropriate for the logit tests of interstate war initiators, I will look at these governments' editorial activity where possible. If a Singer and Small intrastate war escalates into an interstate war through foreign intervention, I have included it in the war data set (two related cases fit this

TABLE 3.5.   Intrastate Wars, 1965–84

	Nation	War	Initiation Date
1.	Philippines	Philippine-MNLF	1/1/72
2.	Ethiopia	Ethiopian-Eritrean	1/1/74
3.	Indonesia	Timor	12/7/75
4.	Morocco	Saharan	12/11/75
5.	Ethiopia	Ogaden	7/1/76

bill—Somalia's support of rebels in the Ogaden region of Ethiopia in 1977 and Cuba's subsequent intervention on behalf of the Ethiopians).[11]

A comparative data set of nations not fighting wars was generated by taking the universe of possible nations (see app. 2.2) over the 20-year period under observation and randomly selecting a nation, a year, and a month (see table 3.6). Since we cannot assume any particular adversary for these nations (other than to say it would be a contiguous state or one in which power has been projected in the recent past), each of these nations is evaluated against all potential adversaries. This has the effect of multiplying the number of individual cases within the no-war sample substantially, as the war sample has only one adversary (the actual opponent) per nation.

For both data sets, then, the research task is to measure newspaper editorial activity within the selected nation for an extended period of time prior to the random month (for the no-war sample) or the war initiation date (for the war sample). Complete data for both the war and no-war samples are reported in appendix 1.2.

Employing a logit regression on this data set, with editorial count as the sole independent variable, yields table 3.7. As with data set 1, the parameter es-

TABLE 3.6.   No War Sample, 1965–84

1.	Egypt	12/79
2.	Zimbabwe	7/67
3.	Venezuela	6/82
4.	Sri Lanka	7/72
5.	Iran	8/77
6.	China (PRC)	3/65
7.	Dominican Republic	5/70
8.	Chile	10/73
9.	Japan	6/76
10.	Israel	1/82
11.	Italy	11/69
12.	Uganda	10/66
13.	Thailand	5/75
14.	Mexico	7/70
15.	Nigeria	10/66
16.	Kenya	4/78
17.	North Korea	3/80
18.	Malaysia	6/77
19.	Peru	2/74
20.	Tanzania	7/78
21.	Uruguay	11/73
22.	Vietnam	2/84
23.	Zambia	3/83
24.	Ethiopia	4/81
25.	Guatemala	4/72

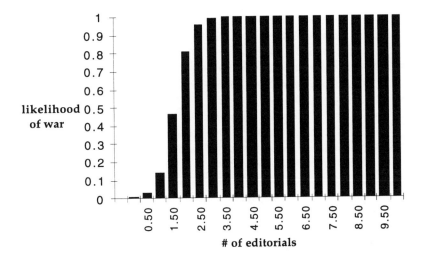

Fig. 3.8.   Data Set 2

timates are very significant and influential. Plugging these estimates into the logit model to generate probabilities of conflict given levels of critical editorial activity generates figure 3.8. Such an analysis provides striking support for hypothesis H1, that wars are preceded by an effort to build public support. Although the relationship between editorial writing and subsequent war is stronger than for data set 1, this chart suggests that wars may be indicated by only two or more critical editorials, rather than the three or more suggested by data set 1. Expressed in tabular form (table 3.8) with such a threshold level, the data is even clearer. Not only is the percentage of cases correctly predicted by the model for data set 2 higher than for data set 1 (98 percent vs. 95 percent), but this higher percentage is more significant. Where less than 10 percent of the sample in data set 1 (9/92 cases) was coded for war (and thus "predictable" with a constant

TABLE 3.7.   Data Set 2
Model: Logit
Dependent variable: War$_t$

Parameter Name	Estimate	S.E.
Constant	−5.031	1.056
Editorial Count$_{t-1}$	3.246	1.058

log-likelihood = −9.4066
$n = 139$
% correctly predicted = 98.56

term), over 15 percent of the sample in data set 2 (21/139 cases) is so coded, making it less likely that the results achieved here are simply by chance.

Even the two cases in which war was not preceded by two or more critical editorials—Iraq before its attack on Iran and Uganda before its move into Tanzania—are understandable outliers. Due to persistent data availability problems, I used the *Baghdad Observer* (a limited-distribution English-language newspaper) rather than the mass dailies *al-Thawra* or *al-Jumhuriyah* to code Iraqi editorial activity. In fact, since the *Baghdad Observer* is almost exclusively read by an international audience, not Iraqi citizens, the lack of critical editorials directed against Iran actually helps confirm the overall model rather than confound it.

Obtaining Ugandan newspapers proved to have no such obstacles, but the content of these papers suggests that the Idi Amin regime was, well, quite mad. Bold-type headlines during October 1978 literally include items such as "Dr. Idi Amin Inspects Two Ambulances." Amin is said to be watching Tanzanian troop movements via secret Ugandan space satellites, and he proclaims himself "Conqueror of the British Empire" during this time. My model assumes a rational decision-making apparatus for a nation that can recognize the benefits of both domestic support and international secrecy; if the national command structure is stupid or crazy, I have little to say. To be fair to Amin, the immediate cause for his attack on Tanzania was in response to an attack made by Ugandan rebels loyal to deposed President Obote and based in Tanzania.[12] Any attempt to rouse public support for moving against the rebels might have given their movement more publicity, reversing the foundation for public support–building efforts hypothesized here. Note that from the Tanzanian side, as my model would suggest, there are no editorials suggesting the idea of war with Uganda prior to the Ugandan army's border crossing, despite the random selection of July 1978 as Tanzania's no-war case.

TABLE 3.8. Data Set 2

	Editorial Count < 2	Editorial Count ≥ 2
War	2	19
No war	118	0

Two war cases come very close to the threshold—the Soviet invasion of Afghanistan (two editorials, examined more closely in chap. 4) and Cuban expeditionary actions in the Ogaden (three editorials). I say three editorials for the Cuban case, even though it is very difficult to say what is and is not an editorial in *Granma*. There are certainly plenty of articles concerning Cuban forces in Africa, and the context is exhortatory rather than descriptive. For example, published "news" pieces during this period bear titles such as "¡La Solidaridad De Cuba Con Los Pueblos De Africa No Se Negocia!" and "¡Ayudamos y Ayudaremos la Revolucion Etiope!"[13] making it hard to say where editorials begin and news ends. Other than U.S. intervention in Vietnam, this is the only case of far-flung power projection of forces. And like U.S. intervention in Vietnam, Cuban involvement in Ethiopia did not happen overnight; the November 1 initiation date is a best guess based on various accounts of events in the Horn of Africa.[14]

The lines between editorials and articles are similarly blurred in Somalia's *Horsed*. Printed half in Italian and half in Arabic, the newspaper is printed infrequently at best. Strangely enough, it is apparently subsidized by North Korea, unless, of course, the editor just enjoys printing Korean War speeches by Kim Il Sung (a remarkably youthful Great Leader to judge by his photograph) with such stirring titles as "Let Us Resolutely Repel the US Imperialist's Armed Invasion." There is no mistaking, however, Siad Barre's desire to take his country into war with Ethiopia. In some issues *every* article deals directly or indirectly with the atrocities committed by Ethiopia in *Somalia Occidentale* and Barre's plans to reclaim the region.

I find it more than a little surprising that *no* nation in the no-war sample writes two or more critical editorials of a potential target nation, despite the existence of crisis situations for several of the dyads involved, not just Tanzania. For example, Thailand in early 1975 is faced with perhaps its greatest foreign policy crisis since World War II—how to deal with the fall of South Vietnam and Kampuchea. In editorials such as "Time for a New Sense of Reality" and "The Sober Truth of a Long War" Thai public opinion is clearly led in the direction of accommodation with the Communist victors, not continued confrontation. The height (or depth) of this effort is reached in mid-April, when in "Cambodia Can Save Her Own Identity" the Khmer Rouge takeover is praised because they are an indigenous Kampuchean group! Little surprise, then, that Thailand immediately sued for peace with the Pol Pot regime.

Likewise, Kenya in 1978 is rather muted in its discussion of the growing war between Ethiopia and Somalia (and Somali editorials in 1977 praise Kenya for its even-handedness), despite irredentist Somali claims on Kenyan territory. Uganda in 1966 has nothing but praise for its neighbors, including Tanzania. Guatemala speaks of the "Splendid Honduran Delegation" and how Britain's problems in Belize will not provoke Guatemalan interest in that territory. Iran speaks warmly of Iraq. Ethiopia in 1981 has special feelings of goodwill toward

Djibouti and the Soviet Union; Eritrea and Somalia are mentioned briefly and dismissively in one editorial comment, the Ethiopian equivalent of declaring victory despite any confounding facts. Where criticism of foreign countries exists in these editorials, it is of countries too far away to be a feasible target. Everyone in Africa (Uganda, Tanzania, Nigeria, Kenya, Ethiopia) criticizes South Africa and Rhodesia—except Zambia, which actually shares a border with Rhodesia. In 1982 Venezuela criticized the United States and the United Kingdom harshly in print for the former's support of the latter's war with Argentina, but editorials are quite tame regarding the neighboring Esequibo region of Guyana, the source of a sharp territorial dispute in April and May. This is an excellent example, in fact, of an international crisis marked by limited yet distinct episodes of violence that did not escalate into war. I think it no coincidence that we see so few critical editorials on the subject in Venezuelan papers.

Criticism is at times present for domestic factions rather than international opponents in these no-war cases, in rough relation to future conflict against those factions. Of course, Sri Lanka does not contemplate war with India in its 1972 editorials, but neither does it call the increasing violence in the north anything more than a political issue surrounding ratification of the new constitution. The "Tamil question" is never discussed directly, just as the government did not direct a military effort against Tamil secessionist groups until much later. Not so in Chile's 1973 editorials, in which the many editorials directed against "Communist elements" are a harbinger of soon realized domestic conflict. Nigerian editorials in late 1966 have nothing to say about international conflict but plenty about how justified the government is in putting down an army revolt.

Again, I am not claiming that the simple presence of more than two critical editorials in a given month is a sure sign to run for the hills. The hypothesis to be confirmed is that a war will not happen unless it is preceded by such editorial effort, not that such editorial effort is a foolproof indicator of future conflict. Editorial effort is presented here as a necessary condition for war initiation, not a sufficient condition.

How long before the outbreak of war does such a necessary condition come to exist? One would expect that the relationship between critical editorials and war initiation would get less clear the farther back one goes from the start of the war but still have some explanatory value. For example, the number of editorials written between two months and one month before war initiation should still have some relationship to that war. These results are summarized in tables 3.9 and 3.10 and figure 3.9.

As expected, the model loses some of its predictive power by using editorials two time periods removed, but they are still a very significant and influential parameter. Moreover, the threshold level of editorial writing followed by war is still about the same. At last we have one example of a no-war case crossing the threshold—Mexico prints two editorials critical of U.S. trade policy—

but even here the substantive issue of complaint does not seem particularly troublesome.

TABLE 3.9. **Data Set 2**
           Model: Logit
           Dependent variable: War*t*

Parameter Name	Estimate	S.E.
Constant	−4.147	0.731
Editorial Count$_{t-2}$	3.538	0.828

log-likelihood = −20.009
$n = 139$
% correctly predicted = 93.53

TABLE 3.10. Data Set 2

	Editorial Count < 2	Editorial Count ≥ 2
War	8	13
No war	117	1

Data Set 2: An Event-Count Operationalization

Although several questions remain unanswered in the analysis of hypothesis H1 (how far in advance do editorials serve as leading indicators of war? how do we get beyond a simple threshold early warning model?), I want to postpone that discussion in favor of a first-cut test of hypothesis H3, that the level of a regime's domestic support–building effort will be commensurate to the degree of conflictual behavior subsequently directed against a target. Graphically, we can think of this process as:

nation *i* complains about nation *j* in media → Time passes → nation *i* initiates conflict proportional to complaints against nation *j*

Again, this is not a causal relationship but a correlative one.

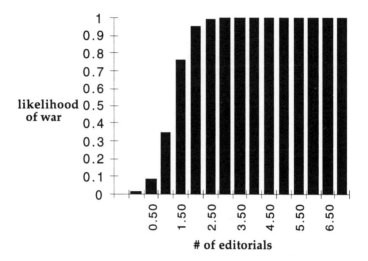

Fig. 3.9.   Data Set 2

An examination of levels of conflict and their temporal pattern requires an event-count methodology. In such an analysis each separate interstate event is counted as a separate case. Thus, a full-fledged war between two nations might generate five or six separate conflictual events each day for months; a border dispute might generate three or four such events over the course of a month. Not only do well-known international incidents generate a large number of conflictual events under this coding scheme, but lesser-known events, such as Argentina and Bolivia recalling their respective ambassadors for a week over a mineral rights squabble or the border disputes between India and Pakistan well before the Bangladesh War, generate an appropriate number of conflictual events as well.

The problem with this scheme for operationalizing conflict is that, unlike newspaper editorials, detailed information on interstate events is not published regularly by every nation in the world. Fortunately, Edward Azar's Conflict and Peace Data Bank (COPDAB) event-count data set of state interactions provides just such a source of information.[15] The COPDAB data set looks at dozens of media sources to code every state interaction from 1948 to 1978. These interactions are coded on a 15-point scale, ranging from a score of 1 for territorial integration to a score of 15 for an all-out warlike act. For the purposes of these initial tests, events coded 11 (defined by Azar as "diplomatic/economic hostile actions") or higher are counted as conflictual events, although other cut-off points, including weighted scale positions, can be tested as well.[16]

Employing these operationalizations, my model relating mass media, time, and conflict is transformed into a functional form of:

$$E(\text{COPDAB Count}_t) = f(\text{Editorial Count}_{t-1})$$

where some function of the independent variable editorial count during month$_{t-1}$ accounts for the variation in COPDAB count during month$_t$. Before I can start to evaluate this expression in a systematic fashion, however, I must first determine the stochastic, or random, component underlying the phenomenon to be explained. Models of planetary motion, cannonball trajectories, or some other relatively deterministic behavior may be decently specified without including a stochastic component, but any model that deals with unpredictable humans must include both a systematic and stochastic component to have any chance of reasonable specification.

Since the dependent variable here can never take on negative values, is not a continuous variable, and has no upper limit, a Poisson distribution much more accurately describes the stochastic process in this case than the commonly used normal distribution.[17] A key assumption, however, of the Poisson distribution holds that the phenomenon in question, conflictual events between states in this case, must accumulate during any particular observation period in an independent and constant manner. This assumption is problematic here, as any single incident of conflictual behavior during a given month is likely to spark another such incident within that same month. Given this sort of contagious behavior in the dependent variable,[18] a reasonable compound distribution to model this particular stochastic process is a negative binomial distribution, where the effect of contagion (really, the rate of occurrence) is accounted for explicitly by an additional parameter, λ, distributed probabilistically, rather than constantly, according to a gamma distribution.[19]

The general form for a negative binomial distribution is as follows:

$$f_{nb}(y_i|\lambda,\sigma^2) = \frac{\Gamma\left|\dfrac{\lambda}{\sigma^2-1} + y_i\right|}{y_i!\Gamma\left|\dfrac{\lambda}{\sigma^2-1}\right|}\left(\frac{\sigma^2-1}{\sigma^2}\right)^{y_i}(\sigma^2)^{\frac{-\lambda}{\sigma^2-1}}$$

To get a feel for this hypothesized distribution of COPDAB count, figures 3.10–13 show a negative binomial distribution under different assumptions for λ and σ^2.

In each of these distributions λ should be thought of as the expected number of conflictual events during the observation period. Thus, if $\lambda = 1$, we expect 1 such event during the month in question; if $\lambda = 10$, we expect 10 such

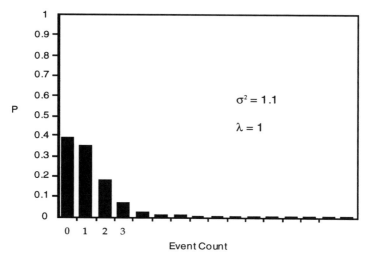

Fig. 3.10

events. As σ^2, a measure of the variation present in the distribution in λ, approaches 1, the gamma distribution collapses to a spike, making λ a constant and creating a Poisson distribution. Thus, figure 3.10 shows a negative binomial distribution very close to a Poisson distribution, with an expected COPDAB count of 1 and a σ^2 verging on the minimum. Figure 3.11 maintains the expected event count but shows how the probability distribution changes when $\sigma^2 = 10$. The basic effect, as one might expect since the higher σ^2 indicates that you are no longer as sure about your best guess for the observed values of COPDAB count, is a spreading out of the distribution. The higher spike for an event count of zero exists because the distribution cannot spread into negative numbers but, instead, accumulates at an event count of zero. Figures 3.12 and 3.13 show how the distribution changes as λ, or the expected number of conflictual events in this case, changes from 1 to 2 and to 10.

We can think of any particular expected editorial count as corresponding to the highest point on some negative binomial distribution. That is, a sample of observations with low editorial counts, and hence a low expected number of conflictual events, might very well look something like figure 3.10 or 3.11, depending on the observed value of σ^2, while a sample of observations with high editorial counts, and hence a high expected number of conflictual events, might look more like figure 3.13.

Now that I have suggested an underlying distribution of the dependent variable, I must specify the appropriate independent variables. In addition to editorial count$_{t-1}$, I want to include both a measure of prior conflict (COPDAB count$_{t-1}$) and a measure of the power resources available to these nations.

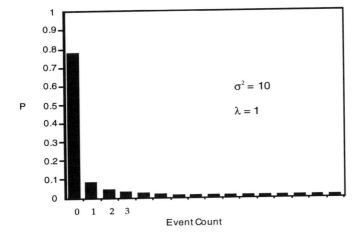

Fig. 3.11

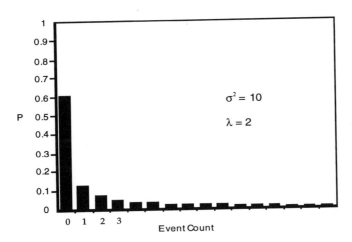

Fig. 3.12

By including power in this predictive calculus, I am trying to incorporate the insights of realist and neorealist conceptions of conflict initiation. In a nutshell these insights revolve around the basic idea that powerful states will move against weak states. Of course, there is great disagreement in the realist/neorealist literature about how power should be measured, and equal disagreement over whether we should be concerned about absolute, relative, or the rate of change of power inequalities. The emphasis on power considerations, however, is common to theorists from Thucydides to Waltz. Although power is a

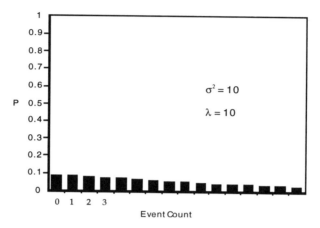

Fig. 3.13

nebulous concept indeed, I will conveniently ignore such questions as fungi-bility in favor of a crude measure designed to be a rough gauge of relative capacities for waging war. In this index each nation's power for any given year is considered to be a function of that year's military expenditures.[20]

Power, however defined, has a poor track record as a solitary predictor of conflict, hence its inclusion as an improvement on the basic model rather than as its base. On the evidentiary side neorealist theory taken alone has a very difficult time accounting for a wide variety of historical events, in particular the fail-ure of some declining systemic or subsystemic hegemons to go to war with the rising hegemon.[21] At best power inequalities might be seen as providing ad-ditional necessary conditions for conflict. Even this rather mild assertion has its problems. Weaker nations, regardless of how power is measured or what type of inequality is involved, have been known to provoke conflict, whether low-level incidents or, as in the case of Pakistan in 1965 or Egypt in 1973, full-scale wars.

Accounting for such puzzling actions is where Bueno de Mesquita's work on war prediction has its greatest value.[22] Employing expected utility theory, Bueno de Mesquita clearly shows how war initiation can at times be a perfectly rational choice by even the weakest nation if the continuation of the status quo is perceived as a worse fate than the expected value of fighting a risky war. In a no-win situation the lesser of two evils can sometimes be losing a war. But, whereas Bueno de Mesquita finds his measure of utility in a systemic variable—dyadic agreement between international alliance portfolios—I use a full-fledged domestic-level measure of the utility associated with war, and I believe that it gives my models both greater explanatory *and* predictive power.

Table 3.11 shows regression statistics for one such specification of a model, including both power comparison (nation *i*'s military spending minus nation *j*'s military spending) and previous conflict (number of COPDAB events coded 11 or higher in the prior month) in addition to editorial count. All variables have the expected sign, and, with the exception of the power comparison variable, all parameter estimates are very significant (at the .001 level) in this regression. Especially influential is the contagion parameter, indicating that the rate of occurrence of conflictual events in month *t* increases as more events occur. Most important for this enterprise, editorial count is both influential and significant, more so than previous conflict, in fact.[23]

The power comparison variable is clearly the least influential and significant variable here (significant at the .1 level), but this is really precisely what we would expect from a broad annual measure asked to make nuanced distinctions between month-to-month likelihoods of conflict initiation. That is, the expectation of neorealist theory for this test would be that having a superiority in military resources would correlate with a small increase in the likelihood of initiating conflict in any given month—precisely the implication of the regression results. All the same, power comparison is clearly not vital to the determination of a short-term prediction of conflict. As we would expect, dropping this variable from the model does not have an appreciable effect on parameter estimates (table 3.12), and 11 cases for which military spending data was missing can be included in the analysis. As in table 3.11, Editorial Count$_{t-1}$ is a more influential variable than COPDAB 11-Count $_{t-1}$. All the same, we cannot know how closely related editorial count is to previous conflict until we run the regression without previous conflict (table 3.13). That is, if the parameter estimate for editorial count goes up sharply when previous conflict is dropped from the model, then we would conclude that it is not as independent a variable as we have hypothesized. Since we are dealing with exponential functions to calculate predicted

TABLE 3.11.   Data Set 2
           Model: Negative Binomial
           Dependent variable: COPDAB 11-Count$_t$

Parameter Name	Estimate	S.E.
Constant	−1.553	0.313
Contagion	1.465	0.266
Editorial Count$_{t-1}$	0.462	0.095
COPDAB 11-Count$_{t-1}$	0.384	0.103
Power Comparison	1.28e-08	7.79e-09

log-likelihood = −140.082
$n = 128$

values, the effect of the parameter estimates should not be compared linearly; instead, since exp(.491) = 1.633 and exp(.559) = 1.748, we should say that the effect of editorial count in table 3.12 is 1.633/1.748, or .934 times that of editorial count in table 3.13, not .491/.559, or .878 as we would say for linear regression. Thus, even when previous conflict is dropped as an explanatory variable, the impact of editorial count does not change appreciably (less than 7 percent in fact), suggesting that this measure is quite independent of prior conflict and is not simply reacting to such events.

Alternative model specifications were tested to check the robustness of measures employed here. Summaries of those alternative specifications and their results are as follows:

> *Poisson distribution:* Dropping the assumption of a negative binomial distribution in favor of a Poisson distribution (losing the contagion parameter of tables 3.11–13) sharply reduces the log-likelihood. Parameter estimates for independent variables are unaffected by the change.
>
> *Alternative COPDAB threshold levels:* Using a dependent variable of the number of COPDAB events coded at some threshold point higher than

TABLE 3.12.   Data Set 2
Model: Negative Binomial
Dependent variable: COPDAB 11-Count$_t$

Parameter Name	Estimate	S.E.
Constant	−1.458	0.308
Contagion	1.602	0.256
Editorial Count$_{t-1}$	0.491	0.109
COPDAB 11-Count$_{t-1}$	0.357	0.104

log-likelihood = −154.729
n = 139

TABLE 3.13.   Data Set 2
Model: Negative Binomial
Dependent variable: COPDAB 11-Count$_t$

Parameter Name	Estimate	S.E.
Constant	−0.819	0.317
Contagion	2.023	0.248
Editorial Count$_{t-1}$	0.559	0.141

log-likelihood = −163.814
n = 139

11 does not significantly change parameter estimates or model specification.

Alternative power comparison variables: None of the demographic, economic, and military measures collected by the Correlates of War project are any more influential or significant than military spending.

Two-month time aggregation: Using either Editorial Count$_{t-2}$ or (Editorial Count$_{t-1}$ + Editorial Count$_{t-2}$) as an independent variable generates results as expected. The farther back one goes from the conflict to be predicted, the less powerful the editorial measure becomes. Aggregating editorial counts provides the highest log-likelihood of any model tested.

Editorial percentage: Operationalizing critical editorials in terms of a percentage of total editorials written is not a more influential or significant variable than a simple count of such editorials. For parsimony, then, count is discussed here rather than percentage.

Alternative previous conflict variables: Using alternative codings of previous conflict—whether from different COPDAB threshold points, earlier months, or events directed at nation i by nation j—shows no real improvement in significance or influence over the measure employed above (threshold scale of 11, directed at j, month prior to conflict). Nor does using any of these measures weaken the influence of critical editorials as an independent variable.

Weighted COPDAB scores: COPDAB events are coded on a 15-point scale, although there is a greater increase in violence moving from, say, 13 to 14 on the scale than from 11 to 12. Azar polled a variety of political scientists to determine a weighting system for the 15-point scale to reflect this disparity.[24] Using this weighted measure does not significantly change the regression results.

The upshot of all of these regression tests is that both H1 and H3 are strongly supported by data set 2. Attempts to mobilize public opinion, as measured by editorial content and activity in regime-sympathetic newspapers, precede every instance of war initiation from 1965 through 1984. Moreover, there is a clear link between editorial activity and subsequent levels of conflict: the more editorials, the more violent events in the following month. Significantly, such activity is statistically independent of prior conflict, suggesting that there is more going on in the publishing of editorials than a simple reaction to previous events.

Sources of Editorial Activity

So what *is* going on in the publishing of editorials prior to war? Thus far I have looked at conflict (war or event-count data) as the dependent variable to be explained, with editorial count as one of several important independent variables. Now I want to treat editorial count as the dependent variable. Chapter 2 established several pathways through which regime type and media system attributes could affect the effort to build public support, summarized in hypotheses H4 and H5. If editorials are indeed part of that effort, then H4 and H5 should provide clues to at least some of the independent variables important to determining the level of editorial activity. In particular, H4 claims that democracies will make a greater effort to build public support (i.e., write more editorials) than nondemocracies; H5 claims that regimes faced with a marketing and/or signaling constraint posed by their domestic mass media system will similarly make a greater effort. Public opinion–building effort, as expressed in either hypothesis, should be affected by the domestic political cost of using such effort as an international signal.

Both of these hypotheses are ceteris paribus arguments. I control for external demand on editorial writing by looking only at those nations that have the same apparent need for public support management. In this instance that means looking at the 21 war cases of data set 2 rather than the entire sample. The logic here is that each of these nations should be writing critical editorials before going to war, but we have yet to specify the function that determines how many editorials a given nation will print given an assumption of similar external constraints and differing regime attributes.

Before including such regime and media variables, table 3.14 shows to what degree editorials are driven by reactive and lagged variables. That is, one might expect that the number of critical editorials written will depend in large part simply on the average number of editorials that newspaper prints in a given time period. One would also expect the number to depend on previous levels of editorial activity and external events that might provoke editorial writing. Of these variables all are significant at the .05 level except COPDAB 11-Count$_{t-2}$ (the sign of this estimate is unlikely as well, showing that high levels of conflict

TABLE 3.14.   Data Set 2: War subset
Model: Negative Binomial
Dependent variable: Editorial Count$_{t-1}$

Parameter Name	Estimate	S.E.
Constant	1.389	0.250
Contagion	−1.561	0.569
Average monthly editorials	0.010	0.004
Editorial Count$_{t-2}$	0.090	0.043
COPDAB 11-Count$_{t-2}$	−0.075	0.059

log-likelihood = −58.122
$n = 21$

in the past are linked to lower levels of editorial writing). As suggested by the regressions on event-count data, previous conflict does not correlate well with editorial activity. Note that I am still assuming a negative binomial stochastic distribution of the data, as I have the same expectations regarding contagious rate of occurrence within observation periods for editorial writing as I did for conflict event initiation. Indeed, the contagion parameter is highly significant here.

I constructed regime and media system independent variables as follows:

Democracy: From the Polity II data set this is a 10-point scale where an absence of democracy is set to 0.[25]

Power Comparison: As in previous regressions, this variable is constructed by subtracting nation *j*'s military spending from nation *i*'s. Of interest for this function is that power comparison should work in two conflicting ways. If nation i is stronger than nation *j*, then there is less need for the force multiplier of strategic surprise and a greater ability to make as strong an effort to build public support as one would possibly want. In this respect power comparison should be positively related to editorial writing. On the other hand, if nation *i* is stronger than nation *j*, then there is less risk to the regime by implementing military intervention and conflict, obviating the need for public support building in the first place.

Media System Constraints: This dummy variable is coded 1 if either the regime has no direct mass media organ (signaling constraint) or if the country has four or more influential daily newspapers or major press holding companies,[26] as listed by UN publications on comparative media systems (marketing constraint).

International Signaling Cost. I assume that, the more factionalized or unstable the polity, the greater the cost of making an opinion-building effort. That is, the greater the ability of opposition groups to work against the regime, the greater the political risk in making policy commitments that go unfulfilled. I use the "regulation of participation" variable in the Polity II data set as a measure of this factionalization. This variable ranges from 1 ("unregulated participation") to 5 ("regulated participation") in Polity II; I use the inverse so that higher measures connote greater cost/risk.

Note that the democracy measure employed here correlates closely with the signaling component of the signaling/marketing measure (Argentina and Pakistan are the only clear examples in this data set of a nondemocratic regime faced with the signaling constraint of a relatively open media system), making it counterproductive to specify both H4 (democratic constraints) and H5 (media marketing/signaling constraints) in the same model. Table 3.15 shows a regression analysis of editorial count testing H4, table 3.16 for hypothesis H5.[27] In the test of H4 (table 3.15) average monthly editorials and the contagion parameter are significant at the .05 level. The lag of editorial count is significant at the .1 level, power comparison at the .2 level, and democracy is insignificant as an explanatory variable. In the regression of table 3.16 all parameter estimates are significant at the .05 level with the exception of power comparison (significant at the .2 level) and lagged editorial count (significant at the .1 level). As expected, the power comparison variable is barely influential or statistically significant, although the negative sign implies that the role of power comparison in eliminating the need for secrecy outweighs its role in eliminating the need for public support. Otherwise, all variables, with the exception of democracy, are reasonably influential and significant. The implication here is that mass media constraints are far more telling in determining editorial activity than a broad measure of democratic institutional structures. In other words, these re-

TABLE 3.15.   Data Set 2: War subset
Model: Negative Binomial
Dependent variable: Editorial Count$_{t-1}$

Parameter Name	Estimate	S.E.
Constant	1.297	0.290
Contagion	−1.622	0.621
Average monthly editorials	0.009	0.004
Editorial Count$_{t-2}$	0.070	0.039
Power comparison	⁵.20e-09	4.41e-09
Democracy	0.010	0.034

log-likelihood = −52.156
$n = 21$

TABLE 3.16.   Data Set 2: War subset
Model: Negative Binomial
Dependent variable: Editorial Count$_{t-1}$

Parameter Name	Estimate	S.E.
Constant	0.721	0.366
Contagion	−2.093	0.746
Average monthly editorials	0.007	0.003
Editorial Count$_{t-2}$	0.055	0.034
Power comparison	−5.43e-09	3.91e-09
Media constraints	0.895	0.388

log-likelihood = −49.591
$n = 21$

sults suggest that there are systematic differences across regimes in the way they handle the mobilization of public support but that these differences are better understood from a perspective that concentrates on media system than on more traditional indicators of regime type.

The test of H4 operationalized with the Polity II data set measure of democracy fails so badly here that it is hardly worth looking at predicted values and outliers. Not so with the test of H5 operationalized with a dummy variable capturing media system constraints. The Soviet Union is the most obvious outlier, with only two editorials directed against Afghanistan, despite a hypothesized marketing problem stemming from the large number of influential mass circulation dailies. As discussed in chapter 2, what I call a marketing problem might be better thought of as a coordination problem for countries in which all media outlets are directly controlled by one government body or another. If the Soviet leadership is not hampered by the wide range of opinion outlets, as suggested by the relatively low number of critical editorials, then it must be rather effective in getting the various opinion sources to toe the same line. I would draw the opposite conclusion from China (well predicted by the model), which, despite having a very closed media system, printed more than 12 critical editorials versus Vietnam in the month before initiating a rather bloody border war in 1979. Not coincidentally, I think, China is faced with more of a coordination problem than any other authoritarian state, according to UNESCO's data on media systems. More than nine separate news dailies have circulations of well over one million, each of which is controlled by a separate People's Liberation Army (PLA), Communist Party, or bureaucratic group (cf. Russia, where most mass dailies were controlled directly by the Central Committee).

A test for the role of international signaling cost is not as simple a matter as including a cost variable in these regression tests of H4 and H5. The data sample here is composed solely of those nations that ended up going to war, but it is only in a comparison of nations that go to war and back down from war that we can generate parameter estimates for international signaling cost. Recall from chapter 2 that these signaling costs are not incurred unless the regime backs down from its demands on a foreign nation; only by reneging on its commitment to fight does a government suffer domestic political retribution for sending such a signal.[28] The costs exist whether or not the regime presses forward, but we cannot see their effect except in a comparison of nations that do and do not press forward. In identical situations of editorial activity, then, we would expect the regime bearing high signaling costs to be more likely to press on with its demands (and more likely to end up in war) than a nation with low signaling costs. Obviously, a data sample composed entirely of nations that ended up in war is inappropriate for testing the role of costs, but even data set 2 as a whole provides little variation for such a test (see table 3.17; cf. table 3.7). Certainly, this interactive term is a powerful and significant predictor (signaling costs are part of an interactive explanatory variable with editorial count because editorial activity must occur for even potential costs to be borne), almost as good a leading indicator as editorial count alone, but our confidence in this test must be muted, because there are hardly any cases in data set 2 that could be considered as examples of backing down from a crisis.

Data Set 3: Israeli Ten-Year Time Series

Data set 2 is incapable of providing the answer to several questions, not just the role of signaling costs. At several points in the analysis of data sets 1 and 2 I incorporated lagged variables to improve the models at hand, even suggesting that editorial count from two prior observation periods was a pretty decent leading indicator itself. What are the roles of time and prior events in this phenomenon? To answer those questions requires a time series, in which editorials and conflict are evaluated for many observation periods in succession. Such an approach is simply not feasible for a large set of nations or wars, so I have taken one nation, Israel, and evaluated it for the 10-year period of 1966 through 1975. Israel was chosen since, as both a frequent initiator and target of conflict, it should present a substantial amount of variation.

This time series provides crucial evidence regarding hypothesis H3: that editorial effort is commensurate to subsequent conflict, that such effort indicates more than just the necessary conditions for war. In other words, if we found equally high levels of editorial activity prior to a mild crisis as before the initiation of war, editorials could not be seen as indicating the presence of sufficient conditions for war. The random sample of nonwarring nations in data set 2 provides some indication that editorial activity is not correlated with subsequent violent events short of war; data set 3 can provide far more compelling evidence, as we know that this time period contains violent crises that do not end up as war. While this data set will also be incapable of testing the role of signaling costs directly (unless we assume—unrealistically, I think—that the Israeli government faced changing signaling costs over time), we can at least get at the

TABLE 3.17.   Data Set 2
            Model: Logit
            Dependent variable: War$_t$

Parameter Name	Estimate	S.E.
Constant	−4.857	0.955
Sig Cost* Ed Count$_{t-1}$	11.079	2.811

log-likelihood = −10.923
$n = 139$
% correctly predicted = 96.19

heart of these issues: How reliable are editorials as an independent leading indicator of crises and/or wars?

A cautionary word on temporal arrangements and leading indicators. I began this book by looking at border shelling incidents as a leading indicator of war. This was, in fact, the approach of Edward Azar, creator of the COPDAB data set, in his efforts to predict war. Azar claimed that an observation of unusual levels of conflictual behavior (levels of activity outside the "Normal Relations Range" of interactions between two states) was in itself a valuable leading indicator of future conflict.[29] Of course, all this is really saying is that conflict in time t is a decent indicator of conflict in time $t + 1$. The limitations of this approach for predicting war should be obvious: it is precisely the abnormal jump out of normal relations, the first major hit, that we would like to anticipate in the first place. To be fair, while not appropriate for predicting initial shocks or foreign policy initiatives, studies of event interaction patterns are certainly valuable in helping us understand why conflict (and cooperation) persists once begun.[30]

But I want to predict the initial shock, not the aftereffects. To do so, I need an indicator of intentions, of what some government plans to do as Prime Mover in its little Thomist universe of some dyadic relationship. As Zeev Maoz puts it, attempts to anticipate crises using only event interaction data "ignores, by and large, intent variables which are crucial for the study of initiation processes."[31] And I think that opinion-leading pieces in mass media, newspaper editorials in particular, are an effective place to look for this measure of independent intent.

At the same time, however, editorial activity is also going to reflect prior events, concurrent events, prior editorial activity, etc. (see fig. 3.14). Editorials are simply an intermediary variable, a way station on a correlative pathway from intentions or past behavior to subsequent behavior. This is not the whole picture, of course, as each component—with the exception of independent intentions—has its own temporally recursive elements. Editorials in time $t - 1$ are a leading indicator regardless of the degree to which any of its four correlative components are responsible for its creation. The point is that editorials are an interesting leading indicator, an independent leading indicator, only when independent intentions rather than past events or behavior is a primary component. Otherwise, editorials are no better or worse than border-shelling incidents as leading indicators.

We can try to disentangle independent intentions from past behavior and events with a variety of statistical tools, but the fact of the matter is that this is a messy relationship I am arguing for, based on messy data, and no amount of Box-Jenkins tests or Cochrane-Orcutt regressions can make up for that underlying messiness. But two claims from this relationship should be visible in the muddiest of time series. First, we should occasionally see editorial activity precede large-scale interstate conflict, perhaps even war, without seeing commensurate preceding violence. If we are really lucky and have a sneak attack in our

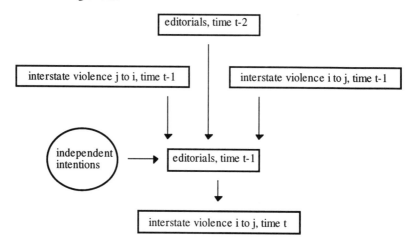

Fig. 3.14

time series, there should be virtually no preceding events of note. Second, we should not see substantial editorial activity (where substantial is defined by activity over the time series) followed by an absence of large-scale interstate conflict.

The graphs in appendix 1.4 show, for each year 1966 through 1975, for each of its four neighbors (Egypt, Jordan, Lebanon, and Syria), month-by-month totals for three pieces of information regarding Israel.

> conflictual events (COPDAB score of 11 or higher) initiated by Israel against a particular neighbor;
> critical editorials in the *Jerusalem Post* directed against that neighbor;
> conflictual events (COPDAB score of 11 or higher) initiated by that neighbor against Israel.

I want to focus attention first on the three wars that took place during this time period: the Six Day War of June 1967, the War of Attrition of March 1969–70, and the Yom Kippur War of October 1973. Of the three the Six Day War is the only one to be clearly initiated by Israel (in anticipation of Egyptian initiation, to be sure) at a distinct point in time. In fact, the time series shows that Israeli actions directed against its neighbors in June 1967 are, more than any other observation, greater than Arab actions against Israel in the same or preceding month. Certainly, there are some events directed against Israel in May (especially from Egypt), but the level of Israeli actions in June go beyond what we would otherwise expect as a response to those Egyptian events. The level of Israeli violence in June is well anticipated, however, by Israeli editorial activity in May.

On the other hand, the Yom Kippur War, by all accounts, came as a shock to Israel in October 1973. What does this mean, that it was a "shock"? It means that neither Egyptian behavior nor Israeli behavior should provide any indication that war was forthcoming. Also, since the war was clearly initiated by Egypt rather than Israel, we should not expect to find a large number of critical Israeli editorials in September.[32] Of course, we should see a tremendous number of editorials in October, both in reaction to the events of that month and as a precursor to continued conflict in November.

The War of Attrition falls somewhere in between the Israeli initiation of the Six Day War and the Egyptian initiation of the Yom Kippur War. This was a muddy war, with no clear "invasion" or "surrender" date. We would expect to see substantial numbers of Egyptian actions directed against Israel, Israeli actions directed against Egypt, and Israeli editorials against Egypt all through this period but probably with no obvious temporal pattern. And, in fact, this is precisely the case.

As important as these war periods are for this model, the time spans of relative peace are equally important. Do we see editorial activity above some threshold (say, three critical editorials), from whatever source, that is not followed by conflict above some threshold (say, five events of interstate violence)? In fact, with one partial set of exceptions there is no case of substantial editorial activity that is not followed by large-scale conflictual events. On the contrary, even nonwar yet violent episodes such as the Israeli-Syrian conflict in 1974 over the Golan Heights or Israeli-Lebanese conflict in late 1974 over PLO camps in southern Lebanon are anticipated by editorial activity.

If there is a partial outlier in this time series—a stretch of months in which unusually high levels of editorial activity did not result in unusually high levels of interstate violence—it would seem to be December 1968 through December 1969. We see at least some editorial activity against each of Israel's neighbors over this span but substantial violence directed only against Egypt. Three factors offset this apparent outlier. First, Israel begins the War of Attrition with Egypt. In fact, if I were to represent conflictual events as a sum of weighted COPDAB events rather than a simple count, this time period of Israel versus Egypt (and vice versa) would be among the most violent in the series. As with other wars over this time period, there is some spillover from editorials critical of Egypt to editorials critical of noncombatant (or less-combatant) neighbors. Second, Jordan was undergoing a virtual civil war as Hussein's army fought to push the PLO out of Jordan (and into Lebanon). Israeli editorials begin 1970 with uncertainty about the effect of all this for Israel; by May, however, editorials are praising Hussein mightily for attacking the PLO. Third, 1969 was perhaps the most tumultuous domestic political year in Israel's history, with two executive and complete ministerial turnovers in a single calendar year. If regime characteristics influence the rate of editorial activity, we would expect 1969 to be different from more stable domestic political periods.

We can perform limited statistical tests on this data, but caution is in order in interpreting these parameter estimates. I used linear regression on this data, as it has the most tractable techniques for ameliorating the effects of the serial correlation inherent to most time series, but it has some drawbacks when used for event-count data (as with all other data set analysis, alternative model specifications were tested for robustness and plausibility comparisons). Since Egypt was Israel's primary adversary during this time period, the regressions examine this dyadic relationship.

It is the nature of time series for past events to have some influence on the present, just as the sound of a plucked guitar string gradually fades out over time. One reasonable approach toward correcting serial correlation given the nature of this data is to use a two-stage least squares regression, where editorial count is treated as a function of certain explanatory variables and where this function is estimated simultaneously with the interstate conflict function (see table 3.18). In this regression, editorial count$_{t-1}$ has been simultaneously estimated as a function of concurrent $(t-1)$ measures of Israeli actions against Egypt, Egyptian actions against Israel, and lagged $(t-2)$ measures of editorial count. The parameter estimate of editorial count is highly significant (at the .001 level), and the coefficient can be read straightforwardly to suggest that one critical editorial printed in January indicates two conflictual events directed against Egypt in February.

A short digression can illustrate my earlier comments on the relative usefulness of events as leading indicators. If our goal were simply to specify the level of interstate conflict directed by Israel against Egypt during any given month, we would do well to use the number of Egyptian violent acts directed against Israel during that same month (see table 3.19).

Parameter estimates are significant at the .001 level, and the r-squared measure is drastically improved. Substantively, there is virtually a one-to-one correspondence between the number of times Israel hits Egypt and Egypt hits Israel in any given month. But there is nothing predictive here (in fact, this is a good example of why r-squared values are often misleading).

On the other hand, using Egyptian actions directed against Israel during the preceding month would be predictive (see table 3.20). Referring back to figure

TABLE 3.18.   **Data Set 3: Egypt subset**
Model: 2SLS
Dependent variable: Israel COPDAB 11-Count$_t$

Parameter Name	Estimate	S.E.
Constant	2.622	1.088
Editorial Count$_{t-1}$	2.276	0.567

R-squared = 0.1405
$n = 118$

3.17, this is the equivalent of drawing a correlative arrow directly from "interstate violence j to i, time$_{t-1}$," to "interstate violence i to j, time$_t$," rather than going through the intermediary variable of editorial activity in time$_{t-1}$. Previous Egyptian violence, like previous editorial count in table 3.18, is an effective leading indicator of current Israeli violence. It is not, however, quite as good a leading indicator as editorial count. When the two-stage least squares regression of table 3.18 is run with Egyptian violence as the sole explanatory variable in the editorial count function (rather than the three variables noted), the r-squared value of that regression is .1425. Judging from the lower r-squared value of table 3.20 (under these circumstances a comparison of r-squared values is meaningful), there is a significant amount of predictive information contained in editorials that is not to be found in preceding events alone.

I say significant because in the vast majority of observation—either months of peace, months of concurrent violence begetting violence, or months of Egyptian first strikes—we would not expect any difference in the informational value of prior editorials or prior violence. For example, neither Israeli editorials nor Egyptian behavior in September 1973 should predict Israeli behavior in October 1973. That such a difference exists in the time series as a whole suggests both that independent intentions strongly outweigh reactive behavior as a source of Israeli conflict initiation (such as June 1967) and that editorials are a salient and valuable mirror of these intentions.

TABLE 3.19. Data Set 3: Egypt subset
Model: OLS
Dependent variable: Israel COPDAB 11-Count$_t$

Parameter Name	Estimate	S.E.
Constant	−0.754	0.447
Egypt COPDAB 11-Count$_t$	−1.106	0.046

R-squared = 0.8277
$n = 120$

TABLE 3.20. Data Set 3: Egypt subset
Model: OLS
Dependent variable: Israel COPDAB 11-Count$_t$

Parameter Name	Estimate	S.E.
Constant	3.082	1.020
Egypt COPDAB 11-Count$_{t-1}$	0.418	0.105

R-squared = 0.1182
$n = 119$

CHAPTER 4

Predicting War in Practice: Crisis and War

Two substantial issues remain with the way I have tried to understand how nations get to war. First, while I have provided some evidence that the level of editorial activity is related to subsequent levels of conflictual behavior (H3) and is independent of prior events, I have done little to go beyond this most basic claim. Is this editorial indicator anything more than an early warning tool? Can editorials and other evidence of support-building efforts tell us anything about the underlying preferences and bargaining strategies of governments facing war? Second, while I have demonstrated that efforts to build public support through the mass media are undertaken by governments prior to initiating a war (H1), I have provided somewhat less evidence that such efforts *only* occur prior to wars. The data sets in chapter 3 have few cases of crises and heightened tensions that do not lead to war. I want to look explicitly at such cases to back up the conclusions of chapter 3.

I make two related arguments in this chapter to respond to these two issues. First, we can get more information out of this editorial measure of support-building effort than a simple measure of the likelihood of subsequent conflict. By reexamining these media complaints for substantive content, we can identify shifts in the bargaining strategy used by governments in times of crisis. Second, by looking at the media activity surrounding linked cases of crises—some that become wars and some that do not—I can show that editorial writing and other mass media behaviors are often independent of external shocks and prior events, particularly those editorials with substantive content indicative of crisis escalation.

Rational choice theory claims that, given knowable, transitive preferences, decisions follow according to the precepts of utility maximization. While procedural rationality has been assailed from a variety of directions, that is not my purpose here. In fact, I have been quite willing to adopt the assumptions of rational choice theory as it pertains to interstate conflict. I claimed that war initiation is the actualization of a decision by political elites, backed by mass support, that war is preferable to peace. Previous chapters presented models of one aspect of this process, in which the demands of building public support create reliable indicators of such a preference for war, despite any conflicting communications to foreign audiences designed to create strategic surprise.

That said, the limitations of procedural rationality make it impossible to ascertain how this preference for war came to exist. Preferences are taken as given, as exogenous to the matter at hand, in microeconomic theory. But, while the notion of *chacun a son gout* might make sense for determinations of supply and demand curves, I want to dig deeper in order to understand why war erupts from time to time. That is, there is a tremendous difference between plotting a bolt-from-the-blue attack for territorial expansion and finding yourself trapped in a downward spiral of deteriorating relations in which war is seized upon as a last alternative. In both scenarios war is the ultimate option, yet the underlying rationale behind the primacy of that option is perhaps quite different. Rational choice theory, in and of itself, does not differentiate between the two scenarios, and neither can the models of chapter 3.

How can I use these tools for identifying the existence of a preference for war to examine the process by which this preference comes about? I move in this direction by taking a second look at the primary component in the conflict prediction models: the newspaper editorial. In the first stage of analysis, editorials were coded simply by whether or not they expressed criticism toward another country. In this second stage the goal is to determine if the nature of these editorials can shed light on the development of conflict. Looking at what editorials are complaining about, rather than just whether they complain or not, is my approach to anticipating the type of future conflict as well as its frequency. For example, let us assume that the number of U.S. editorials written against Iraq following the invasion of Kuwait indicates future conflict. The sheer number of editorials, however, tells us nothing about what form that conflict would take, whether U.S. action would be an embargo or an all-out attack. I argue that evaluating these editorials for substantive content, and linking those patterns with the process of conflict, allows us both to anticipate what kind of conflict we can expect as well as to understand the path to that conflict a bit better.

As operationalized in chapter 3, the set of critical editorials vis-à-vis some foreign country is not equal to the entire set of editorials about that foreign country. Sometimes an editorial will simply comment on a foreign country without focusing on the threat that country poses. This is what we usually consider to be the traditional role of the editorial: to notice some practice and present reasons for either applauding or condemning that practice. In fact, practically every editorial in major U.S. newspapers fits this description; only under relatively rare circumstances will a critical editorial appear. One primary characteristic of such ordinary editorials—which I will refer to as "analytic"—is a concern with the actions of the foreign nation rather than the actions of the home nation. Such an editorial might very well discuss the possible options open to the home country in response to a foreign misstep, but the tone should be conciliatory and cautious. In general, the level of vitriol in these editorials should be lower than in their "critical" cousins, assumedly because the need to generate such passion is less. The role of editorials in this case is as an immediate response to perceived iniquities in another nation's policy. Critical editorials, on the other hand, focus on justifying a unilateral action rather than calmly discuss an adversary's actions; they should either threaten some escalation or, if dealing with a recent aggressive action, defend it in a nonconciliatory fashion.

Despite the apparent subjectiveness of this coding scheme, the results are remarkably consistent across coders. Thirty editorials were shown to three coders. Each coder was told that each editorial had to be assigned to one of two categories, analytic or critical. Full instructions for coding are found in appendix 2.1, but, in brief, coders were told that analytic editorials would calmly discuss events in or involving some foreign country. Analytic editorials would emphasize external actions, would seek to preserve the status quo or return to a recent status quo ante, and would tend to react to a recent foreign action rather than present a case for escalatory behavior. Critical editorials would emphasize unilateral actions, would threaten to change the status quo or return to a long past status quo ante, and would tend to make a case for aggressive behavior. Finally, coders were told that analytic editorials are more common than critical.[1] Coder 1 identified 20 editorials as analytic and 10 as critical; coder 2 identified 12 as critical editorials, including the same 10 identified by coder 1; coder 3 identified 11 as critical editorials, 9 shared with coder 1, all 11 shared with coder 2. Of the 30 editorials all three coders agreed on 27.

The consistency across these criteria is more easily understood with a few examples.[2] An Israeli editorial of March 17, 1967, entitled "Israel Raises the Stakes," is critical, with its justification of escalatory hot pursuit of Fatah terrorists to their Syrian and Jordanian bases. An editorial of a few days earlier, noting the effect Egyptian actions in Yemen had on Arab unity and British plans to leave Aden, is coded as analytic. Likewise, an October 1973 Indian editorial discussing the soft line taken by the USSR toward Pakistan in a communiqué with Algeria is analytic, whereas an editorial printed two weeks later calling for military support of the Mukti Bahini (the anti-Pakistani guerrilla forces in Bangladesh / East Pakistan) is critical. These differences in editorial type change little over time. For example, a 1917 editorial calling for the United States to join the Allies in order to fight the German "spirit of militarism and aggression" that threatens the well-being of the entire world is as clearly critical as a 1915 editorial discussing the legality of German blockade plans for Britain is clearly analytic.

Looking for Patterns

I examined the pattern of editorial type in detail for almost all of the countries involved in the Singer and Small data set of chapter 3, looking at both the wars from that data set as well as crisis periods that did not flare into full-scale war.

No attempt was made to examine the universe of crises as I did with the universe of interstate wars, nor is a random sample possible given the uncertainty surrounding starting dates of crises as well as the data collection effort such a sample would entail.[3] Instead, discrete and researchable crises, listed in the International Crisis Behavior Project, 1918–1988,[4] were matched with nations from the interstate war data set. I paid special attention to the months preceding the initiation of four wars—the Six Day War (Israel 1967), the Bangladesh War (India 1971), the Falklands War (Argentina 1982), and the Lebanon War (Israel 1982).

Argentina

With the fewest critical editorials involved Argentina in 1982 is the simplest of the interstate wars to analyze. As we saw in chapter 1, the Argentine junta mounted a comprehensive media campaign to build public support for its moves. Hostile editorials began to appear in early March, surpassing the predicted threshold for violent interstate conflict by March 12. Of the four hostile editorials directed by *La Prensa* against Britain in March, two speak in general terms of Argentina's just cause in combating the horrible affront to Argentine sovereignty presented by British occupation of the Malvinas over the past 199 years. One deals with Argentina's wise proposal to push for an accelerated negotiation process to reclaim the Malvinas. The final editorial, on March 29, refers proudly to the landing of Argentine workers on South Georgia Island in violation of British immigration laws, claiming that England would no longer be able to drag matters along. All four attempt to justify some concrete Argentine action designed to upset the status quo or force Britain's hand. Note that these editorials were written in the absence of hostile behavior by the United Kingdom. In fact, the months and years prior to Argentine initiation showed Britain withdrawing military support from the Falklands and agreeing to negotiate with the junta on a transferal of sovereignty over the islands.

A very different pattern of editorial writing exists for Argentine disputes with Chile over the Beagle Channel and associated islands. Although widely reported to be on the brink of war several times over this issue, especially in late 1978,[5] there is little evidence in the Argentine press of an effort to build public support for war. There are editorials discussing Chilean relations, to be sure, but all are of the analytic type, calling for peace and mediation throughout the supposed worst days of the crisis. Indeed, those that are critical during this period (December 19 and 22) concern the Falklands more than the Beagles. A list of these editorials, all from *La Prensa,* is as follows:

> 10/19/78, "La Argentina y Chile," Analytic. Best wishes for an equitable conclusion to current negotiations and further integration of interests in the future.

10/31/78, "Conciliacion argentino chilena," Analytic. Urges moderation on both sides. Encourages both governments to drop any absolute demands.

11/4/78, "Tercera fase en las negociaciones con Chile," Analytic. Calls for direct communications between the presidents of both countries, and no more military maneuvers on either side.

11/10/78, "La mediacion," Analytic. Mediation of international issues (silent on what issues—Beagles or Falklands) is the best path to take.

11/17/78, "La respuesta Argentina a Chile," Analytic. Applauds Chilean proposal to submit Beagle issues to third-party arbitration.

12/19/78, "La conciencia territorial," Critical. Argentina's self-esteem has been damaged by long-standing territorial disputes with Chile and United Kingdom.

12/22/78, "Nuestros derechos sobre las islas Malvinas," Critical. Argentina is impatient to see this ancient dispute resolved. Argentina's sovereign rights to the Falkland islands are very clear (no mention of Chile or Beagles).

12/24/78, "Una mision de paz," Analytic. The pope is concerned with the suspension of talks between Chile and Argentina. He will help resolve this issue peacefully.

12/28/78, "Situacion creada en el conflicto del Beagle," Analytic. More praise for papal intercession and mediation. Calls for level heads on all sides, no provocative actions.

1/9/79, "La gestion del enviado papal," Analytic. Mediation efforts continue. Bravo to papal legate.

1/28/79, "La mediacion papal," Analytic. Mediation efforts continue. Success and peaceful resolution are almost certain.

Based on the sheer number of editorials mentioning Chile over these months, I would expect some level of interstate conflict to develop, but without the clarion call of critical editorials I would not expect the crisis to escalate to war. In fact, the editorials indicative of military conflict are directed against Britain during this time, although not of a quantity that would presage actual war. In March 1982, however, we see both a continuation of the critical, hostile editorial line against Britain *and* a large enough number to trip an early warning system.

India

The growth in tensions with Pakistan over the breakaway of East Pakistan / Bangladesh, culminating in declared war on December 2, 1971, follows an archetypal pattern of a security dilemma path to war. That is, we see a long, drawn-out period of diplomatic and military brinkmanship, in which each side pushes the other for concessions and is pushed back in turn. As we see in table 4.1 and figure 4.1, analytic editorials mirror this process for the first nine months of the crisis. In January and February hostile editorials are very specific and quite petty; the January 22 editorial complains about Pakistan's successful efforts in disqualifying an Indian field hockey team from an international tournament. Even in March, as tensions between East and West Pakistan mount, the editorials treat the entire issue as a domestic Pakistani affair. The tone is quite detached, as if the editorial writers were pollsters trying to predict the outcome of some electoral contest. Both the pace and anger of editorials begin to pick up in April, as Bangladesh declares its independence and refugees begin to stream across the border. We see occasional editorials focusing on domestic actions, even escalatory ones. For example, the April 28 editorial commends the Indian government's decision to grant asylum to Pakistani diplomats with Bangladesh sympathies. Still, the vast majority are still analytic, making disparaging comments about the Khan regime. May, June, July, August, and September continue this general style of editorial, as the most prevalent subject now becomes third-party nations supporting "the genocidal generals" of Pakistan.[6] In August we see the first editorials justifying genuinely hostile actions on India's part—the training and supply of Bangladesh guerrillas.

Yet two months before hostilities truly begin in earnest, the relative and absolute frequency of editorial types changes drastically. By October very few calm analyses of Pakistani actions and internal affairs turn up; instead, the *Times* presents justifications of the steps India has taken to remove the Pakistani threat. A massive troop buildup is explained on October 22, and by late November the editorials defend India's refusal to accede to the United Nation's call for mutual withdrawals from the borders.[7]

In retrospect, is there evidence that the Indian government decided in late September or early October to initiate a full-blown war as soon as public opinion would allow? It appears that India consciously decided not to go to war in

TABLE 4.1.   Indian Editorials vs. Pakistan, 1971

Month	Total Editorials	Analytic Editorials (%)	Critical Editorials (%)
January	2	2 (100)	0 (0)
February	4	3 (75)	1 (25)
March	8	8 (100)	0 (0)
April	13	10 (77)	3 (23)
May	6	5 (83)	1 (17)
June	8	6 (75)	2 (25)
July	10	9 (90)	1 (10)
August	6	4 (67)	2 (33)
September	4	4 (100)	0 (0)
October	6	2 (33)	4 (67)
November	8	2 (25)	6 (75)

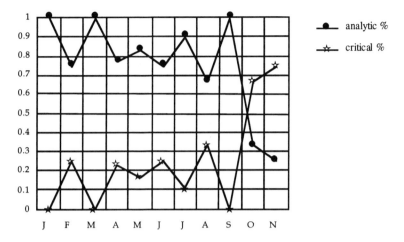

Fig 4.1.   Indian editorials vs. Pakistan, 1971

the spring of 1971 but, instead, to consider such action later in the year.[8] In early October the Soviet Union successfully pressured India into giving up its categorical demand for East Bengali independence if Pakistan would release Sheikh Mujib. When Yahya Khan declared his intention on October 12 to move on with the East Pakistani by-elections without Mujib, thus dashing the Soviet peace plan, India apparently decided that enough was enough and that all-out war was the answer.[9] I will consider the implications of this shift in media behavior for our understanding of crisis bargaining later in this chapter.

Israel

This same shift in decision makers' preferences, as evidenced by a change in the kind of editorial written, can also be seen in the Israel 1967 case (see table 4.2 and fig. 4.2). Here the shift is not as pronounced, as editorials do not occur with any frequency more than four months before the war, as opposed to almost a full year in the India 1971 case, but the clear trend is for more and more critical editorials, both relatively and absolutely, to focus on potential Israeli breaks with the status quo.

The trend in these editorials is a shift from an analysis of Egyptian misadventures in Yemen and Syrian foot-dragging in the Mixed Armistice Commission to clear threats of unilateral escalation in response to Egyptian and Syrian force postures. On May 18 the *Post* writes that

it is of utmost importance that it should be pressed home to the Syrians that, in the event of renewed terror, Israel would choose both the timing

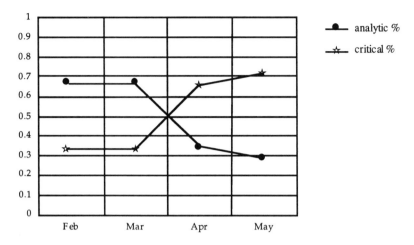

Fig 4.2.   Israeli editorials vs. Syria and Egypt, 1967

and the manner of her reaction in a manner most advantageous to Israel.[10]

On the Egyptian front the *Post* threatens a military strike if Israeli shipping is restricted in any fashion and goes on a week later to write:

> We insist on free passage to and from the Red Sea. And we are determined to prevent violence along our borders. If there will be no alternative, the Israeli Defense Forces will be put into action. However, we will not allow Egypt to dictate the timing, place, method, or scope of such action.[11]

Although the nature and tone of the Israeli editorials is overwhelmingly analytic in the early days of this crisis period, by the end of May the editorials are indistinguishable in critical content from those in the latter days of the Indian and Argentine cases.

From the Egyptian side there is only one critical editorial versus Israel in April 1967. Granted, it calls for the eradication of Israel from the face of the

TABLE 4.2.   Israeli Editorials vs. Syria and Egypt, 1967

Month	Total Editorials	Analytic Editorials (%)	Critical Editorials (%)
February	3	2 (67)	1 (33)
March	3	2 (67)	1 (33)
April	6	2 (33)	4 (67)
May	18	5 (28)	13 (72)

Earth—certainly a nationalistic call to arms—but it is not followed by others and is not, by itself, an indicator of much. In fact, the lion's share of critical Egyptian editorials during this time are directed against Saudi Arabia and their "reactionary meddling" in Yemen. By late May, however, Egyptian criticism of Israel skyrockets, with almost one call for war per day from May 20 until the Israeli attack on June 6. I surmise from this spate of critical editorials that Israel had good reason to conclude that Egypt was planning an attack against Israel and that the June 6 initiation could be justified as a preemptive rather than preventive attack. Yet, judging from Israel's record of critical editorials—which start in April, well *before* the Egyptian media blitz—I also conclude that Egypt had good reason to assume that Israel was planning a military strike against Syria certainly and Egypt possibly.

In 1973, prior to the October War clearly initiated by Egypt, we do not see this mix of critical editorials on both sides. Instead, the editorial pages in Israel are rather clear of any mention of Egypt, critical or analytic. In Egypt, however, editorials against Israel are few in June, pick up somewhat in July and August, and are stridently critical in September. In fact, if there is any decline in this steady pattern of increasing numbers and increasing virulence from June onward, it is in the first week of October, as if Egypt sought at least tactical surprise by limiting criticism in the days immediately prior to the attack in the Sinai.

The close quarters of the Levant, where the lines between domestic and international communications are more blurred than anywhere else in the world, makes it difficult for nations to overcome the secrecy/support dilemma in the usual fashion, by telling lies through diplomatic channels and the truth in domestic media. Given that Egyptian newspapers hit the stands in Tel Aviv almost as fast as they do in Cairo, a regime seeking to maintain surprise must be creative in its management of information regarding its intentions. One such strategy might be to "cry wolf" repeatedly in the domestic media until domestic media signals are no longer taken seriously by your adversaries. This is what Chaim Herzog claimed Egypt did throughout the early 1970s, occasionally creating what Herzog called a "war atmosphere" in its domestic media so that Israel would be unable to judge when the threat was real.[12] A related strategy, which I think looks a great deal like actual media behavior in 1973, would be to mobilize public opinion until you are confident that support for war is high, then intentionally stop those efforts long enough to create at least a touch of surprise without losing too much domestic support. Still, there is little doubt among observers of the Egyptian media system that its role is far greater as a domestic signaler of regime intentions than as an international signaler.[13] In fact, a nonstrategic interpretation of *al-Ahram*'s relative curtailment of critical editorials immediately prior to the 1973 attack could plausibly focus on the falling out between *al-Ahram*'s influential editor, Muhammed Hassanain Haykal, and President Nasser over the conduct of the October War. So, while Egyptian editorials are perhaps the best example (if not the only example) of opinion leading efforts being used as part of an international signaling game, even here we cannot say that an international strategic purpose came close to outweighing domestic considerations of public opinion management and regime power struggles.

Israel 1982 is very close to Argentina 1982 as an example of a straightforward bolt-from-the-blue path to war, and the editorial pattern leading up to the invasion is just what would be expected in such a case (see table 4.3). The editorials are clearly focused on Israeli threats rather than events in Lebanon, they begin to appear in earnest two months before the initiation date, and the clear implication is for a sharp break with the status quo. As early as March 4, we see muted calls for scrapping the existing cease-fire agreement as no longer in Israel's best interests:

> These facts [the PLO buildup in Lebanon] may not in themselves entitle Israel to initiate military action against the terrorists, in view of the existence of a cease-fire. The cease-fire agreement may have been badly drafted and hastily endorsed, and it may now be working to Israel's disadvantage. But it is a commitment. On the other hand, no one with any knowledge of the character, programme and record of the PLO can write off these facts as lacking military significance.[14]

By May 17 the cease-fire is characterized as an out-and-out "bad deal" that Israel should not continue to abide by.[15]

These editorials in the *Jerusalem Post* concerning the prospects of war delve into the governmental decision-making process deeply enough to shed light on when and how the decision to invade was made. As early as February, *Time* magazine in the United States printed a story claiming that Ariel Sharon had set a plan for the invasion of Lebanon into effect; the *Post* claimed that "senior defense officials" denied the charge that a decision had been reached, although the officials agreed that "an expanded version of the Litani Operation, designed to crush, once and for all, the rearmed and regrouped terrorists in Lebanon, even at the risk of conflict with Syria" was an option to consider if terrorist attacks continued.[16] By May the *Post* is providing a breakdown of

TABLE 4.3. Israeli Editorials vs. Lebanon, 1982

Month	Total Editorials	Analytic Editorials (%)	Critical Editorials (%)
February	1	0 (0)	1 (100)
March	1	0 (0)	1 (100)
April	3	0 (0)	3 (100)
May	3	0 (0)	3 (100)

the cabinet's position on moving into Lebanon, with the majority, including Begin, convinced of the necessity of the invasion and a "vocal minority" opposed.[17]

Many of the same pressures that led to an Israeli invasion in 1982 were also present in 1981. The immediate *casus belli,* PLO shelling of Israeli settlements, is identical. In fact, there is the added provocation of Syrian installation of advanced SAM systems in Lebanon in 1981. The tensions in 1981, however, led to a cease-fire agreement, whereas the tensions in 1982 led to war. An examination of the pattern of editorials in 1981 suggests that the potential for mediated crisis bargaining existed in this case, to be successfully achieved by Philip Habib's shuttle diplomacy (see table 4.4).

The tone and content of editorials in 1981 is completely different than in 1982. Discussing the Israeli government's announcement that the destruction of the Christian community in Lebanon was unacceptable to Israel, the *Post* writes that "trying to halt the escalation, even at this late hour, Mr. Begin insisted it was not a war, and that the aim of Israel's action was not to oust the Syrians from Lebanon altogether."[18] Israel is just as clearly attempting to maintain the status quo in 1981 as it is trying to break with it in 1982. The *Post* explicitly acknowledges this desire, claiming that "Israel is intent upon restoring the status quo ante" in 1981.[19] Five editorials across this time span talk about the fine job Habib is doing in reducing tensions and how domestic opinion within Israel will simply not support a war at this time.[20]

Soviet Union

I examine paired cases of war and crisis for the United States in chapter 5. As the other superpower during the Cold War but a nondemocracy, the USSR serves as a useful comparison case to U.S. diplomatic history. How does Soviet media effort differ, if at all, for a case of war (Afghanistan 1979), military intervention (Czechoslovakia 1968), and crisis (China 1969)?

The editorial position of *Pravda* during the initial stages of the Dubček liberalization measures appears to have been almost exclusively analytic, precisely as we would expect. As Jiri Valenta writes:

TABLE 4.4. Israeli Editorials vs. Lebanon, 1981

Month	Total Editorials	Analytic Editorials (%)	Critical Editorials (%)
March	3	3 (100)	0 (0)
April	4	4 (100)	0 (0)
May	3	3 (100)	0 (0)
June	4	3 (75)	1 (25)

Even the CPSU's most important periodical, *Pravda,* had for several months of the crisis adopted a cautious stand on Czechoslovakia, presenting the critical events in Prague in a selective but more or less calm manner until mid-June 1968. The positions of these periodicals [*Kommunist* and other CPSU publications] seemed to reflect the cautious attitude of some Soviet bureaucracies, particularly those concerned with the detrimental effects of the Soviet hard line toward Czechoslovakia.[21]

Pravda was not alone in its cautious tone toward the changes in Czechoslovakia, but it was not the only opinion expressed in the mass media, either. Other periodicals, according to Valenta, particularly those linked to the Ukrainian Party bureaucracy and Russian State Party officials, took quite a hard line toward the Dubček regime from the beginning.[22] This is strong evidence that the Soviet regime was faced with a marketing (or coordination) problem, in that different groups within the Soviet leadership expressed their differing views on appropriate policy toward Czechoslovakia through various media outlets. Still, to Valenta that debate is entirely internal to the regime; he does not link this media debate to efforts to mobilize a broader public's support for a faction's position.

The reflection of such internal regime debate in the Russian media is interesting in and of itself (and the bread and butter of Kremlinologists), but did the Soviet regime make an active attempt to channel domestic opinion and preserve international secrecy once the decision to intervene was made? According to Valenta, the final decision to intervene was not made until August 17, only three days before the tanks rolled across the border.[23] But we see strong evidence in *Pravda* of attempts to lay the foundation for this intervention from late July onward:

>7/22/68, "Suspicious Visit," Critical. West Germany is maintaining an actively subversive role in Czechoslovakia and must be stopped. The forces of Imperialism are contained only through the solidarity of the Warsaw Pact. Socialist countries will never yield their accomplishments or risk their territorial integrity.
>7/23/68, "Black Lion," Critical. The purpose of large-scale NATO exercises near Czechoslovakia is clear. NATO forces are trying to subvert that country from the socialist path.
>7/28/68, "Horseshoe in a Wrap," Critical. They try to conceal their plans, but NATO forces are on secret alert on Czech border. "All this reveals Western plans—aggressive and hostile towards socialist Czechoslovakia."
>8/11/68, "NATO Trying to Gain Control," Analytic. NATO accelerates its military buildup and lies about the Warsaw Pact threat.

8/12/68, "With Provocative Purpose," Critical. Socialist nations must be vigilant against imperialist military threats. We have all seen what they are trying to accomplish in Czechoslovakia.

Given these editorial comments, it comes as little surprise that Soviet intervention masqueraded as a military exercise to counter the NATO forces on "secret alert." Note also that the Brezhnev Doctrine, claiming the USSR's right to prevent any socialist nation from backsliding, is clearly enunciated for domestic consumption in the editorials of July 22 and 23, well before its international announcement in late August.

On the other hand, Soviet clashes with China over the Ussuri River had a very different media etymology. For years the USSR had used intimidation tactics to keep Chinese settlers off contested river islands. On March 2, 1969, however, China challenged this policy with military firepower, resulting in 31 dead Soviet soldiers and an unknown number of Chinese casualties.[24]

On the Chinese side there was little media activity of any sort during 1969, as the Cultural Revolution was at its peak, and editorials were printed perhaps once per month as a direct order to the people from Mao Tse-tung. All the same, two editorials critical of the Soviet Union were printed in February prior to the border incident.[25] Immediately following the attack on March 4 a joint editorial in both *People's Daily* and *Liberation Army Daily,* titled "Down with the New Tsars," said that Chenpao Island belonged to China from an 1860 treaty, that Chinese troops had a "sacred" right to patrol their territory, and that the USSR had been massing troops on its side of the border. No further editorial effort materialized, however.

Given that the clash was initiated by China, we would not expect Soviet editorials to anticipate the conflict, and indeed there was no *Pravda* article even remotely critical of China in the months prior to the incident.[26] In fact, even after the incident no *Pravda* editorial blasted the Chinese in a critical manner. A diplomatic protest note went out over TASS (the Soviet international press agency) on March 2, but not through the domestic news services.

Yet, by March 7, the Soviet decision to retaliate with a limited military strike against the Chinese was reflected in an effort to build public support.[27] A March 8 *Pravda* editorial calls the border clash indicative of China's hostility to socialists everywhere. Also on March 8 *Red Star* devoted half of its front page to a warning that future Chinese aggression would be met with extreme force, and on March 9 that same newspaper printed a clearly critical editorial against China titled "Stern Warning to the Adventurists."[28] On March 15 a second clash broke out on the Ussuri, this time from the Soviet side of the river, with several dozen casualties on both sides.

Immediately after the March 15 incident, however, both sides made over-tures to begin negotiations. Chinese newspapers were virtually silent about this second clash, as were their Soviet counterparts. And at the subsequent Party meetings in both China and the USSR, substantial movement was made toward compromise. By October China made a final confirmation that it would nego-tiate the island's future peacefully, and, while relations stayed chilly afterward, no clashes were to break out along the border again. Soviet and Chinese media efforts during this period were similarly restrained. Do we have any indication in the Soviet or Chinese press about why their respective leadership decided against pursuing these territorial disputes? No. What we do have is a media in-dicator that accurately signals both the intensity and type of subsequent initiated conflict.

We also have the supportive results of a largely forgotten data set on Soviet and Chinese perceptions of each other and the United States from 1950 through 1967. Collected by researchers at the Social Sciences Department of the Ben-dix Corporation, "Project Triad" compiled indices of perceived threat in these two countries as determined by a function of statements made in their news-paper editorials, public speeches, and diplomatic notes.[29] The statement data was aggregated into annual cumulative scores, making it noncompatible with the quantitative tests of this research (the original data from which the indi-ces are compiled are no longer available), but we should see support for the claims made here in the broadest terms—that critical media statements concern-ing each other should be minimal between the USSR and PRC throughout the 1950s but grow as the 1960s progress and incidents such as the Ussuri conflict develop (see figs. 4.3 and 4.4).

The Project Triad data does not go past 1967, so we cannot directly compare this operationalization of Soviet and Chinese media statements to the level of activity immediately prior to the Ussuri conflict in 1969. All the same, we can pull some applicable information from this effort. Looking at COPDAB event count scores of interactions between the USSR and PRC over this time period, I find *no* events coded 11 or higher prior to 1961. The years 1961 through 1966 have a total of 10 such events over the six-year time span, with no year containing more than three. In 1967, however, we see both the highest "threat perception" measure for the USSR and the PRC versus each other as well as 17 COPDAB events scored 11 or higher. We cannot tell whether or not higher levels of media activity directly preceded higher levels of conflict in the manner of a leading indicator, but we can tell that higher levels of critical media activity—even aggregated on an annual basis—are not unrelated to higher levels of conflict.

In many ways the Soviet invasion of Afghanistan in December 1979 would seem to parallel 1968's intervention in Czechoslovakia, the primary difference

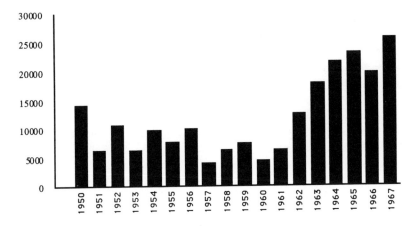

Fig. 4.3.   USSR media threat perception of PRC

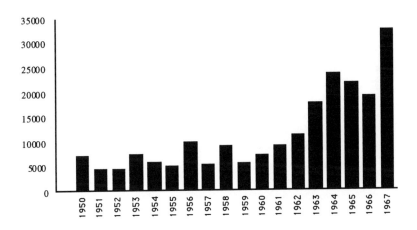

Fig. 4.4.   PRC media threat perception of USSR

being that the Afghans fought back and the Czechs gave up. Just as Moscow quickly tired of Alexander Dubček's policies in Czechoslovakia, so did the USSR became disenchanted with the ostensibly Communist leaders of Afghanistan following their takeover of the country in late April 1978. Rebuffed in their efforts to install a more malleable puppet government through diplomatic means, the Soviet army crossed the border into Afghanistan on December 24, taking Kabul three days later.[30]

Perhaps because the South Asian theater was not as crucial to the USSR as its East European buffer, there are not as many critical editorials concerning

Afghanistan in the months immediately preceding the invasion as there were concerning Czechoslovakia. But, although not as concentrated as in the Czech case, *Pravda* editorials from mid-August onward give substantial evidence of Soviet attempts to channel domestic support in favor of potential intervention in Afghanistan.

> 7/18/79, "For Defense of the Revolution,"Analytic. Afghan National Democratic Party is hard at work to institute reforms and fight off counterrevolutionaries.
>
> 8/10/79, "A Righteous Cause of the Revolution," Critical. The USSR must arm the Afghan people in their worthy struggle to throw off the influence of Western imperialists and Chinese hegemonists, who support evil counterrevolutionary forces.
>
> 8/30/79, "Hands Off Afghanistan!"Critical. USSR will not allow "Western Imperialists and Chinese Hegemonists . . . to kill the Revolution and reverse its achievements."
>
> 10/7/79, "For Protection of the Revolution," Critical. Given the strong counterrevolutionary forces at work in Afghanistan, the Afghan people have established a defense organization that may need our help.
>
> 11/4/79, "Mutually Beneficial Cooperation," Analytic. With the victory of the Afghan Revolution, we are now seeing an acceleration of Soviet-Afghan economic and technological cooperation.
>
> 11/17/79, "Steps of Reform," Analytic. First stage of land reform completed in Afghanistan. Revolutionary leaders there expressed confidence that they would be able to overcome formidable counterrevolutionary terrorists and blackmailers.
>
> 11/28/79, "Dangerous Activity," Critical. Growing American military presence in the Indian Ocean Basin and surrounding territories is a grave threat to peace.
>
> 12/7/79, "Guarding the Revolution," Critical. Inspired by imperialist forces, counterrevolutionary groups are wreaking havoc in Afghanistan. The Afghan workers have authorized a new national defense organization that may need Soviet help.

As in Czechoslovakia, intervention in Afghanistan is initially presented as necessary to preserve socialist gains that were difficult to achieve and must not be squandered. On November 28 *Pravda* presents a second rationale to justify intervention, also similar to that used for Czechoslovakia: given American troop buildups and maneuvers in the region, the USSR must counter with its own exercises and power projection.

Unlike the Israeli and Indian cases, we do not see clear evidence of a shift in editorial types, from analytic and toward critical, in these three Soviet cases.

Instead, the trend in media activity is much closer to that found in Argentina prior to the Falklands War. Not coincidentally, perhaps, the Soviet and Argentine regimes are much more authoritarian than their Israeli and Indian counterparts. Although the Polity II measure of democracy provided little support for hypothesis H4 (that democracies should make a greater opinion-building effort than nondemocracies) in chapter 3's data sets that looked only at critical editorials, we see some tentative evidence that regime type does indeed make a difference in editorial activity when the entire set of editorials—analytic and critical—is considered. Note also that there is a far more visible crisis period prior to the Israeli and Indian wars, a crisis period that mirrors the predominance of analytic editorials.

Between the analysis here and in the preceding chapter I can now make three responses to the claim that this editorial measure is not really independent of crisis levels of conflict, that at best editorials pick up the same necessary conditions for war found in crisis behavior:

A few wars are best characterized as bolts from the blue and are not preceded by drawn-out crisis. All the same we still see a significant number of editorials of a critical sort prior to such sneak attacks.

When looking at paired cases of crises that escalated to war and crises that did not (and this point will be reinforced in the next chapter), we see fewer editorials in general associated with crises that do not escalate. Moreover, we see a very different *type* of editorial alongside nonescalating crises.

During a crisis editorials react very little to prior or contemporary crisis events. Instead, the number and type of editorial effort is strongly related to the intensity of *future* conflictual events.

There is a related potential criticism that these paired cases can shed some light on: that the media indicator developed here should really be considered a predictor of crises or militarized disputes rather than a predictor of war.[31] Given that the class of events known as "militarized disputes" differs from the class of events known as "war" only in scope rather than in type, this media indicator is inevitably a predictor of both crises *and* war. And, given the relative distribution of militarized disputes and wars (with the former being far more common), it is also inevitable that we will see a stronger statistical relationship between media indicators and crises than media indicators and war. All the same, I claim that a qualitative difference exists between media activity immediately prior to full-blown wars and media activity prior to and concurrent with disputes. This distinction is necessarily less robust and statistically significant than chapter 3's conclusion that editorial activity is a leading indicator of conflictual events (whether in war or crisis)—not because any evidence is contradictory but because the phenomenon in question does not allow as rigorous an examination.

Pattern Implications

Regardless of regime type, the pattern consistent with all these cases is a world in which wars are immediately preceded by relatively high levels of critical editorials, but that crises—whether eventually escalating into war or not—are marked more by analytic editorials. This is an inductive finding, to be sure, based on relatively few cases (although consistent with both the far-ranging cases of data set 2 and the time series observations of data set 3). Is there a theoretical foundation that would suggest such a pattern?

Recall that the original purpose of this book was to identify the timing of a national command structure's decision to initiate war. This was not to say that all wars start out of the blue, with a single nation making a unilateral decision to fight no matter what concessions the other side might make. But I did suggest that, regardless of whether a country is "dragged" into war or rushes headlong into it, at some point national leaders must decide (barring some last-minute miracle or adversary capitulation) that in all likelihood they will have to fight. Sometimes this decision will be made only after a drawn-out process in which the identity of the initiator is not very clear and in which the status quo deteriorates over an extended period of time. Sometimes this decision will be made in the absence of such a downward spiral in relations, in which the initiator can be clearly identified as breaking with the status quo in an aggressive attack. Both decisions are concurrent with a "crisis," although the crisis will be far more visible in the former set of circumstances.

These classifications are not original to this work. A host of theorists, both in quantitative and nonquantitative fashion, have argued that warring nations are typically caught in a vicious circle in which nation i's perceptions of threat demand actions that are, in turn, perceived as threatening by nation j, leading to further destabilizing actions by nation j, leading to still greater perceptions of threat by nation i. In this vision, often referred to as a "security dilemma,"[32] neither nation prefers war to peace at the onset of this circle, but each finds itself sliding down the slippery slope to war because of the logic of defense within a self-help system.

Other theorists, again with a variety of methodologies, have argued that wars are not so much the result of pernicious state interactions in an anarchic system as they are the result of a deliberate and independent decision for aggrandizement. This strategy might be based on concerns of an imminent power transition; it might be based on simple greed for new territory or trade routes; it might be based on a desire to halt the genocidal domestic policies of another state. Regardless, the key facet to this vision of conflict is that in the relative absence of immediate threats one nation decides unilaterally and conclusively that war is the best means to the desired end.[33]

For example, we can see both of these broad visions of conflict attempt to account for the outbreak of World War I. To Dina Zinnes and others, acts perceived as aggressive and reactions to those acts magnified initial tensions over time until reactions became troop mobilizations and territorial annexations.[34] Arguments that the participants were dragged into war or that offensive strategies were driven by the nature of the alliance system are other manifestations of the idea that this devastating war was the unfortunate and largely unforeseen consequence of a security dilemma.[35]

On the other hand, Fritz Fischer argues that the Versailles treaty was largely correct in assigning war guilt to Germany.[36] Fearful of Continental encroachment and decline of empire, Germany initiated a preventive war. Likewise, arguments that this war was the result of a power transition imply either that the heretofore dominant nation intentionally began the war in order to protect its preeminent position or that the challenging nation intentionally began the war in an attempt to hurry things along.[37] Arguments that a "cult of the offensive" so pervaded the minds of European military leaders that conflict initiation was to be welcomed rather than feared also rest on the idea that unilateral decisions drove events in 1914.[38]

The concept of a bargaining space provides an intuitive summary of the pertinent forces at work. Figure 4.5 illustrates such a space. In the utility continuum for i and j there are any number of future negotiated settlements of a dispute, each of which possesses some mix of utility for the two states. Unfortunately, not all of these future settlements are achievable. The dividing line between those that are theoretically achievable and those that are not is the frontier of possible negotiated settlements.[39] I now hypothesize some reservation utility level for i (and j, if we wish). This is the lowest utility level i will accept rather than walk away from the bargaining table. If i's reservation utility level intersects the frontier at any point, then a negotiated settlement is at least a possibility (at some point to the right of the reservation line and at or below the frontier); if i's reservation level does not intersect the frontier at any point, then no settlement is even conceptually attainable.

If we are associating the paths to war with a bargaining space, we might represent two of the many possibilities as in figure 4.6. I assume that in a security dilemma road to war, i's reservation utility level intersects the frontier of negotiated settlements, making some sort of diplomatic bargain possible. I assume that in a unilateral road to war, i's reservation utility level does not intersect the frontier. In this scenario there is no negotiated settlement that satisfies i's minimal expectations. Note that the nature of the strategic interaction

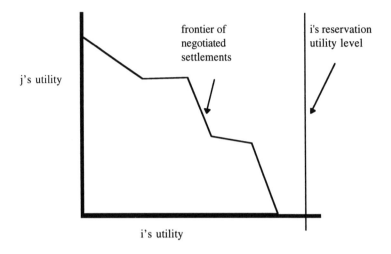

Fig. 4.5

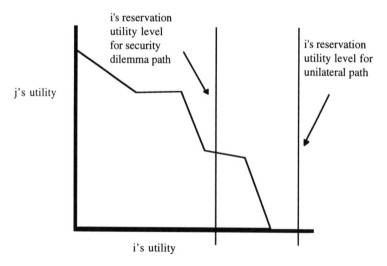

Fig. 4.6

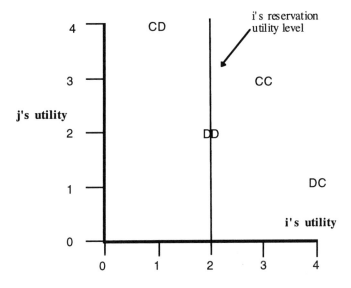

Fig. 4.7.   Prisoner's dilemma

at work within a bargaining space will differ for each case. I am simply using the term *security dilemma* as shorthand for any such case of international dispute in which mixed motives and a bargaining space over outcomes exist.

The Prisoner's Dilemma and Deadlock games are very specific manifestations of a bargaining situation. To get a better feel for bargaining theory, figures 4.7 and 4.8 express these two types of games on a bargaining space.

In a Prisoner's Dilemma the set of possible outcomes consists of the points (3,3), when both *i* and *j* cooperate, (4,1), when *i* defects and *j* cooperates, and (1,4), when *i* cooperates and *j* defects. Mutual defection (2,2), is also within the set of achievable outcomes, but is not as efficient as (3,3). In this game *i*'s reservation price is an expected utility of 2, as *i* is guaranteed such a minimum result with a strategy of defect. Thus, the reservation price does indeed intersect the frontier to the left of a cooperative outcome, making a solution of CC at least possible. Unfortunately, the logic of Prisoner's Dilemma games suggests that the final outcome may well be the inefficient outcome of DD. In Deadlock not only is *i*'s reservation level of utility 3 rather than 2, but the frontier now contains mutual defection at (3,3) rather than mutual cooperation. In this bargaining space, assuming *j*'s reservation level is similar, mutual defection is both the expected and the efficient outcome.

While normal form two-by-two games and bargaining spaces are useful heuristic device for my purposes, I do not intend to model the road to war in formal theoretic terms. A voluminous literature exists on modeling crisis

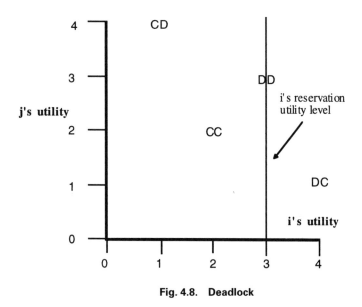

Fig. 4.8. Deadlock

behavior through game theory and/or bargaining theory, and I will not try to summarize or duplicate that here.[40] My point is that any given bargaining structure is fluid, not set in stone, and that a set of preference orderings that allows a bargaining space to exist today may well change to create a set of functions that does not allow a bargaining space tomorrow. As Frederick Mayer argues, one can understand this aspect of international conflict in terms of bargaining theory by thinking of any crisis period as an opportunity for the determination and alteration of utility reservation levels, not just as an argument over where within the bargaining set (if one exists) the outcome will settle.[41]

Immediately prior to a war, if initiation is a procedurally rational process, preference orderings must be such that a unilateral decision for war has been made. Sometimes there will be a very short period of time between the unilateral decision and quantum escalation; most of the time (since public opinion needs to be prepared) not. Sometimes there will be a highly visible and perhaps lengthy crisis period preceding that decision; sometimes (as in a sneak attack) not. During the crisis stage preceding a unilateral decision, whatever its duration, a bargaining space will exist, and if a settlement is reached (by definition at some point within the bargaining space) then the crisis may be defused. As time passes without a settlement, however, the cumulative likelihood of one or both parties choosing to take the unilateral escalatory path increases.[42] By focusing on the transition from analytic to critical editorials, I argue, we can determine the timing of this transition.

Identifying shifts in the strategies of decision makers as they consider going to war is as important for preventing conflict as identifying a basic leading indicator for war. At some point in their considerations, governments must stop trying to justify continued reactive moves and start trying to build popular support for unilateral, highly escalatory attacks. But external behavior through-out—in the form of diplomatic communiqués, troop movements, etc.—remains reactive throughout the entire crisis period, regardless of whether analytic or critical editorials are being printed domestically. This continuation of external reactive behavior even as support is built for unilateral action is important, for it suggests that the accepted paradigm for the security dilemma descent to war is flawed. Instead of an image of two nations getting angrier and angrier, pushing each other back and forth, harder and harder, until the pushes become blows, the better image seems to be two nations pushing back and forth until one party de-cides to continue pushing and being pushed only in order to disguise a new and hidden intention to deliver a really devastating blow in the near future. The old image suggested that nations were captives of the process—precisely the essence of the dilemma in the security dilemma. This new image suggests that nations have greater control over their destinies, that a substantial segment of the process is devoted to preparing for unilateral escalation while continuing on as if a prisoner to the security dilemma. The continuation of prior external be-havior while building internal support for sharp escalation is the sort of media/ foreign policy interaction we would expect if my model of that relationship is sound.

A great deal of effort in the political science literature, in a variety of meth-odologies, has been devoted to portraying the horrors of the security dilemma. This work suggests that the security dilemma itself is not such a bad situation, that tremendous conflict arises only when one or both nations decide that it no longer wishes to play the game. Granted, such a decision might arise only after the reactive process had gone so far as to make unilateral escalation the only hope for national survival, but this is not what happens in the cases examined in this chapter. Instead, the decision seems to be made on the basis of a growing perception that national aims could be better accomplished through a major attack, perhaps with the advantage of strategic surprise, rather than on a percep-tion that unilateral escalation was the only remaining option.

To Robert Jervis the key to ameliorating the security dilemma is to estab-lish a clear difference between offensive and defensive weapons and then to work toward a world in which the defense is dominant.[43] To Robert Axelrod the key is to insure repeated plays of the game so that a tit-for-tat strategy can evolve, moving both players to joint cooperation.[44] Regardless of the strategy, the shared message is that the security dilemma is to be defused if at all possible. This work suggests that, barring a method of creating an outbreak of peace and mutual cooperation, the best way to prevent major war from erupting is to maintain the potential for contingent bargaining strategies, even if this means encouraging the existence of a prisoner's dilemma. So long as hostile actions are confined to reacting to the adversary's actions, violence remains at limited levels; when hostile actions are taken in support of a unilateral attack strategy, we see conflict escalate to levels we consider to be war. This pattern of behavior suggests that defection within a security dilemma is less aggressive or violent than defection within deadlock, that the potential for cooperation only needs to be encouraged enough to keep states locked into a relatively benign pattern of defection within a security dilemma framework.

This is not an altogether original thought—that there are worse fates than to be in a prisoner's dilemma. Kenneth Oye makes the case that conflict during the early 1930s over monetary policy stemmed from a pernicious transition from a prisoner's dilemma situation to one of deadlock, in which each participant prefers defection regardless of any possible adversarial response.[45] Downs, Rocke, and Siverson point out that arms races characterized by deadlock are both more common than generally assumed and more difficult to resolve without war than arms races under the security dilemma.[46] Arthur Stein shows how concerns about misperception and other bogeymen often blamed for conflict initiation are irrelevant when pure strategies for defection replace situations such as the security dilemma, in which shared interests play some meaningful role.[47]

But what does this mean, to keep adversaries in the security dilemma? How can decision makers be persuaded to continue walking within the frustrating confines of a bargaining space when unilateral attack plays its siren song? The driving element behind the security dilemma, as I am using the term, is that nation i cares whether or not nation j will defect or cooperate. When nation i no longer cares about what nation j does, when mutual defection is as attractive as mutual cooperation, the bargaining space crumbles, albeit in a frightening direction. Efforts to keep nation i locked in the bargaining space, then, should focus on maintaining the importance of nation j's potential actions to nation i's decision makers. Even if the subsequent choice is still to defect, I suggest that there is a qualitative difference between defection when j's potential actions are at least relevant and when they are not.

There are two ways to maintain the importance of nation j's potential actions. Either nation j's defection must be made exceedingly painful to i if i defects, or nation j's cooperation must be made exceedingly valuable if i cooperates. The first course is relatively easy to accomplish: nation j must build up its punitive abilities,[48] either through its own efforts or the support of third parties with a stake in keeping the relative peace.[49] Since nation i is often in the mirror-image position of nation j in these security dilemma situations, with each nation getting close to deciding on a unilateral strategy, nation i would also have to be

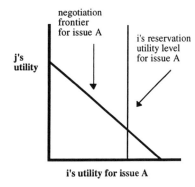
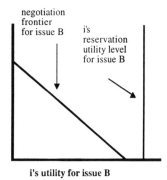

Fig. 4.9

well poised to defect in a truly destructive manner. This is a problematic solution, to recommend arms races as a relatively healthy policy choice, but perhaps not as problematic as a pernicious removal of the security dilemma altogether.

The other method of keeping nation i in the bargaining space—making nation *j*'s cooperation more valuable given *i*'s cooperation—does not have as clear-cut a method of implementation. In fact, this is the traditional goal of analysts of the prisoner's dilemma, making mutual cooperation the sole equilibrium of the game and moving the parties out of the dilemma entirely. Since our goal is merely to keep the adversaries within the dilemma, our task is not as rigorous. Instead of making mutual cooperation the most preferred outcome for both parties, I am quite willing to let *i*-defect/*j*-cooperate remain as the most preferred outcome for *i* (and vice versa for *j*), so long as mutual cooperation is preferred to mutual defection by both parties.

We can easily imagine ways of increasing the payoff of mutual cooperation relative to mutual defection—for example, bribes made contingent on good behavior. But what is the theoretical foundation for such strategies? How can negotiators increase the relative value of cooperation for a deadlocked issue? What I am suggesting here can be thought of as contingent linkage, in which negotiators seek to inject shared motives from a separate bargaining space into a situation where few such motives otherwise exist.[50] To illustrate this idea in terms of bargaining theory,[51] let us assume two different issues under contention between nations *i* and *j* (see fig. 4.9). For issue A let us assume that *i*'s reservation level of utility for any settlement falls within the negotiation frontier for such agreements; for issue B let us assume that the reservation level is outside the frontier. Now let us assume that issues A and B can be linked to create a single issue A-B. Since we are interested in how such a linkage can alter *i*'s perception of the negotiation, I will illustrate the linkage as a three-dimensional

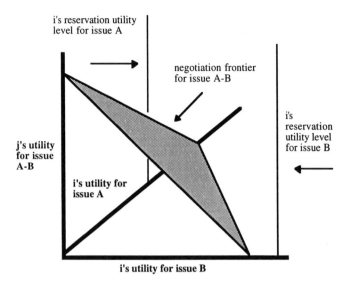

Fig. 4.10

bargaining space (*j*'s utility for A-B, *i*'s utility for A, and *i*'s utility for B) whose frontier is a triangular area (fig. 4.10).[52] Given this structure, the unlinked reservation utility levels held by nation *i* for the single issues A and B can now be represented as a reservation utility plane intersecting the bargaining space (fig. 4.11). In terms of figure 4.11 the volume behind the reservation utility plane and underneath the triangular negotiation frontier provides a bargaining set for issue A-B that is both satisfactory to *i* and achievable relative to *j*. This bargaining set is relatively smaller than that for issue A alone but obviously greater than the nil bargaining set for issue B taken alone. In the real world, of course, there may be many issues linked together (creating a new dimension for each additional linked issue), the utility functions will not be as well defined, and nation *j* will have its own reservation utility levels to model and include. But, so long as both nations have a utility reservation level sufficiently inside the frontier for one of the separate issues, creating a multidimensional bargaining space through linkage can provide a bargaining set in which a negotiated settlement is at least possible. The existence of this set is the necessary condition for the maintenance of a security dilemma.

Recent diplomatic history provides many examples of the creation of just such a single linked issue out of previously separate issues. For instance, Kissinger's persistent use of most-favored-nation (MFN) trading status as a carrot for arms control negotiations with the USSR employed precisely this sort of linkage to connect a strong Soviet preference for economic cooperation with

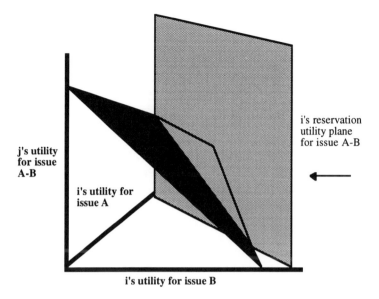

j's utility
for issue
A-B

i's utility for
issue A

i's reservation
utility plane
for issue A-B

i's utility for issue B

Fig. 4.11

a Soviet security preference ordering that had few motives for cooperation. Negotiators must certainly be careful with the nature of their offers, as some carrots may both increase the payoff for mutual cooperation and reduce nation *j*'s punitive capabilities, perhaps to the point where mutual cooperation actually loses ground to mutual defection in nation *i*'s calculations.[53] For example, even at the height of détente Kissinger never offered to link separate arms control issues into a broader security issue, such as ground troops in Europe and MIRV technology for strategic missiles. Instead, nuclear weapons, conventional forces, and naval armaments all have their own discrete set of agreements and negotiations. Mutual arms reduction across weapon types is perhaps a wise policy choice for other goals, but it does not necessarily make an efficient tool to increase the relative attraction of mutual cooperation.[54] Gains through economic cooperation (such as the extension of MFN status) are ultimately transferable into military gain,[55] but the lag time involved suggests that they will not greatly lessen the sanctions associated with mutual defection or increase the probability of *j*'s succeeding in war. Social policy linkages, such as the Soviet Union's offers to allow increased Jewish emigration, would seem to be even more efficient in making mutual cooperation attractive relative to mutual defection.

But such linkage strategies to maintain conditional strategies are only part of any crisis management effort. What forces are pushing governments out of the bargaining space in the first place and toward a unilateral solution through military escalation? One possible answer to this question requires a look at psychological studies of issue framing, in which the tendency to choose a possible yet large loss (say, a 20 percent chance of losing 100 dollars) over a certain yet small loss (a 100 percent chance of losing 10 dollars) but to opt for a certain yet small gain (a 100 percent chance of winning 10 dollars) over a possible yet large gain (a 20 percent chance of winning 100 dollars), is a robust observation.[56] Such behavior may be crucial for our concerns, as participation in the security dilemma resembles accepting an assured yet limited loss while initiating a war resembles accepting only the risk of an extremely large loss.

That is, during the crisis stage marked by analytic editorials, decision makers want to change the behavior of their adversary but are unwilling to take the forceful steps necessary to secure that change with any certainty because intense conflict as marked by mutual defection is still a relatively unpleasant future. Instead, decision makers take incremental, responsive, limited steps that serve to signal displeasure and mark time as the crisis persists. On the other hand, during the crisis stage marked by critical editorials, decision makers are building the popular support necessary to take action sufficiently forceful to elicit permanent change in the adversary's objectionable behavior. Such action is, of necessity, more violent, nonincremental, and unlimited than responsive steps and also carries with it the chance of violent, nonincremental, and unlimited defeat. Analysts who focus on the cognitive shortcomings and misperceptions of decision makers claim that national leaders tend to reduce artificially the odds associated with losing the war that they start.[57] Such a tendency only serves to magnify the potential of this disposition to trade small yet assured losses for extremely large yet probabilistic losses.

The connection between this aversion to assured losses and issue framing rests on the ability of negotiators to portray the glass as half-full rather than half-empty. For example, we can think of vaccinating entire populations as a small yet certain loss, in which more than a few people are going to die from the vaccination process itself, or we can think of it as probably saving a great many more people from the ravages of disease.[58] Likewise, we can think of reactive policy as a small yet certain loss, in which foreign misbehavior is sure to continue to nag and annoy, or we can think of it as making concrete strides toward other, more important or fundamental goals. Of course, if foreign misbehavior is striking at the very heart of a nation's most cherished goals, such as self-preservation, then such attempts at positive framing are likely to be wasted efforts. More likely, it will require an element of contingent linkage to focus decision makers' attention on the benefits of reactive policy.

For example, I think it would be fair to assume that the Indian government in 1971 was less concerned about domestic Pakistani politics than it was about potential insurrections, perhaps aided by Pakistan, in Kashmir and Jammu. Had India been convinced that restraining its support of Sheikh Mujib might serve to reduce Pakistani influence in Kashmir and Jammu, it seems less likely that India would have opted for unlimited support for Bangladesh. I am not suggesting that such a bargaining stance would have brought peace to the region. I am suggesting, however, that a contingent linkage of Indian support for East Pakistani rebels and Pakistani support for Kashmir rebels could have worked to frame the issues for Indian and Pakistani decision makers in such a way as to maintain the limited conflictual behavior characteristic of a security dilemma paradigm longer than otherwise would have been the case.

In fact, I suggest that an alternative form of contingent linkage—Soviet economic, military, and diplomatic support for India in exchange for limited reactive policies vis-à-vis Pakistan—was at least partially responsible for maintaining the bargaining space for as long as it lasted. On August 9, 1971, the Soviet Union and India signed a Treaty of Peace, Cooperation, and Friendship. Although previously rather ambivalent in public over the Indo-Pakistani grievances, the Soviet Union now began to support India publicly, to the extent of successfully backing Indian rejection of UN border supervision on September 28. Indira Gandhi finished an official visit to Moscow on September 29, and a few days later, publicly acceding to a Soviet "suggestion," India gave up its categorical demand for Bangladesh independence in exchange for a return to the limited pursuit of Sheikh Mujib's release from prison. On October 12, however, Yahya Khan announced his intention to move on with the assembly by-elections without releasing Mujib, repudiating the Soviet and Indian proposal. More important, the Soviet Union backed off a bit from its unqualified support of India during these weeks, at least in the eyes of Indian decision makers, by sending Podgorny to meet with Khan and stating that the treaty with India did not preclude closer relations with Pakistan as well. By October 19, when Gandhi rejected the Pakistani proposal for a mutual withdrawal from its borders (a proposal tacitly supported by the USSR), the Indian leadership had apparently concluded that Soviet support was too fickle and impotent to counteract the continuing frustration of Pakistani behavior. Human history is, of course, a very imperfect laboratory, and we will probably never know whether Soviet attempts to link closer relations with limited Indian policy truly postponed the Indian decision to escalate unilaterally. At the very least, however, the timing of Indian actions vis-à-vis Pakistan and the timing of Indo-Soviet diplomatic relations indicate that this may well have been the case.

Still, the fact of the matter is that India did apparently change its preference ordering over time, that diplomatic efforts were not successful in maintaining a relatively peaceful security dilemma over a prolonged crisis. And, unfortunately, the evidence from every case in this chapter, not just India in 1971, suggests that the reservation utility level will move over time to eliminate the bargaining set, not maintain or strengthen it. Although much of the literature on crises suggests that preferences and bargaining foundations are essentially constant over the course of the process,[59] the clear suggestion here is that prefer-ence orderings tend to change during crises usually considered to be driven by a security dilemma, to the point that a security dilemma no longer exists but is replaced by a unilateral, decisive march to war.[60]

This new vision of the security dilemma poses a vexing problem for crisis bargaining. If a bargaining strategy is designed with one set of preference order-ings in mind, then obviously a change in that ordering creates grave difficulties for that strategy. At the very least the window of opportunity for successful bar-gaining is smaller than would exist if preferences did not shift several months before major hostilities. And since these revised preferences are largely hidden from the outside world, revealed only through domestic mass media in order to build public support for an escalatory move, it is little wonder that attempts to resolve crises through diplomatic offices fail as often as they succeed.

Crisis management techniques for a security dilemma generally revolve around extending the shadow of the future or promoting defense over offense. Once a crisis has transformed itself into a unilateral path to war, however, simply working to overcome the dilemma of a security dilemma is not enough. Before even considering the salutary effects of multiple plays or the potential for increasing defensive dominance, a negotiator in these circumstances must first make mutual cooperation more attractive than mutual defection, either by increasing the sanctions connected with mutual defection or increasing the rewards gained by mutual cooperation. Looking at this situation on a bargaining space, negotiators must find some way to get each nation's reservation utility level to intersect the frontier of negotiated settlements before they can even begin to get the parties to agree on a diplomatic solution. Note that the addi-tional difficulties posed by the unilateral paradigm are compounded by the rel-ative lack of warning time for these intentions. Once critical editorials appear (whether preceded by analytic editorials or not), typically only one or two months remain before sharply escalated, aggressive attacks begin.

If we stay focused on issue framing as a political tool, as a close relative of agenda setting, or "spin control," in public relations, we get a better sense for how framing affects the relationship between media and conflict initiation. Re-gardless of the apparent road to war, extreme conflict is not initiated until the contending issues are publicly stated as deserving aggressive, unilateral action rather than responsive, tit-for-tat reaction. Clearly, these patterns point out the importance of how issues are presented by decision makers. So long as Indian opinion leaders portrayed the East Pakistani turmoil as fallout from the re-cent Pakistani election, all-out war was not an option. When Yahya Khan was portrayed as a genocidal maniac, however, war became the sanest course. Here issue framing is more of a strategy for opinion manipulation than a constraint on individual decision making.[61]

If we assume that opinion leaders are not omniscient, then they cannot know precisely which message will arouse the greatest possible public support for their desired actions. The media behavior we should see under this assumption is a series of different messages to justify reactive action and another series to justify unilateral action. That is, unless opinion leaders are lucky enough to stumble immediately upon the best message to foment optimal support for whatever sort of action is desired, the message will need some tinkering and improvement before the most effective message or blend of messages is identified.[62] For example, the U.S. administration tried out a litany of reasons why U.S. forces should be committed to mounting an attack to dislodge Iraq from Kuwait, from the effect of Iraqi control over oil reserves on the U.S. economy to the potential nuclear capability of Iraq to the Hitlerian characteristics of Saddam Hussein.[63]

In fact, this is precisely the sort of editorial behavior we see in each of the cases in this chapter. Argentine editorials, critical throughout, change the specific content of their message from long-standing claims of Malvinas sovereignty to praise of Argentine moves to thwart British imperialism and intransigence. Israeli editorials prior to the Six Day War shift from complaints about Egyptian adventures in Yemen to complaints about Syrian foot-dragging over an armistice agreement during the reactive stage of the prewar period, and from justifications of Israeli action against Syrian force postures to justifications of action in support of Israeli shipping rights during the unilateral stage. Prior to the Lebanon War critical Israeli editorials shift from defending future Israeli action against terrorist bases in southern Lebanon to announcing the potential annihilation of the Lebanese Christian bloc unless Israel were to move in. Indian editorials during the reactive phase of their road to war start by complaining about possible Pakistani support for terrorists, move to discussions of Pakistani election fraud, and end by criticizing the high-handed moves of Yahya Khan against Sheikh Mujib. During the aggressive stage Indian editorials start by announcing support for the righteous struggle of East Pakistani guerrillas, move to a discussion of the crushing economic burden placed on India by the stream of refugees, and end by proclaiming Khan a genocidal maniac bent on the liquidation of East Pakistan.

The possibility that framing contentious issues with a certain spin is a conscious strategy to build public support past the level possible by some other framing raises the question of whether the content of editorials actually reflects the opinions of decision makers. If the message changes from week to week, are we to assume that the messenger's thoughts are equally malleable? So long as we lack the technology to read minds, we will never be able to answer this question with absolute precision. In fact, so long as we lack effective research access to decision makers, we cannot even get close.[64] Still, it seems unlikely that President Bush became captivated with the idea of saving American jobs by going to war in the Gulf and then changed his minds about the intrinsic wisdom of that motivation the next day. Far more likely, it seems, the White House realized that framing the Gulf issue in terms of recessionary pressures was not building public support for aggressive moves, so that argument was dropped in favor of more compelling complaints.

Even if opinion leaders don't really believe the opinions they espouse, does it matter? We may think of the precise content of editorial arguments as molded to touch whatever popular nerves opinion leaders believe are particularly vulnerable. The overall tone, however—analytic or aggressive—must mimic the intentions of opinion leaders for this model to work. In a sense a government's media messages to its public are much like a human's instructions to her pet dog; the tone of the voice is as important as the actual message. For my predictive purposes, in fact, the tone is more important than the actual message, because the tone is hypothesized to be an accurate, revealed signal of decision makers' beliefs, while the message is hypothesized to be an adjustable tool for opinion manipulation.

The dilemma, then—to what degree does editorial content reflect actual opinions—is both unanswerable and, fortunately, immaterial so long as the editorial tone matches the intentions of national decision makers. Not only does independent evidence exist in each of the cases I examined in this chapter that government intentions were matched by editorial tone, but the simple observation that aggressive actions were always preceded by an aggressive tone suggests that, whether or not governments actually believe the specifics of the arguments they make, they certainly believe the underlying gist.

## CHAPTER 5

Getting to War in U.S. Diplomatic History

Pre–Twentieth Century

The manipulation of national media by U.S. administrations to build public support for foreign policy actions is by no means a twentieth-century aberration. Newspapers were avowedly propagandistic tools in the early days of the Republic, and almost every prominent politician had at least one virulent editor in his pocket.[1] While secretary of state in a Federalist-dominated administration, Thomas Jefferson mounted attacks on Washington and Hamilton through the *National Gazette* by giving its editor a job in the State Department and offering him "the perusal of all my letters of foreign intelligence."[2]

Andrew Jackson was noted for his use of sympathetic newspapers to marshal support both for his election and his administration's policies. Richard Barnet, in his work on the relationship between American popular opinion and political policy, writes:

> Andrew Jackson was the first American politician to build a political machine on a national network of friendly newspapers. . . . His closest political advisers were newspapermen. His famous Kitchen Cabinet was composed of Amos Kendall, former editor of the Frankfort, Kentucky, *Argus;* Kendall's associate, Francis P. Blair; and another newspaperman, John C. Rives. Jackson was the only president to start his own organ of news and opinion [the *Globe*], mostly the latter, while in the White House.[3]

Jackson used the press with particular skill to promote his Indian relocation policy, successfully reframing the issue from domesticating the Indians in order to integrate them into white society to forcing the Indians west in order to slow their inexorable extinction.[4]

Still, the economies of scale for the news media were not sufficiently developed until the mid-nineteenth century for editorials to provide effective opinion leadership for more than the already converted partisans of one faction or another. According to Barnet:

> The expansionist sentiments of the day [1845] were reflected in the "penny press." With the invention of the revolving-cylinder press, a machine that

could throw off ten thousand papers a hour, metropolitan dailies began developing large circulations in Boston, Philadelphia, New York, and Baltimore. Thanks to the telegraph and faster transportation, smaller papers all around the country began reprinting articles from the big-city newspapers. Creating public opinion by planting articles in the press became more feasible.

One of the first to take full advantage of the new realities of the news media was William Seward following the purchase of Alaska from Russia in 1867.

But the treaty of purchase solemnizing "Seward's Folly," the bargain of the age at $7.2 million, would probably not have been ratified had not Secretary of State William Seward launched a careful "campaign of education." He produced enthusiastic letters of endorsement for buying Alaska from prominent people all over the United States, which he then planted in leading newspapers along with extravagant hints of the riches to be found in that vast domain, about which almost nothing was known. Seward even had a clerk copy some of the foolish comments that the opponents of the Louisiana Purchase had made in 1803 and sent these to the newspapers. He was charged with trying to bribe the press into creating a ground swell for the treaty, but he swore that the budget for the whole campaign came to no more than $500.

Other politicians quickly caught on to the power of newspapers to reach a wide, heretofore politically untapped audience. Horace Greeley's *Weekly Tribune,* for example, was, as Walter Dean Burnham notes, "indispensable to the Republican mobilization in the 1850s."[5]

The turn of the century saw this new appreciation for the power of the press extend to the White House. Barnet writes:

McKinley was the first president to understand the power of the mass media. His was the first inauguration to be preserved on film. When he moved into the White House the entire presidential staff consisted of six typists and clerks, one of whom was assigned to the First Lady. McKinley tripled the staff and created the post of secretary to the president, which was largely a public relations job. Unlike his predecessors, McKinley cultivated the press. He attended the press corps' annual Gridiron Dinner, invited editors and reporters to receptions, and encouraged them, particularly the Washington representatives of the newly expanded national wire services, to call on him and his cabinet for information. The White House began to put out regular press releases. McKinley kept track of public opinion with a scrapbook of clippings from newspapers that his secretaries prepared for him each day.[6]

As for the Spanish-American War itself, the role of newspapers such as Hearst's *New York Journal* and *San Francisco Examiner* and Pulitzer's *New York World* in egging on the American public and Congress is well-known. Less well-known, however, is that, despite a popular portrayal as squarely against the war, as forced into aggression against his will,[7] McKinley used the press to create a public perception of statesmanlike prudence coupled with a willingness to attack.

In Robert Hilderbrand's study of McKinley's actions he finds that:

As far as Cuba was concerned, McKinley's policy had been determined months before, in a time of relative quiet. One by one, his demands had gone unmet, and now even the Maine disaster had failed to bring the Spanish around. By early April McKinley knew that they must pay the consequences.[8]

Just as my models would predict, Hilderbrand finds that aggressive editorials suggesting war preceded U.S. hostilities (see table 5.1).[9] In summarizing his results, Hilderbrand claims that:

To a remarkable extent, local editorial arguments reflected elements of administration policy. Redefinition of Spanish responsibility followed the announcement of the Sampson investigation, which centered its inquiries on the location of the explosion. Although external detonation hardly proved Spain caused the disaster, it appeared so to editors who knew only the general terms of the navy's investigation. Similarly, editorials placing the Maine disaster in the context of Spain's Cuban difficulties mirrored the reality of McKinley diplomacy. And finally, the editors' appreciation of American arms increased only after the president requested and received his $50 million emergency military appropriation. The strength this measure implied may have had some effect upon the Spanish; it certainly did

TABLE 5.1. Iowa Newspaper Editorial Position on Prospects of Spanish-American War following Maine Explosion (*n* = 45)

	Pro War	Pro War with Doubts	Slightly against War	Strongly against War
First two weeks	51.1	28.9	17.8	2.2
Second two weeks	55.5	31.1	13.4	0.0
Third two weeks	88.9	11.1	0.0	0.0

upon Iowa editors. In weeks following its passage, the press took on a tone of confidence in America's ultimate victory and found the risk of war much easier to accept.

Still, *editorial desire for war preceded McKinley's request for a declaration,* prompting some historians to see newspaper pressures as playing a part in his decision. Iowa editors did call for action from their president, and they did show some impatience with his conservative diplomacy. But this was surely the way of the cautious McKinley: he made very certain of his support before taking the country into war. Nor was editorial impatience a sign of the president's inability to control newspaper opinion. McKinley remained the symbol of national unity and purpose, and Iowa editors tempered their prowar arguments with willingness to follow his direction.[10]

Likewise, David Green's analysis of McKinley's media behavior prior to the Spanish-American War finds that McKinley did a masterful job in framing the issues at stake in such a way as to bolster his own position domestically while allowing himself the freedom to move to war at his own speed.[11]

Although these eighteenth- and nineteenth-century examples suggest a general pattern of media management by American leaders to garner public support, the twentieth century is even more fertile ground for this sort of analysis. Not only are the pertinent data more available, both for the media and government decision making, but developments in media technology and management, coupled with change in American electoral politics, have led to even greater efforts to build public support for foreign policy decisions.

The 1983 invasion of Grenada provides a good example of the type of analysis this chapter will attempt. The premier of Grenada, Maurice Bishop, was placed under house arrest by more militant Marxists on October 13. Six days later Bishop was freed by supporters, only to be recaptured and executed by the forces of Gen. Hudson Austin. On the morning of October 25 approximately 1,800 U.S. troops, joined by a smaller number of soldiers from other Caribbean nations, landed on the island and installed a more sympathetic regime after several days of fighting.[12] This intervention is neither an appropriate case for a detailed look at the support/secrecy equilibrium, as Washington did not anticipate any effective resistance and hence never saw any need for secrecy, nor an appropriate example of interstate war, as indeed no effective resistance ever materialized (other than a few scattered platoons of visiting Cuban soldiers). On the other hand, given these constraints, it shows striking support for the primary claim of this book—that domestic media provide a leading indicator of conflict initiation.

Even with such a rapid turn of events in Grenada and the relatively insignificant risks posed by military intervention, we see clear evidence in the U.S. national media of an attempt to prepare domestic opinion for the military option. With an area of 133 square miles, a population of 95,000, and a GNP of slightly over 100 million dollars, Grenada, one of the world's largest exporters of nutmeg, was probably well-known to eggnog manufacturers prior to the U.S. invasion but to few others. As early as March 1983, however, President Reagan attacked Grenada, particularly the new airport being built with Cuban help, in a televised speech.[13] *Time* magazine followed the speech with an investigative article on the airport.[14] An editorial written in the *Wall Street Journal* on October 21, 1983, condemned the recent convulsions in Grenada and suggested that U.S. interests in the Caribbean demanded a non-Marxist regime sympathetic to the United States.

The justifications presented by the Reagan administration following the landing proceeded according to the hypothesized pattern of issue framing, in which several rationales are trotted out to the public before settling on the most effective. Although the underlying tone of these statements remained one of defending aggressive action to remove a grave security threat, the precise nature of that threat changed over time from the bodily danger posed to approximately 600 Americans enrolled in a Grenadian medical school to the danger posed to Grenada's neighbors should Cuba be allowed to cement its hold on the island. Both issues played simultaneously for a time in the national media, with the former threat bolstered by pictures of U.S. students kissing the ground upon their safe return. The Cuban threat took the foreground with the revelation of discoveries of Cuban weapons and secret treaties.

To look at U.S. diplomatic history in light of the media/government models developed earlier, I want to examine cases similar in situation but different in policy, and to look for associated similarities or differences in media activity. The analysis here does not rely on the pairing of cases; each case could just as easily be analyzed individually. These pairings are made solely to provide a very rough comparison of two crises with passing similarity in date and target yet marked difference in response. From recent years I compare the media and foreign policy events surrounding the forceful response to Iraq in 1991 and the tepid response to Iran in 1980. As an example from the early Cold War period, I look at the first Berlin crisis and U.S. entry into the Korean War; from the early twentieth century, I examine the 1915 response to German submarine warfare, culminating in the sinking of the *Lusitania,* and the 1917 response to the second such declaration of submarine warfare, culminating in an American declaration of war against Germany. (For each of these cases a summary of all editorials analyzed here can be found in app. 3.)

Iran 1980 and Iraq 1991

Iran 1980

On September 7, 1978, the Shah of Iran imposed martial law in response to growing disturbances and riots. Late November saw a crippling general strike, followed by increased demonstrations for the Shah's ouster. The Shah attempted several conciliatory moves, including the pardon of dissidents (even the Ayatollah Khomeini) and the creation of a coalition government led by a civilian prime minister, but each step was too little and too late. During this period the Carter administration vacillated between supporting the Shah, the civilian government under Bakhtiar, or Khomeini, eventually losing the trust of each.[15]

The Shah left Iran on January 16, 1979, traveling through Egypt and Morocco before settling down for a time in the Bahamas and Mexico. Khomeini arrived in Tehran on February 1. He announced his support for Mehdi Bazargan as prime minister, leading to Bakhtiar's resignation on February 11. Although Bazargan announced his intention to resume normal oil shipments and cultivate good relations with the West, his position was continually undermined by more revolutionary Khomeini supporters. At this point there were still several thousand Americans in Iran, and a variety of kidnapping incidents took place, none of them long-lived. Most notably, 20 Air Force employees were taken prisoner at one of the electronic monitoring sites along the Iranian-Soviet border, to be released after an imprisonment of several days.[16]

On October 20 Carter was advised that the Shah was seriously ill with a malignant lymphoma that could only be treated effectively in a U.S. hospital. Advised by Mexican president López Portillo that the Shah could return to Mexico once the medical procedures ran their course, and advised by Secretary of State Cyrus Vance that the Bazargan government had reacted "with moderation" to the Shah's possible U.S. visit, Carter allowed the Shah to enter the country.[17] On November 4 the American embassy was overrun by approximately 3,000 Iranians, with the subsequent capture of 50 to 60 American staffers, amid demands of returning the Shah and his money to Iran. Khomeini publicly commended the demonstrators, and Bazargan was completely ineffectual in attempts to remove them.

In the next few weeks the Carter administration moved to expedite the deportation of Iranian students with expired visas, forbade Iranian demonstrations on federal property, terminated Iranian oil purchases, and sought to freeze Iranian assets in U.S. banks. The slow pace with which these actions took place is in sharp contrast to the freezing of Iraqi and Kuwaiti funds in 1990, which took place in the dead of night, within hours of the Iraqi invasion.[18] With the exception of putting a higher priority on satellite photographs of Iranian forces, no military options were seriously explored or undertaken during the first three weeks of the crisis, despite Khomeini's threats to try the hostages as spies on November 17.[19]

On November 23 Carter finally met with his top advisors at Camp David to explore military options. Their decision was to impose a blockade on Iranian commerce should a public trial of the hostages begin and to carry out a limited punitive action against an oil refinery or two should the hostages be executed. Otherwise, efforts to free the hostages centered on negotiations via UN secretary-general Kurt Waldheim, who was authorized to offer the Iranians access to U.S. courts to pursue claims against the Shah if the hostages were released.[20] Shortly before Christmas the Shah left the United States for Panama, but his departure did not ameliorate the crisis.

On January 28 the successful smuggling of six hostages out of Iran through the Canadian embassy gave a brief boost to U.S. hopes, as did the February 4 secret communiqué from newly elected Iranian president Bani-Sadr saying that he personally favored releasing the hostages. The release plan centered on a six-step process, according to Carter's memoirs:

1. Following a public request from Iran's Revolutionary Council, a five member United Nations commission would be formed, its members to be approved by Bani-Sadr and me.
2. The commission would be a fact-finding body and not conduct any kind of trial. Its members would listen in private sessions to grievances from both sides, and would visit Iran to obtain evidence.
3. The members would visit the hostages, but only to determine their condition and not to interrogate them in any way.
4. The hostages would then be transferred to a hospital, thus being removed from control of the militants and coming under the custody of the Iranian government.
5. The commission would make its report to Secretary General Waldheim, and the hostages would be allowed to leave Iran simultaneously.
6. Subsequently, other disputes between the United States and Iran would be discussed by a joint commission formed by the two governments.[21]

Despite the unclear benefits such a plan would provide to Iran, the UN delegation arrived in Tehran on February 23. Khomeini announced, however, that the Iranian parliament would have to make the final decision about whether to release the hostages; unfortunately for the Carter/Bani-Sadr plan, this new government would not be elected and in place before mid-April. Dashing the plan entirely, Khomeini refused to allow the UN delegation to visit the hostages as planned and forbade the transfer of the hostages from the militants to the government until the UN delegation condemned the United States and the Shah for unspecified illegal acts.[22]

Even then the Carter administration did not take steps toward a military solution, much less break diplomatic relations. The United States imposed additional economic sanctions in early March, and Carter recalls investigating the possibility of confiscating Iranian assets rather than merely impounding them.[23] For the most part, however, the administration concentrated on another negotiating initiative.

By March 22, however, the White House was reviewing the military option, as defined by a rescue mission.[24] With the failure of the latest diplomatic attempt to see the hostages transferred to government authorities in early April, Carter met with advisors on April 11 to plan a military operation. Secretary of State Vance resigned on April 21 in protest, but the rescue attempt went ahead as scheduled on April 23, only to be aborted, as several helicopters were disabled from a variety of mechanical failings.

Following the rescue fiasco, the hostage situation remained moribund for months, with neither side willing to take bold action or give in to the other's demands. The Iraqi invasion of September 22 gave some impetus to the Iranians to settle the hostage issue, and the Iranian parliament debated the issue in late October, eventually agreeing to free the hostages provided the frozen funds and additional moneys ("the Shah's wealth") were made available for the Iranian war effort. Although Carter clearly hoped (and Reagan feared, perhaps to the point of intervening with negotiators of his own) for some sort of "November surprise" in which the hostages would be released just before the presidential election, agreeing to the *majlis'* economic demands was an untenable solution. With Algerian mediation the Iranian demands were slowly diminished over the following months. Finally, on January 20, minutes after Reagan was sworn into office, the hostages were released.[25]

As for media behavior during the hostage crisis, we clearly see that the message presented to the American public mirrors the actions of the administration. Table 5.2 shows the number and qualitative breakdown of editorials of the *New York Times* during this period; figure 5.1 shows the relationship of analytic and critical editorials graphically. The sheer number of editorial complaints suggests that some conflictual behavior is to be expected, although the count never reaches the level we see immediately prior to full-scale wars initiated by the United States. I hypothesized in chapter 3 that the greatest level of editorial activity should be associated with the months preceding the highest levels of violence directed against the target nation. In this case the highest number of critical editorials appear at the onset of the crisis in November and in April, the month of the rescue attempt. Although the early months were indeed marked by a relatively high number of conflictual events directed against Iran, in support of the chapter 3 hypothesis, the April editorials should have appeared in March if we are to take a strict construction of that hypothesis. I take some solace in the

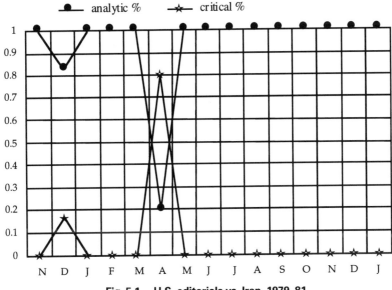

Fig. 5.1.   U.S. editorials vs. Iran, 1979–81

fact that defining observation periods by the calendar month is a completely ar-
tificial method of looking at the basic insight of this research program, that more
editorials should precede more conflictual events. That is, the only rationale for
aggregating observations on a month-by-month basis is that the method is rela-

TABLE 5.2.   United States vs. Iran, 1980–81 (*New York Times*)

Month	Total Editorials	Analytic Editorials	Critical Editorials
November	8	8	0
December	6	5	1
January	2	2	0
February	1	1	0
March	2	2	0
April	5	1	4
May	1	1	0
June	1	1	0
July	3	3	0
August	0	0	0
September	2	2	0
October	2	2	0
November	3	3	0
December	2	2	0
January (through Jan. 20)	1	1	0

tively tractable. In this instance, since the critical editorials were in the same month as the conflict, the finding that relatively high numbers of critical editorials in early April did indeed precede the relatively significant conflict directed against Iran in late April (which is quite supportive for the thrust of this research project) would be obscured were I to employ strictly a monthly aggregation.

In chapter 4 I suggested that just looking at the count of editorials was not sufficient to determine what form the predicted conflict would take, that we needed more information to judge the road to conflict followed by the combatants. I found that a preponderance of analytic editorials was associated with a bargaining structure in which a negotiated settlement was at least possible, that the associated preference ordering at least allowed the prospects of a cooperative outcome. The almost exclusively analytic tone of these editorials (with the exception of April) predicts that any conflictual events directed at Iran by the United States would take precisely the diplomatic and economic forms initiated by the Carter administration.

Editorials throughout this period speak of the wisdom of diplomatic approaches, of the virtues of patience. One of the first editorials of the crisis, a November 9 piece titled "The Stakes in Iran," claims that a hostage rescue would require a costly attack with many casualties, with the end result that Khomeini would be even more powerful and obdurate than before. One of the last editorials, written on November 11 and titled "Seeking the Hostages in Algeria," claims that, though difficult, negotiations are the only way to win the hostages' release, that eventually diplomacy will succeed where force would fail.

Note, however, the one exception to the preponderance of analytic editorials in the months examined. During April, the month of the abortive rescue attempt, the ratio of analytic to critical editorials abruptly shifts. Editorials here are quite aggressive. For example, an April 8 editorial, titled "Let Iran Begin to Worry," states that we should create "real penalties for holding the hostages" and that, although force might not work, we have been too cautious; now is the time to act. Other editorials, such as "Past the Point of No Result" and "Allies Are What Allies Do," call for a solid Western front against Iran as the United States prepares to use force to free the hostages. Note also that each of these critical editorials appeared *before* the rescue attempt and despite apparently strict secrecy within the White House.[26] Perhaps, despite the claims of Carter, Vance, and Brzezinski, word of the impending operation was leaked to the *Times*. More likely, as I hypothesized in chapter 1, the shared worldview, background, and sentiments of White House decision makers and the *Times* editorial staff led to this outcome. In any event a systematic analysis of editorials in the *Times* would have provided an effective indicator of the extent and nature of conflictual events directed against Iran throughout the crisis, including military intervention to rescue the hostages.[27]

Iraq 1990–91

American satellite photographs first picked up Iraqi troop movements to the Kuwaiti border on July 16, 1990.[28] By July 19 three tank divisions from the Republican Guards were poised there. By the end of the month over 100,000 troops, composing eight divisions, had been moved into aggressive posture next to Kuwait.

Official communications from the White House to Iraq failed to get across the message that the United States would not accept an annexation of Kuwaiti territory. According to Woodward's account of the contents of U.S. State Department records of ambassador April Glaspie's July 25 meeting with Saddam Hussein, Glaspie accepted at face value Hussein's statements announcing successful Egyptian mediation of the Kuwaiti dispute. A State Department cable from James Baker on July 27 merely stated that the United States was willing to work with Iraq for a regional settlement and that Iraq must find some way to reciprocate these good intentions.[29]

The lack of a more forceful U.S. response to the initial Iraqi troop buildup is directly attributable to a mistaken reading of Hussein's intentions. Kuwait had no independent means of recognizing these troop movements, and U.S. analysis consistently attributed the Iraqi actions to signaling behavior over Iraqi demands for debt forgiveness and higher oil prices. In addition, until August 1 Iraqi logistical support was not in place to allow an aggressive move into Kuwaiti territory. Even after this support appeared, however, the U.S. military and political leadership suspected that invasion was simply not in the cards.[30]

Perhaps most important, Hussein successfully utilized direct communications with foreign governments, including the United States, to preserve strategic surprise concerning his true intentions. As early as April 1990, Hussein was sending direct messages to President Bush and King Fahd, through the Saudi ambassador to the United States, that Iraq would not attack Israel, despite recent inflammatory words,[31] so long as Israel would pledge not to attack Iraq. Such an assurance was highly valuable to Hussein, as deploying his troops along the Kuwaiti border required removing troops and matériel from the western border, where Israeli combat flights would arrive. As late as July 27:

> Bandar [the Saudi ambassador] told Powell that Saudi King Fahd was being assured by everyone in Iraq and the Middle East that Saddam was not going to invade Kuwait. Saddam had given personal assurances to Mubarak of Egypt and King Hussein of Jordan. It isn't going to happen, Bandar said confidently. Saddam was saying it was only a military exercise of his crack divisions. Saddam's summons to U.S. Ambassador Glaspie

was a positive sign, he said. Clearly, the dispatch of the KC-135s to the United Arab Emirates had caught Saddam's attention.[32]

Bandar's upbeat assessment was coupled with Egyptian President Mubarak's personal message to Bush that Hussein was merely maneuvering for leverage in the debt and oil production ceiling debates. According to Staniland, Hussein told Mubarak:

> As long as discussions last between Iraq and Kuwait, I won't use force. I won't intervene with force before I have exhausted all the possibilities for negotiation. But don't tell it to the Kuwaitis, Brother Mubarak. It'll only make them conceited.[33]

Of course Hussein knew that Mubarak would tell others, maintaining the strategic secrecy of his attack on Kuwait despite visible troop movements. Once again the diplomatic stage proved itself to be an inherently suspect arena for gathering information regarding intentions.

On the morning of August 2 (approximately 9 P.M., August 1, EST) Iraqi forces did indeed cross the Kuwaiti border en masse, overwhelming the indigenous defenses and taking Kuwait City within a matter of hours. Hussein's army was quickly resupplied and moved into a threatening posture near the Kuwait-Saudi border, with a total force concentration of over 100,000 men.

A public statement denouncing the invasion and calling for the withdrawal of Iraqi forces was out of the White House within a few hours. Iraqi and Kuwaiti assets in the United States were frozen early the next morning. Unlike the Iranian crisis, military options were discussed seriously from the outset, although they were based on contingency plans dating back to the early 1980s. In fact, there was apparently real concern among Bush's nonmilitary advisors over the lack of options provided by the Joint Chiefs of Staff (JCS) and over the slow pace with which those options were developed.[34]

On August 3, following an Aspen, Colorado, meeting between Bush and British prime minister Thatcher, the National Security Council (NSC) met again to explore further possible U.S. responses. Following Brent Scowcroft's lead, the NSC fell in line behind the general assessment that the United States would have to use force to stop Iraq from further aggression. In addition, Bush authorized the CIA to begin planning covert activities to topple Hussein. One day later Bush authorized a Pentagon plan sending approximately 200,000 men to Saudi Arabia in a protective and deterrent role, contingent upon Saudi approval.[35] Following an August 6 meeting between Defense Secretary Cheney and CENTCOM commander Schwartzkopf with King Fahd, the Saudis agreed to the plan to bring massive numbers of U.S. troops into their country. On August 25 the UN Security Council approved a resolution to give the U.S. Navy, and any other navy, the right to enforce a trade embargo against Iraq, using force if necessary.

Although this defensive buildup and economic embargo was not fully in place until late November, plans to increase the American force commitment to allow aggressive action began almost immediately after the first troops arrived on Saudi soil. Despite JCS chairman Powell's recommendation of holding the line with current deployments and relying on economic sanctions to force Iraq out of Kuwait, Bush ordered a briefing on possible offensive options against Iraq. On October 11 Schwartzkopf's chief of staff, General Johnston, presented a four-phase plan of attack to the president, consisting of three air campaigns and a final ground campaign. According to Woodward:

> Phase One would be an air attack on Iraqi command, control and communications, attempting to sever Saddam in Baghdad from his forces in Kuwait and southern Iraq. Simultaneously, airpower would destroy the Iraqi Air Force and air defense system. In addition, Phase One would include an air attack to destroy Iraqi chemical, biological, and nuclear weapons facilities.

> Phase Two would be a massive, continuous air bombardment of Iraqi supply and munitions bases, transportation facilities and roads, designed to cut off the Iraqi forces from their supplies.

> Phase Three would be an air attack on the entrenched Iraqi ground forces of 430,000 men, and on the Republican Guard.[36]

The phases would overlap somewhat. As early as a week after the beginning of the first air phase, the phase 4 ground assault would be launched on the Iraqi forces in Kuwait. One of Johnston's slides was a map with three large arrows showing the three attack points where coalition forces would hit the Iraqis. One arrow represented U.S. Marines in an amphibious assault from the Gulf; another was the U.S. Army on the ground attacking directly into Iraqi lines; and the third was an Egyptian ground division, also going straight into enemy forces while protecting one of the U.S. flanks.

All three air campaigns survived in essentially this form. The ground campaign was agreed to be unacceptable, requiring U.S. light infantry to march into the teeth of fortified heavy tanks, and was so suicidal as to suggest that Schwartzkopf proposed the plan only in order to demonstrate his inability to mount an attack given current deployments.[37] The meeting concluded with orders to the Joint Chiefs to develop both a less dangerous strategy and to ascertain the additional forces necessary to implement an aggressive strategy.

On October 22 Powell met with Schwartzkopf in Saudi Arabia to put together the requirements of an offensive force. They decided to insist on twice the air power, three more aircraft carriers for a total of six, and twice the army and marine deployment, including two additional heavy tank and two additional mechanized infantry divisions. Bush was briefed on the requirements on October 30 and gave final approval to the offensive deployments on October 31.[38] Despite continued suggestions by Schwartzkopf and Powell simply to maintain the blockade, by this point Bush was clearly favoring a unilateral attack on Iraqi forces to push them out of Kuwait.

With the decision effectively made to pursue the offensive option, by mid-November debate within the White House was effectively limited to whether to put the potential for offensive action to a vote in Congress. On November 13 Senator Nunn vowed to open public hearings to force the options and ramifications into the open. Support within Congress for the offensive option dropped precipitously on November 28, when former JCS chairmen Crowe and Jones testified that they, too, believed sanctions to be the most appropriate course of action for the foreseeable future. Despite the vote in the United Nations on November 29 to approve "all necessary means," including force, to remove Iraq's forces from Kuwait if they had not been removed voluntarily by January 15, congressional leaders refused in a private briefing with Bush to promise their support if a similar measure were introduced to Congress.[39] Cheney and Powell testified before Nunn's Senate committee on December 3, however, and by December 17 Nunn's House counterpart, Les Aspin, was convinced that the offensive option was called for. On January 7 Speaker Foley announced that the House would start debate on a resolution approving the use of force, and on January 12 both houses approved a joint resolution authorizing military force.

The White House's offers to negotiate a settlement via direct talks between Baker and Hussein or Iraqi foreign minister Aziz, first made on November 30 following the UN vote authorizing force, appear to have been shams. As early as December 18, according to Woodward: "'Basically the President has made up his mind,' Scowcroft confided. Referring to the diplomatic efforts, he told Bandar, 'These are all exercises.'"[40] The decision to move to war was officially finalized in the White House at a Camp David meeting of January 1, well before the January 15 negotiating deadline and before any serious communications with Iraq over a possible diplomatic meeting date. Bush ordered a national security directive written up to document the reasoning behind the offensive action he planned to take and directed Baker to drop any plans to go to Baghdad but to meet Aziz in Switzerland, instead, between January 7 and 9, when Baker would be in Europe anyway.[41] To the surprise of no one in the administration, the January 9 meeting failed even to get Aziz to transmit Bush's ultimatum to Hussein.

Even Colin Powell, who was as reticent as anyone in the Bush administration to pursue a military offensive against Iraq, had apparently concluded almost immediately that such a policy would be necessary. In a letter reacting to a 1995 *New York Times Magazine* article portraying Powell as rather dovish on Iraq, Lt. Gen. Thomas Kelly writes:

> I recall clearly entering Powell's office on August 5, 1990, and finding him staring out the window, obviously in a pensive mood. We had been up to Camp David the previous day to brief President Bush on the situation and make recommendations on an appropriate course of action. I asked Powell what he was thinking. He replied that he was considering the end game with regard to Saddam Hussein. He said that we were going to go to war with Iraq, that it was not in our best interest to destroy Iraq since that would generate further Middle East problems, but that their teeth had to be pulled. He also stated that he'd like to see their combat power reduced to the point where they could defend themselves against their neighbors but not sufficient to project power outside their borders. Guess what? That's exactly what we did.[42]

Note that Powell's expression of certainty that the United States will go to war comes all of three days after the initial Iraqi invasion.

In fact, the clear implication is that every U.S. offer of a diplomatic solution was made for domestic political reasons rather than any expectation that it might actually be a road to a peaceful resolution. Baker recommended the original Baghdad visit to Bush for the express reason of shoring up domestic support by demonstrating a willingness to work for peace.[43] His argument was supported when a *Washington Post* poll showed that 90 percent of the American public approved of the offer and that a higher percentage approved of Bush's handling of the crisis.[44] The Baker-Aziz meeting in Geneva was announced to Congress on January 3, together with a renewed request for support on a resolution of authorization for use of force.

The Bush administration's general use of the media throughout the prewar period reflects the early decision for aggressive military action rather than defense of Saudi Arabia and maintenance of economic sanctions. As early as August 5, Bush made a public announcement that the invasion of Kuwait must be reversed, not simply contained. In his words: "This will not stand. This will not stand, this aggression against Kuwait."[45]

On August 8 Bush made a nationally televised speech on the invasion in which he repeatedly drew on World War II parallels, such as "blitzkrieg" and the failed appeasement of Munich, to make the point that force was the only sensible and moral choice to accomplish the American goal, "the immediate, unconditional and complete withdrawal of all Iraqi forces from Kuwait."[46] At an August 15 speech to Pentagon employees Bush made an even fierier speech, framing the issue for the first time as an attempt to save the Kuwaitis from the atrocities of the marauding Iraqi occupation forces.[47] From September on, Bush made public and private statements indicating that the only acceptable outcome of the crisis was the liberation of Kuwait.

The importance of framing was recognized early on by the administration. According to Woodward:

> Several times in October, Robert Teeter, Bush's chief pollster, talked with the President about the Gulf policy. Teeter said he thought the administration had too many messages flying around. There was a lack of focus. He suggested that Bush return to the fundamentals that he had stated in August. The two with the strongest appeal were fighting aggression and protecting the lives of Americans, including the more than 900 Americans being held hostage in Iraq and Kuwait.

> Baker felt the foundation for the Gulf policy was not solid enough. The plight of the emir of Kuwait, his people, aggression and oil were not selling to the American people. The polls showed that the greatest concern was over the American hostages in Iraq and Kuwait. Baker had argued that the focus of the Gulf policy should be shifted to the hostage issue. It was the one issue that would unite Americans and the international community because most nations, including the Soviets, had hostages held in Iraq. It was the one issue that might justify a war.[48]

Following this advice, the administration began an intense effort to build support for the use of aggressive force on the grounds of mistreatment of American hostages. On October 29 Baker made a speech emphasizing the squalid living conditions of the "human shields" and the degradation heaped upon them by their Iraqi captors, concluding that "we will not rule out a possible use of force if Iraq continues to occupy Kuwait."[49] Bush made the same points in a briefing of congressional leaders the next day, to a very mixed response. Some even directly questioned whether the hostages were not just a flimsy pretext for war initiation.[50] By December 16, in a television interview with David Frost to be shown on January 2, Bush was back to emphasizing the human rights atrocities being perpetrated in Kuwait as well as the moral similarities to World War II.[51] In fact, right up until the initiation of hostilities on January 17 we see continual and varied efforts by the administration to channel public opinion in support of military action.[52]

My model of the relationship between government policy and media suggests that governments will attempt to maintain strategic surprise for their actions via foreign communications and attempt to build public support through domestic communications. We saw how Hussein successfully maintained the element of strategic surprise through the manipulation of direct foreign communications to Mubarak, Fahd, and others, and we see the same intentions in U.S.

actions. Proposing diplomatic negotiations after the decision was already made for war was one such deceiving action. Another was the intentional uncertainty generated concerning when the offensive U.S. forces would be fully deployed and ready to move on Kuwait. Although the administration made every effort to present reasons to the American public why they should support a war, it also attempted to maintain at least tactical surprise through its military press conferences.[53] At a December 19 interview Schwartzkopf's deputy, Lt. Gen. Waller, was asked what he would tell the president if Bush wanted to attack on January 15. Waller replied, "I'd tell him, 'No, I'm not ready to do the job.' "[54]

Although not a spoken or printed communication to Iraq, the American amphibious training exercises in December were a clear signal that marine forces intended to make a landing behind Iraq front lines in the Kuwait City area. The exercise was not only the largest such amphibious training effort in the history of the American armed forces, but also the press pool was provided unheralded access to the mission in order to insure that Iraq would get the message. Just as the United States was caught off guard by Iraq's strategically surprising invasion, so was Iraq misled by the American efforts to build tactical surprise. Iraqi air defenses were not on heightened alert on January 16, and tremendous forces were deployed around Kuwait City to repel the amphibious landing that never came.

Of course, it is rather easy to look back at the media record and select statements that support the general model linking policy decisions and media efforts. Did the systematic model, based on newspaper editorials, provide the same conclusion before the actual initiation of U.S. attacks on January 16?

Tables 5.3A and 5.3B show the *Wall Street Journal* and *New York Times* editorials discussing Iraq for the period from August 2, 1990, through January 15, 1991. Although the operationalizing hypothesis for newspaper choice suggests using the *Wall Street Journal* for Republican administrations and the *New York Times* for Democratic administrations, both newspapers are examined here out of curiosity. The results imply that I am correct to assume both that the *Journal* is a better indicator of the Bush administration's preferences and that the *Times* editorial pattern paints a clearer picture of the preference orderings of Democratic congressional leaders. The total number of editorials, for either newspaper, clearly indicates that conflict of some sort is due to be initiated by the U.S. against Iraq. The decline in *Wall Street Journal* editorials in the months between the start and end of the prewar period is not too surprising. The August editorial count and intensity are unheard of for the *Journal,* and even the September count rivals World War II. The November elections take up the lion's share of the *Journal's* editorial attention during October, November, and December, much more so than in the *Times.*

Total editorial count only tells us whether we can expect some sort of conflict; we cannot tell from this measure alone whether the conflict identified is an all-out attack or an embargo under UN auspices. By going back to the editorials and evaluating them for critical or analytic content, however, we can determine more precisely the form of administration policy. Tables 5.3A and 5.3B break down the editorials for the *Journal* and *Times* along these lines,[55] and figures 5.2 and 5.3 display the information graphically.

The *Journal* editorials are, with one exception over 22 editorials and five and a half months, extremely critical. A typical editorial, from August 22, reads:

> Saddam's threat [hostages] is the final evidence that he is nothing more than an international thug who needs to be removed if there is to be any peace in the Middle East now or in the foreseeable future. Negotiating with him, which many in the West surely would support, would leave his military machine intact. That would leave the Gulf at his mercy and the world at the mercy of any future pirate who can lay his hands on some Americans.

An August 29 editorial claims that the optimum resolution is to "take Baghdad and install a MacArthur regency." The vitriol in the *Journal* editorials is undiminished over the November elections, even if the number of editorials declines somewhat. A December 7 editorial claims that "Americans will never be safe traveling the world or economically secure at home" if Saddam gets away with the invasion of Kuwait. A January 1 editorial claims that a short, successful war would do wonders for the prestige of the Bush administration.

TABLE 5.3A.   United States vs. Iraq, 1990–91 (*Wall Street Journal*)

Month	Total Editorials	Analytic Editorials	Critical Editorials
August	8	0	8
September	4	0	4
October	2	1	1
November	2	0	2
December	1	0	1
January (through Jan. 15)	5	0	5

TABLE 5.3B.   United States vs. Iraq, 1990–91 (*New York Times*)

Month	Total Editorials	Analytic Editorials	Critical Editorials
August	17	13	4
September	9	7	2
October	6	4	2
November	9	8	1
December	7	6	1
January (through Jan. 15)	6	5	1

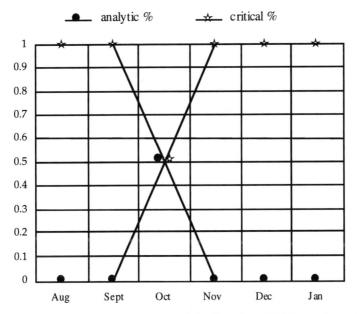

Fig. 5.2.   U.S. editorials vs. Iraq, 1990–91 (Data from *Wall Street Journal*)

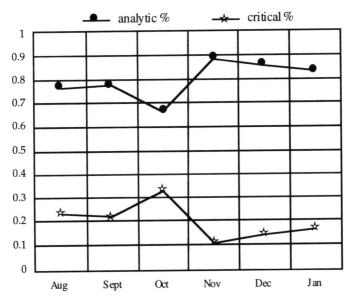

Fig. 5.3   U.S. editorials vs. Iraq, 1990–91 (Data from *New York Times*)

The *Times* editorials reveal an almost mirror image pattern, in which analytic editorials dominate. Initial editorials appear to show some uncertainty over which course to advise. Although most editorials in August and September take an analytic approach, suggesting a preference ordering consistent with a security dilemma view of the invasion, some elements of critical editorials intrude. For example, an August 17 editorial comments that, "however great the provocation and however ominous the detention of foreigners in Kuwait, the wise course for the United States is to press tirelessly for collective condemnation, collective sanctions and collective force." While the emphasis here is on mediated settlement, aggressive military force—so long as it is under UN auspices—is a serious option. Some editorials during this initial period go even further. An August 23 editorial praising the unified Arab front against Iraq states that "unilateral American military action may ultimately prove necessary, and President Bush was surely right in his news conference yesterday in refusing to rule it out."

By October, however, this initial uncertainty has been resolved in favor of a uniformly analytic approach, with a clear emphasis on sanctions rather than attack. An October 1 editorial titled "The Siege Is Only Eight Weeks Old" claims that it is "dangerously premature to beat the drums of war." An October 25 editorial does suggest ultimate peace terms that are "perhaps not achievable under the UN umbrella, and that require pushing at the limits of Iraqi sovereignty," but this is the strongest critical argument made in any *Times* editorial after October 1. Far more common are editorials with titles such as "Too Far Too Fast in the Gulf," "What's Wrong with the Siege," and "A Weak Case for War."

Again, I should note that we do not expect the *Times* to mirror administration preferences as we expect the *Journal* to do. Instead, I believe that this editorial pattern in the *Times* closely mimics the decision-making process of opposition party leaders. The *Times* editorials move away from a growing tendency to frame the Iraqi invasion in critical terms at precisely the same time that Senators Nunn and Mitchell make clear their preference for a continued embargo rather than an offensive military action.[56]

Berlin 1948 and Korea 1950

Berlin 1948

On March 20, 1948, Russian marshal Sokolovsky abruptly walked out of the Allied Control Council, raising American fears of a showdown over Berlin. Initial responses to the potential for a Berlin crisis included Truman's decision to ask General Clay, who had planned to retire at the end of the year, to retain his dual positions as American military governor in Germany and commander of U.S. forces in Europe for a while longer. Also, on March 26 Truman ordered the imposition of an embargo on trade in certain goods between West and East Germany through the denial of export licenses.[57]

Fears of a Berlin crisis were confirmed on April 1, when the Soviets instituted a partial blockade of the American, British, and French positions in Berlin, limiting Western access to those areas. The United States had been warned to expect such a move,[58] and Truman had authorized Clay to start sending test trains through the Russian checkpoints. Guards were instructed to prevent Soviet personnel from entering the trains but not to shoot, except in self-defense. The situation simmered for the next seven weeks, as more and more routes to the city were cut off, and Clay moved forward with a controversial unified currency plan for the Western zones of Germany and, starting June 23, the Western zones of Berlin.[59]

On June 24, however, all Western access to the American, British, and French zones of occupation in Berlin was severed. General Clay initiated a small-scale airlift to supply Berlin on June 25, and that same day Truman decided against either sending a note of protest to Moscow or instigating some form of retaliation away from Berlin. The next day Truman ordered that Clay's impromptu airlift be increased and put on a permanent basis until further notice.[60]

On June 28 Truman and his top advisors met and decided that a continued American presence in Berlin was of paramount importance, that the precedent set by withdrawing from Berlin would have extremely grave consequences for future relations with the Soviet Union. General Clay was authorized to meet with his Russian counterpart to initiate a diplomatic solution, and preliminary authorization was given to move B-29 bombers to Europe. The negotiations between the military governors proved fruitless, and on July 15 final authorization was granted for the transfer of B-29s to England. Further meetings of Truman and his advisors that month redoubled their resolve to stay in Berlin, although Truman specifically denied requests by the Joint Chiefs to transfer custody of atomic weapons to the military command.[61]

With significant British support, and over the initial objections of the air force, the airlift to Berlin was augmented over the following weeks, to the point where the needs of the Western zones of the city were almost completely supplied. By September 7 approximately 200 American transport planes were taking part in the airlift. The Soviets remained intransigent in every diplomatic avenue, however, and by mid-September tensions had re-escalated to the point where the utility of transfer of control of atomic weapons to the military command was again debated in the White House.[62]

Even so, diplomatic negotiation was clearly still Truman's preferred strategy. By transferring the negotiation venue from the Allied Control Council to the United Nations on September 26, the talks were given fresh impetus. Despite Soviet attempts to foment unrest in the Western zones of Berlin, by the beginning of 1949 the Soviet Union was no longer demanding control over Berlin's currency and was proposing a mutual withdrawal of access restrictions. By April the Soviets had given up on all demands and acceded to the American plan to set up a West German state with its capital in Bonn. A May 5 accord officially ended the Berlin blockade, with full access restored on May 12.[63]

The editorial record for the first six months of the crisis is just as we would expect, given the administration actions. As we see in table 5.4 and figure 5.3, the number of editorials written suggests some conflict short of all-out war, and the mix of analytic and critical editorials suggests that this conflict will indeed be on a diplomatic or economic level.

Although characterizing the Berlin blockade as "reckless" and a "direct challenge to the Great Powers" (April 2), early editorials during the crisis, such as "Focus on Germany" (April 26) and "The 'Inevitable War'" (April 29), claimed that the blockade was unlikely to determine the struggle between the West and Russia, and that "a shooting war can and will be averted by victory in the political field." Despite occasional editorials warning that the West should actively increase its military capacities to counter the Russian threat ("Deeds; Not Words" [April 13]) or that the "showdown" with Russia may now be at hand ("Struggle over Germany" [June 25]), the overwhelming majority of these editorials concentrate on the progress of diplomatic negotiations with the Soviet Union. Typical of these editorials is the August 27 "Moscow in Berlin," explaining how the Moscow negotiation over Berlin may be moved to Berlin at the suggestion of Stalin, with a focus on the currency disputes.

Just as the United States sent false signals to Iraq with its amphibious exercises while sending true signals to the American public via the domestic press, so did Truman send false signals to the Soviet Union with the transfer of B-29s to British bases. Not only were the planes not configured to carry nuclear weapons, but the bombs were not released to the military command.[64] The effect of the repositioning of the bombers was to bluff the Soviets that the United States was prepared to launch a first-strike nuclear attack rather than capitulate on the Berlin issue. While Truman was certainly resolute in his determination to remain in Berlin, he makes it quite clear that he was not willing to start another

TABLE 5.4.   United States vs. Soviet Union, 1948 (*New York Times*)

Month	Total Editorials	Analytic Editorials	Critical Editorials
April	3	3	0
May	8	7	1
June	9	7	2
July	13	11	2
August	12	11	1
September	10	8	2

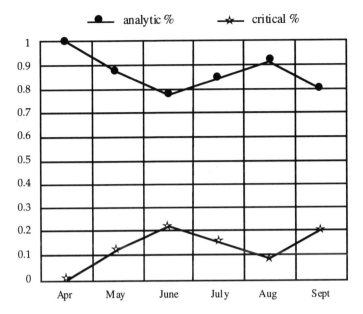

Fig. 5.4.   U.S. editorials vs. USSR, 1948. (Data from *New York Times*)

world war.[65] In both cases direct communications or signaling of military strategy was misleading, while indirect communications via the domestic press was on target.

Korea 1950

On June 24, 1950, North Korean army units crossed the 38th parallel and invaded South Korea. Upon learning of the invasion, the United States immediately requested a meeting of the UN Security Council, which approved a resolution the next day ordering the North Koreans to withdraw. In his memoirs Truman recounts his immediate determination to back up the UN resolution with force, and on June 27 he made a public pronouncement to that effect:

> In Korea the Government forces, which were armed to prevent border raids and to preserve internal security, were attacked by invading forces from North Korea. The Security Council of the United Nations called upon the invading troops to cease hostilities and to withdraw to the 38th parallel. This they have not done, but on the contrary have pressed the attack. The Security Council called upon all members of the United Nations to render every assistance to the United Nations in the execution of this resolution. In

In these circumstances I have ordered United States air and sea forces to give the Korean Government troops cover and support.[66]

The use of ground troops was approved on June 28.

U.S. and South Korean forces were significantly outnumbered in the early weeks of the fighting and were forced back into a defensive position around the coastal city of Pusan. As the war proceeded poorly, Truman called for a removal of restrictions on the size of the armed forces on July 19 as well as for new taxes and an immediate 10 billion dollar supplemental defense appropriation. On July 31 he called up four National Guard divisions.[67]

Although the relationship between Truman and MacArthur began to show intense signs of strain in August, as MacArthur publicly disagreed with Truman over proper U.S. policy toward the Chinese nationalists,[68] MacArthur's plan to break out of the Pusan perimeter and simultaneously mount an amphibious landing at Inchon was approved by the president on September 11. The September 15 operation was wildly successful, and by September 27 MacArthur was given the new objective of "the destruction of the North Korean Armed Forces," with approval to move north of the 38th parallel to accomplish that goal, provided no Russian or Chinese troops entered the fray.[69]

By October 2 South Korean forces were moving rapidly north of the 38th parallel to little resistance. Although Chinese foreign minister Chou En-lai threatened on October 3 to intervene massively if UN forces, as opposed to South Korean forces, crossed the 38th parallel, MacArthur discounted the threat completely. Truman traveled to Korea for a personal meeting with MacArthur on October 15, where the general assured Truman that the war was essentially over and that the chances of Chinese or Russian intervention was nil. Pyongyang was captured on October 19, and regular U.S. units were now operating well above the 38th parallel.[70]

Unfortunately for the U.S. forces, China did indeed begin to send its army units across the Yalu River into Korea on October 16, and by October 31 it was clear that the Chinese intended to fight. On November 7 MacArthur reported that the Chinese intervention was far larger than he had thought possible, and their intentions to do more than merely secure a buffer zone were soon clear.[71] By November 28 UN forces had been forced south of the 38th parallel, following a ragged retreat from North Korean territory.

Although Truman did not actively seek to build a popular consensus for his deployment of U.S. forces in Korea prior to his June 27 announcement, we must take into account the time pressures imposed by the initial pell-mell retreat of South Korean forces. In fact, not only does the newspaper editorial record in the initial weeks of the fighting show an amazing amount of media manipulation to build support for American troop deployment (see table 5.5), but we can also analyze the actual war-fighting strategy through the editorial record. That is, instead of just testing the base hypotheses of critical editorials immediately preceding the initiation of military action, this case allows us to see if defensive and offensive strategies within a military action are mirrored by the appropriate editorial type.[72] If so, we should expect to see critical editorials surrounding both the initial deployment and the escalatory move across the 38th parallel following Inchon; we should expect to see analytic editorials surrounding the initial retreat to Pusan and the retreat from the Yalu following Communist China's entry into the war. To an extent we see the same observation aggregation problem in these editorial counts that we saw with the April rescue attempt during the Iranian hostage crisis. That is, since the North Korean invasion took place on June 24, there was only one week during that month to accumulate editorials mentioning the invasion. Still, seven editorials within one month is a large number indicative of conflict; seven editorials within one week, especially with a preponderance of critical editorials, is a sure sign of military conflict. We see a similar problem in the November data, as they are based only on editorials written through November 7, the day the extent and purpose of the Chinese intervention became clear.

In figure 5.5 we see graphically how the relative frequency of critical and analytic editorials relates to the war-fighting strategy of the United States: Editorials during the first five weeks of the war, through the end of July, are predominantly critical, just as we might expect with the initial unilateral deployment of troops. In "War in Korea," published on June 26, the *Times* claims that the United States cannot afford to "lose" Korea and that world peace is at risk. With Truman's declaration of military support, the June 28 editorial "Democracy Takes Its Stand" praises the action and calls for the rest of the world to "close ranks" to meet this "threat of brutal aggression."

As the troops are steadily pushed back to Pusan, the editorial balance shifts strongly to favor analytic editorials, in keeping with now sharply lowered expectations and reduced war aims. The focus in editorials such as "Reply to Mr. Nehru" (July 19) and "The UN's Gravest Test" (June 31) switches from the Korean war fighting to the diplomatic maneuverings in the United Nations.

TABLE 5.5.   United States vs. Korea, 1950 (*New York Times*)

Month	Total Editorials	Analytic Editorials	Critical Editorials
June (from June 24)	7	1	6
July	20	6	14
August	14	11	3
September	16	11	5
October	11	4	7
November (through Nov. 7)	4	4	0

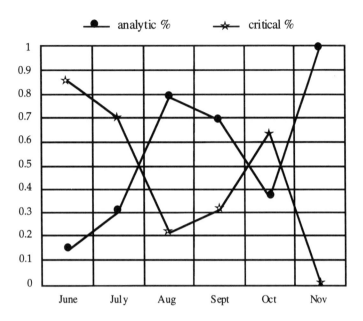

Fig. 5.5.   U.S. editorials vs. Korea, 1950. (Data from *New York Times*)

With the Inchon landing of September 15, however, both the tide of the war and the tone of editorials at home change drastically. All five critical editorials in September follow the Inchon offensive, with more to follow through October. The September 26 editorial "The Liberation of Seoul" claims that "the tables have been turned." Four successive editorials from September 29 through October 2 deal with the 38th parallel. In "A Plan for Korea," "The 38th Parallel," "Korea: A Test of Policy," and "North of the 38th," expansion of war aims to take all of Korea is argued. The end of the war is near, and Chinese intervention would be "folly beyond belief."

Yet, by November 1 it was clear that the Chinese did indeed plan to intervene in some capacity; the question was how far. During this period of uncertainty before November 7 all four editorials on the war are analytic, just as we would expect if a contraction of war aims were being considered. In "Red China and Korea" (November 1) and "A United Nations Task" (November 7) the focus again shifts away from the battlefield and toward international diplomatic negotiations.

All the same, I cannot claim that a change in editorial type precedes a change in war-fighting strategy, or at least not with the same confidence that I claim that change in editorial type precedes a change in prewar strategy. Rather, editorial type appears to mirror the fortunes of war, with battlefield successes leading to critical editorials pressing for an extension of war aims, such as crossing the 38th parallel, and battlefield failures leading to analytic editorials focusing on nonmilitary aspects of the war, such as negotiations in the United Nations. In truth, this is really all we can expect of wartime editorials. National decision makers cannot predict the success or failure of military operations and are necessarily forced to see the battlefield outcome before selling the public on a change in war aims. For example, Truman had no idea whether the Inchon offensive would be a grand success or a horrible fiasco; he had to wait until its success became clear before he could decide to push beyond the 38th parallel and before his administration could begin to push for popular acceptance of such an expansion via the domestic media.

Germany 1915 and Germany 1917

Germany 1915

International law regarding naval blockades is clear in wording and hopelessly muddy in application. A blockade is legal—and enforceable on neutral merchants—if it is "effective." To be effective a blockade must be enforceable against everyone, including neutrals. Such a circular definition creates obvious diplomatic problems. For combatants, blockade actions are legal only if they're successful. For neutrals, blockade running is illegal only if you're caught. As the largest neutral merchant nation in the world after World War I broke out in Europe, the United States was caught squarely in the middle of this impossible situation.[73]

From the earliest days of World War I Britain sought to keep neutral shipping, especially that of the United States, from reaching Germany. Britain quickly placed some mines outside of principal German ports (illegal under international law, as an effective blockade had not been established), imposed strict import quotas on non-German ports (also illegal), and declared practically every commodity bound for the Continent to be "conditional contraband" (even without a legal blockade, warring parties may legally search neutral merchant ships for contraband, such as munitions, and seize any such cargo).[74] Although Britain did not declare an official blockade until March 1915, the importation of most goods into Germany was effectively halted some time earlier. With the official declaration of a British blockade and American recognition of the blockade as "effective," Germany countered with a few mines of its own off Ireland and proclaimed a submarine blockade of England.

To make its blockade effective Germany announced on February 4 that, beginning February 18, enemy merchant ships would be destroyed without warning in a zone around the British Islands. Since English ships often flew neutral flags, including that of the United States, Germany warned that neutral ships would enter the zone at the risk of being mistaken for English ships. The German ambassador to the United States did assure the White House that German submarines would do everything possible to avoid sinking truly neutral ships.[75]

In a reply dated February 10 Wilson objected to the sinking of merchant ships without warning, even if they were those of an enemy. Germany countered by claiming that many English merchant ships were armed and that submarines, strong while hidden under the surface but weak once above, would provide an easy target to even these merchant ships if the submarines came up to search and board before firing. Wilson proposed a compromise solution, as the now official British blockade of Germany and neutral Continental ports chafed American free trade sensibilities almost as much as the German pseudo-blockade. Under this proposal both sides would stop flying neutral flags, German submarines would search and board, and England would allow the shipment of foodstuffs to Germany. Germany rather heavy-handedly demanded a more liberal spectrum of admissible items, and this round of talks soon collapsed.[76]

On May 7, 1915, a German submarine sank the English passenger liner *Lusitania* off the coast of Ireland. One hundred and twenty-eight Americans were on board and perished. Wilson sent three diplomatic notes to Germany: on May 13, June 9, and July 21. Secretary of State William Jennings Bryan resigned his post after the second *Lusitania* note, complaining that its sentiments were far too pro-British.[77] Still, it seems clear that Wilson was determined to stay out of war at this point. In the fall of 1915, according to Henry Breckinridge, then acting as secretary of war, Wilson promised to dismiss every officer on the General Staff if the rumors he had heard that they were preparing contingency plans for war with Germany were true.[78]

Wilson's general handling of the media during this prolonged road to war was quite purposeful. Wilson was the first president to give regular press conferences,[79] and, as George Juergens writes, he and Teddy Roosevelt were "the first presidents to base their leadership on direct appeals to the public, and to do so, moreover, using newspapers and magazines as their sole instruments of communication."[80] The editorial record bears out this concern with public opinion manipulation in the domestic media, as the content and number of editorials in the *New York Times* from February through June 1915 reflect his policy of economic pressure without military struggle (see table 5.6 and fig. 5.6).

The sheer number of editorials is indicative of some form of conflict. As for the ratio of analytic to critical editorials, analytic editorials maintain a clear preponderance, even immediately after the sinking of the *Lusitania* on May 7. In fact, the tone of editorials following the sinking of the *Gulflight* a few days earlier, now less than a footnote in the history texts, is much more threatening. None of these editorials makes any concrete threats about what will happen if Germany does not give up its submarine warfare policy, but the May 4 editorial

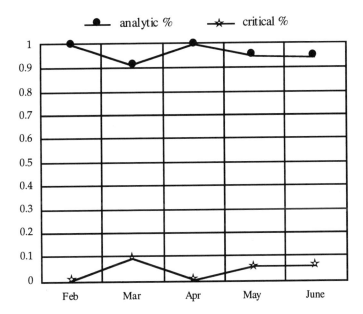

Fig. 5.6. U.S. editorials vs. Germany, 1915. (Data from *New York Times*)

"The Case of the Gulflight" at least says that the U.S. will be forced to take steps to protect its ships should Germany not change its policy. The editorials following the *Lusitania* sinking, interestingly enough, do not even go this far. Instead, they ask for Germany to return to the path of "sense and reason." Demands were practically nonexistent, at least in these domestic communications. For example, in the May 10 editorial "Stand by the President" we read that:

TABLE 5.6. United States vs. Germany, 1915 (*New York Times*)

Month	Total Editorials	Analytic Editorials	Critical Editorials
February	13	13	0
March	11	10	1
April	12	12	0
May	19	18	1
June	17	16	1

> If she [Germany] has become our enemy, if she has resolved to make war on us, . . . then we cannot too soon be advised of her purposes. But we have no such belief. We have faith that in response to our demand Germany will give us assurances that will remove doubt as to the continuance of our friendly relation. But to do that she must not only give pledge for the future; she must, difficult as it may be, disavow and denounce the act of her naval commander who sank the *Lusitania*.

Difficult terms indeed. Within a month the *Times* dropped any reference to the sinking of the *Lusitania;* instead, the few editorials on Germany discussed the "ridiculous" German accusations that some secret understanding existed between the United States and England and predicted that Germany would sue for peace soon.

From July 1915 through December 1916, editorials did not deviate from this pattern of analytic editorial dominance, despite several events that kept U.S.-German relations in the forefront of domestic political debate. In February 1916 twin resolutions in the House and Senate warning U.S. citizens against traveling on English and French merchant ships were opposed by Wilson and narrowly defeated. Just more than a month later, on March 24, 1916, the French steamer *Sussex* was sunk (whether by English mine or German torpedo was uncertain at first, with the latter eventually blamed); out of 25 American passengers, 4 were injured. In response, Wilson sent yet another diplomatic cable to Germany, the "Sussex note," calling for Germany to return to a strict observance of the naval rules of war. As with the second Lusitania note, Wilson rewrote a far more aggressive draft penned by his staff in order to leave the door open for meaningful international negotiations on the issue.[81] Wilson was rewarded for his diplomatic overtures in May, when Germany agreed to compensate the wounded American passengers of the *Sussex* and to give warning to all unarmed merchant ships, belligerent and neutral alike.

Germany 1917

On January 8, 1917, the German military command issued a secret order to its naval commanders to resume unrestricted submarine warfare, effective February 1, against all ships sailing in waters from the North Sea to the eastern Mediterranean. On January 31 the German ambassador informed the White House of the policy as well as of an exemption for the United States to send one passenger ship per week to England. On February 3 Wilson severed diplomatic relations with Germany.

The resumption of submarine attacks came as quite a blow to the peacemaking efforts of Wilson. Just a few days earlier, on January 22, he had made his "peace without victory" speech, in which he called for a new sort of war resolution process, one in which no side would run roughshod in victory over the vanquished. Both the Allies and the Germans wanted no part of such a settlement, the difference being that the English declined gracefully, while the Germans nixed the idea clumsily.[82]

Following the leak of the Zimmermann telegram to the State Department on February 24 and its presentation to the American press on March 1, U.S. relations with Germany soured still further.[83] Despite a Senate filibuster, Wilson ordered merchant ships armed on March 4. Three American ships were sunk on March 18, leading Wilson to convene a special session of Congress to discuss a declaration of war on April 2. The Senate passed such a declaration on April 4, and, with House approval on May 6, 1917, the United States entered World War I on the side of the Allies.

We might expect that, given Wilson's peace initiative of late January and the lack of any single incident as incendiary as the sinking of the *Lusitania,* the editorial record might not predict the swift move to war following the Germans' resumption of a submarine warfare policy. This is not the case. As we see in table 5.7 and figure 5.7, both the absolute number of editorials and the number of critical editorials reach unprecedented levels in the months prior to a declaration of war. The sharply lower totals for April are simply an artifact of the observation aggregation problem. If I were simply to extrapolate from the six days of editorials that constitute the April data forward to a month of editorials, I would generate an editorial count as indicative of severe conflict as the February and March results.

The pattern shown in figure 5.7 is an archetypal switch from analytic editorial predominance to critical predominance immediately prior to the abandonment of diplomatic negotiations and the decision for unilateral military action. In my examination of recent wars in chapter 4 I hypothesized that the paths to wars described as security dilemmas were transformed into completely new bargaining situations a few months before all-out war. With both the Six Day War and Bangladesh Wars we saw the same pattern of figure 5.7 in the months immediately preceding the initiation of sharply escalated hostilities. The drawn-out entry of the United States into World War I would appear to be another example of this sort of security dilemma gone awry.

TABLE 5.7. United States vs. Germany, 1917 (*New York Times*)

Month	Total Editorials	Analytic Editorials	Critical Editorials
January	18	14	4
February	36	6	30
March	24	6	18
April (through Apr. 6)	5	0	5

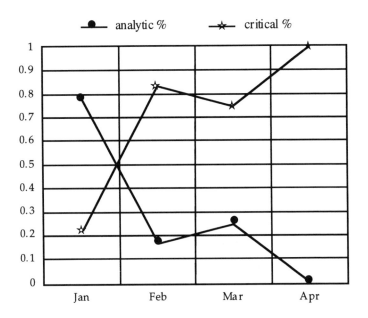

Fig. 5.7.   U.S. editorials vs. Germany, 1917. (Data from *New York Times*)

Editorials in January are convinced that peace is close at hand. In editorials such as "The Open Door of Peace" (January 1), "Enforcing Peace" (January 2), and "Daybreak in Germany" (January 22), the *Times* claims that Germany realizes it cannot achieve its original war aims and that its best hope is to sue for peace. Starting with the February 1 editorial "Germany Wars against the World," however, the tone of editorials is unstintingly critical and war hungry. In sharp contrast to the 1915 opinion pieces, the 1917 editorials explicitly suggest that the United States actively enter the war on the side of the Allies. In editorials such as "The Nation's Duty" (February 3), "In Defense of Our Rights" (February 4), and "In Defense of American Liberty" (February 28) the *Times* claims that the United States must discard its neutrality in order to save the world from the militaristic German threat. Even a prompt disavowal of the submarine policy is no longer enough according to "The Doom of the Hohenzollerns" (March 4); since "the Hohenzollerns are outside civilization's pale," the only hope for peace is for the United States to join the Allies and sweep away the existing German state.

Conclusion

In each of these cases we see clear support for the working hypothesis of this chapter: that media opinion pieces of newspapers especially sympathetic to the incumbent administration accurately reveal the preference ordering and future behavior of that administration. Analytic editorials dominate throughout the Iranian hostage crisis, suggesting that economic embargo and diplomatic initiatives would be the course set by the Carter White House. When we move to the Iraqi crisis of 1990–91 we see markedly different media behavior, at least in the newspaper closest to the Republican administration, the *Wall Street Journal*. Not only are as many (or more) editorials in absolute numbers written, the relative frequency of analytic and critical editorials is reversed. The relationship between government action and media behavior, however, is precisely the same. Just as the analytic editorial predominance during the Iranian crisis presaged economic and diplomatic moves against Iran, so did the critical editorial preponderance during the Iraqi crisis predict the military action against Iraq.

The similarities between Korea and Berlin were not lost on Truman. He wrote, "I told my advisers that what was happening in Korea seemed to me like a repetition on a larger scale of what had happened in Berlin."[84] In both cases Truman claimed his overriding objective was to prevent a new world war; the means of that prevention, however, turned out to be completely different. Whereas aggressive military action was never seriously contemplated in Berlin, such a response was Truman's gut response in Korea. Notably, just as the media record suggests diplomatic conflict and solution in 1948, so does it suggest military conflict in 1950.

Despite the similarities in the 1915 and 1917 German decisions to unleash their submarines, both Wilson's response and the *New York Times* editorial patterns are completely different. Even though the *Lusitania* was sunk under the 1915 submarine program, even though Wilson had just launched a peace initiative in 1917, diplomatic negotiations were both the preferred policy of the administration and the policy suggested by the editorial record in 1915, while the 1917 military intervention was presaged by the dramatic shift in the ratio of analytic to critical editorials in early 1917.

I should note that these results are especially compelling because they are individual cases. That is, the lower the sample size of any phenomenon, the greater the likelihood that the phenomenon will not show up. For example, although we know the odds of tossing a true coin "heads" are 50 percent, one or two tosses of the coin will perhaps not suggest such a relationship. That the operational calculus developed in previous chapters for predicting both the initiation and form of conflict sheds light on each of these cases suggests that it is remarkably robust. With the possible exception of the Gulf War, there is no

154 Getting to War

smoking gun here to show that American political leaders consciously employed information management techniques to grease the skids to war. All the same, the limited process tracing of this chapter provides strong circumstantial evidence that such techniques, particularly for garnering domestic opinion (less so for maintaining international secrecy), have been among the most salient aspects of foreign policy making in the United States.

CHAPTER 6

Conclusion and Implications for Theory

I began this work with an examination of an interesting political dilemma first noted by Karl Deutsch. Modern governments face a perplexing problem when they seek to initiate conflict: how to maintain strategic surprise vis-à-vis some target state while at the same time generating domestic support for such a risky future action. Deutsch suggested that the domestic mass media of states preparing for war should give reliable signals of their intentions that will be lacking in statements and actions on the international stage. I proposed that a systematic evaluation of domestic mass media would provide precisely the affective, domestic-level indicator that existing models of conflict prediction lack, and even a cursory look at events in Argentina prior to the Falklands War gave support to these propositions.

Chapter 2 took this domestic political dilemma and developed a formal equilibrium model between maintaining international secrecy and maintaining domestic support. Using this political equilibrium, I deduced a set of hypotheses that explain the way governments approach war once the decision for conflict is made. Most important among these were the claims that: (1) efforts to build public opinion should precede all wars, and (2) the level of opinion-building effort should be commensurate with the level of subsequent interstate conflict. Other hypotheses dealt with the effect of regime type on opinion-building effort as well as the role of international signaling when domestic media is used as part of a broader strategic interaction between nations.

Chapter 3 tested these hypotheses, giving particular attention to the central claim of this project—that mass media efforts should provide a leading indicator of war initiation. I operationalized the indicator by means of a systematic analysis of newspaper editorials and found that this measure was a significant and influential indicator of conflictual events, providing information that captured both the effect of prior events and the effect of independent intentions. I found that the indicator was robust in its predictions and that reformulating the dependent variable of conflictual events in a variety of ways did not reduce its significance or power, whether the tested data set consisted of a wide range of war and nonwar cases or an extended time series of observations from one particular country.

Chapter 4 took a new look at the editorial measure that drives the predictive models in order to see what this indicator says about the roads to war. In this second cut at the key indicator I recoded editorials in an attempt to identify the nature of the affective complaint as well as its existence. I found that editorials fell into one of two general types: analytic, in which foreign countries were calmly discussed, and critical, in which the prospects of violent conflict were raised. I also found analytic editorials to occur prior to and concurrently with diplomatic and economic conflict and critical editorials prior to major escalation and military conflict. The pattern of occurrence of the two editorial types suggests both a new vision of the way nations approach conflict as well as an improved indicator capable of predicting what form conflict is likely to take.

The cases of U.S. policy in chapter 5 provided a nonrigorous confirmation of the claim that taking two cuts on the mass media variable indicates both when conflict is imminent as well as what form that conflict may likely take. Military intervention in Iraq in 1991 is clearly predicted by the number and type of editorials in the *Wall Street Journal,* and the pattern of editorials in the *New York Times* provides an interesting insight on the opposition party's decision-making process. The lack of military intervention in Iran in 1979–80 is just as clearly predicted by the editorial pattern, and the indicators show themselves to be sensitive enough to pick up the transitory shift in U.S. strategy prior to the abortive military rescue attempt. Evaluating the nature of the affective complaint during the Korean campaign of 1950 provides some indication of U.S. war-fighting strategy, while such an evaluation of U.S. editorials in 1948 suggests a diplomatic/economic conflict with the Soviet Union over Berlin rather than a substantial military engagement. Despite the identical issue of unrestricted German submarine warfare, U.S. editorial patterns suggest strong diplomatic conflict in 1915, even after the sinking of the *Lusitania,* while the patterns suggest war in 1917.

My prescriptions for crisis bargaining on the basis of these findings are twofold. First, pay more attention to indirect sources of information on adversarial decision makers, particularly sources in the domestic media (where decision makers have intrinsic incentives to tell the truth) and less attention to direct diplomatic communications (where such incentives rarely exist). The existing literature on the failings of intelligence services,[1] with its emphasis on cognitive and organizational constraints, tends to ignore the overall culture surrounding ordinary information transfers between nations. Indirect sources of information are usually only examined when the costs of failure are extremely high, as witnessed by the U.S. intelligence community's strong efforts to read the media tea leaves stirred by Moscow (and weak efforts to develop such a system for other nations), and even then the emphasis is usually placed on collecting huge mounds of data rather than analyzing that data in a deductively rigorous fashion.[2]

Second, move quickly to stabilize a crisis at the security dilemma level if at all possible. In other words, the mere possibility of negotiated settlements that at least satisfy minimal expectations on both sides is a situation to be treasured and preserved rather than a situation to be particularly feared. The existence of contingent strategies and shared interests should give observers reason to hope, as it suggests the existence of a feasible bargaining space. Far more dangerous to any hope of peace is the collapse of a bargaining space and the unilateral plan for military escalation such a collapse engenders on one or both sides, although such a situation receives relatively short shrift in the literature. Time is of the essence within the security dilemmas that usually mark the existence of bargaining space, however, as nations faced with the grinding pressures of reactive policies may quickly search for a more radical solution.

I want to conclude my analysis by returning to the theoretical issues broached in the introduction. Have I identified only an interesting predictive tool, or can I also say something new about the sources of war? Even if my answer were that this was solely a prior indicator of conflict, by no means would I accept the pejorative assertion that this is "merely" an indicator.[3] Predicting wars is at least as worthy a goal as predicting earthquakes, and, just as a highly reliable earthquake indicator based on something as implausible as nematode activity would have great value, so would a reliable conflict indicator qua indicator have significant value. Still, we must understand why an approach works before we can truly accept it; models need a plausible theoretical basis regardless of the strength of statistical test results. To continue with the seismology analogy, we would have much more confidence in an earthquake prediction model based on a theory of plate tectonics than on astrology. I claim not only that this predictive calculus is firmly based on theory but also that it does indeed give us new insights on a comprehensive theory of how and why nations fight.

The theoretical assumption on which my indicators are based is a domestic politics argument that modern governments require at least some degree of popular support for their actions in order to remain in power and that they behave in a manner that seeks to maximize that support given other constraints. One of those constraints is a concurrent desire to maximize strategic surprise in any initiation of conflict with another nation. The tension between these desires creates an equilibrium situation in which governments attempt to maximize each with respect to the other. Thus, even when strategic surprise is a paramount concern, reliable information regarding intentions should appear in the domestic press in an attempt to influence domestic opinion, even if contrary information is presented in other arenas. In and of itself this is certainly no comprehensive theory of conflict initiation, nor is it intended to be. Yet this manner of taking advantage of a middle-level theory, of a theory about how the parts of the international system behave internally, allows me to make some observations about what a comprehensive theory of international conflict might include.

At its most basic level, without a consideration of the system/unit interaction, this work supports the claims of social science as a potential source of general explication and prediction of even the most complex political behaviors. As a close relative of the humanities, the study of politics is not as strongly based on a faith in the scientific method as the study of physics or geology. While few geologists would doubt the potential existence of a predictive calculus of earthquakes, many political scientists doubt even the possibility of a predictive calculus of war.[4] As Stanley Hoffmann points out, human behavior is less deterministic than the behavior of molecules. Given the potential for meaningful choice in human behavior, given the multitude of causal effects in social systems and the impossibility of choosing or weighting them objectively, he claims that science is incapable of saying more about war than pointing out the "limits of our knowledge" and providing "tools for the analysis of concrete situations." More general theories or assertions concerning the causes of war are not possible in this view of social science; as Hoffmann goes on to say:

> we should not expect to be able to answer definitively why a certain war, why certain types of wars, happen when they did. . . . What social science can do is show how the logic of human drives, ideas, impersonal forces, state calculations and reactions, leaders' personalities in a certain milieu— how all these made the resort to war as instrument, outlet, or outcome likely. More it cannot do, because reality itself does not lend itself to greater certainty.[5]

I certainly do not deny the role of free will in human behavior, and of course I agree with Hoffmann's general assessment that there are inherent limits on the deterministic, predictive abilities of any scientific analysis. Even in the largely deterministic world of atomic physics, researchers cannot conceivably know the position and velocity of particles simultaneously. I agree that all science can hope to do is show the likelihood of conflict under certain circumstances. I disagree with Hoffmann, however, about the *extent* of these inherent limits; I disagree about the confidence we can potentially have in predictions of conflict likelihood. It does not require some ultra-Calvinist view to see a large enough role for the constraints of domestic and systemic forces to allow a meaningful answer through social scientific analysis to why certain wars happened when they did. Instead, it requires a certain assessment of the relative degree to which stochastic and systematic factors account for the social phenomenon of international conflict. Hoffmann assumes that random or stochastic factors dominate the ratio; I assume the opposite. To the degree that I have been successful in demonstrating the effectiveness of this approach to predicting conflict, I have also demonstrated that my conception of the ratio between what can and cannot be systematically explained is more correct.

As for Hoffmann's other objection to the potential for substantive scientific prediction of international conflict—the multitude of causal events involved in the initiation of conflict—it is precisely via the use of domestic mass media that I hope to aggregate this morass of domestic sources of conflict into a single, effective indicator. Driven by the political demands of simultaneously maintaining international surprise and domestic support, domestic media serves as an intermediary variable between the virtually infinite set of unit-level causes of war and the quite limited set of systemic causes.

Although a purely systemic focus may yield an understanding of the necessary conditions for such conflict to come about, as Bueno de Mesquita claims to have done, the tremendous overprediction inherent with such a focus, together with the associated lack of variation from observation period to observation period, provides extremely little meaningful prediction for any particular case. On the other hand, attempts to get inside the systemic level by finding ad hoc amendments to systemic rules run the risk of providing meaningful explanation for only the particular case under examination; such efforts lack both the power and parsimony of systemic explanations. In modeling terms the danger posed by delving beneath the systemic level is roughly equivalent to the danger of including more independent variables than either theory or data can support. Imagine an extreme example, in which a separate independent variable is included for each observation; the resulting model would show tremendous fit with the data, but its significance would certainly be nil. In fact, such a construct is not a model at all but is merely a recapitulation of the pieces of the system under study.

In this work I did indeed dig beneath the systemic level to answer the question of conflict timing. Yet, instead of supplying dummy variables to account for the particular quirks of particular cases, instead of including a multitude of unit-level variables, I tried to elucidate one crucial domestic characteristic that applies across time and geography, that applies to some degree regardless of other characteristics of the domestic regime. My domestic media indicator is a unit-level attribute, to be sure, but it is not an ad hoc addition to a systemic theory; instead, it is determined deductively from a theory of the behavior of regimes and serves to aggregate an indeterminate number of unit-level sources of conflict. I believe that this kind of variable largely preserves both the power and parsimony of a systemic focus as well as the substantive predictions for particular cases of a unit-level focus.

I am not suggesting a reductionist theory of international conflict, in which the behavior of the system is determined wholly by the behavior of the parts. I am suggesting that a greater appreciation of the regular and predictable aspects of the internal behavior of the parts is a necessary addition to general theory and does not inexorably lead to hopelessly ad hoc or nonparsimonious argument. Just as I disagreed with Stanley Hoffmann about the extent to which scientific analysis can provide substantive explanation of international conflict, so do I disagree with Kenneth Waltz about the extent to which bringing in unit-level attributes leads to inelegant and weak analysis.[6] Granted, the resulting hybrid theory will not, by definition, be a purely general one; granted, the power and parsimony of such a "pure" theory will inexorably be reduced somewhat. But, if including a special type of unit-level variable leads to a quantum leap in specificity at the cost of an exceedingly negligible reduction in parsimony, what benefit is there in holding obstinately to a goal of theoretical purity? I believe that this mass media indicator, conceptualized in terms of a theory of regime behavior, is just such a "special" unit-level variable.[7]

Waltz's systemic balance of power theory explicitly holds that preferences stem from position in the international system, as determined by the distribution of power within that system.[8] The basic model presented here, on the other hand, evaluates preferences by looking at a full-fledged unit-level variable,[9] newspaper editorials. Although some neorealist theories of war look explicitly at unit-level attributes for their source of conflict,[10] these unit-level attributes are based on changes in traditional power indices such as population or military spending. Since these indices are also used to determine the systemic distribution of power, editorials simply provide a far more independent source of information on preferences based on unit-level attributes.

For this reason it seems clear why those theorists who emphasize the growth of power relative to some adversary[11] have difficulty distinguishing between peaceful and wartorn transitions of power as well as why they disagree on when war is most likely to break out during the transition period. By ignoring independently determined unit-level preferences, they cannot tell whether a transition will be peaceful or not. By ignoring the manner in which such preferences can modify power considerations, they cannot know the timing of conflict initiation. The same observations can be made about those theories of war that rely on economic or economic leadership cycles as the primary source of conflict.[12]

Does this analysis tell us which unit-level causes of war apply in which situations? Not directly. If so, we would be well on our way to a comprehensive theory of international conflict, but I make no such claims. To be sure, my methods suggest not only when conflict will occur but also what general form— diplomatic/economic or military—international conflict will take under the circumstances in question. By comparing these existing circumstances with the anticipated form of conflict, we might well inductively determine the possible set of domestic causes of diplomatic/economic conflict and the possible set of domestic causes of military conflict. Perhaps informative comparisons between the two sets could be made, but I suspect that the difficulty in confidently assigning any nonaggregated unit-level attribute as even a partial causal factor of conflict, not to mention the difficulty of identifying each pertinent causal factor, will sharply diminish the utility of such set comparisons.

Still, this work advocates an indirect way of determining what domestic sources of conflict apply under what conditions, by suggesting a new conception of the interplay between unit-level and systemic causes of conflict. My theoretical assumptions regarding the existence of regime constraints based on the dictates of public opinion maintenance are, in and of themselves, neither true nor false. The degree to which data analysis supports the hypotheses derived from the theoretical assumptions determines the degree to which that theory helps us understand the world as it is. I think that my analysis has, to a large extent, supported these theoretical assumptions, implying that the desires for foreign secrecy and domestic support are extremely important constraints on international behavior.

For this to be a progressive research program, in a Lakatosian sense, looking at international behavior through the lens of the support/secrecy equilibrium needs to provide new questions or avenues of inquiry. In general, this work suggests that more attention should be paid to the interaction between domestic and international constraints on how regimes get to war. In particular, I believe that the apparent strength of measures of opinion-building effort as an indicator of war shows that the desires for domestic support and (to a lesser extent) strategic surprise serve as gatekeepers or modulators of how unit-level causes manifest themselves into a decision for war.

Imagine the set of unit-level sources of international conflict. Its number is legion, incorporating such disparate issues as social and economic tension caused by refugee flows, the pressures of nationalism, and religious intolerance. For each member of this set we can find historical examples in which its presence clearly contributed to the development of conflict as well as examples in which its presence did not. I believe that an answer to the questions "Why this issue, why this causal factor, why now?" must take into account, in addition to the constraints of the international system, the degree to which these social and historical causal factors serve the public support requirements of the regime in power.

A decision for war does not spring, like Athena, full grown from the minds of national leaders; it must be encouraged, nurtured, and constrained, partially by an appreciation for the dictates of position in the international system but also by an appreciation for the political dictates of modern government. This vision of the development of conflict does not require that leaders sit back in their chairs and malevolently choose that particular issue with which they can simultaneously maximize both public support and strategic secrecy for the achievement of some international goal through conflict (although some leaders might). It requires that leaders pay great attention to the demands of support and secrecy and that they, to whatever degree possible, modulate or channel existing unit-level causal factors of conflict in light of those demands.

By no means do I claim that the public support constraint identified by Deutsch and employed here is the only such domestic phenomenon that regulates the transformation of social and historical sources of conflict into war. Nor do I suggest that this is the only methodology for parsimoniously aggregating unit-level causes of war into a prior indicator of conflict. In fact, I suspect that a variety of such domestic and international phenomena exist and that an effective comprehensive theory of international conflict will need to use the theoretical assumptions and implications of each to tie systemic forces to the forces within state and society. I only hope that this analysis will prove to be one strand of such a rope.

Appendixes

Appendix 1: Data Sets

1.1: Data Set 1

Variable	Description
#	case number
actor	initiating nation
target	target nation
date	yy/mm/dd of conflict initiation
war	dummy variable; 1 if Singer and Small war
edt-1	number of critical editorials in prior time period
i-power	power resources of initiating nation
j-power	power resources of target nation
s-power	power resources of neighboring nations to i and j
avgeds	average number of editorials printed in time period
autoc	regime autocracy measure from Polity II; 1 to 10 scale
democ	regime democracy measure from Polity II; 1 to 10 scale
conc	regime concentration measure from Polity II; 1 to 7 scale
coher	regime coherence of policy measure from Polity II; dummy variable

#	actor s-power	target avgeds	date autoc	war democ	edt-1 conc	i-power coher	j-power
1	Pakistan	India	650806	1	5.5	1.327	5.894
	36.158	37	1	4	3	0	
2	Pakistan	India	670606	0	3	1.308	5.833
	35.108	37	1	4	3	0	
3	Pakistan	India	711203	1	10	1.364	5.919
	37.368	37	1	4	5	0	
4	Pakistan	India	731007	0	1	1.364	5.865
	38.629	37	1	4	5	0	
5	Pakistan	India	820402	0	1	0.801	5.923
	35.503	37	5	0	4	0	
6	Pakistan	India	820604	0	1	0.801	5.923
	35.503	37	5	0	4	0	
7	India	Pakistan	650806	1	3	5.894	1.327
	36.158	75	0	10	3	1	
8	India	Pakistan	670606	0	0.5	5.833	1.308
	35.108	75	0	10	3	1	

#	actor s-power	target avgeds	date autoc	war democ	edt-1 conc	i-power coher	j-power
9	India	Pakistan	711203	1	8.5	5.919	1.364
	37.368	75	0	10	3	1	
10	India	Pakistan	731007	0	2.5	5.865	1.364
	38.629	75	0	10	3	1	
11	India	Pakistan	820402	0	3	5.923	0.801
	34.792	75	0	10	3	1	
12	India	Pakistan	820604	0	2	5.923	0.801
	34.792	75	0	10	3	1	
13	Israel	Egypt	650806	0	3.5	0.136	0.463
	0.765	25	0	10	5	1	
14	Israel	Egypt	670606	1	5.5	0.168	0.425
	0.772	25	0	10	5	1	
15	Israel	Egypt	711203	0	3	0.287	0.506
	0.977	25	0	10	5	1	
16	Israel	Egypt	731007	0	0.5	0.529	1.000
	1.820	25	0	10	5	1	
17	Israel	Egypt	820402	0	1	0.343	0.662
	1.356	25	0	10	5	1	
18	Israel	Lebanon	650806	0	1	0.136	0.045
	0.765	25	0	10	5	1	
19	Israel	Lebanon	711203	0	0	0.287	0.050
	0.977	25	0	10	5	1	
20	Israel	Lebanon	731007	0	0	0.529	0.100
	1.820	25	0	10	5	1	
21	Israel	Lebanon	820402	0	0.5	0.343	0.053
	1.356	25	0	10	5	1	
22	Israel	Lebanon	820604	1	3	0.343	0.053
	1.356	25	0	10	5	1	
23	Argentina	Chile	650806	0	0.5	0.524	0.169
	5.407	75	4	3	6	0	
24	Argentina	Chile	670606	0	0	0.503	0.169
	5.139	75	9	1	7	1	
25	Argentina	Chile	711203	0	1.5	0.504	0.172
	5.046	75	9	1	7	1	
26	Argentina	Chile	731007	0	1.5	0.495	0.153
	5.097	75	1	6	7	0	
27	Argentina	Paraguay	650806	0	0	0.524	0.028
	5.407	75	4	3	6	0	
28	Argentina	Paraguay	670606	0	0	0.503	0.027
	5.139	75	9	1	7	1	
29	Argentina	Paraguay	711203	0	0	0.504	0.026
	5.046	75	9	1	7	1	
30	Argentina	Paraguay	731007	0	0	0.495	0.025
	5.097	75	1	6	7	0	

#	actor s-power	target avgeds	date autoc	war democ	edt-1 conc	i-power coher	j-power
31	India	Nepal	670606	0	0	5.833	0.116
	35.108	75	0	10	3	1	
32	India	Nepal	731007	0	0	5.865	0.114
	38.629	75	0	10	3	1	
33	India	Nepal	820402	0	0	5.923	0.123
	35.503	75	0	10	3	1	
34	India	Nepal	820604	0	0	5.923	0.123
	35.503	75	0	10	3	1	
35	Argentina	Bolivia	650806	0	0	0.524	0.051
	5.407	75	4	3	6	0	
36	Argentina	Bolivia	670606	0	0	0.503	0.049
	5.139	75	9	1	7	1	
37	Argentina	Bolivia	711203	0	0	0.504	0.055
	5.046	75	9	1	7	1	
38	Argentina	Bolivia	731007	0	0	0.495	0.055
	5.097	75	1	6	7	0	
39	India	Sri Lanka	670606	0	0	5.833	0.128
	35.108	75	0	10	3	1	
40	India	Sri Lanka	731007	0	2	5.865	0.124
	38.629	75	0	10	3	1	
41	India	Sri Lanka	820402	0	0	5.923	0.123
	35.503	75	0	10	3	1	
42	India	Sri Lanka	820604	0	0	5.923	0.123
	35.503	75	0	10	3	1	
43	India	Burma	670606	0	0	5.833	0.280
	35.108	75	0	10	3	1	
44	India	Burma	731007	0	0	5.865	0.287
	38.629	75	0	10	3	1	
45	India	Burma	820402	0	0	5.923	0.276
	35.503	75	0	10	3	1	
46	India	Burma	820604	0	0	5.923	0.276
	35.503	75	0	10	3	1	
47	Argentina	Uruguay	650806	0	0	0.524	0.063
	5.407	75	4	3	6	0	
48	Argentina	Uruguay	670606	0	0	0.503	0.058
	5.139	75	9	1	7	1	
49	Argentina	Uruguay	711203	0	0	0.504	0.057
	5.046	75	9	1	7	1	
50	Argentina	Uruguay	731007	0	0	0.495	0.054
	5.097	75	1	6	7	0	
51	Israel	Jordan	650806	0	0	0.136	0.041
	0.765	25	0	10	5	1	
52	Israel	Jordan	670606	1	2.5	0.168	0.041
	0.772	25	0	10	5	1	

#	actor s-power	target avgeds	date autoc	war democ	edt-1 conc	i-power coher	j-power
53	Israel 0.977	Jordan 25	711203 0	0 10	0 5	0.287 1	0.041
54	Israel 1.820	Jordan 25	731007 0	0 10	0 5	0.529 1	0.080
55	Israel 1.356	Jordan 25	820402 0	2 10	0 5	0.343 1	0.060
56	Israel 0.765	Syria 25	650806 0	0 10	0 5	0.136 1	0.080
57	Israel 0.772	Syria 25	670606 1	4 10	0 5	0.168 1	0.085
58	Israel 0.977	Syria 25	711203 0	1 10	0 5	0.287 1	0.093
59	Israel 1.820	Syria 25	731007 0	1.5 10	0 5	0.529 1	0.111
60	Israel 1.356	Syria 25	820402 0	0 10	0 5	0.343 1	0.238
61	Pakistan 35.108	Afghanistan 37	670606 1	0 4	0 3	1.308 0	0.165
62	Pakistan 38.629	Afghanistan 37	731007 1	1 4	1 5	1.364 0	0.167
63	Pakistan 35.503	Afghanistan 37	820402 5	1 0	1 4	0.801 0	0.115
64	Pakistan 35.503	Afghanistan 37	820604 5	0 0	0 4	0.801 0	0.115
65	Pakistan 35.108	Iran 37	670606 1	0 4	0 3	1.308 0	0.464
66	Pakistan 38.629	Iran 37	731007 1	0 4	0 5	1.364 0	0.723
67	Pakistan 35.503	Iran 37	820402 5	1 0	1 4	0.801 0	1.094
68	Pakistan 35.503	Iran 37	820604 5	1.5 0	0 4	0.801 0	1.094
69	India 35.108	China 75	670606 0	1 10	1 3	5.833 1	10.088
70	India 38.629	China 75	731007 0	1.5 10	1.5 3	5.865 1	10.932
71	India 35.503	China 75	820402 0	0 10	0 3	5.923 1	8.908
72	India 35.503	China 75	820604 0	0 10	0 3	5.923 1	8.908
73	Argentina 5.407	Brazil 75	650806 4	0 3	0 6	0.524 0	1.258
74	Argentina 5.139	Brazil 75	670606 9	0 1	0 7	0.503 1	1.281

#	actor s-power	target avgeds	date autoc	war democ	edt-1 conc	i-power coher	j-power
75	Argentina 5.046	Brazil 75	711203 9	0 1	0 7	0.504 1	1.412
76	Argentina 5.097	Brazil 75	731007 1	0 6	0 7	0.495 0	1.467
77	India 35.108	USSR 75	670606 0	0 10	0 3	5.833 1	16.726
78	India 38.629	USSR 75	731007 0	0 10	0.5 3	5.865 1	18.362
79	India 35.503	USSR 75	820402 0	0 10	1 3	5.923 1	17.429
80	India 35.503	USSR 75	820604 0	0 10	0.5 3	5.923 1	17.429
81	Pakistan 35.108	USSR 37	670606 1	0 4	0 3	1.308 0	16.726
82	Pakistan 38.629	USSR 37	731007 1	0 4	0 5	1.364 0	18.362
83	Pakistan 35.503	USSR 37	820402 5	1 0	0 4	0.801 0	17.429
84	Pakistan 35.503	USSR 37	820604 5	0 0	0 4	0.801 0	17.429
85	Argentina 5.407	U.K. 75	650806 4	0 3	0 6	0.524 0	3.314
86	Argentina 5.139	U.K. 75	670606 9	0 1	1 7	0.503 1	3.052
87	Argentina 5.046	U.K. 75	711203 9	0 1	0 7	0.504 1	2.820
88	Argentina 5.097	U.K. 75	731007 1	0 6	0 7	0.495 0	2.848
89	Argentina 4.826	U.K. 75	820402 8	1 1	4 7	0.518 1	2.499
90	India 38.629	Bangladesh 75	731007 0	0 10	0 3	5.865 1	0.691
91	India 35.503	Bangladesh 75	820402 0	0 10	1 3	5.923 1	0.711
92	India 35.503	Bangladesh 75	820604 0	0 10	0 3	5.923 1	0.711

1.2: Data Set 2

Variable	Description
#	case number
actor	initiating nation
target	target nation
date	yy/mm/dd of conflict initiation or test date

war   dummy variable; 1 if Singer and Small war
edt-1   number of critical editorials in prior time period
edt-2   number of critical editorials in twice removed time period
c15   count of COPDAB events coded 15 or higher
c11   count of COPDAB events coded 11 or higher
d15   COPDAB events coded 15 or higher; prior time period
d11   COPDAB events coded 11 or higher; prior time period
e15   COPDAB events coded 15 or higher; twice removed time period
e11   COPDAB events coded 11 or higher; twice removed time period
imil   military expenditures of initiating nation
jmil   military expenditures of target nation
avg   average number of editorials printed in time period
autoc   regime autocracy measure from Polity II; 1 to 10 scale
democ   regime democracy measure from Polity II; 1 to 10 scale
conc   regime concentration measure from Polity II; 1 to 7 scale
coher   regime coherence of policy measure from Polity II; dummy variable
reg   regime regulation of participation measure; 1 to 5 scale
mktg   # of influential dailies or press holding cos.
sig   dummy variable; 1 if no regime mass media organ

| # | actor | target | date | war | edt-1 | edt-2 | c15 | c11 |
| | d15 | d11 | e15 | e11 | imil | jmil | avg | autoc |
	democ	conc	coher	reg	mktg	sig		
1	Israel	Lebanon	820604	1	3.0	3.0	15	17
	0	5	0	6	8241308	331000	25	0
	10	5	1	5	4	1		
2	Argentina	UK	820402	1	5.0	1.0	5	10
	0	0	0	0	4147000	2.42E+07	75	8
	1	7	1	1	2	1		
3	Iraq	Iran	800922	1	1.0	1.0	37	46
	0	8	0	4	3386780	3386907	25	8
	1	7	1	4	1	0		
4	USSR	Afghanistan	791222	1	2.0	2.0	5	10
	0	0	0	0	1.80E+08	58000	25	7
	1	6	1	4	7	0		
5	China (PRC)	Vietnam	790201	1	12.5	3.5	18	21
	0	4	0	1	3.00E+07	—	25	7
	1	5	1	4	9	0		
6	Uganda	Tanzania	781030	1	0.0	0.0	0	8
	0	1	0	0	1031579	66719	25	7
	0	7	1	4	0	0		
7	Cuba	Somalia	780130	1	3.0	2.0	0	1
	0	1	0	0	31771	135265	25	7
	0	7	1	4	1	0		
8	Somalia	Ethiopia	770801	1	7.0	5.0	5	11
	0	5	0	1	—	-9	12	7
	0	5	1	4	0	0		

#	actor d15 democ	target d11 conc	date e15 coher	war e11 reg	edt-1 imil mktg	edt-2 jmil sig	c15 avg	c11 autoc
9	Vietnam 0 1	Kampuchea 0 7	781215 0 1	1 0 4	3.0 156012 1	1.0 264913 0	0 25	9 9
10	Turkey 0 10	Cyprus-Greece 0 5	740720 0 1	1 0 5	8.0 1136713 2	4.0 1049967 1	18 25	21 0
11	Egypt 0 1	Israel 1 5	731006 1 1	1 1 4	13.0 3194479 4	14.5 3121718 0	37 37	46 7
12	Syria 0 2	Israel 4 5	731006 0 0	1 0 3	10.0 388408 5	5.0 3121718 0	18 25	35 5
13	India 13 10	Pakistan 28 3	711203 1 1	1 5 5	8.0 1924810 4	6.0 727215 1	47 75	54 0
14	Pakistan 7 4	India 16 5	711203 1 0	1 7 2	10.0 727215 4	8.0 1924810 1	12 37	21 1
15	El Salvador 0 8	Honduras 6 6	690714 0 1	1 0 5	15.0 10480 2	2.0 7100 1	1 50	6 0
16	Israel 0 10	Egypt 0 5	690306 0 1	1 0 5	3.0 680798 4	1.0 975161 1	6 25	8 0
17	Israel 0 10	Egypt 4 5	670605 0 1	1 0 5	5.5 491616 4	1.0 570377 1	25 25	33 0
18	Israel 0 10	Syria 2 5	670605 2 1	1 5 5	4.0 491616 4	3.5 95812 1	7 25	9 0
19	Egypt 2 1	Israel 8 6	670605 0 1	1 0 4	17.0 570377 4	1.0 491616 0	6 37	14 7
20	Pakistan 0 4	India 0 3	650805 0 0	1 5 2	5.0 428512 4	1.0 1804170 1	10 37	13 1
21	U.S. 3 10	N. Vietnam 4 4	650302 5 1	1 5 5	18.0 5.18E+07 9	5.0 375170 1	14 150	16 0
22	Egypt 0 1	Israel 0 5	791201 0 0	0 0 3	0.5 1714530 —	1.0 4517002 —	0 37	0 5
23	Egypt 0	Libya 0	791201 0	0 0	0.5 1714530	0.0 3000000	0 37	0 5

#	actor d15 democ	target d11 conc	date e15 coher	war e11 reg	edt-1 imil mktg	edt-2 jmil sig	c15 avg	c11 autoc
	1	5	0	3	—	—		
24	Egypt	Sudan	791201	0	0.0	0.0	0	1
	0	0	0	0	1714530	329566	37	5
	1	5	0	3	—	—		
25	Zimbabwe	Botswana	670701	0	0.0	0.0	0	
	0	0	0	0	201600	0	50	3
	7	4	1	4	—	—		
26	Zimbabwe	Mozambique	670701	0	0.0	0.0	0	0
	0	0	0	0	20160	—	50	3
	7	4	1	4	—	—		
27	Zimbabwe	S. Africa	670701	0	0.0	0.0	0	0
	0	0	0	0	20160	325462	50	3
	7	4	1	4	—	—		
28	Zimbabwe	Zambia	670701	0	1.0	1.0	0	0
	0	0	0	0	20160	40325	50	3
	7	4	1	4	—	—		
29	Venezuela	Brazil	820601	0	0.0	0.0	0	0
	0	0	0	0	1142338	1838775	25	0
	8	6	1	5	—	—		
30	Venezuela	Colombia	820601	0	0.0	0.5	0	1
	0	0	0	1	1142338	420228	25	0
	8	6	1	5	—	—		
31	Venezuela	Guyana	820601	0	1.0	1.0	0	1
	0	3	0	0	1142338	23000	25	0
	8	6	1	5	—	—		
32	Sri Lanka	India	720701	0	0.0	0.0	0	0
	0	0	0	0	28328	2133921	37	0
	8	3	1	2	—	—		
33	Iran	Afghanistan	770801	0	0.0	0.0	0	0
	0	0	0	0	7972585	52289	25	10
	0	7	1	4	—	—		
34	Iran	Iraq	770801	0	0.0	0.0	0	0
	0	0	0	0	7972585	2008127	25	10
	0	7	1	4	—	—		
35	Iran	Kuwait	770801	0	0.0	0.0	0	0
	0	0	0	0	7972585	1040139	25	10
	0	7	1	4	—	—		
36	Iran	Oman	770801	0	0.0	0.0	0	0
	0	0	0	0	7972585	686161	25	10
	0	7	1	4	—	—		
37	Iran	Pakistan	770801	0	0.0	0.0	0	0
	0	0	0	0	7972585	878485	25	10
	0	7	1	4	—	—		

#	actor d15 democ	target d11 conc	date e15 coher	war e11 reg	edt-1 imil mktg	edt-2 jmil sig	c15 avg	c11 autoc
38	Iran	Saudi Arabia	770801	0	0.0	0.0	0	0
	0	0	0	0	7972585	8961448	25	10
	0	7	1	4	—	—		
39	Iran	Turkey	770801	0	0.0	0.0	0	0
	0	0	0	0	7972585	2765803	25	10
	0	7	1	4	—	—		
40	Iran	UAE	770801	0	0.0	0.0	0	0
	0	0	0	0	7972585	—	25	10
	0	7	1	4	—	—		
41	Iran	USSR	770801	0	0.0	0.0	0	0
	0	0	0	0	7972585	1.49E+08	25	10
	0	7	1	4	—	—		
42	China (PRC)	Afghanistan	650301	0	0.0	0.0	0	0
	0	0	0	0	1.38E+07	13865	25	9
	1	7	1	4	—	—		
43	China (PRC)	Myanmar	650301	0	0.0	0.0	0	0
	0	0	0	0	1.38E+07	107747	25	9
	1	7	1	4	—	—		
44	China (PRC)	China (ROC)	650301	0	0.0	0.0	0	1
	0	0	0	0	1.38E+07	319202	25	9
	1	7	1	4	—	—		
45	China (PRC)	India	650301	0	0.0	1.0	0	0
	0	0	0	0	1.38E+07	1804170	25	9
	1	7	1	4	—	—		
46	China (PRC)	Japan	650301	0	1.0	0.0	0	0
	0	0	0	0	1.38E+07	852603	25	9
	1	7	1	4	—	—		
47	China (PRC)	N. Korea	650301	0	0.0	0.0	0	0
	0	0	0	0	1.38E+07	350000	25	9
	1	7	1	4	—	—		
48	China (PRC)	S. Korea	650301	0	1.0	0.0	0	0
	0	0	0	0	1.38E+07	111990	25	9
	1	7	1	4	—	—		
49	China (PRC)	Laos	650301	0	0.0	0.0	0	0
	0	0	0	0	1.38E+07	26600	25	9
	1	7	1	4	—	—		
50	China (PRC)	Mongolia	650301	0	0.0	0.0	0	0
	0	0	0	0	1.38E+07	25000	25	9
	1	7	1	4	—	—		
51	China (PRC)	Nepal	650301	0	0.0	0.0	0	0
	0	0	0	0	1.38E+07	5499	25	9
	1	7	1	4	—	—		

#	actor d15 democ	target d11 conc	date e15 coher	war e11 reg	edt-1 imil mktg	edt-2 jmil sig	c15 avg	c11 autoc
52	China (PRC)	Pakistan	650301	0	0.0	0.0	0	0
	0	0	0	0	1.38E+07	428512	25	9
	1	7	1	4	—	—		
53	China (PRC)	Thailand	650301	0	0.0	0.0	0	0
	0	0	0	0	1.38E+07	94287	25	9
	1	7	1	4	—	—		
54	China (PRC)	U.K.–Hong Kong	650301	0	0.0	0.0	0	0
	0	0	0	0	1.38E+07	—	25	9
	1	7	1	4	—	—		
55	China (PRC)	USSR	650301	0	0.0	0.0	0	1
	0	0	0	0	1.38E+07	4.60E+07	25	9
	1	7	1	4	—	—		
56	China (PRC)	Vietnam	650301	0	0.0	0.0	0	0
	0	0	0	0	1.38E+07	—	25	9
	1	7	1	4	—	—		
57	Domin. Rep.	Haiti	700501	0	1.0	0.0	0	0
	0	0	0	0	31600	7160	50	4
	2	4	0	3	—	—		
58	Chile	Argentina	731001	0	0.0	0.0	0	0
	0	0	0	0	378378	468085	50	6
	0	5	0	1	—	—		
59	Chile	Bolivia	731001	0	0.0	0.0	0	1
	0	1	0	0	378378	20900	50	6
	0	5	0	1	—	—		
60	Chile	Peru	731001	0	0.0	0.0	0	0
	0	0	0	0	378378	324470	50	6
	0	5	0	1	—	—		
61	Japan	Australia	760601	0	0.0	0.0	0	0
	0	0	0	0	4972179	2751572	50	0
	10	5	1	5	—	—		
62	Japan	China (PRC)	760601	0	0.0	0.0	0	0
	0	0	0	0	4972179	3.17E+07	50	0
	10	5	1	5	—	—		
63	Japan	China (ROC)	760601	0	0.0	0.0	0	0
	0	0	0	0	4972179	1202631	50	0
	10	5	1	5	—	—		
64	Japan	Indonesia	760601	0	0.0	0.0	0	0
	0	0	0	0	4972179	1404819	50	0
	10	5	1	5	—	—		
65	Japan	N. Korea	760601	0	0.0	1.0	0	0
	0	0	0	0	4972179	1003962	50	0
	10	5	1	5	—	—		

#	actor d15 democ	target d11 conc	date e15 coher	war e11 reg	edt-1 imil mktg	edt-2 jmil sig	c15 avg	c11 autoc
66	Japan	S. Korea	760601	0	0.0	0.0	0	0
	0	0	0	0	4972179	876033	50	0
	10	5	1	5	—	—		
67	Japan	Malaysia	760601	0	0.0	0.0	0	0
	0	0	0	0	4972179	479619	50	0
	10	5	1	5	—	—		
68	Japan	New Zealand	760601	0	0.0	0.0	0	0
	0	0	0	0	4972179	209247	50	0
	10	5	1	5	—	—		
69	Japan	P. New Guinea	760601	0	0.0	0.0	0	0
	0	0	0	0	4972179	25000	50	0
	10	5	1	5	—	—		
70	Japan	Singapore	760601	0	0.0	0.0	0	0
	0	0	0	0	4972179	313259	50	0
	10	5	1	5	—	—		
71	Japan	U.S.	760601	0	0.0	0.5	0	0
	0	0	0	0	4972179	9.10E+07	50	0
	10	5	1	5	—	—		
72	Japan	USSR	760601	0	0.0	0.5	0	0
	0	1	0	0	4972179	1.38E+08	50	0
	10	5	1	5	—	—		
73	Japan	Vietnam	760601	0	0.0	0.0	0	0
	0	0	0	0	4972179	—	50	0
	10	5	1	5	—	—		
74	Israel	Egypt	820101	0	0.0	0.0	0	0
	0	0	0	0	8241308	2494532	25	0
	10	5	1	5	—	—		
75	Israel	Jordan	820101	0	0.0	0.0	0	0
	0	0	0	0	8241308	518769	25	0
	10	5	1	5	—	—		
76	Israel	Lebanon	820101	0	0.0	0.0	0	2
	0	2	0	2	8241308	331000	25	0
	10	5	1	5	—	—		
77	Israel	Syria	820101	0	0.5	0.0	0	2
	0	0	0	0	8241308	2548606	25	0
	10	5	1	5	—	—		
78	Italy	Ethiopia	691101	0	0.0	0.0	0	0
	0	0	0	0	2265000	37400	37	0
	10	5	1	5	—	—		
79	Italy	France	691101	0	0.0	0.0	0	0
	0	0	0	0	2265000	5761015	37	0
	10	5	1	5	—	—		
80	Italy	Switzerland	691101	0	0.0	0.0	0	0

#	actor d15 democ	target d11 conc	date e15 coher	war e11 reg	edt-1 imil mktg	edt-2 jmil sig	c15 avg	c11 autoc
	0	0	0	0	2265000	439098	37	0
	10	5	1	5	—	—		
81	Italy	Yugoslavia	691101	0	0.0	0.0	0	0
	0	0	0	0	2265000	558400	37	0
	10	5	1	5	—	—		
82	Uganda	Kenya	661001	0	0.0	0.0	0	0
	0	0	0	0	14282	13162	25	6
	1	6	0	1	—	—		
83	Uganda	Rwanda	661001	0	0.0	0.0	0	0
	0	0	0	0	14282	4800	25	6
	1	6	0	1	—	—		
84	Uganda	Sudan	661001	0	0.0	0.0	0	0
	0	0	0	0	14282	45089	25	6
	1	6	0	1	—	—		
85	Uganda	Tanzania	661001	0	0.0	0.0	0	0
	0	0	0	0	14282	8121	25	6
	1	6	0	1	—	—		
86	Uganda	Zaire	661001	0	0.0	0.0	0	0
	0	0	0	0	14282	32000	25	6
	1	6	0	1	—	—		
87	Thailand	Indonesia	750501	0	0.0	0.0	0	0
	0	0	0	0	512193	1195180	37	0
	8	3	1	2	—	—		
88	Thailand	Kampuchea	750501	0	0.0	1.0	0	0
	0	1	0	0	512193	67008	37	0
	8	3	1	2	—	—		
89	Thailand	Laos	750501	0	0.0	0.0	0	0
	0	0	0	0	512193	19000	37	0
	8	3	1	2	—	—		
90	Thailand	Malaysia	750501	0	0.0	0.0	0	0
	0	0	0	0	512193	547135	37	0
	8	3	1	2	—	—		
91	Thailand	Myanmar	750501	0	1.0	0.0	0	0
	0	0	0	0	512193	138049	37	0
	8	3	1	2	—	—		
92	Mexico	Guatemala	700701	0	0.0	1.0	0	0
	0	0	0	1	218014	17200	25	6
	1	4	0	4	—	—		
93	Mexico	U.K.-Belize	700701	0	0.0	0.0	0	0
	0	0	0	0	218014	—	25	6
	1	4	0	4	—	—		
94	Mexico	U.S.	700701	0	0.0	2.0	0	0
	0	0	0	0	218014	7.78E+07	25	6

#	actor	target	date	war	edt-1	edt-2	c15	c11
	d15	d11	e15	e11	imil	jmil	avg	autoc
	democ	conc	coher	reg	mktg	sig		
	1	4	0	4	—	—		
95	Nigeria	Benin	661001	0	0.0	0.0	0	0
	0	0	0	0	61327	3646	25	7
	0	6	1	4	—	—		
96	Nigeria	Cameroon	661001	0	0.0	0.0	0	0
	0	0	0	0	61327	17825	25	7
	0	6	1	4	—	—		
97	Nigeria	Chad	661001	0	0.0	0.0	0	0
	0	0	0	0	61327	5777	25	7
	0	6	1	4	—	—		
98	Nigeria	Niger	661001	0	0.0	0.0	0	0
	0	0	0	0	61327	2783	25	7
	0	6	1	4	—	—		
99	Kenya	Ethiopia	780401	0	0.0	0.0	0	0
	0	0	0	0	205000	202898	50	7
	1	6	1	4	—	—		
100	Kenya	Somalia	780401	0	1.0	1.0	0	0
	0	0	0	0	205000	66719	50	7
	1	6	1	4	—	—		
101	Kenya	Sudan	780401	0	0.0	0.0	0	0
	0	0	0	0	205000	206814	50	7
	1	6	1	4	—	—		
102	Kenya	Tanzania	780401	0	0.0	0.0	0	0
	0	0	0	0	205000	264913	50	7
	1	6	1	4	—	—		
103	Kenya	Uganda	780401	0	0.0	0.0	0	0
	0	0	0	0	205000	156012	50	7
	1	6	1	4	—	—		
104	N. Korea	China-PRC	800301	0	0.0	0.0	0	0
	0	0	0	0	1416585	2.85E+07	25	8
	1	7	1	4	—	—		
105	N. Korea	Japan	800301	0	0.0	0.0	0	0
	0	0	0	0	1416585	9297521	25	8
	1	7	1	4	—	—		
106	N. Korea	S. Korea	800301	0	0.0	0.0	0	1
	0	0	0	0	1416585	3308760	25	8
	1	7	1	4	—	—		
107	N. Korea	USSR	800301	0	0.0	0.0	0	0
	0	0	0	0	1416585	2.01E+08	25	8
	1	7	1	4	—	—		
108	Malaysia	Indonesia	770601	0	0.0	0.0	0	0
	0	0	0	0	616341	2183132	50	0
	10	3	1	5	—	—		

#	actor d15 democ	target d11 conc	date e15 coher	war e11 reg	edt-1 imil mktg	edt-2 jmil sig	c15 avg	c11 autoc
109	Malaysia	Philippines	770601	0	0.0	0.0	0	0
	0	0	0	0	616341	549792	50	0
	10	3	1	5	—	—		
110	Malaysia	Thailand	770601	0	0.0	0.0	0	0
	0	0	0	0	616341	637255	50	0
	10	3	1	5	—	—		
111	Peru	Bolivia	740201	0	0.0	0.0	0	0
	0	0	0	0	364041	39350	50	7
	0	6	1	4	—	—		
112	Peru	Brazil	740201	0	0.0	0.0	0	0
	0	0	0	0	364041	1287187	50	7
	0	6	1	4	—	—		
113	Peru	Chile	740201	0	0.0	0.0	0	0
	0	1	0	0	364041	530048	50	7
	0	6	1	4	—	—		
114	Peru	Colombia	740201	0	0.0	0.0	0	0
	0	0	0	0	364041	113183	50	7
	0	6	1	4	—	—		
115	Peru	Ecuador	740201	0	0.0	0.0	0	0
	0	0	0	0	364041	71600	50	7
	0	6	1	4	—	—		
116	Tanzania	Burundi	780701	0	0.0	0.0	0	0
	0	0	0	0	264913	16000	25	7
	1	5	1	4	—	—		
117	Tanzania	Kenya	780701	0	0.0	0.0	0	0
	0	0	0	0	264913	205000	25	7
	1	5	1	4	—	—		
118	Tanzania	Malawi	780701	0	0.0	0.0	0	0
	0	0	0	0	264913	21097	25	7
	1	5	1	4	—	—		
119	Tanzania	Mozambique	780701	0	0.0	0.0	0	0
	0	0	0	0	264913	—	25	7
	1	5	1	4	—	—		
120	Tanzania	Rwanda	780701	0	0.0	0.0	0	0
	0	0	0	0	264913	11327	25	7
	1	5	1	4	—	—		
121	Tanzania	Uganda	780701	0	0.0	0.0	0	0
	0	0	0	1	264913	156012	25	7
	1	5	1	4	—	—		
122	Tanzania	Zaire	780701	0	0.0	0.0	0	0
	0	0	0	0	264913	45455	25	7
	1	5	1	4	—	—		

#	actor	target	date	war	edt-1	edt-2	c15	c11
	d15	d11	e15	e11	imil	jmil	avg	autoc
	democ	conc	coher	reg	mktg	sig		
123	Tanzania	Zambia	780701	0	0.0	0.0	0	0
	0	0	0	0	264913	76000	25	7
	1	5	1	4	—	—		
124	Uruguay	Argentina	731101	0	0.0	0.0	0	0
	0	0	0	0	68571	468085	75	8
	1	6	1	4	—	—		
125	Uruguay	Brazil	731101	0	0.0	0.0	0	0
	0	0	0	0	68571	1100229	75	8
	1	6	1	4	—	—		
126	Zambia	Angola	830301	0	0.0	0.0	0	0
	0	0	0	0	378665	—	25	7
	1	6	1	4	—	—		
127	Zambia	Botswana	830301	0	0.0	0.0	0	0
	0	0	0	0	378665	26000	25	7
	1	6	1	4	—	—		
128	Zambia	Malawi	830301	0	1.0	0.0	0	0
	0	0	0	0	378665	23945	25	7
	1	6	1	4	—	—		
129	Zambia	S.A.-Namibia	830301	0	1.0	0.0	0	0
	0	0	0	0	378665	3306705	25	7
	1	6	1	4	—	—		
130	Zambia	Tanzania	830301	0	0.0	0.0	0	0
	0	0	0	0	378665	123131	25	7
	1	6	1	4	—	—		
131	Zambia	Zaire	830301	0	0.0	0.0	0	0
	0	0	0	0	378665	140080	25	7
	1	6	1	4	—	—		
132	Zambia	Zimbabwe	830301	0	0.0	0.0	0	0
	0	0	0	0	378665	378076	25	7
	1	6	1	4	—	—		
133	Ethiopia	Kenya	810401	0	0.0	0.0	0	0
	0	0	0	0	440032	222000	25	5
	0	4	0	4	—	—		
134	Ethiopia	Somalia	810401	0	0.0	0.0	0	0
	0	0	0	0	440032	162042	25	5
	0	4	0	4	—	—		
135	Ethiopia	Sudan	810401	0	0.0	0.0	0	0
	0	0	0	0	440032	311009	25	5
	0	4	0	4	—	—		
136	Guatemala	El Salvador	720401	0	0.0	0.0	0	0
	0	0	0	0	22500	12520	25	1
	5	3	0	3	—	—		

#	actor d15 democ	target d11 conc	date e15 coher	war e11 reg	edt-1 imil mktg	edt-2 jmil sig	c15 avg	c11 autoc
137	Guatemala 0 5	Honduras 0 3	720401 0 0	0 0 3	0.0 22500 —	0.0 15450 —	0 25	0 1
138	Guatemala 0 5	Mexico 0 3	720401 0 0	0 0 3	0.0 22500 —	0.0 260800 —	0 25	0 1
139	Guatemala 0 5	UK-Belize 0 3	720401 0 0	0 0 3	0.0 22500 —	0.0 — —	0 25	0 1

1.3: Data Set 3

Variable	Description
case	case number
year	year
mnth	month (1–12)
ecnt	count of COPDAB events (score > 10) from Egypt to Israel
jcnt	count of COPDAB events (score > 10) from Jordan to Israel
lcnt	count of COPDAB events (score > 10) from Lebanon to Israel
scnt	count of COPDAB events (score > 10) from Syria to Israel
esum	sum of weighted COPDAB events from Egypt to Israel
jsum	sum of weighted COPDAB events from Jordan to Israel
lsum	sum of weighted COPDAB events from Lebanon to Israel
ssum	sum of weighted COPDAB events from Syria to Israel
iecnt	count of COPDAB events from Israel to Egypt
ijcnt	count of COPDAB events from Israel to Jordan
ilcnt	count of COPDAB events from Israel to Lebanon
iscnt	count of COPDAB events from Israel to Syria
iesum	sum of weighted COPDAB events from Israel to Egypt
ijsum	sum of weighted COPDAB events from Israel to Jordan
ilsum	sum of weighted COPDAB events from Israel to Lebanon
issum	sum of weighted COPDAB events from Israel to Syria
eted	number of critical editorials directed against Egypt
jted	number of critical editorials directed against Jordan
lted	number of critical editorials directed against Lebanon
sted	number of critical editorials directed against Syria

case iecnt	year ijcnt	mnth ilcnt	ecnt iscnt	jcnt iesum	lcnt ijsum	scnt ilsum	esum issum	jsum eted	lsum jted	ssum lted	sted
1 0	1966 0	1 0	0 5	0 0	0 0	5 0	0 212	0 0	0 0	148 0	0

| case | year | mnth | ecnt | jcnt | lcnt | scnt | esum | jsum | lsum | ssum | |
iecnt	ijcnt	ilcnt	iscnt	iesum	ijsum	ilsum	issum	eted	jted	lted	sted
2	1966	2	2	1	0	2	32	65	0	100	
0	1	0	3	0	50	0	165	0	0	0	1
3	1966	3	0	1	0	0	0	29	0	0	
0	1	0	0	0	50	0	0	0	0	0	0
4	1966	4	1	2	0	1	16	130	0	50	
1	3	0	2	16	116	0	130	0	0	0	1
5	1966	5	1	3	1	4	16	76	29	77	
0	3	0	1	0	95	0	16	0	1	0	0
6	1966	6	0	0	1	1	0	0	50	29	
0	0	1	0	0	0	65	0	0	0	0	0
7	1966	7	1	1	1	4	16	16	16	111	
1	0	0	3	16	0	0	97	0	0	0	2
8	1966	8	1	0	0	5	29	0	0	161	
0	0	0	5	0	0	0	129	0	0	0	3
9	1966	9	0	0	0	7	0	0	0	180	
0	1	0	2	0	16	0	32	1	0	0	2
10	1966	10	1	5	0	12	16	163	0	367	
0	7	0	5	0	229	0	129	0	0	0	2
11	1966	11	1	5	1	9	16	191	16	327	
1	4	0	6	65	175	0	194	0	1	0	1
12	1966	12	0	3	0	1	0	76	0	50	
1	2	0	3	50	32	0	97	0	0	0	0
13	1967	1	3	3	0	17	97	82	0	578	
3	1	0	23	134	65	0	760	0	0	0	2
14	1967	2	1	0	1	11	16	0	16	278	
0	0	1	7	0	0	44	244	0	0	0	1
15	1967	3	0	1	0	1	0	65	0	16	
0	2	1	5	0	66	16	129	0	0	0	1
16	1967	4	1	2	0	12	16	94	0	411	
0	1	1	9	0	50	44	512	0	0	0	4

| case | year | mnth | ecnt | jcnt | lcnt | scnt | esum | jsum | lsum | ssum | |
iecnt	ijcnt	ilcnt	iscnt	iesum	ijsum	ilsum	issum	eted	jted	lted	sted
17	1967	5	22	4	3	10	821	132	95	233	
10	3	1	5	284	61	16	129	7	1	0	6
18	1967	6	27	16	3	32	917	545	95	1427	
53	17	2	18	3144	839	204	988	2	4	0	0
19	1967	7	17	4	1	9	899	64	16	212	
23	3	0	6	1006	74	0	194	3	1	0	0
20	1967	8	3	7	0	2	134	210	0	32	
6	10	0	3	179	280	0	97	0	3	0	0
21	1967	9	16	5	1	2	853	157	16	32	
11	3	0	3	425	108	0	125	1	2	0	0
22	1967	10	11	2	1	4	370	115	16	64	
9	5	0	4	384	161	0	98	2	1	0	2
23	1967	11	3	8	0	5	61	260	0	114	
4	7	0	3	113	297	0	82	0	2	0	0
24	1967	12	4	3	1	3	175	110	29	48	
6	4	0	0	184	124	0	0	0	0	0	0
25	1968	1	4	9	0	0	190	340	0	0	
6	7	0	0	145	327	0	0	1	0	0	0
26	1968	2	0	5	0	1	0	240	0	16	
2	4	0	0	81	147	0	0	0	2	0	0
27	1968	3	2	9	0	0	32	389	0	0	
1	9	0	0	50	393	0	0	0	1	0	0
28	1968	4	7	10	0	2	210	407	0	66	
2	8	0	0	81	390	0	0	0	0	0	0
29	1968	5	6	4	4	1	207	211	77	16	
7	3	0	0	276	165	0	0	1	0	0	0
30	1968	6	6	10	2	1	271	418	66	16	
9	7	1	1	495	244	50	16	0	0	0	0
31	1968	7	9	4	0	0	402	175	0	0	
4	2	0	0	179	130	0	0	1	0	0	0

case / iecnt	year / ijcnt	mnth / ilcnt	ecnt / iscnt	jcnt / iesum	lcnt / ijsum	scnt / ilsum	esum / issum	jsum / eted	lsum / jted	ssum / lted	sted
32	1968	8	3	8	0	3	180	373	0	95	
3	7	0	2	116	389	0	66	2	1	0	0
33	1968	9	12	7	0	2	559	342	0	100	
9	3	0	3	381	195	0	174	3	0	0	0
34	1968	10	10	5	0	5	443	246	0	182	
12	4	1	3	512	209	50	165	1	1	0	0
35	1968	11	6	11	1	2	190	557	29	66	
4	8	0	1	147	377	0	50	2	1	0	0
36	1968	12	6	4	3	0	158	211	76	0	
4	10	2	1	184	492	60	44	0	1	3	0
37	1969	1	1	3	4	0	65	174	145	0	
0	4	1	0	0	209	65	0	1	0	1	0
38	1969	2	4	2	0	1	98	66	0	50	
2	5	1	3	32	197	16	183	0	0	1	0
39	1969	3	10	6	0	2	454	292	0	66	
11	4	0	2	704	233	0	81	3	0	0	0
40	1969	4	13	4	0	0	600	260	0	0	
16	8	0	3	931	358	0	48	2	0	0	0
41	1969	5	9	6	1	2	438	228	16	79	
10	5	0	1	405	182	0	65	3	2	1	1
42	1969	6	11	6	1	0	517	130	16	0	
12	11	0	2	953	440	0	32	2	0	0	0
43	1969	7	22	5	0	3	1134	227	0	82	
22	3	1	2	1245	165	65	130	8	1	0	0
44	1969	8	11	4	6	4	553	211	145	166	
14	7	3	6	776	293	97	179	1	2	2	1
45	1969	9	1	0	1	0	16	0	16	0	
5	1	1	0	338	65	65	0	3	0	0	3
46	1969	10	5	0	0	0	227	0	0	0	
2	2	0	2	167	130	0	81	0	0	2	1

case	year	mnth	ecnt	jcnt	lcnt	scnt	esum	jsum	lsum	ssum	
iecnt	ijcnt	ilcnt	iscnt	iesum	ijsum	ilsum	issum	eted	jted	lted	sted
47	1969	11	11	0	0	0	600	0	0	0	
8	2	2	0	496	130	32	0	2	0	1	0
48	1969	12	2	2	2	1	115	115	115	50	
6	3	1	2	397	195	65	115	3	0	1	0
49	1970	1	13	2	0	2	668	130	0	115	
23	4	2	1	1675	230	130	50	2	1	3	0
50	1970	2	16	1	0	4	893	16	0	132	
12	1	0	4	793	65	0	245	6	1	0	1
51	1970	3	6	2	1	3	311	66	50	150	
13	2	4	4	833	130	162	211	2	0	2	1
52	1970	4	5	0	0	2	276	0	0	115	
12	1	1	2	790	50	65	130	5	1	0	3
53	1970	5	12	2	3	2	744	130	110	79	
17	3	5	0	1340	165	227	0	2	0	3	1
54	1970	6	11	2	0	6	617	94	0	390	
17	0	1	8	1325	0	65	407	3	1	0	1
55	1970	7	12	0	0	1	682	0	0	50	
16	3	1	0	1521	165	65	0	3	1	0	0
56	1970	8	5	2	0	1	212	32	0	16	
5	2	2	0	142	94	130	0	5	0	0	0
57	1970	9	3	0	3	0	48	0	97	0	
5	1	1	1	80	16	65	16	0	0	0	1
58	1970	10	1	1	0	0	16	16	0	0	
5	0	0	0	80	0	0	0	2	0	0	0
59	1970	11	1	0	0	0	16	0	0	0	
4	1	0	0	64	65	0	0	1	0	0	0
60	1970	12	2	1	0	0	73	16	0	0	
2	0	1	0	81	0	65	0	0	0	0	0
61	1971	1	13	5	1	2	305	157	16	45	
9	1	3	0	241	50	195	0	0	1	0	0

case	year	mnth	ecnt	jcnt	lcnt	scnt	esum	jsum	lsum	ssum	
iecnt	ijcnt	ilcnt	iscnt	iesum	ijsum	ilsum	issum	eted	jted	lted	sted
62	1971	2	3	1	1	1	48	29	44	16	
6	0	0	0	109	0	0	0	4	0	0	0
63	1971	3	7	2	0	1	146	32	0	16	
4	1	1	0	64	16	65	0	0	0	0	0
64	1971	4	7	1	2	0	153	16	45	0	
3	0	2	1	110	0	94	16	0	0	0	0
65	1971	5	0	0	0	0	0	0	0	0	
0	0	0	0	0	0	0	0	0	0	0	0
66	1971	6	1	0	1	0	16	0	50	0	
0	0	0	0	0	0	0	0	1	1	0	0
67	1971	7	1	0	0	0	16	0	0	0	
0	0	0	0	0	0	0	0	1	0	0	0
68	1971	8	0	0	1	2	0	0	50	32	
3	0	0	1	110	0	0	16	0	1	0	0
69	1971	9	6	1	0	2	271	16	0	66	
6	0	0	1	228	0	0	16	1	0	0	0
70	1971	10	9	1	0	3	232	16	0	61	
1	0	0	0	16	0	0	0	0	0	0	0
71	1971	11	7	1	0	0	164	50	0	0	
2	0	0	0	32	0	0	0	2	0	0	1
72	1971	12	5	2	1	2	106	32	16	32	
5	1	1	1	178	29	16	16	2	0	0	0
73	1972	1	8	1	4	4	167	16	111	126	
1	1	4	7	16	16	199	259	0	0	0	0
74	1972	2	7	0	8	4	112	0	128	98	
2	2	4	2	66	81	199	115	0	0	0	0
75	1972	3	5	1	4	3	80	16	64	144	
2	2	2	3	32	45	81	146	0	0	1	0
76	1972	4	3	0	0	0	61	0	0	0	
1	0	0	0	16	0	0	0	0	0	0	0

| case | year | mnth | ecnt | jcnt | lcnt | scnt | esum | jsum | lsum | ssum | |
iecnt	ijcnt	ilcnt	iscnt	iesum	ijsum	ilsum	issum	eted	jted	lted	sted
77	1972	5	2	0	1	1	32	0	16	16	
2	1	1	1	32	16	16	16	3	0	0	0
78	1972	6	10	2	11	2	290	32	223	66	
1	0	6	5	50	0	247	163	0	0	0	1
79	1972	7	5	0	1	2	148	0	16	32	
2	0	2	1	45	0	66	29	1	0	2	1
80	1972	8	1	1	0	0	65	16	0	0	
0	0	0	2	0	0	0	81	0	0	0	0
81	1972	9	3	1	8	11	48	16	196	559	
2	1	8	14	32	29	294	473	0	0	1	0
82	1972	10	5	0	2	5	166	0	32	163	
1	0	1	3	16	0	50	131	1	0	0	0
83	1972	11	2	0	4	19	45	0	77	634	
2	1	0	14	66	16	0	537	2	0	0	2
84	1972	12	1	2	1	5	29	45	29	161	
3	0	0	8	48	0	0	309	0	0	0	0
85	1973	1	3	2	1	7	48	60	29	229	
1	0	0	12	29	0	0	484	1	0	0	1
86	1973	2	7	1	1	1	245	16	16	50	
2	0	2	2	81	0	32	60	0	0	1	0
87	1973	3	4	0	1	0	77	0	50	0	
0	1	1	1	0	29	50	16	3	0	0	1
88	1973	4	6	2	2	2	135	32	32	45	
4	1	1	1	77	50	16	16	0	0	0	0
89	1973	5	3	0	0	0	162	0	0	0	
1	1	1	3	16	16	16	48	2	0	2	0
90	1973	6	7	1	0	5	232	16	0	114	
3	0	1	4	48	0	29	111	0	0	0	0
91	1973	7	2	1	1	2	32	29	16	45	
0	1	0	2	0	16	0	32	2	0	0	0

| case | year | mnth | ecnt | jcnt | lcnt | scnt | esum | jsum | lsum | ssum | |
iecnt	ijcnt	ilcnt	iscnt	iesum	ijsum	ilsum	issum	eted	jted	lted	sted
92	1973	8	5	0	6	1	166	0	96	50	
7	0	2	3	195	0	58	82	0	0	0	0
93	1973	9	1	2	0	6	16	45	0	205	
1	0	0	5	16	0	0	129	0	0	0	1
94	1973	10	70	10	5	56	4525	419	93	3205	
77	4	2	43	4604	211	81	2860	14	0	0	8
95	1973	11	11	0	2	12	480	0	66	294	
16	0	2	10	538	0	115	258	5	0	0	1
96	1973	12	15	1	0	12	840	29	0	294	
13	0	1	5	632	0	50	197	4	0	0	2
97	1974	1	11	0	0	9	554	0	0	416	
14	0	0	10	612	0	0	567	0	0	0	1
98	1974	2	0	1	0	7	0	16	0	472	
0	0	0	11	0	0	0	580	0	1	0	5
99	1974	3	0	1	0	15	0	16	0	593	
1	0	0	13	16	0	0	721	2	0	0	2
100	1974	4	2	0	7	23	32	0	310	1366	
1	0	4	21	16	0	267	1192	0	0	2	1
101	1974	5	2	0	4	22	81	0	334	1351	
2	0	8	21	66	0	520	1105	0	0	0	2
102	1974	6	3	1	7	2	48	16	257	45	
1	0	7	1	16	0	391	44	0	0	2	0
103	1974	7	0	1	1	0	0	16	102	0	
0	0	6	1	0	0	311	16	0	0	1	0
104	1974	8	1	0	3	5	16	0	131	127	
1	1	7	1	16	29	419	50	0	0	0	2
105	1974	9	7	1	3	4	146	16	131	98	
0	0	8	3	0	0	439	95	0	0	0	0
106	1974	10	1	0	2	0	16	0	100	0	
1	0	5	2	16	0	295	45	1	0	0	0

case iecnt	year ijcnt	mnth ilcnt	ecnt iscnt	jcnt iesum	lcnt ijsum	scnt ilsum	esum issum	jsum eted	lsum jted	ssum lted	sted
107	1974	11	3	0	5	0	76	0	182	0	
1	0	9	4	16	0	525	64	1	0	0	0
108	1974	12	0	0	7	4	0	0	270	113	
1	0	4	2	16	0	181	32	1	0	0	0
109	1975	1	2	0	11	1	32	0	376	16	
0	0	8	2	0	0	366	32	2	0	2	0
110	1975	2	2	0	0	0	32	0	0	0	
1	0	0	1	16	0	0	16	2	0	0	1
111	1975	3	3	0	0	0	61	0	0	0	
1	0	2	0	16	0	79	0	2	0	0	2
112	1975	4	1	0	0	1	16	0	0	16	
0	0	0	0	0	0	0	0	0	0	1	0
113	1975	5	1	2	4	0	16	60	196	0	
0	2	4	0	0	45	209	0	0	0	1	1
114	1975	6	2	2	3	2	45	45	82	45	
2	1	2	2	45	16	115	45	1	0	0	0
115	1975	7	1	0	2	0	16	0	115	0	
2	0	2	0	45	0	100	0	0	0	2	0
116	1975	8	0	0	1	0	0	0	50	0	
0	0	3	0	0	0	150	0	0	0	1	0
117	1975	9	0	0	1	2	0	0	16	32	
0	0	2	1	0	0	152	16	0	0	1	0
118	1975	10	1	0	0	1	16	0	0	50	
0	0	0	0	0	0	0	0	0	0	1	1
119	1975	11	1	0	1	1	50	0	65	16	
1	0	1	0	65	0	65	0	0	0	1	3
120	1975	12	1	0	1	1	16	0	16	50	
0	0	1	0	0	0	65	0	0	0	2	1

1.4: Israeli Time Series

1966   1967

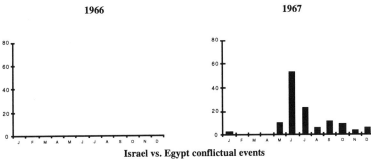

Israel vs. Egypt conflictual events

Israel vs. Egypt editorials

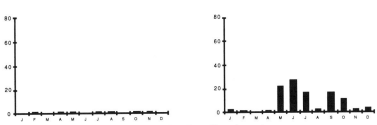

Egypt vs. Israel conflictual events

1968   **1969**

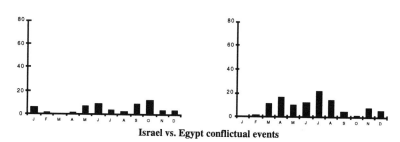

Israel vs. Egypt conflictual events

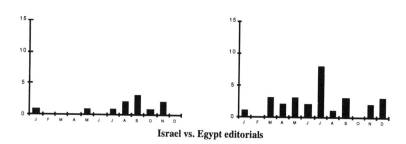

Israel vs. Egypt editorials

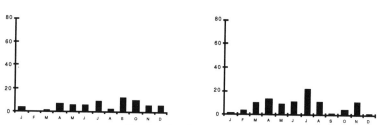

Egypt vs. Israel conflictual events

1970   **1971**

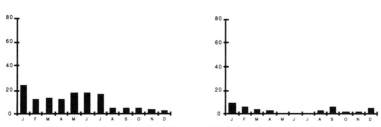

Israel vs. Egypt conflictual events

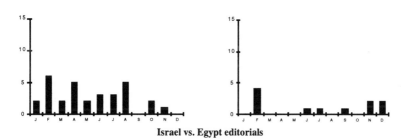

Israel vs. Egypt editorials

Egypt vs. Israel conflictual events

1972   **1973**

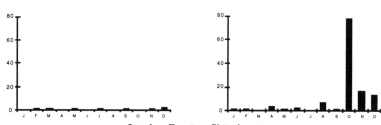

Israel vs. Egypt conflictual events

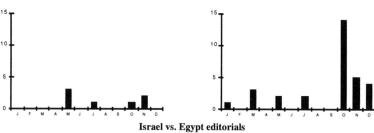

Israel vs. Egypt editorials

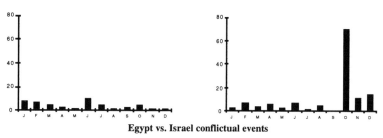

Egypt vs. Israel conflictual events

1974   **1975**

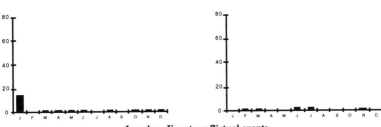

Israel vs. Egypt conflictual events

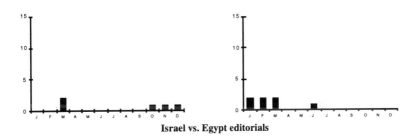

Israel vs. Egypt editorials

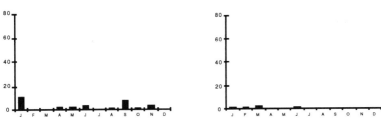

Egypt vs. Israel conflictual events

1966 **1967**

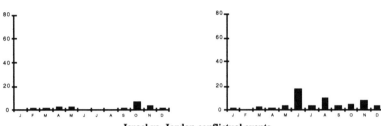

Israel vs. Jordan conflictual events

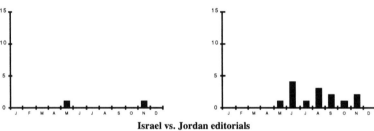

Israel vs. Jordan editorials

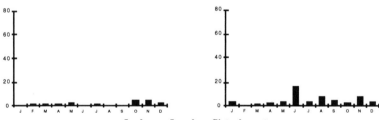

Jordan vs. Israel conflictual events

1968   **1969**

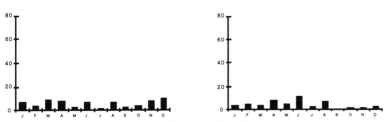

Israel vs. Jordan conflictual events

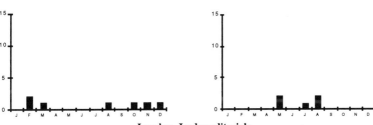

Israel vs. Jordan editorials

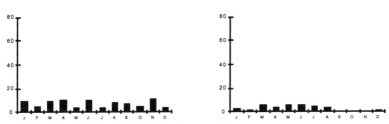

Jordan vs. Israel conflictual events

1970   **1971**

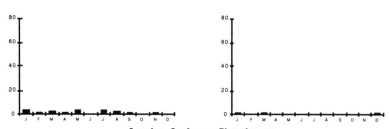

Israel vs. Jordan conflictual events

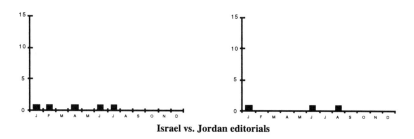

Israel vs. Jordan editorials

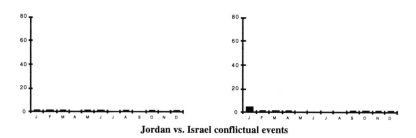

Jordan vs. Israel conflictual events

1972   1973

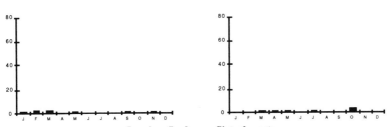

Israel vs. Jordan conflictual events

Israel vs. Jordan editorials

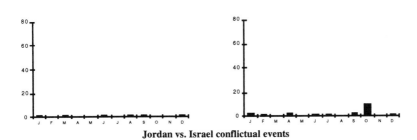

Jordan vs. Israel conflictual events

1974   **1975**

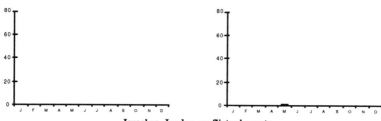

Israel vs. Jordan conflictual events

Israel vs. Jordan editorials

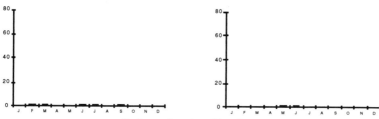

Jordan vs. Israel conflictual events

1966   **1967**

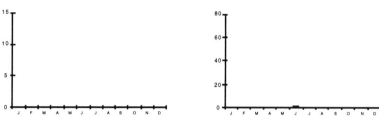

Israel vs. Lebanon conflictual events

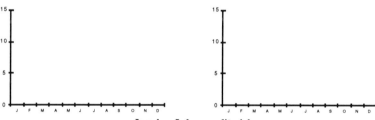

Israel vs. Lebanon editorials

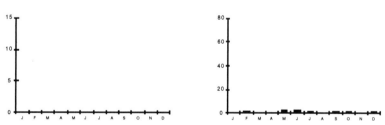

Lebanon vs. Israel conflictual events

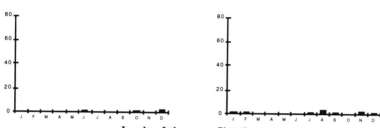

Israel vs. Lebanon conflictual events

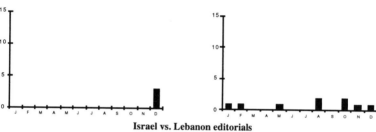

Israel vs. Lebanon editorials

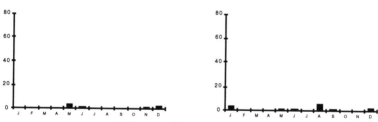

Lebanon vs. Israel conflictual events

1970　　　　　　　　　　**1971**

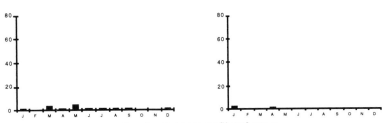

Israel vs. Lebanon conflictual events

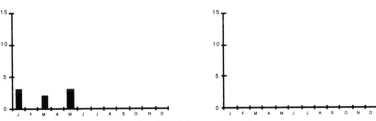

Israel vs. Lebanon editorials

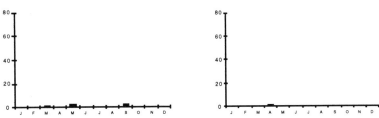

Lebanon vs. Israel conflictual events

1972   **1973**

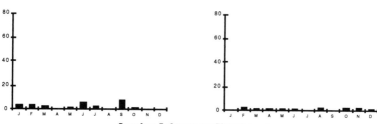

Israel vs. Lebanon conflictual events

Israel vs. Lebanon editorials

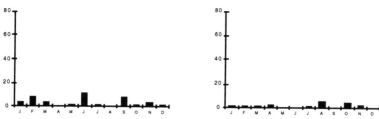

Lebanon vs. Israel conflictual events

1974   **1975**

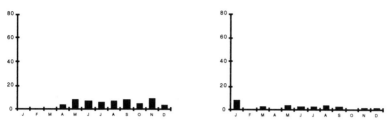

Israel vs. Lebanon conflictual events

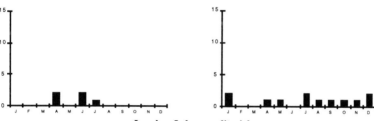

Israel vs. Lebanon editorials

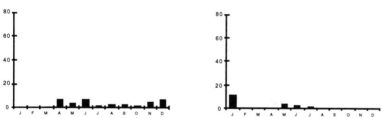

Lebanon vs. Israel conflictual events

1966   **1967**

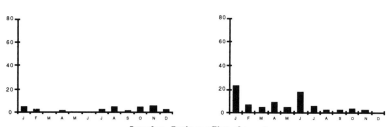

Israel vs. Syria conflictual events

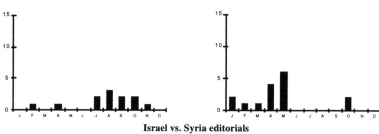

Israel vs. Syria editorials

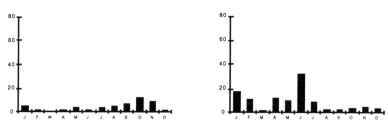

Syria vs. Israel conflictual events

1968   **1969**

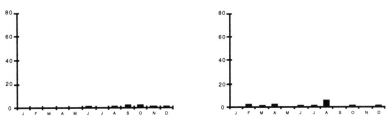

Israel vs. Syria conflictual events

Israel vs. Syria editorials

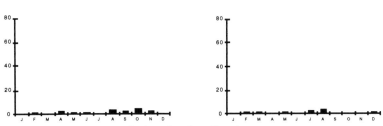

Syria vs. Israel conflictual events

1970   **1971**

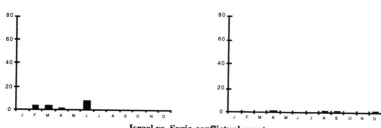

Israel vs. Syria conflictual events

Israel vs. Syria editorials

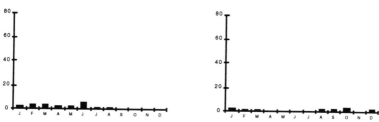

Syria vs. Israel conflictual events

1972   **1973**

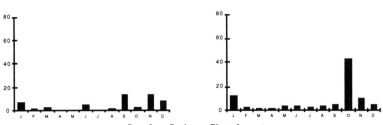

Israel vs. Syria conflictual events

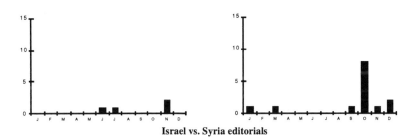

Israel vs. Syria editorials

Syria vs. Israel conflictual events

1974   **1975**

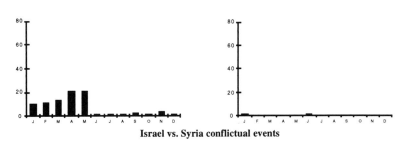

Israel vs. Syria conflictual events

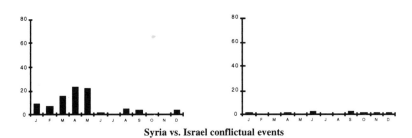

Israel vs. Syria editorials

Syria vs. Israel conflictual events

Appendix 2: Coding Instructions, Nations and Newspapers

2.1: Guide for Translators

Part A

This research project deals with the causes of international conflict. The backbone to this project is a model of state behavior, and editorials are one of the key variables in this model. Editorials provide a convenient way of measuring how much the nation in question likes or dislikes other nations. That is, if the national newspaper of the United States (for the sake of argument assume the *New York Times*) writes 100 editorials critical of Panama and 2 editorials critical of Mexico, then we can conclude that, all other things being equal, the United States dislikes Panama more than Mexico.

Using editorials in this manner allows us to calculate how much the nation in question would like to alter the behavior of some foreign nation. Other variables, such as GNP and military spending, are used to determine how much the nation in question is actually able to alter that nation's behavior. Both sets of variables are indispensable. For example, even if Cuba truly hates the United States, even if every editorial expresses wild hatred for the United States, the likelihood of Cuba starting a war with the United States is very low, since Cuba has very little actual ability to attack the United States. On the other hand, even though the United States has great ability to do harm to Cuba, unless the United States is very upset about Cuban behavior, as measured by editorials, the likelihood of conflict is again very low. The model combines the two sets of variables to determine the likelihood of conflict between the two nations. This measurement has shown great accuracy in a wide variety of tests on past conflicts and provides an excellent tool for predicting future conflicts.

The coding of these editorials requires a basic reading knowledge of the language in question and a rudimentary knowledge of current affairs. Detailed translations are not necessary nor are subjective evaluations of the issues raised by the editorials. If you can read the language in question with the aid of a dictionary and recognize the foreign nations and organizations mentioned in the editorials, you are qualified for this work.

For each day evaluated I need three pieces of information. First, how many editorials were published that day? Second, what foreign nations or organizations, if any, are mentioned that day? Third, why are they mentioned? Let's look at each of these questions in turn.

I need to know the total number of editorials written on any given day. Note that we are not interested in letters to the editor or opinion pieces written by guest columnists. All that requires evaluation here are those opinion pieces written under the direct auspices of the newspaper in question. In most Western newspapers these appear directly under the masthead on a specified and regular page. Some newspapers are problematic in this regard. If you are at all unclear about what actually constitutes the editorials in the paper you are assigned, please discuss the issue with one of the supervisors.

I am only interested in foreign nations and organizations mentioned by the paper in question. If an editorial is concerned with some domestic issue, skip it. If an editorial is concerned with international issues, write down any foreign nations or organizations mentioned by the editorial. If more than one foreign actor is discussed in one editorial, mark them all down, separating them with slash marks. If more than one editorial mentions foreign actors, evaluate each editorial separately. The most difficult evaluation for any translator comes when an editorial vaguely discusses some foreign actor. Try to resolve this problem with the following criteria. First, do not report some foreign actor unless it is mentioned by name. For example, if a Chinese editorial mentions "imperialist powers," do not assume it means the United States; instead, report a criticism of a foreign actor called "imperialist powers." Second, if a foreign actor is mentioned only in passing and is not the central subject of the editorial in question, report the foreign actor with a .5 before its name. Examples of all of these situations can be found on the sample data sheet included with this guide.

Please include a short (one sentence or two) summary of any editorial that you evaluated as containing a criticism of some foreign actor.

Sample Data Sheet

Chosun Ilbo	South Korea	Yenching Library	Translator
Date	**Total No. of Editorials**	**Foreign Actor Criticized** **(Summary of Critical Editorial)**	
1/1/86	3	—, —, —	
1/2/86	3	U.S., —, — (U.S. should reduce defense budget)	
1/3/86	2	U.S./Japan, — (U.S. and Japan should not limit imports)	
1/4/86	3	—, —, —	
1/5/86	—		

Chosun Ilbo	South Korea	Yenching Library Translator
Date	Total No. of Editorials	Foreign Actor Criticized (Summary of Critical Editorial)
1/6/86	2	NATO, — (NATO should unilaterally reduce forces)
1/7/86	3	—, —, —
1/8/86	2	—, —
1/9/86	3	—, —, —
1/10/86	3	—, —, —
1/11/86	2	—, —
1/12/86	3	—, —, —
1/13/86	2	.5 Japan, —, — (We must increase production of cars and Japan should allow us to export more)
1/14/86	3	—, —, —
1/15/86	—	
1/16/86	2	—, —
1/17/86	3	—, —, —
1/18/86	2	—, —, —
1/19/86	3	—, —, —
1/20/86	3	—, —, —
1/21/86	2	N. Korea, China (N. Korea is behaving in warlike fashion) (China should allow students to protest)
1/22/86	3	—, —, —
1/23/86	2	—, —
1/24/86	3	—, —, —
1/25/86	3	China, N. Korea/USSR, — (China should allow students to protest) (N. Korea and USSR are promoting international terrorism)

Chosun Ilbo	South Korea	Yenching Library	Translator
Date	Total No. of Editorials	Foreign Actor Criticized (Summary of Critical Editorial)	
1/26/86	2	—, —	
1/27/86	3	—, —, —	
1/28/86	2	—, —, —	
1/29/86	3	—, —, —	
1/30/86	3	—, —, —	
1/31/86	2	—, —	

2.1: Guide for Translators

Part B

The second coding phase of this research project is to look more closely at the content of critical editorials. In this phase we are classifying editorials as either "analytic" or "critical." The intention here is to go beyond simple identification of a preference for conflict and determine what sort of conflict we might expect.

There are five criteria by which this classification is made, although there is often a great deal of overlap between them. These criteria should be thought of as spectra, with "pure" analytic at one end and "pure" critical at the other. Actual editorials will rarely fall so neatly. Thus, unlike phase 1, this coding process is more subjective and requires a somewhat greater knowledge of the history and events of the country examined. In general, you may expect analytic editorials to be more common than critical, although this may vary from country to country and month to month.

You will be given 10 test editorials to be coded. You may mark the coding on the sheet. If you are unsure about how to code a particular editorial, note your thoughts on the sheet and discuss the case with me. Return your test editorials to me before going to the library for your assignment. Remember to make photocopies of the editorials you code in the library.

The primary characteristic of analytic editorials should be a focus on the actions of the potential adversary rather than the actions of the home nation. Such an editorial might very well discuss the possible options open to the country in response to this foreign misstep, but the tone is conciliatory and cautious. In general, the level of vitriol in these editorials should be lower than in their critical cousins. Analytic editorials are what you might consider the traditional editorial—they note some practice, in this case that of a foreign nation, and present reasons for either applauding or condemning that practice.

In a critical editorial the continuation of the current state of affairs is unacceptable, even if military conflict results from attempts to change the situation. Critical editorials should focus on justifying a unilateral action rather than discuss or complain about an adversary's actions; they should either threaten some escalation or, if dealing with a recent aggressive action, defend it in a nonconciliatory fashion. Keep a few caveats in mind. Even the most aggressive critical editorial tries to couch the proposed escalatory action in terms of responding to some evil perpetrated by the opposing nation, and an editorial advocating unilateral action generally mentions some foreign action as a precipitating event.

Summary of Criteria (in loose order of importance)

1. Suggested action: an analytic editorial will not suggest a violent response to a neighbor's actions; a critical editorial will perhaps hold out the prospect for such behavior. An analytic editorial usually suggests no action at all or some sort of diplomatic or economic sanction at most; a critical editorial may suggest the use of military force or at least an escalation in force posture, such as calling up reserves. For example a U.S. editorial recommending diplomatic negotiation to free the hostages seized by Iran is analytic; an Israeli editorial promising to use "all means necessary" to protect settlements is critical.

2. Tone: an analytic editorial will take a dispassionate, calm approach; a critical editorial has much more venom in its words. For example, an Indian editorial discussing the winning and losing factions in a Pakistani election is analytic; an Indian editorial calling for the removal of "the genocidal maniac, Yahya Khan" is critical.

3. Status quo: an analytic editorial will usually seek a return to a recent, balanced status quo; a critical editorial may seek radical change in the existing state of the world. For example, a Soviet editorial advocating a return to prewar borders for Iran and Iraq is analytic; a U.S. editorial seeking the overthrow of the Hohenzollerns in Germany is critical.

4. Responsiveness: an analytic editorial will be written in response to some concrete action by a neighbor; a critical editorial will concentrate on unilateral action directed against a target nation. For example, a Japanese editorial criticizing the statements of a visiting American trade representative is analytic; an Ethiopian editorial praising the imposition of new borders with Somalia is critical.

5. Timeliness: an analytic editorial will usually discuss a nation's recent action; a critical editorial may complain about chronic behavior or long-standing complaints. For example, an Israeli editorial complaining

about yesterday's PLO bombing is more analytic than an Argentine editorial complaining about Britain's seizure of sovereignty over the Falklands 150 years ago.

2.2: List of Nations and Newspapers

Nation	Newspaper	Language
Algeria	*El-Moudjahid*	French
Angola	*Jornal de Angola*	Portuguese
Argentina	*La Prensa*	Spanish
Australia	*Sydney Morning Herald*	English
Austria	*Die Presse*	German
Bangladesh	*Bangladesh Observer*	English
Barbados	*Advocate News*	English
Bolivia	*El Diario*	Spanish
Botswana	*Botswana Daily News*	English
Brazil	*O Estado de São Paulo*	Portuguese
Burma	*Guardian*	English
Canada	*Globe and Mail*	English
Chile	*El Mercurio*	Spanish
China (PRC)	*Remin Ribao*	Chinese
China (ROC)	*Chung Yang Jih Pao*	Chinese
Colombia	*El Tiempo*	Spanish
Cuba	*Granma*	Spanish
Czechoslovakia	*Prace*	Czech
Denmark	*Politiken*	Danish
Dominican Rep.	*El Caribe*	Spanish
Ecuador	*El Comercio*	Spanish
Egypt	*Al-Ahram*	Arabic
El Salvador	*El Diario de Hoy*	Spanish
Ethiopia	*Ethiopian Herald*	English
Finland	*Uusi Suomi*	Finnish
France	*Le Monde*	French
Germany (FRG)	*Zeit*	German
Germany (GDR)	*Neues Deutschland*	German
Ghana	*Ghanaian Times*	English
Greece	*Ta Nea*	Greek
Guatemala	*El Imparcial*	Spanish
Haiti	*Le Matin*	French
India	*Times of India*	English
Indonesia	*Kompas*	Indonesian
Iran	*Kayhan*	English
Iraq	*Al-Jumhuriyah*	Arabic
Ireland	*Inniu*	Gaelic
Israel	*Jerusalem Post*	English
Italy	*Corriere Della Sera*	Italian

Nation	Newspaper	Language
Ivory Coast	*Fraternite Matin*	French
Japan	*Asahi Shimbun*	Japanese
Kenya	*Daily Nation*	English
Korea (DPRK)	*Nodong Sinmun*	Korean
Korea (ROK)	*Chosun Ilbo*	English
Lebanon	*Al-Hayat*	Arabic
Libya	*Al-Zahaf Al 'Akhdar*	Arabic
Malaysia	*New Straits Times*	English
Mexico	*Excelsior*	Spanish
Morocco	*Al-'Alam*	Arabic
Mozambique	*Diario de Mocambique*	Portuguese
Nicaragua	*Barricada*	Spanish
Nigeria	*Daily Times*	English
Pakistan	*Dawn*	English
Panama	*La Estrella*	Spanish
Peru	*El Commercio*	Spanish
Philippines	*Bulletin Today*	English
Poland	*Trybuna Ludo*	Polish
Portugal	*A Rua*	Portuguese
Romania	*Lunceafarui*	Romanian
Saudi Arabia	*Al-Jazirah*	Arabic
Singapore	*Straits Times*	English
Somalia	*Horsed*	Italian/Arabic
South Africa	*The Star*	English
Spain	*Pais*	Spanish
Sri Lanka	*Sunday Times*	English
Sweden	*Expressen*	Swedish
Switzerland	*Neue Zuercher Zeitung*	German
Syria	*Al-Ba'th*	Arabic
Tanzania	*Daily News*	English
Thailand	*Bangkok Post*	English
Turkey	*Cumhuriyet*	Turkish
Uganda	*Argus / Voice of Uganda*	English
U.K.	*Times*	English
Uruguay	*El Dia*	Spanish
U.S.	*N.Y. Times / Wall St. Journal*	English
USSR	*Pravda*	Russian
Venezuela	*Diario de Caracas*	Spanish
Vietnam	*Nhan Dan*	Vietnamese
Zambia	*Zambia Daily Mail*	English
Zimbabwe	*Herald*	English

Appendix 3: U.S. Editorial Information

Each entry in Appendix 3 is structured in the following manner: the first line lists the date the editorial appeared (month/day/year), the title, the source, and the coding; the entry concludes with a summary of the editorial.

Germany 1915

2/1/15, "The German Propaganda in This Country," *New York Times*—Analytic
"Vexed by the total failure" of its war effort, Germany is attempting a heavy-handed propaganda effort in the United States. Will not influence us at all; we will stay carefully neutral.

2/3/15, "Germany's 'Blockade' of England," *New York Times*—Analytic
German announcement of blockade of England. Will not be accepted by neutrals because it is not effective.

2/6/15, "The War-Zone Blunder," *New York Times*—Analytic
Announcement of blockade by Germany could be interpreted as a declaration of war on neutrals. However, "It is not to be assumed that the German admiralty entertains any such monstrous purpose."

2/7/15, "Atrocities," *New York Times*—Analytic
Granted, the German army did not do the bad things it was said to have done in Belgium. Still, naval actions (mines and blockade) are atrocities in a different sense.

2/8/15, "Within the Empire," *New York Times*—Analytic
It is appropriate that the *Lusitania's* Captain Dow falsely flew the American flag, but do not let it happen again. Appropriate in this instance because of the horrible German submarine threat.

2/10/15, "Was Soll Es Bedeuten?" *New York Times*—Analytic
Germans now realize that the rest of the world is not in their corner. Germans will doubtless sue for peace this spring or summer as this realization and Allied offensive sink in.

2/11/15, "The Cable to Germany," *New York Times*—Analytic
Will Germany please allow the reestablishment of cable communications to its country via the Azores?

2/13/15, "Our Diplomacy at Its Best," *New York Times*—Analytic
Note to Germany warning against sub attacks against neutral shipping is just right; threat is unstated, as it should be. Good that we also complain to Britain about flying the American flag.

2/16/15, "Germany's Food Supply," *New York Times*—Analytic
Sorry we cannot do anything about the British blockade of Germany. Our diplomatic note to Germany is on target: if you are hungry, sue for peace.

2/18/15, "Germany's Purpose," *New York Times*—Analytic
Germany is stupid to complain to us about the British blockade. Only effect will be to redouble the British effort to maintain that blockade.

2/19/15, "The German Reply," *New York Times*—Analytic
German reply to our diplomatic note is very courteous and polite, but they persist in threatening sub attacks on neutral shipping. Germany's blockade is contrary to international law, as it is ineffective.

2/23/15, "The Evelyn Incident," *New York Times*—Analytic
Too bad that the U.S. ship *Evelyn* has been blown up by a mine while transporting cotton to Bremen, Germany. Still, serves Germany right because we assume that the mine was a stray German one. "The incident serves to emphasize the folly of the German action in regard to navigation on the North Sea and the English Channel."

2/25/15, "Negotiations about the War Zone," *New York Times*—Analytic
Both the *Evelyn* and the *Carib* have been sunk on the way to Germany. "England will exercise her own judgment as to permitting the free import of grains and meat by Germany, but we certainly have the right to ask that if we are to send food to the Germans they shall take adequate measures to ensure the safety of our ships nearing their coast" from their stray mines.

3/2/15, "The Blockade of Germany," *New York Times*—Analytic
"England's announcement of her purpose to prevent all trade with Germany is at least more definite and understandable than Germany's declaration of a war zone." England will be held, however, to the same strict interpretation of international law we have used to invalidate the German blockade.

3/4/15, "What Germany Offers," *New York Times*—Analytic
The prevailing American opinion is that the latest German diplomatic offers to England concerning shipping are quite reasonable. We should be wary, however, of giving them too much credit for simply behaving in a civilized fashion.

3/8/15, "A Baffled Peacemaker," *New York Times*—Analytic
Chancellor Bethmann-Hollweg's recent interview shows how the Kaiser and the German government badly misunderstood the diplomatic imperatives driving Austria and Russia.

3/12/15, "A German Commander's Blunder," *New York Times*—Analytic
"After due investigation of the destruction of the American ship *William P. Frye,* we have no doubt that it will appear that Germany must disavow the act of the commander. . . . The commander of the *Eitel Friedrich* appears to have taken it upon himself to make law to fit the case in hand."

3/21/15, "Geist, Ungeist, and Kultur," *New York Times*—Analytic
The German national culture raised its industry to the most efficient in the world. Unfortunately, it also pervaded German society with an efficient militarism.

3/22/15, "One of the War's Surprises," *New York Times*—Analytic
Winter was supposed to be Germany's ally on the Eastern front and enemy on the Western. The opposite has turned out to be true.

3/26/15, "When Will the War End?" *New York Times*—Analytic
"It would be well nigh impossible to discover the basis of the very general impression that the European war will soon be over. Yet that impression is widely prevalent, it seems to be growing."

3/27/15, "A New German Policy," *New York Times*—Analytic
Germany, despite a growing change in popular beliefs, still holds to "the doctrine of might, that a nation should take what it needs and keep what it can."

3/28/15, "The Germany of Bismarck and the Old Germany," *New York Times*—Analytic
The militaristic Germany of today stems from the efforts of Bismarck. Its government should realize that the rest of the world does not agree with their militaristic ways.

3/30/15, "Was Es Bedeutet," *New York Times*—Analytic
Why do the Germans need the Kaiser and his imperial organization? If Germany were the United States, the Kaiser would be under much greater control, both from the people and the Congress.

3/31/15, "Murder on the High Seas," *New York Times*—Critical
The sinking of the *Falaba* is even worse than the atrocities perpetrated against Belgium. The U.S. government has been largely silent in the past, as befits a neutral nation. Now, however, we need to take action to prevent this sort of behavior from continuing.

4/6/15, "Our View of the Blockade," *New York Times*—Analytic
We take a very legalistic view of the competing blockades and have sent very friendly notes to both sides explaining our position. We will continue to export to Britain, as there is no legal German blockade, and we will export to Germany via ports outside the English blockade's legal boundary. We are asking for reparations for the value of the *Frye* and its cargo, wheat bound for England. "Nothing could be more businesslike."

4/7/15, "What Shall Germany Pay?" *New York Times*—Analytic
Recent English and French suggestions of appropriate German war reparations are ridiculous. Although responsible for the war, Germany's obligations should be much less.

4/8/15, "New Aspects of the War," *New York Times*—Analytic
Analysis of the potential for campaigns this spring on Western and Eastern fronts.

4/9/15, "The Change in Germany," *New York Times*—Analytic
The German people have come to realize that they must sue for peace soon and that they were wrong to start the war.

4/10/15, "Possibilities of Early Peace," *New York Times*—Analytic
Peace is in the air. The German people realize that they will not prevail in their original ambitions, and it would be prohibitively expensive for the Allies to try to throw the Germans back behind their defensive positions. Thus, sane statesmen will pursue peace soon.

4/13/15, "What Does It Mean?" *New York Times*—Analytic
The German destroyer *Kronprinz Wilhelm* put into Newport News yesterday, removing the last German surface threat to shipping. At the same time, the German ambassador's claim that the United States is not being strictly neutral is clearly put down.

4/18/15, "Disenchantment," *New York Times*—Analytic
Prussian militarists have cruelly suppressed the writings of socialist members of the Reichstag.

4/19/15, "The True Position of Germany," *New York Times*—Analytic
Even prominent German writers now acknowledge what the *Times* has been saying for quite a while now—that Germany cannot hope to succeed in its original war aims and that its best hope is to sue for peace now.

4/22/15, "New German Ideas," *New York Times*—Analytic
The German government has misled its own people in the past. Now it is slowly coming around to admitting publicly that Germany cannot win the war as it was originally conceived.

4/23/15, "The Soft Answer," *New York Times*—Analytic
Wilson and Bryan's most recent diplomatic note is a "gentle admonition," written as "a big hearted teacher" might scold a naughty pupil. Germany must not interfere with our rights as a neutral; we have a perfect right to continue exporting ammunition.

4/27/15, "Rights and Wrongs of War," *New York Times*—Analytic
Thousands are dying every day on the battlefields of Europe. Germany could sue for peace with its European neighbors, and it has absolutely nothing to fear from other nations such as the United States.

4/29/15, "An Illogical Protest," *New York Times*—Analytic
We object to the use of poison gas regardless of who employs it, not just when the Germans use it. Their protests to the contrary are just wrong.

5/4/15, "The Case of the Gulflight," *New York Times*—Critical
The German submarine attack on the *Gulflight* is a flagrant violation of our neutral shipping rights. Perhaps the German commander could not see our flag or markings in the fog, but this is little excuse. Germany must explain and apologize, or we will be forced to take steps to protect our ships.

5/5/15, "Where Germany Leads," *New York Times*—Analytic
Germany leads the world in chemical and dyestuff production. It has just announced plans to open two new plants in New Jersey.

5/8/15, "War by Assassination," *New York Times*—Analytic
In the history of war there is no single deed comparable to the sinking of the *Lusitania.* The American people, led by Wilson, will not rush into hasty action, but we are tremendously aggrieved by this dastardly act. Our intention is to recall the German government to the path of "sense and reason."

5/9/15, "The Law of the Lusitania Case," *New York Times*—Analytic
It was clearly a violation of international law to sink the *Lusitania.* Some senators claim mitigating circumstances, but it was really an evil deed. We do not believe that the German government intended its policy to go this far, and we will try to get its leaders to return to their previous course.

5/10/15, "Stand by the President," *New York Times*—Analytic
We have full confidence in Wilson to show wise statesmanship in the current crisis. "If she [Germany] has become our enemy, if she has resolved to make war on us, . . . then we cannot too soon be advised of her purposes. But we have no such belief. We have faith that in response to our demand Germany will give us assurances that will remove doubt as to the continuance of our friendly relations. But to do that she must not only give pledge for the future; she must, difficult as it may be, disavow and denounce the act of her naval commander who sank the *Lusitania.*"

5/11/15, "Not the Final Word," *New York Times*—Analytic
Wilson made no direct reference to Germany in a speech last night, but this is the president's way, to hold back his innermost thoughts and opinions. We are confident that Wilson will lead us peacefully through this crisis, without failing to gain compensation for this incident.

5/11/15, "Germany's Defenses," *New York Times*—Analytic
Germany's protestations of a legal blockade are absurd. The sinking of the *Lusitania* has no justification under international law.

5/12/15, "President Wilson's Decision," *New York Times*—Analytic
"The nation has heard with deep satisfaction of the President's resolve to demand of Germany reparation for their wrongs and guarantees that they shall not be repeated. . . . His note will give no provocation to war. Its whole purpose will be to avert misunderstandings that might sever friendly relations."

5/12/15, "German Atrocities," *New York Times*—Analytic
Our newspapers have published only a small number of the atrocities that the Germans have committed in Belgium and elsewhere.

5/14/15, "The President's Note," *New York Times*—Analytic
Wilson's note to Germany is firm yet peaceful and just. "The President brings clearly into view Germany's way out. He is conciliatory to the point of clearly indicating the terms of a reply that will meet our demands. She may disavow the acts of her naval commanders, which he with the greatest candor assumes to have been committed without orders or approval, and she is asked to prevent effectually the recurrence of such acts." We appeal to Germany's "sense of honor" and justice to follow the path of humanity.

5/15/15, "The Appeal to German Pride," *New York Times*—Analytic
The German people approve of Wilson's note. They know that their own high traditions and sense of honor demand that they stop this submarine warfare and make reparations for the *Lusitania.*

5/15/15, "The German-American Myth," *New York Times*—Analytic
The Germans' "genius for history" ought to tell them that, while sympathetic, Americans of German descent will give their loyalties to the interests of the United States.

5/16/15, "Our Justifications," *New York Times*—Analytic
We base our demands for reparations and a cessation to submarine warfare on our Treaty of 1828 with Germany.

5/18/15, "The German Answer," *New York Times*—Analytic
We do not know yet how Germany will respond to Wilson's note, but some of the suggestions floating around the United States are strange. For example, arbitration has no meaning here.

5/18/15, "The Warnings," *New York Times*—Analytic
If the German naval commander were subject to the same rules Austria used in convicting Princip of the assassination of Archduke Ferdinand, he would be convicted just as surely.

5/19/15, "One Point in the Note," *New York Times*—Analytic
Wilson has annexed one German justification of submarine warfare: the impossibility of search of merchant ships.

5/21/15, "The Maw," *New York Times*—Analytic
The cost of this war in human lives is unprecedented in human history.

5/26/15, "The Last Argument," *New York Times*—Analytic
"Germany's forensic methods are those of the wolf. From the beginning of the war she has made a pitiful showing in argument, but her last word is so terrible that her opponents have learned to beware of it." It was this way with Belgium, Austria, and now Italy.

5/31/15, "Germany's Disappointing Reply," *New York Times*—Analytic
"The German reply is not responsive to our demand. . . . Germany does not want war with the United States. . . . The two nations are in accord in seeking the way of peace, and, being in that temper, the way will necessarily be found."

6/1/15, "For German Consumption," *New York Times*—Analytic
The German reply to Wilson's latest note was possibly intended to fool the German people. That's really the only way to explain "its fathomless stupidity and ineptitude, its total lack of adaptation to diplomatic ends."

6/1/15, "Germany's Nightmare," *New York Times*—Analytic
The latest German diplomatic note is like a bad dream. Germany will never be able to erase the Lusitania sinking from our memory; it was truly a barbaric act. So why does the German government claim mitigating factors? "The tormented German soul cannot bear to see itself. It hides behind a veil of things it knows are false. . . . The tragedy is German."

6/2/15, "The Use of Submarines in War," *New York Times*—Critical
The latest note from Wilson to Germany makes clear that submarine attacks must be stopped. "The language of the President's note appeals not merely to Germany but to civilization, to all humanity." Should the Germans not acquiesce, we expect Wilson will get other neutral nations to join with the United States in collective action to stop the sub threat.

6/3/15, "The Twist in the German Mind," *New York Times*—Analytic
It is just bad luck for Germany that it cannot supply enough food domestically but must try to import through an effective British blockade. It is not some U.S. conspiracy to side with Britain.

6/4/15, "The Reichstag Defined," *New York Times*—Analytic
There is a great deal of misunderstanding in this country about the role of the Reichstag. It is not really that democratic.

6/6/15, "False Counselors," *New York Times*—Analytic
Bravo to the British for maintaining a high level of military preparedness in the face of German military growth over the past years. This German military strength poses great dangers to England, and we should not shirk our properly neutral role of exporting ammunition to combatants, especially Britain.

6/6/15, "A Thin Allegation," *New York Times*—Analytic
German claims that there is some secret treaty or understanding between the United States and Britain are simply ludicrous.

6/8/15, "A Phantom Treaty," *New York Times*—Analytic
German claims that there is some secret treaty or understanding between the United States and Britain are simply ludicrous.

6/11/15, "Germany's Opportunity," *New York Times*—Analytic
Our latest diplomatic note makes no new demands on Germany, and it actually makes it easier for Germany to set herself right in the minds of neutral nations. Our note "makes for peace, not for strife."

6/11/15, "A German Absurdity," *New York Times*—Analytic
If it is true that German agents are trying to buy controlling interests in our largest corporations, it just goes to show how they do not understand us. There is no possible way that they could even make a dent in the ownership of our industry.

6/17/15, "The Main Point," *New York Times*—Analytic
The German press has praised Wilson's latest note of June 9, and we expect that these views mirror those of the German government.

6/17/15, "Retaliation at Last," *New York Times*—Analytic
Both the Germans and the British, but mostly the Germans, have resorted to the awful practice of retaliation, via air bombardment, against civilian populations following battlefield setbacks.

6/18/15, "Waterloo," *New York Times*—Analytic
Today is the anniversary of Waterloo, where an imperialist autocrat was finally defeated. We hope that German imperialism will be similarly defeated, because the Kaiser doesn't even have the limited good points of Napoléon.

6/20/15, "Two Opinions in Germany," *New York Times*—Analytic
The president's note of June 9 appears to have had a marked effect within Germany. No longer is there a monolithic opinion within Germany supporting its governments actions.

6/24/15, "The Fighting in Galicia," *New York Times*—Analytic
The Germans and Austrians have indeed succeeded in pushing the Russians out of Galicia, but it was not a total rout. The Russians were able to save their artillery.

6/27/15, "The Change in Germany," *New York Times*—Analytic
Germany went to war to conquer Europe. Now it is fighting for its very survival. We expect that it will sue for peace soon.

6/29/15, "A Great Stroke for Peace," *New York Times*—Analytic
It is little wonder that the German government is suppressing its Socialist Party, for its latest manifesto shows that party to be solidly in favor of working for an armistice.

Germany 1917

1/1/17, "The Open Door of Peace," *New York Times*—Analytic
Discusses Germany's offer of a peace proposal for the first time since war started, a hopeful sign of potential peace.

1/2/17, "Enforcing Peace," *New York Times*—Analytic
Disputes claim of Kaiser that his forces are victorious. Allies will continue to "enforce the peace" until Germany submits to Allied terms. Peace is near.

1/5/17, "Imperiling Peace," *New York Times*—Critical
Urges senators and wealthy private individuals to leave peace negotiations to the president and the Allies. "Peace now would be a German victory." Peace must not be sought for its own sake.

1/6/17, "Not a Victor," *New York Times*—Analytic
Germany's militarism is a failure. "Germany's offering peace in the tone of a victor" is silly because Germany hasn't won anything.

1/7/17, "The 'Conda,'" *New York Times*—Analytic
Discusses the success of British naval blockade of Germany. The Allies should use the blockade ("conda") to "squeeze the Central Alliance to a peace which will be on their terms."

1/9/17, "The Unchanged Kaiser," *New York Times*—Critical
The Kaiser's call for renewed vigor in the war against the Allies is an example "of the spirit of militarism and aggression that must be destroyed in the peace that the arms of the allies will bring to the world."

1/11/17, "Mr. Gerard's Speech," *New York Times*—Critical
German interpretation of a speech given by the American ambassador in Berlin, suggesting that the United States no longer blames Germany for the war and wants peace, is pure propaganda.

1/11/17, "With the Aid of Allah," *New York Times*—Analytic
Disputes claims by the sultan to the Turkish army that the Allies are responsible for the failure to reach a peaceful solution to the war. Turks are weaker than they admit.

1/12/17, "The Terms of the Allies," *New York Times*—Analytic
Germany cannot blame the Allies for the continuation of the war. Germany can only end the war by agreeing to Allied terms.

1/14/17, "What Are Germany's Terms?" *New York Times*—Analytic
War/peace aims of Germany are questionable. Germany must "put its cards on the table" in order to achieve peace.

1/17/17, "Germany's Mistake," *New York Times*—Analytic
"Germany wants peace." Germany's failure to publish peace terms or war aims has cost Germany in terms of the view that neutral countries take.

1/19/17, "More Questions for Germany," *New York Times*—Analytic
Germany must answer the diplomatic note sent by the Allies asking what its terms for peace are and stating the Allied positions. The good opinion that many neutral countries have of Germany is suffering.

1/20/17, "The Battle of the Somme," *New York Times*—Analytic
Allied attack at the Somme has been "stifled in blood and mud." In spite of this, the battle was a success for the Allies.

1/22/17, "Daybreak in Germany," *New York Times*—Analytic
Discusses the statement of a German newspaper publisher. Shows that many Germans understand that Germany should make its peace terms clear.

1/23/17, "The President's Ideals," *New York Times*—Critical
Discusses Wilson's address to the Senate. Applauds speech as Wilson's "greatest utterance." Agrees with Wilson that peace without a victory over German military aggression will be worthless.

1/25/17, "Peace with Victory," *New York Times*—Analytic
Disagrees with Wilson's suggestion that peace on the terms put forward by the Allies will be a "peace without victory."

1/26/17, "For Years to Come," *New York Times*—Analytic
Discusses German claims that they have only lost 2 million of 10 million soldiers and that the Germans will be able to fight for many years to come. Germany should state the aims for which it is carrying on the war.

1/28/17, "Russia Approves," *New York Times*—Analytic
Russia's position on peace is the same as Wilson's. This is reassuring.

2/1/17, "Germany Wars against the World," *New York Times*—Critical
German threats to attack neutral shipping in the North Atlantic are an attack on all the countries of the world. The United States cannot put up with it. The threats are an "act of desperation" that may signal that the end of the war is near.

2/2/17, "For a Just Cause," *New York Times*—Critical
Germany has arrayed herself against the whole world. Wilson has the support of the whole country to resist Germany's blockade.

2/2/17, "Germany Stakes All," *New York Times*—Analytic
Agrees with Germans that they have staked everything on their decision to renew submarine warfare. German decision to do so is despicable.

2/3/17, "The Nation's Duty," *New York Times*—Critical
United States must not accept German blockade. "England and the Allies fight our battle now." Germany leaves us no choice but to discard our neutrality.

2/3/17, "Shortening of the War," *New York Times*—Critical
Discusses German claim that their new policy will shorten the war. War will not be shortened, as the new German policy will force the United States to join the war against Germany.

2/4/17, "In Defense of Our Rights," *New York Times*—Critical
German decision to resume destruction of neutral shipping will cause all neutrals to declare war against Germany. United States will make war in defense of rights that Germany has violated.

2/4/17, "The Milestones," *New York Times*—Critical
Wilson has consistently shown Germany that the United States will not accept the blockade. Germany has mistaken "patience for timidity."

2/5/17, "Germany's Sacrifice," *New York Times*—Critical
Germany has thrown away a very positive relationship with the United States.

2/5/17, "Making Ready," *New York Times*—Critical
"If war does come it will find a united nation." American mood is not one of excitement but, rather, one of sober resolution.

2/5/17, "The President Answered," *New York Times*—Critical
Discusses German reply to Wilson's speech in which he announced the severing of diplomatic relations with Germany. Reply was unhelpful and "a threat against the future peace of the world."

2/6/17, "Germany Must Make Her Choice," *New York Times*—Critical
German "surprise" at U.S. response to blockade is feigned and not believable. Seas must be kept open "no matter what the cost."

2/6/17, "Starvation," *New York Times*—Critical
Both England and Germany have the right to blockade the other, but the German "slaughter of neutrals" is unacceptable. United States should respond vigorously to German threats.

2/7/17, "By Permission of Germany," *New York Times*—Critical
Discusses "concessions" made by Germans to Spanish and Dutch ships. United States doesn't need German permission to ship goods on the open sea.

2/8/17, "The Overt Act," *New York Times*—Critical
Discusses Wilson's speech in which he said that he would ask the Congress for power to use any means necessary to protect U.S. seamen if Germans sink a U.S. ship. Says actual sinking of a ship should not be necessary for such a granting of power.

2/8/17, "Has Germany Gone Mad?" *New York Times*—Analytic
Criticizes Germany's treatment of American ambassador. Incident is "grave and extraordinary."

2/8/17, "Blockading the Neutrals," *New York Times*—Critical
German decision to resume blockade will necessarily cause United States to join the war. Decision will cut off all trade to Europe and accelerate "starvation" of Germany.

2/10/17, "The Verdict," *New York Times*—Critical
The entire world agrees that Germany's actions are a violation of international law.

2/11/17, "How Germany May Avoid War," *New York Times*—Critical
Germany "must desist from piratical and murderous acts on the high seas" in order to avoid war with the United States.

2/12/17, "The World's Navies," *New York Times*—Critical
"The lawless methods she [Germany] has adopted and is using are condemned by the United States, and other neutral nations."

2/13/17, "The Right Answer," *New York Times*—Critical
Applauds U.S. government's decision to refuse to negotiate with Germany until Germany stops attacking U.S. ships.

2/13/17, "Preparedness for Defeat," *New York Times*—Critical
Disagrees with antiwar movement's opposition to preparing for war. "No referendum on war is needed."

2/14/17, "The Pacifist Propaganda," *New York Times*—Critical
Criticizes pacifists in no uncertain terms.

2/15/17, "The Scandinavian Protest," *New York Times*—Analytic
Discusses protest of blockade by Scandinavian countries. Says that the protests of these and other countries should convince Germans that their government is carrying on the war "by criminal methods."

2/15/17, "A Three-Year's Truce," *New York Times*—Critical
Agrees with claims by some that peace with Germans now would only mean a resumption of the war in a few years' time.

2/16/17, "Other Neutral Nations," *New York Times*—Analytic
Denmark, Sweden, and Norway agree with the United States that German actions are unacceptable and that they must defend themselves.

2/16/17, "New Blockades for Old," *New York Times*—Critical
Countries of the world are telling Germany that they blame Germany for the war that it, and its blockade, is causing. World is learning to hate Germany.

2/17/17, "Misplaced Emphasis," *New York Times*—Critical
Criticizes statement by Senator Mann that United States should continue to seek to avoid war.

2/17/17, "The Kaiser's Inspiration," *New York Times*—Analytic
Discusses the men that the kaiser has said are his heroes, all conquerors who failed. The kaiser will fail, just as his heroes have.

2/18/17, "A German Warning," *New York Times*—Critical
Discusses German warning to United States not to arm merchant ships. United States must resist German blockade, or it will mean "peace with dishonor."

2/19/17, "Beginning to Get Ready," *New York Times*—Critical
U.S. participation in war may "still be avoided"; United States should prepare for war immediately.

2/20/17, "Seeking Peace, Inventing War," *New York Times*—Critical
All Americans must trust Wilson with the decision of whether to wage war. Criticizes pacifists. President is "resolved to defend our rights upon the sea."

2/22/17, "The Dangers of Delay," *New York Times*—Critical
Discusses dangers of delaying our response to German blockade. Support for a firm stance may slowly wither away.

2/26/17, "German Freedom of the Seas," *New York Times*—Analytic
Discusses contrast between British and German blockades as evidenced by German's sinking of seven Dutch ships in one day. Germans are "savage and ruthless."

2/27/17, "The Germans Withdraw," *New York Times*—Analytic
Discusses first small German retreats in Somme region since 1914. War is going well for the Allies.

2/27/17, "For the Defense of Our Rights," *New York Times*—Critical
Agrees with Wilson that United States cannot accept German blockade. Says "the time and the occasion for action have come."

2/28/17, "In Defense of American Liberty," *New York Times*—Critical
German U-boats are killing Americans and must be stopped. Congress should confer the power on Wilson "to employ arms to defend our rights."

3/1/17, "Prussian Reasoning," *New York Times*—Analytic
It is impossible to tell whether German statesmen actually believe the ridiculous statements they make or whether they are deliberately trying to deceive their citizens.

3/2/17, "Action Not Talk," *New York Times*—Critical
Congress must formally give Wilson the power to resist Germans militarily without further delay.

3/4/17, "The Doom of the Hohenzollerns," *New York Times*—Critical
The removal from power of the German emperor and his family should be a condition of peace as "the Hohenzollerns are outside civilization's pale."

3/5/17, "The Power to Arm Ships," *New York Times*—Critical
Wilson must be given the power to arm and protect U.S. merchant ships. "The prosperity of the Nation" is threatened.

3/7/17, "German Reasoning Outdone by Austria," *New York Times*—Analytic
Austrian response to U.S. complaints about blockade is evasive and contemptible. Austria is simply a "vassal State subject to the German will."

3/10/17, "The Nation's Will," *New York Times*—Critical
U.S. public has demanded that the German blockade be raised. Germany should be treated like any other "pirate."

3/11/17, "Let the House Show Its Patriotism," *New York Times*—Critical
There is an "imminent danger of war," and Congress must do its "duty as a Patriot."

3/13/17, "The German Plots," *New York Times*—Critical
"Every day some new German activity, conspiracy, or espionage" against the United States comes to light. United States will be "swift to punish offenses."

3/13/17, "The Merciful Way," *New York Times*—Critical
United States refusal to allow German blockade to stand is merciful because it means war will end sooner, and it will end with a German defeat. United States protection of its merchant ships is a "boon to mankind."

3/14/17, "Unfortunate Accidents," *New York Times*—Critical
Germany, not the United States, will bear responsibility from any unfortunate accidents that occur as a result of the U.S. decision to arm merchant ships.

3/15/17, "The German Retreat," *New York Times*—Analytic
The Allies are beating Germany and forcing a retreat.

3/18/17, "Apologetic Preparedness," *New York Times*—Critical
Criticizes government statements that appear to apologize for preparing for war. United States must prepare now and doesn't need to apologize.

3/19/17, "Germany's Acts of War," *New York Times*—Critical
"By the repeated acts of Germany, a state of war exists between that country and the United States." German leaders "exhibit the recklessness of madmen, the depravity of irreclaimable criminals."

3/20/17, "Moloch Has Vanished," *New York Times*—Analytic
Germany's "only plausible excuse for plunging the world into war, an excuse that was never valid, . . . has now lost the faintest semblance of plausibility."

3/21/17, "The Last Card," *New York Times*—Critical
The war is going badly for Germans, and "the end, too, may be sooner than they expected" as the United States should enter on the Allied side.

3/20/17, "Making Ready for War," *New York Times*—Critical
Discusses Wilson's decision to call Congress back together sooner than expected. This must be done to deal with German "acts of war." "It is necessary that the existence of war should be proclaimed."

3/24/17, "What Is the Motive?" *New York Times*—Critical
German motives for "acts of savagery" on the seas cannot be understood. Maybe Germany has a "monstrous form of rabies" that we should forcibly cure.

3/25/17, "How to Help the Allies," *New York Times*—Critical
United States should give the Allies food, clothing, and ammunition.

3/26/17, "Wise Defensive Measures," *New York Times*—Critical
Agrees with Wilson's decision to order the mobilization of the National Guard. Says "great enterprises are afoot."

3/27/17, "Our Treaty with Germany," *New York Times*—Critical
Agrees with U.S. government that, in light of repeated violations of current treaties by Germany, any new treaties with Germany would be useless. Old treaties are "void."

3/28/17, "Explaining the Retreat," *New York Times*—Analytic
German efforts to explain its retreat as a victory to its people is evidence of the grimness of Germany's cause.

3/29/17, "The Only Way," *New York Times*—Critical
German decision to take American relief workers prisoner in Belgium "removes any doubt as to the course the U.S. government should pursue."

3/30/17, "An Ancient Tale," *New York Times*—Analytic
German claims that they are not responsible for war with the United States are untrue.

4/2/17, "The Deliverance of Germany," *New York Times*—Critical
Prussian militarism is at the root of this war, and it must be destroyed so that the German people and the rest of the world can be free from it.

4/2/17, "For Freedom and Civilization," *New York Times*—Critical
United States must unite with Allies and "hew down and cast into the fire" the "poisonous tree" of Germany. Congress should declare war.

4/4/17, "The War Resolution," *New York Times*—Critical
Congress should declare war on Germany.

4/5/17, "Democratic Germany," *New York Times*—Critical
Germany must throw off the "Hohenzollern incubus" and take its place among the democratic nations.

4/6/17, "The Nation Speaks," *New York Times*—Critical
Applauds Congress' decision to declare war on Germany.

Berlin 1948

4/2/48, "Berlin under Siege," *New York Times*—Analytic
Soviet decision to blockade West Berlin is "reckless." This is a "direct challenge to the Great Powers." West cannot withdraw without a loss of face; doubt that the Soviets will risk the anger of the West by forcibly evicting the West from Berlin.

4/26/48, "Focus on Germany," *New York Times*—Analytic
If Soviet efforts to cut off Berlin are successful, it will be a fatal blow to democracy and recovery throughout Europe. Berlin crisis is unlikely to determine the struggle between the West and Russia.

4/29/48, "The 'Inevitable War,'" *New York Times*—Analytic
Talk of "inevitable war" between United States and Soviets is "reckless" and generally untrue. "A shooting war can and will be averted by victory in the political field."

5/12/48, "Discussions with Russia," *New York Times*—Analytic
Discusses new talks between United States and Russia. They are a good sign, but it's doubtful whether Russians have changed their views in any concrete way. Urges United States and the rest of the West to be on guard in dealing with the Russians.

5/13/48, "Deeds; Not Words," *New York Times*—Critical
Once again discusses the "exchange of notes" between United States and Russia. United States simply asked Russia to abide by certain treaties and agreements it had already made; if the Soviets do not abide by them, the West will continue to build up its military power to defend against Russian aggression.

5/16/48, "The Issue with Russia," *New York Times*—Analytic
Exchange of notes with Russia hasn't done any harm and may do some good in the long run.

5/20/48, "Lets Look at the Record," *New York Times*—Analytic
Discusses the most recent "peace initiative" from Russia and dismisses it as unhelpful propaganda.

5/24/48, "Russia's Peace Offensive," *New York Times*—Analytic
Latest Russia propaganda efforts are an attempt to split Western opposition to the Soviet Union.

5/26/48, "Curtailing the Veto," *New York Times*—Analytic
Russia is abusing its veto rights in the Security Council with its actions to suppress condemnation of the Czech coup.

5/29/48, "The Search for Peace," *New York Times*—Analytic
Russia is linking its cold war with a propaganda attempt to split the Western allies. Al-

though the immediate issue is Austria, we must get Russia to participate in good faith in conferences on a variety of issues.

6/1/48, "Russia Invented It First," *New York Times*—Analytic
Russia takes credit, falsely, for every invention and advancement under the sun.

6/2/48, "Edited by Moscow," *New York Times*—Analytic
Russia jams all our attempts to spread information in that country, but a variety of publications here are directly controlled by Russia.

6/8/48, "The New Plan for Germany," *New York Times*—Analytic
The Western plan to set up a separate German state proceeds apace. Perhaps the Russian controlled zones will be able to join one day to form a united Germany.

6/14/48, "Russia against the World," *New York Times*—Analytic
The Russians are more subtle than Hitler but just as evil. Truman's recent diplomatic note effectively refutes the recent Soviet "peace offensive."

6/16/48, "Russia 'Accepts,'" *New York Times*—Analytic
Russia is now willing to participate in an international conference on navigation of the Danube but only one in which it will have more votes.

6/17/48, "Russia and the West," *New York Times*—Analytic
Russia, as expected, does not like the Western plan to set up a German state and is even now tightening the noose around the Western zones in Berlin and fomenting strife in those zones. "In the face of this situation, the best and for the moment the only weapon against Russian pressure available to the Western Powers is a firm, consistent, and united foreign policy."

6/21/48, "The New German Currency," *New York Times*—Analytic
The West has finalized plans for a new currency for their zones of Germany. Unfortunately, it is intensifying the split between us and Russia, as they have seized on this issue to push us out of Berlin.

6/25/48, "Struggle over Germany," *New York Times*—Critical
Russians have begun to apply the final pressure to drive the West out of Berlin. General Clay says the United States will not be driven out by anything short of war. Problem can only be solved by the reestablishment of communications and supply lines to Berlin. "Showdown" with Russia may now be at hand.

6/28/48, "The Russian Challenge," *New York Times*—Critical
Berlin crisis is as grave as that faced by the Allies 10 years ago at Munich. Loss of Berlin would lead to the loss of Germany. Discusses the options of the West (appeasement, diplomacy, and military action). West must remain united.

7/2/48, "Unity of Germany," *New York Times*—Analytic
Berlin crisis has unified the West in its views on Germany. Discusses plans to give Germans limited autonomy.

7/4/48, "Operation Vittles," *New York Times*—Analytic
Recounts "the greatest air lift in history." Applauds the decision to airlift food into Berlin.

7/6/48, "Moscow and Berlin," *New York Times*—Analytic
Discusses the formal demand by the West to Russia to end the blockade of Berlin. Airlift of food has removed the threat of starvation. Russia has made it plain that it seeks control over all of Germany, not just Berlin. West must prepare for negotiations on Germany with Russia.

7/7/48, "Protest to Moscow," *New York Times*—Critical
Discusses the formal demand by the West to Russia to end the blockade of Berlin. Showdown with Russia is imminent, but the door is still open for an amicable settlement. Any move by Russians to send troops into Berlin "would be an act of military force which the West could not accept."

7/11/48, "Firm but Not Belligerent," *New York Times*—Analytic
Discusses the formal demand by the West to Russia to end the blockade of Berlin. "The Russian attempt to blockade Berlin cannot stand." "The firmness shown in these notes has diminished rather than increased the danger of armed conflict."

7/16/48, "The Russian Answer," *New York Times*—Analytic
Soviet answer to formal demand to end blockade further aggravates the situation. Blockade is Russian "blackmail" and an attempt "to impose Russia's will on the Western powers as it has already been imposed on Eastern Europe."

7/20/48, "The Berlin Crisis," *New York Times*—Analytic
"Tension over Berlin crisis" is mounting. This "is a situation which demands . . . wise statesmanship." West must stand firm and "stay in Berlin at any cost." West must also show restraint so that Russia will clearly be seen as the aggressor if it comes to a military clash.

7/21/48, "France and Berlin," *New York Times*—Analytic
Discusses the effect of the resignation of the French cabinet (over military disputes with Socialists) on the Berlin crisis. French must bear their share of the burden of stopping Soviet aggression.

7/22/48, "No Time to Lose," *New York Times*—Analytic
New French cabinet must be formed swiftly so that the Berlin crisis can be dealt with by the West. West is open to general discussions with the Soviets on all of Germany if the blockade is lifted.

7/23/48, "Compromise on Berlin," *New York Times*—Analytic
West is open to general discussions with the Soviets on all of Germany if the blockade is lifted. Before such general discussions can take place, the Western allies must decide exactly what they would like Germany to look like.

7/26/48, "New Approach on Germany," *New York Times*—Critical
Berlin is the key to Germany, and Germany is the key to Europe; as a consequence, "Germany must be restored an integral part of a democratic Europe," albeit with certain procedural safeguards in place. West must remain in Berlin.

7/28/48, "Western Joint Strategy," *New York Times*—Analytic
West remains unified in its demand that the blockade be ended. Willing to discuss all German issues with Russia if the blockade is ended.

7/29/48, "Why Stay in Berlin?" *New York Times*—Analytic
"It can be argued that Berlin is not worth the risk of war. It is not. . . . It cannot be argued, however, that the risk is lessened by leaving Russia in sole possession."

8/2/48, "Working for Peace," *New York Times*—Critical
The "Western Powers have left no doubt in Russian minds that they are determined to remain in Berlin, whatever the costs."

8/3/48, "Light on Russian Aims," *New York Times*—Analytic
Discusses the Belgrade Conference on administration of the use of the Danube River. The conference is an attempt "to convert the Danube into a private Russian river."

8/4/48, "The Moscow Conference," *New York Times*—Analytic
Discusses conference between Stalin and representatives of Western powers. Conference has rekindled hopes that "diplomacy may yet find a way to save the peace." Optimism must be kept within bounds.

8/13/48, "Deadlock in Moscow," *New York Times*—Analytic
Negotiations with Soviets over Berlin and Germany are deadlocked even before they have begun in earnest.

8/16/48, "Germany and Korea," *New York Times*—Analytic
The idea of a "West-German project" should not be dismissed just because the Russians dislike it so. The abandonment of the idea of a West Germany would "imperil the recovery of Europe." Korea is a good example of how such a plan could be made to work.

8/18/48, "Failure in Belgrade," *New York Times*—Analytic
Belgrade Conference has ended as a complete failure, and the Russians are to blame. United States should not have even participated.

8/20/48, "Decision Due in Moscow," *New York Times*—Analytic
Russian response to Western overtures for negotiations on Berlin/Germany will be made soon. Nobody knows what the response will be.

8/22/48, "No Time for Hysteria," *New York Times*—Analytic
Events of the past week have witnessed a deterioration in relations between the "Russian Empire" and the West. "Patience as well as firmness, insistence on justice but no hysteria over "incidents," are what is now required of us."

8/23/48, "A New German State," *New York Times*—Analytic
Organization of West German government is proceeding despite Russia's dislike. West Germany is crucial to economic restoration of Europe.

8/25/48, "New Hope in Moscow," *New York Times*—Analytic
Meetings between representatives of the Western powers and Stalin are encouraging.

8/27/48, "Moscow in Berlin," *New York Times*—Analytic
Negotiations in Moscow over Berlin/Germany may be moved to Berlin at the suggestion of Stalin, with a focus on currency disputes. This is an encouraging sign. West must make sure that Berlin Conference is not used merely as a stalling tactic.

8/28/48, "Waiting for the North Wind," *New York Times*—Analytic
There are some hopeful signs in U.S.-Soviet negotiations over Germany. Patience of Western allies shows that they want peace.

9/1/48, "Negotiations in Berlin," *New York Times*—Analytic
Resumption of negotiations in Berlin is a hopeful sign. Failure of negotiations cannot leave the West any worse off than it already is, but success could be a breakthrough in relations with the Soviets.

9/8/48, "Russian Tactics in Berlin," *New York Times*—Analytic
Russian actions, the organization of mobs to besiege key government offices and the kidnapping of policemen from the Western sector, have strained negotiations in Berlin.

9/10/48, "While Negotiations Go On," *New York Times*—Critical
Russian tactics to disrupt local Berlin government belie their negotiating posture and suggest that peaceful negotiations may not be able to solve the Berlin crisis.

9/11/48, "The Berlin Air Lift," *New York Times*—Analytic
Soviet demands for air traffic regulations show that they have lost hope that the airlift will fail. United States must not abandon our position on freedom of the air.

9/13/48, "The Battle of Berlin," *New York Times*—Analytic
Mass demonstration staged by Russians in Berlin were a fiasco. Demonstration shows that Russia will continue to seek to take over Berlin as it did Czechoslovakia, even while negotiations are going on.

9/15/48, "The Deadlock on Berlin," *New York Times*—Analytic
In light of deadlock on Berlin crisis the West is preparing to submit the issue to the United Nations. Russians have lost far more than they have gained in the Berlin crisis so far.

9/17/48, "Russia and Europe," *New York Times*—Critical
It is becoming clear that Russia doesn't want to reach an agreement with the West so that the world will remain in turmoil and be ripe for a communist world revolution. West should continue to negotiate while also developing its military power.

9/23/48, "Last Call to Moscow," *New York Times*—Analytic
Discusses final efforts of Western powers to solve the Berlin crisis before submitting the issue to the United Nations. Time is on the side of the West, and the unity among the Western powers that the Berlin crisis has created will serve the West well in any "cold war" with Russia.

9/27/48, "Russia before the UN," *New York Times*—Analytic
Discusses end of Berlin negotiations by the West and the submission of the issue to the United Nations. Soviet response to the last Western proposal was completely unsatisfactory. Berlin subjects the United Nations to its greatest test.

9/28/48, "Russia and the West," *New York Times*—Analytic
Discusses speech of Foreign Secretary Bevin to the United Nations on Russian duplicity in the Berlin negotiations. "Only when the West demonstrates that it cannot be frightened is there hope that the Russians will abandon their present tactics."

9/30/48, "Russia before the Council," *New York Times*—Analytic
Discusses formal call of Western powers for the United Nations to step in and resolve the Berlin crisis. "Russian actions endanger the security of the United States, whose soldiers stand in Berlin."

Korea 1950

6/26/50, "War in Korea," *New York Times*—Critical
Discusses attack by North Korea on South Korea. United States is right to recognize that this is not a "local" dispute and that world peace is at risk. United States cannot afford to "lose" Korea, because all of Asia would be threatened.

6/26/50, "Warning to the West," *New York Times*—Critical
Soviet support of North Korea's invasion shows the West must be on its guard against Soviet attacks elsewhere in the world. West must come up with a coordinated, aggressive defense plan.

6/27/50, "At Stake in Korea," *New York Times*—Critical
Prestige and character of the United Nations is at stake in Korea. U.S. government has not yet indicated a willingness to intervene militarily. U.S. prestige in Asia is also at stake.

6/28/50, "Democracy Takes Its Stand," *New York Times*—Critical
Praises decision of Truman administration to give air and sea military support to the South Koreans. Rest of the world should "close ranks" to meet this "threat of brutal aggression."

6/29/50, "The Choice Is Russia's," *New York Times*—Critical
Discusses whether Russia will back down from a fight with the United States and the rest of the world.

6/29/50, "Support from the Free World," *New York Times*—Critical
Discusses decision of many countries (Netherlands, Australia, Britain) to send military support to the South Koreans. Praises these governments.

6/30/50, "The Soviet Replies," *New York Times*—Analytic
Suggestions by Russia that United States is responsible for Korean War is crazy. Soviet absence from the Security Council meeting doesn't mean the United Nations resolutions are invalid.

7/1/50, "For the Sake of Koreans," *New York Times*—Critical
U.S. involvement in Korea is necessary not only to stop Soviet expansionism but also to help the Korean people be free.

7/1/50, "Ground Troops Move In," *New York Times*—Critical
Supports U.S. decision to send ground troops in. United States must do whatever is necessary to save Korea.

7/2/50, "The Task Ahead," *New York Times*—Critical
U.S. task in Korea will be a hard and difficult one. Final outcome not in doubt, however, as the United States will eventually triumph.

7/4/50, "Fourth of July, 1950," *New York Times*—Critical
Korean "war" is actually a police action undertaken for the United Nations. United States must do everything in its power to win the war quickly in order to prevent its spread.

7/5/50, "The Russian Case," *New York Times*—Analytic
Russian suggestions that the United States is to blame for the war are ludicrous. Some solace can be gained from the fact that the Russians are only arguing with us and aren't entering the war themselves.

7/6/50, "Korean Battlefront," *New York Times*—Critical
Discusses war; says the fighting is difficult and everything depends on how fast we can deploy our forces.

7/9/50, "The First Two Weeks," *New York Times*—Critical
Discusses first two weeks of the war. The "high resolution" of the United States must continue if we are to win the war.

7/10/50, "The United Nations at War," *New York Times*—Analytic
Soviets have unwittingly created problems for themselves by their actions in Korea, because the United Nations has been made into a potentially powerful military tool over which they have no control.

7/12/50, "Ordeal of Battle," *New York Times*—Critical
Korean campaign will be a long and difficult one, but, "in the words of Senator Taft, once we are in it, we must also go all out for victory."

7/13/50, "Anniversary in Korea," *New York Times*—Critical
Notes two-year anniversary of adoption of Korean Constitution. Blames Russia for destroying South Korea and starting the war.

7/14/50, "Men to Do the Job," *New York Times*—Critical
Applauds Truman's decision to call reserves and National Guard to serve in Korea. Forces are needed to prevent spread of war by freeing South Korea quickly.

7/17/50, "The Lesson of Korea," *New York Times*—Critical
Korean situation should teach us that "the Soviets cannot be contained by mere guarantees." West must build up its military might in order to deter Russia from starting such "little wars" in the future.

7/19/50, "Reply to Mr. Nehru," *New York Times*—Analytic
Applauds U.S. rejection of suggestion by Mr. Nehru that communist China should be admitted to the United Nations as a prelude to Korean peace negotiations.

7/21/50, "Moscow, China, and Korea," *New York Times*—Analytic
Admission of Red China to the United Nations and the North Korean invasion are unrelated. Soviets are linking them for purely selfish reasons. Russia is attempting to use "blackmail."

7/22/50, "On the Korean Front," *New York Times*—Critical
Discusses the many contributions made to the UN cause in Korea by various countries.

7/25/50, "Korean Balance Sheet," *New York Times*—Critical
So far the North Koreans are winning. United Nations must increase the strength of its forces.

7/27/50, "The Enemy," *New York Times*—Critical
Discusses characteristics of North Korean army; high level of training and support from Red China and Russia is one reason for the difficulties UN forces are having.

7/29/50, "Mr. Malik to Return," *New York Times*—Analytic
Discusses why Soviet representative to the United Nations (Malik) is returning to the United Nations. Reasons for return are unclear. Issue of admittance of Red China to the United Nations will surely come up, but the United States should not change its policy.

7/31/50, "The UN 's Gravest Test," *New York Times*—Analytic
United Nations must not give in to pressure to give Red China a seat in United Nations and accept the Soviet "peace" proposal.

8/2/50, "A Soviet Defeat," *New York Times*—Analytic
UN Security Council vote of 8-3 against Russia's motion to admit Red China to the United Nations was a big victory in the "most bitter clash between East and West ever staged within the UN."

8/4/50, "Russia Gets Her Answer," *New York Times*—Analytic
Vote shows Russia is the "real villain" in Korean War.

8/5/50, "The Propaganda Battle," *New York Times*—Analytic
Russia is not benefiting from the lies it is spreading about the Korean War.

8/6/50, "Checks to Aggression," *New York Times*—Analytic
In past two weeks Soviet aggression has been dealt two strong blows. One on battlefield in Korea and the other in the United Nations. Russians may see Korea as a test of the world's resistance to their aggression.

8/6/50, "The Offensive in Korea," *New York Times*—Critical
Chronicles first offensive action by UN forces in Korea. Success of action is a good sign.

8/10/50, "Malik's Ten Big Lies," *New York Times*—Analytic
Suggestion by Malik (Soviet UN representative) that United States is responsible for the Korean War is ludicrous.

8/11/50, "Appeal to World Opinion," *New York Times*—Analytic
Criticizes Malik and says his actions show the Soviets are engaged in a "policy of expansion by means which include open and aggressive warfare."

8/12/50, "The Man Who Came Too Late," *New York Times*—Analytic
Malik's actions in the United Nations are not and will not help the cause of the Soviets.

8/17/50, "How to Deal with Russia," *New York Times*—Critical
Discusses suggestion that Russia should be "warned" against starting any other "little wars" like Korea. Primary objective of U.S. policy must be to keep the Korean War from spreading; such a warning might upset the Russians too much.

8/19/50, "Imperialism in Asia," *New York Times*—Analytic
Despite Soviet claims, Russia is the only world power that has imperialistic ambitions in Asia.

8/19/50, "What We Fight For," *New York Times*—Critical
U.S. soldiers are fighting because "our liberty and our whole way of life are at stake." "There is no ground for compromise between Soviet communism and Western democracy."

8/23/50, "The Battle of Lake Success," *New York Times*—Analytic
No further United Nations action on Korea is likely while Malik enjoys his month-long tenure as president of the United Nations.

8/28/50, "No 'Preventive War,'" *New York Times*—Analytic
"No war is inevitable, and as long as the Kremlin abstains from a direct attack, we can afford to wait while doing everything in our power to frustrate its designs."

8/30/50, "Malik's Last Big Lie," *New York Times*—Analytic
Chronicles further derogatory statements about the United States that were made by Malik and his failure to achieve anything during his month-long tenure as UN president.

9/1/50, "The Month of Malik Ends," *New York Times*—Analytic
Recounts Malik's derogatory statements about the United States and his attempts to blame the United States for the Korean War.

9/1/50, "Our Attitude toward China," *New York Times*—Analytic
"This country has no hostility toward the Chinese people." United States must deny the baseless charges of imperialism that are being made by the Chinese communists.

9/5/50, "Korea and Lake Success," *New York Times*—Analytic
Discusses UN situation now that Malik's term as president is over. North Korean military success is directly linked to the high level of support from Russia and Red China. United States is doing everything it can to avoid expansion of the war.

9/6/50, "A Test for the Soviets," *New York Times*—Analytic
UN Security Council must take up possible problem of further involvement by Russia and Red China in the Korean War. UN action is needed to avoid expansion of the war.

9/7/50, "Soviet Veto," *New York Times*—Analytic
Chronicles growing involvement of the Russians in the war and their increasingly hostile attitude toward the United States.

9/8/50, "Mr. Malik's Latest Line," *New York Times*—Analytic
Recounts most recent Russian charges that U.S./UN planes are attacking Chinese civilians in China. Accusations are lies.

9/9/50, "The Aircraft Incidents," *New York Times*—Analytic
Recounts most recent Russian charges that U.S./UN planes are attacking Chinese civilians in China. Accusations are lies.

9/10/50, "Red China's Tactics," *New York Times*—Analytic
Discusses Red China's refusal to allow UN observers to enter its territory. Red China is simply trying to gain leverage in its efforts to be admitted to the United Nations.

9/18/50, "Hard Fighting Ahead," *New York Times*—Critical
Recounts latest battlefield events. Outcome may depend on how much outside help is given to North Korea. "Idea of aggression" must be halted in North Korea.

9/21/50, "American Program," *New York Times*—Critical
Recounts speech by Acheson to the United Nations calling for action to prevent "a new world war." Blames "New Imperialism of the Soviet Government" for heightened danger of a world war. West's system of collective defense must be strengthened.

9/21/50, "The Vote on China," *New York Times*—Analytic
Applauds efforts of United States to postpone UN consideration of admitting Red China to the United Nations. The actions of Red China in Korea cast doubt on its trustworthiness.

9/22/50, "'Expansionism' in Asia," *New York Times*—Analytic
Soviet claims of Western expansionism in Asia "are not merely false" but "ridiculous" in their "impudence."

9/24/50, "The Assembly Takes Over," *New York Times*—Analytic
"In time . . . the Russians may have a change of mind or heart . . . [about] the policy of infiltration and aggression they are now following."

9/26/50, "The Liberation of Seoul," *New York Times*—Critical
Recounts Inchon campaign and the liberation of Seoul. "Tables have now been turned."

9/29/50, "A Plan for Korea," *New York Times*—Critical
Applauds U.S. plan in the United Nations to create a united, free, and democratic Korea. Thirty-eighth parallel can be discounted.

9/30/50, "The 38th Parallel," *New York Times*—Critical
Discusses whether UN forces should cross the 38th parallel in their advance. Says they should, as the line is not really a national frontier, as the Russians are claiming.

10/1/50, "Korea: Test of Policy," *New York Times*—Critical
Korea is a "test" of the strength of the world's nations. All of Asia is looking to see how the United States will handle Korea. Foresees quick end to the war.

10/2/50, "North of the 38th," *New York Times*—Critical
Question of whether the 38th parallel should be crossed is now settled (as it already has been crossed). South Koreans have dismissed threats by Red China as "bluster," and "we must hope they are right." Chinese intervention would be "folly beyond belief."

10/3/50, "The Soviets and Korea," *New York Times*—Analytic
Discusses Soviet proposal for peace in Korea. Soviets may be laying the basis for a later disclaimer of responsibility if Red China invades.

10/4/50, "For a Free Korea," *New York Times*—Critical
United States must not lose the peace by allowing the Russians to "Balkanize" Korea once it is free and united.

10/6/50, "China and Korea," *New York Times*—Analytic
Red China will not intervene in the war.

10/14/50, "Closing In," *New York Times*—Analytic
"It now seems unlikely that there will be direct intervention by either the Chinese communists or the Soviet Union."

10/16/50, "Words Are Not Enough," *New York Times*—Critical
Discusses recent statements by the Soviets and their conciliatory nature. West must still be on its guard, and the Russians cannot be trusted.

10/18/50, "Mr. Truman's Speech," *New York Times*—Analytic
Discusses Truman's latest speech in which he warns the Soviets against further aggression and says the Soviets must prove their desire for peace with their actions.

10/20/50, "Pyongyang Yields," *New York Times*—Critical
Recounts taking of Pyongyang. Next goal will be to remove the threat of "prolonged communist guerrilla opposition."

10/22/50, "Mopping Up," *New York Times*—Critical
War in Korea is over, and only "mopping up" remains to be done.

10/27/50, "The Problem of Disarmament," *New York Times*—Critical
Disarmament talks with the Soviets do not make sense right now because of the relative strength of the Soviets and the current hostile atmosphere in the world as a result of the Korean War.

11/1/50, "Red China and Korea," *New York Times*—Analytic
There is little doubt that some Chinese communists are joining the war in Korea. The "intentions of the Chinese Communist Government . . . remain a mystery." Doubts that Red China will intervene in force. United Nations should warn Red China not to intervene.

11/3/50, "New Turn in Korea," *New York Times*—Analytic
Recounts stiffening resistance of the North Koreans. "The ultimate intentions of both the Soviets and the Chinese Communists remain unclear."

11/5/50, "Chinese Troops in Korea," *New York Times*—Analytic
There is no longer any question that Chinese communists have intervened in large numbers in Korea. Chastises Red China for its actions.

11/7/50, "A United Nations Task," *New York Times*—Analytic
United Nations must do something about intervention of Red China in the Korean War. United States will do everything in its power to avoid a third world war. Chinese communists are taking the "way of madness."

Iran 1980

1/7/79, "The Friend That Failed," *New York Times*—Analytic
Discusses need for United States to be perceived as supporting the shah, despite the tension such support creates with the other powers in Iran. Such support is necessary to soothe other allies that might otherwise see us as weak.

1/17/79, "The Shah Departs, Finally," *New York Times*—Analytic
Discusses departure of the shah from Iran. Regrets that shah waited so long to leave. Khomeini promises to return from his exile and establish Islamic government. Khomeini's government will be hostile to United States. Civilian government put in place by the shah should be given a chance.

2/13/79, "The Inevitable in Iran," *New York Times*—Analytic
Shah's downfall is dangerous for United States. Discusses strategic problems caused by revolution in Persian Gulf. Recognizes possibility that Iran may turn toward Soviets.

3/15/79, "Behind the Veil of Iran," *New York Times*—Analytic
Discusses protests in Iran by thousands of women who reject Khomeini's request that they wear chadors (traditional robes and veil) rather than blue jeans and skirts. Iranian society is growing tired of revolutionary government's repressive policies.

4/10/79, "Of Law, Life, and Death," *New York Times*—Analytic
Discussing purge of the supporters of the shah by the new revolutionary government in Iran. Suggests that "government and execution ought to be recognized as incompatible."

4/19/79, "Trial by Komiteh," *New York Times*—Analytic
Discusses rash of executions in Iran carried out by ad hoc local bodies of Islamic fundamentalists loyal to Khomeini. Suggests that government cannot control these "komitehs." Worries that old dictatorship is simply being replaced with a new one.

5/22/79, "By the Light of the Ayatollah's Oil," *New York Times*—Analytic
Discusses general relations between Iran and United States after revolution. Mentions Khomeini criticism of United States ("Our relationship with them is that of a tyrant with an innocent, that of a ravaged victim with a plunderer"), particularly his criticism of Senator Javits and his wife, who had close ties to the shah and have criticized Khomeini.

7/24/79, "Opiates of the People," *New York Times*—Analytic
Discusses decision of the Iranian government to ban the broadcast of music on radio and television. Highlights the censorship and repression carried out by the revolutionary government. Mentions the inability of the Bazargan government to control Khomeini.

8/16/79, "The Ayatollah Draws the Curtain," *New York Times*—Analytic
Discusses press censorship in Iran and reports of violent unrest. Says that Khomeini is creating a dictatorship by rigging elections and repressing people.

8/27/79, "Of Arms and the Ayatollah," *New York Times*—Analytic
Discusses Carter administration's decision to sell spare military parts and kerosene to Bazargan government. Policy questioned in light of fragility of the new revolutionary government.

11/6/79, "Doing Satan's Work in Iran," *New York Times*—Analytic
Khomeini has recklessly opened a Pandora's box. In a sense Iran is hurting itself by reducing oil exports; the United States can retaliate against the Iranian embassy and block spare part weapon supplies to Iran.

11/9/79, "The Stakes in Iran," *New York Times*—Analytic
A hostage rescue would require a large force of American troops in the Middle East; this is costly and will result in many casualties. In addition, a rescue attempt may positively influence Khomeini's political position in Iran. Waiting seems to be the best alternative.

11/13/79, "The Right Way to Get Tough," *New York Times*—Analytic
Conservation is better than fighting. "Driving less and shivering a little" will not release the hostages but will force Americans to unite. The message is that the United States can manage without oil if it has to. This step will clarify the American position and show Iran that we cannot be blackmailed.

11/16/79, "Food Is No Weapon against Iran," *New York Times*—Analytic
Food is a "poor diplomatic weapon." A food embargo will not work because nations can easily guard themselves against a shortage by reducing the amount of grain used to feed livestock. The effect of an embargo is reduced and will tend to "strengthen the nation's resolve to fight on." More so, such an embargo inevitably hurts the wrong people, the poor.

11/20/79, "The Ayatollah Discovers Law," *New York Times*—Analytic
In an attempt to extradite the shah of Iran from the United States, Khomeini has considered a new weapon, international law. Khomeini's recognition of a law may aid his adherence to other international laws and court systems, which will eventually help resolve the hostage crisis.

11/21/79, "The Rights of Iranians," *New York Times*—Analytic
The obvious route of retaliation against Iran would be to evict Iranian students who lack appropriate visas. Although a poor diplomatic tool, targeting Iranian students will appease American sentiments for "something" to be done and will also buy time to secure hostage release.

11/25/79, "Words of Violence, Paths of Reason," *New York Times*—Analytic
Khomeini has threatened to conduct spy trials for the hostages. Such an action would invoke American military attack, causing shedding of Iranian blood and making the Ayatollah more favored in Iran. However, "he cannot exploit his prisoners and murder them, too." If the shah returns to Mexico, it is hoped that the crisis will be resolved in international courts.

11/27/79, "Throwing Matches in Iran: Holiness and Hate," *New York Times*—Analytic
Ayatollah Khomeini is viewed as a man of holiness and hate. On one side Ayatollah seeks to unify Iran and calls other Muslims (and even American blacks) to rise against the United States and Israel. His charge is that the United States and Israel have seized the Grand Mosque in Mecca and are evil and corrupt. The undertone of this message, however, speaks racism and hate.

12/2/79, "Hostages to What?" *New York Times*—Critical
The imprisonment of the hostages has allowed Khomeini to place himself in a position to fuel a cultural and racial revolution that could preface a Holy War. The American decision to restrain a response to the tyranny imposed by Ayatollah will save the lives of the 50 remaining hostages, but we must grimly realize that the United States cannot hold this position indefinitely.

12/5/79, "Hindsight in America, Foretaste in Iran: Enough of Guilt," *New York Times*—
    Analytic
Iran's inner conflicts, although somewhat embarrassing, are not a reflection of U.S. ties with Iran. Iran is free to choose its friendships, and the United States has not and will not influence this choice. Our focus should be the hostages. We ought to maintain the course that allows for their safety.

12/5/79, "Hindsight in America, Foretaste in Iran: Too Much Guardian," *New York
    Times*—Analytic
Iran has recently granted Ayatollah the office of Faghi (trustee or guardian). Under the new constitution, his authority is unchecked; "he is allowed to declare to war, appoint jurists who can veto laws of elected parliaments, etc." Although history has recorded the devastation wrought by many absolute rulers, authoritarianism still continues. Unfortunately for Iran, it seems to be something new and improved.

12/8/79, "Hostage Taking as a World Crime," *New York Times*—Analytic
United Nations should ratify and adopt procedures established during the international convention against the taking of hostages. The adoption of the convention on hostages will build on the United Nations' present appeal to Iran.

12/22/79, "Boycotting Iran, Buying Time," *New York Times*—Analytic
The hostages may be killed if the United States uses force against Iran. An embargo is the next reasonable step. It will buy time, but only at the cost of cutting trade—a step many nations are reluctant to take. An embargo may not be effective if Iran finds a secret friend willing to barter oil for food and other goods. Without an embargo, however, the prospects of a peaceful solution decrease.

12/30/79, "Patience Is Strength in Iran," *New York Times*—Analytic
"Patience is a character of a strong man. It is not the character of a weak man." Carter's hesitation to use force and seek a peaceful resolution is not favored by the U.S. people. By standing still, President Carter decreases the risk of confrontations with not only Iran

but also powers that may aid Iran, namely, the Soviet Union. This stance may not bring immediate results, but it will buy time toward a "face-saving solution."

1/16/80, "The Teheran Stage Goes Dark," *New York Times*—Analytic
U.S. news reporters have been expelled from Iran in an attempt to ease tensions.

1/30/80, "Better News from Islam," *New York Times*—Analytic
Canada has assisted the escape of six U.S. hostages from Iran. Iran has elected a new president, who appears willing to reach an agreement with the United States. Iran's Muslim neighbor's are pleading for a resolution to the crisis in an attempt to focus on the threat of Soviet aggression in Afghanistan. Unfortunately, we are unaware of Ayatollah Khomeini's position on these current events.

2/26/80, "The Hostages' Bad Deal, Continued," *New York Times*—Analytic
More delays. There is hope that the new Iranian president will help secure a hostage release. According to Ayatollah Khomeini, their release is dependent upon the next parliament, which unfortunately will not meet until April. This news casts a shadow of doubt on the progress of resolving the hostage crisis. The losers are the hostages. There is nothing to do but wait.

3/12/80, "Mr. Bani-Sadr Needs Some Help," *New York Times*—Analytic
It appears that there are still more delays that prevent the release of the hostages. This delay is primarily due to opposition between Ayatollah Khomeini and Iranian president Bani-Sadr. "Encourage Moslem nations to denounce Khomeini; complicate trade relations between the West and Iran; close the Iranian Embassy in Washington; but do not use military force."

3/26/80, "The Jetsam of Foreign Policy," *New York Times*—Analytic
It seems as if the burdens of U.S. affairs are falling on the shoulders of Egyptian president Anwar Sadat. The shah has been admitted to Egypt for treatment of an enlarged spleen. As a result, tensions in Iran have increased. It is unclear whether this new turn of events will favor a hostage release. United States should still be firm in its policy to harass Iranian trade and diplomacy.

4/3/80, "Tell Them Almost Anything, Clearly," *New York Times*—Analytic
In desperation for a resolution "President Carter is willing to say almost anything that will result in the freedom or comfort of the hostages." He is willing to cease further action against Iran if negotiations are actively discussed. Unfortunately, there are two voices coming from Iran (President Bani-Sadr and Ayatollah Khomeini), and President Carter is selective in his response.

4/8/80, "Let Iran Begin to Worry," *New York Times*—Critical
"The objective should be to influence the debate in Teheran by creating real penalties for holding the hostages." Although force against Iran may not free the hostages, and might stir strife in Teheran, we have worried too much and too long. For the past five months President Carter has shown cautious restraint; it is now time to act.

4/13/80, "Allies Are What Allies Do," *New York Times*—Critical
"If the allies want to help steer American policy, they need first to show a willingness to share the risks and the costs." U.S. force against Iran may be used soon and may not only hurt America but also its allies; thus, it's in allies best interest to lend support and get involved now.

4/20/80, "Past the Point of No Result," *New York Times*—Critical
Carter is biting the bullet and will not back away from new pressures on Iran to release the hostages. The situation is tense, and it is unclear what will occur as a result of Carter's threats, but one thing is sure: the president is on the right course.

4/23/80, "The Alliance Groans On," *New York Times*—Critical
Until now the United States has withstood many internal and international criticisms concerning its actions against Iran. United States has stood alone on most issues because of a lack of harmony between allied forces. Europeans claim that the disunity stems from Carter's global goals and "wider interests (reelection)," yet they fail to realize that they have much more to lose if oil prices surge and if the hostages are kept for ransom. Soon we will be compelled to action, and it will be of great interest to see how the allies will react.

5/7/80, "What London Proves," *New York Times*—Analytic
In London the hostage rescue was executed with force because terrorists were starting to murder them by the clock. It does not prove that force is useful at all times. It was easy to dispel five terrorists holding the Iranian embassy in London; it is very difficult, however, to overthrow terrorists supported by hoards of people and a weak government. In reality, there is no comparison between the two hostage crises. "What it should prove to Iran is that wise differs from reckless, bravery from bluster, and that law differs from crime."

6/12/80, "To and Fro on the Road to Iran," *New York Times*—Analytic
Things are looking up. "If civil relations with the U.S. and the resumption of oil exports with the West are recognized as benefits rather than threats to the revolution, Americans should encourage those calculations, with wise and measured words."

7/12/80, "Waiting for the Release of Richard Queen," *New York Times*—Analytic
"Carter has recently been biting his tongue when it comes to the hostages, and wisely so. . . . For the moment, the best chance of freeing the hostages lies in Iran's politicians coming to see the consequences of their obsession with the hostages. . . . waiting is the least bad present policy."

7/16/80, "On Understanding the Abominable," *New York Times*—Analytic
We refuse to accept the cultural validity of such practices as death by stoning, as happened yesterday in the Iranian town of Kerman. Also, do not forget the traditional Islamic acceptance of slavery.

7/21/80, "The Darkness in Teheran," *New York Times*—Analytic
Iran is filled with firing squads. Religious minorities, particularly the Bahai, are especially persecuted.

9/17/80, "Signals and Static from Iran," *New York Times*—Analytic
Discusses fate of the American hostages and the possibility of their release. Reagan favors consenting to certain conditions (release of eight billion dollars in assets, etc.) set by Iran. While no one really knows what will happen, economic pressures caused by Iran's inability to produce enough oil may make Iran accept diplomatic overtures from the United States.

9/23/80, "Iraq v. Iran," *New York Times*—Analytic
Discusses growth of hostilities between Iran and Iraq. "Americans have an interest in helping the parties negotiate a settlement and impressing on Iran the importance of its return to normal diplomatic and trade relations with the West."

9/30/80, "Riptides in the Persian Gulf," *New York Times*—Analytic
Discusses continuation of the Iran-Iraq war. American diplomacy should "contain the war." Need for Soviet help with diplomatic efforts. United States will not allow the "dismemberment of Iran." Moscow and United States should refuse to supply either side.

10/17/80, "The Thief in Search of a Judge," *New York Times*—Analytic
Discusses pleas by Iranian prime minister Ali Rajai to the United Nations for help in the Iran-Iraq war. Such pleas are diplomatically impertinent. The taking of hostages has not helped Iran in any way. Hostages must be released before Iran can get any help from the United Nations or the United States.

10/24/80, "What Price the Hostages," *New York Times*—Analytic
Discusses hostage crisis. Iranians would probably trade hostages for weapons to use in war against Iraq; would be in President Carter's personal political interest. Possibility of diplomatic solution to hostage crisis is increased by Iran's involvement in war against Iraq. Carter should wait until after election if he intends to trade arms for hostages.

11/4/80, "The Voter Is Not a Hostage," *New York Times*—Analytic
Lauds Reagan and Carter for not making the hostages a political tool. Whoever wins should be able to obtain the release of the hostages via diplomacy.

11/11/80, "Seeking the Hostages in Algeria," *New York Times*—Analytic
Discusses efforts of Carter administration to arrange for the release of the hostages via diplomacy in Algeria. Negotiations are not pointless, just difficult. It may take weeks or months, but eventually diplomacy will secure the release of the hostages.

12/23/80, "Quit the Haggling with Iran," *New York Times*—Analytic
Americans have named their highest price for the release of the hostages and should "walk away from the haggling in disgust" if Iran doesn't accept. Iran cannot decide what

it wants, and Carter administration is unlikely to gain the release of the hostages in its one remaining month. There is little that can be done outside of further economic sanctions.

12/30/80, "Teheran Is Outraged," *New York Times*—Analytic
Agrees with the decision of Carter (and Reagan) to turn down Iran's offer to trade the hostages for approximately $24 billion (thought $2.5 billion enough). "The word 'barbarian' may indeed sound harsh in Iran, but the shouting match had its start there." There remains a "fleeting chance for a civilized settlement."

1/20/81, "Unscrambling the Egg," *New York Times*—Analytic
End of hostage crisis. "Escape from the hostage trauma should be a blessing for both peoples." "The hostage-taking was an outrage. . . . To understand is not to forgive."

Iraq 1991: *New York Times*

8/3/90, "Iraq's Naked Aggression," *New York Times*—Analytic
Iraq's unprovoked attack on Kuwait is truly a horrible action. Shows that raw force has not disappeared as a weapon, despite thaw in U.S.-USSR relations.

8/5/90, *New York Times*—Analytic
"Collective diplomacy to isolate Iraq could finally realize what the UN Charter envisioned: collective security."

8/7/90, *New York Times*—Analytic
We should encourage the Saudis to help contain Iraq. An economic embargo is the wise policy choice.

8/9/90, *New York Times*—Analytic
The United States should work harder to get other nations on board with the embargo. "Collective security cannot work unless it is collective."

8/10/90, *New York Times*—Analytic
We should keep on with the embargo. Let us hope that we have the patience and will to see the embargo through to its conclusion.

8/12/90, *New York Times*—Critical
Bush needs to "trumpet" the need for U.S. forces to be in the Gulf and the need for other nations to join in the embargo.

8/15/90, *New York Times*—Analytic
We should use the United Nations to set up a "collective effort at sea" to maintain the embargo. Do not go it alone.

8/17/90, *New York Times*—Analytic
Analysis of Iraq's actions. "However great the provocation and however ominous the detention of foreigners in Kuwait, the wise course for the United States is to press tirelessly for collective condemnation, collective sanctions and collective force."

8/20/90, *New York Times*—Analytic
Collective action is the only way to go. Delaying the naval embargo is worth it if that will secure such collective action.

8/21/90, "Time Squeezes Iraq," *New York Times*—Analytic
Time is on our side as the embargo will soon start to bite.

8/22/90, *New York Times,* Analytic
Bush would be foolish to initiate hostilities.

8/23/90, *New York Times*, Critical
Arab unity against Iraq is a wonderful development. Also, "unilateral American military action may ultimately prove necessary, and President Bush was surely right in his news conference yesterday in refusing to rule it out."

8/25/90, *New York Times*—Analytic
Laundry list of awful things Iraq has done in its invasion of Kuwait.

8/26/90, *New York Times*—Critical
The United States must resist the temptation to initiate hostilities. Still, any peace settlement will have a hard time getting at basic problem of future Iraqi military power. Any solution will require Iraq to destroy some weapons and submit to international inspection.

8/28/90, "This Embargo Can Work," *New York Times*—Analytic
United States has time on its side with the embargo. Constant economic pressure will allow United States to achieve its goals.

8/29/90, *New York Times*—Critical
World will not be safe if Iraq simply withdraws from Kuwait, because its military might will remain intact. "UN resolution [condemning aggression and authorizing naval embargo] doesn't go far enough."

8/30/90, *New York Times*—Analytic
Although we cannot overlook the danger Iraqi arms will pose even after they withdraw from Kuwait, Iraqi arms reductions can be negotiated. This future danger does not warrant going beyond embargo.

9/2/90, *New York Times*—Critical
Our prescription for a resolution: "Keep uniting the UN; nurture the enforcing coalition; do not rise to Baghdad's bait; give the embargo a chance to work; begin now to shape peace terms." Last element raises doubt that future Iraqi military threat can be removed under UN auspices, may require unilateral U.S. action.

9/7/90, *New York Times*—Critical
USSR and United States must send a joint message to Iraq: "Get out of Kuwait."

9/8/90, *New York Times*—Analytic
Brazil is selling missiles to Iraq; we should try to get them to stop.

9/10/90, *New York Times*—Analytic
Hussein must be worried that the United States and the USSR are working together to defuse the Gulf crisis.

9/13/90, *New York Times*—Analytic
Congress and the U.S. people are firmly behind a cautious embargo approach.

9/15/90, *New York Times*—Analytic
The seizure of embassies is an awful thing, and we must hope that our Kuwaiti embassy will not be threatened.

9/18/90, *New York Times*—Analytic
General Dugan's announced strategy of decapitation and massive air strikes is the wrong strategy for the United States to follow. His comments deserved his sacking.

9/23/90, *New York Times*—Analytic
Analysis of historical State Department perceptions of Iraq.

9/25/90, *New York Times*—Analytic
Do not discount Hussein's threats of a preemptive strike, but let's not go that route ourselves. Instead, we should maintain the embargo.

10/1/90, "The Siege Is Only Eight Weeks Old," *New York Times*—Analytic
Patience should be exercised in dealing with Iraqi invasion. It is "dangerously premature to beat the drums of war." No deals should be made with Saddam so that economic sanctions can continue to work.

10/2/90, "'Opportunities' for Peace in the Gulf," *New York Times*—Analytic
Bush's plan is a "sensible diplomatic solution to the Persian Gulf crisis." The ball is now in Saddam's hands, and he should have the sense to respond positively.

10/8/90, "Who Will Pay for the Gulf Crisis?" *New York Times*—Critical
"There's increasing room to hope that Saddam Hussein will have to withdraw from Kuwait . . . either because of the embargo or battlefield defeat." United States will pay the most in dollars and blood. Bush has let the allies get away with paying less than their fair share.

10/21/90, "America's Best Weapon: Patience," *New York Times*—Analytic
Once again counsels against making any hasty moves in the Gulf. Urges United States to be patient and give economic sanctions a chance to work. The economic siege of Iraq needs time to work.

10/25/90, "Gulf Peace: On Tough Terms," *New York Times*—Critical
Raises the difficulties that Saddam's withdrawal from Kuwait might create for the coalition and the Middle East. Suggests plan in the event this happens whose elements

include an Arab peacekeeping force, U.S. involvement, a military arms embargo on Iraq, and diplomatic efforts to solve regional problems.

10/27/90, "Escalation, 1990 Style," *New York Times*—Analytic
Says Bush needs to explain to America why 100,000 more U.S. troops have been sent to the Gulf. Doesn't criticize the deployment, but "the burden is on President Bush to show that a significant increase in American forces will make less likely their use in battle."

11/1/90, "How to Rattle Iraq," *New York Times*—Critical
Bush should invite Congress to consider the prospect of war. This will make the threat of war more credible to Iraq. Public support for war will increase if it is debated and explained.

11/2/90, "The Big Lie about Kuwait," *New York Times*—Analytic
Iraqi historical claims to Kuwait are complete nonsense. Iraqi claims that Kuwait was unfairly overproducing oil are similarly untrue. All such Iraqi claims are pure propaganda.

11/4/90, "War? Make the Case," *New York Times*—Analytic
Bush's threats of war are hollow. Bush needs to explain his policy to the American people. Bush must make his case for the use of force at home before the military option is fully credible to Iraq.

11/11/90, "Too Far Too Fast in the Gulf," *New York Times*—Analytic
Bush's decision to send 150,000 additional troops to Iraq is premature. Bush needs support of Congress before war can be waged. Buildup may "create irresistible pressures for war." Saddam's aggression cannot be abided, but Bush is too impatient.

11/14/90, "Desert Sword: Time for Answers," *New York Times*—Analytic
Congress is right to call for a public debate on the Iraqi crisis and the possibility of war. "Calls for a declaration of war seem premature." Bush should mobilize political support for war.

11/16/90, "Double Insult from the President," *New York Times*—Analytic
Criticizes Bush for asking senators to restrain their criticism of his Iraqi policy. "True strength" can be shown by vigorous democratic debate.

11/18/90, "What's Wrong with the Siege," *New York Times*—Analytic
Criticizes Bush for wanting to rush the buildup of U.S. forces in the Gulf. Embargo hasn't been given enough time to work. Embargo has been more effective than most people realize.

11/25/90, "Taking Out Iraq's Nukes," *New York Times*—Analytic
Discusses view of those who call for a preemptive strike against Iraq to take out their nuclear capabilities. Concerns are justified, "but military action should be the last resort, not the first and certainly not the best." True Iraqi nuclear threat is low; the only long-term solution is a diplomatic one.

11/29/90, "Once Again: What's the Rush?" *New York Times*—Analytic
More patience is needed. Criticizes new and more militaristic stance of United States
and United Nations. January 15 deadline puts time on the side of Saddam rather than the
allies. Agrees with Nunn and Gephardt that more patience is called for.

12/1/90, "Mr. Bush's Extra Mile for Peace," *New York Times*—Analytic
Applauds Bush's offer to send Baker to meet with Saddam. Suggests that Bush continue
to be patient and let economic sanctions work. Congress should also urge Bush to be patient.

12/2/90, "A Weak Case for War," *New York Times*—Analytic
Bush administration's arguments that force may soon be necessary are wrong. Urges patience. The threshold at which fighting becomes necessary has not yet been crossed.

12/7/90, "How to Choke Iraq," *New York Times*—Analytic
Saddam's decision to release the hostages is a sign that he is weakening; this proves that
economic sanctions are working. War will erode security and stability in the Gulf; only
diplomatic means can check Saddam.

12/16/90, "War by Default," *New York Times*—Analytic
Bush is risking war prematurely; sanctions must be given more time to work. Congressional approval is necessary to wage war, and Congress should begin debate on the war
immediately.

12/19/90, "Israel and Iraq, Unlinked," *New York Times*—Analytic
Applauds Bush administration for its policy that the Iraqi and Palestinian crises are not
linked. There must be no linkage, and any call from third world countries for a new UN
resolution calling for Israel to get out of the occupied lands should be skillfully avoided.
International peace conference is premature and would be seen as linkage.

12/21/90, "The General Is Telling the Truth," *New York Times*—Analytic
Applauds Gen. Waller's comments that the January 15 deadline is premature. Fantasies
of an antiseptic air war must be publicly dismissed by men such as General Waller if the
public is to understand the war. More time is necessary to prepare troops.

12/24/90, "No Booty for Iraq. None," *New York Times*—Critical
Potential Iraqi proposal of peace in return for certain islands and oil fields is unacceptable. Saddam's aggression must not be rewarded.

1/3/91, "Where Is Congress on the Gulf?" *New York Times*—Analytic
Congress has a constitutional duty to debate the war. "Mr. Bush's brinksmanship is running out of time to show results."

1/5/91, "How to Bargain with a Blackmailer," *New York Times*—Analytic
Both sides must "walk the last mile for peace." Iraq must unconditionally withdraw
from Kuwait. Bush has set forth "honorable terms" for peace.

1/10/91, "The Larger Patriotism," *New York Times*—Analytic
Counsels against war. American "interests would not be served by the offensive use of military force to expel Iraq from Kuwait." Sanctions should be given more time; "the wise, brave vote on war is no."

1/11/91, "Iraq's Untenable Argument," *New York Times*—Analytic
Disputes Iraqi claims that its invasion of Kuwait is linked in any way to the Palestinian crisis. The right response is to refuse to link the two disputes.

1/11/91, "The Message Stronger," *New York Times*—Critical
Congressional support of war may force Saddam to seek a bargain in return for his withdrawal from Kuwait, but the allies should be "tough-minded" in their response. Saddam's withdrawal must be unconditional.

1/15/91, "The Stakes in the Gulf," *New York Times*—Analytic
Both militarists and pacifists in United States have some good points and bad points; they must learn to understand each other. The blame for the crisis lies in Baghdad.

Iraq 1991: *Wall Street Journal*

7/26/90, *Wall Street Journal*—Critical
"In today's exquisitely interdependent world, we need to think again about the ancient military mission known as suppression of piracy." Iraq certainly qualifies as a pirate nation.

8/3/90, "The Thief of Baghdad," *Wall Street Journal*—Critical
The United States must do something to stand up to this "pirate." His seizure of Kuwait cannot be allowed to stand.

8/6/90, *Wall Street Journal*—Critical
The world reaction to Iraqi invasion suggests that our diplomats may be able to put together a coordinated military effort to rectify Hussein's "piracy."

8/8/90, *Wall Street Journal*—Critical
Strong, aggressive action on the Iraqi invasion will give Bush increased world and domestic influence.

8/9/90, *Wall Street Journal*—Critical
Bush will pacify the entire Gulf region by crushing Hussein. Good to see that Bush is headed in this direction.

8/15/90, *Wall Street Journal*—Critical
"The ultimate objective ought to be the overthrow of the Saddam government." If this requires military action, so be it.

8/22/90, *Wall Street Journal*—Critical
The United States should move against Hussein with a massive military attack. "Saddam's threat [hostages] is the final evidence that he is nothing more than an international thug who needs to be removed if there is to be any peace in the Middle East now or in the foreseeable future. Negotiating with him, which many in the West would surely support, would leave his military machine intact. That would leave the Gulf at his mercy and the world at the mercy of any future pirate who can lay hands on some Americans."

8/28/90, *Wall Street Journal*—Critical
Bush should not support Perez de Cuellar's peace mission, as it just "confuses matters." An immediate military attack on Iraq is called for.

8/29/90, *Wall Street Journal*—Critical
The Kissinger-Haig school is correct: launch a preemptive strike now. Their rationale, however, that the public will "wimp out" if we wait, is wrong. The American public will support a military action if the goals are clear. The optimum resolution is to "take Baghdad and install a MacArthur regency."

9/7/90, *Wall Street Journal*—Critical
Bush should definitely remove the "pirate regime" in Iraq with a military attack.

9/11/90, *Wall Street Journal*—Critical
The United States must remove Hussein from power.

9/13/90, *Wall Street Journal*—Critical
The war objectives as recently stated in the *New York Times* are simply not achievable as they are based on hopes of successful negotiation. You cannot negotiate with a pirate such as Hussein; instead, you must attack with military force and dictate terms.

9/26/90, *Wall Street Journal*—Critical
U.S. Treasury needs to get in line behind the war effort. We need to mount a massive attack on Iraq, and the Treasury must find the money to finance the operation.

10/10/90, *Wall Street Journal*—Critical
United States should not tolerate Iraqi threats of chemical weapons. We should take them out now if we can locate them. If Iraq uses such weapons, the United States should retaliate in kind.

10/22/90, *Wall Street Journal*—Analytic
The Israeli response to the Palestinian provocation at the Temple in Jerusalem, while justified, allows Hussein the pretext he needs to link the Gulf and Israel. Such a link makes U.S. efforts to remove Hussein that much more difficult.

11/7/90, "Aims in the Gulf," *Wall Street Journal*—Critical
"History will judge the success or failure of his [Bush's] presidency on the outcome of the confrontation with Saddam Hussein." While United States cannot punish every act

of aggression, Iraq is a special case and should be punished. Saddam is a "pirate," "to secure the future someone should stop him. . . . the Americans are the only ones who can."

11/19/90, "Lawyers for Iraq," *Wall Street Journal*—Critical
Criticizes legalisms such as whether the United Nations or Congress or the president should control negotiations. Even if Saddam's "armies cannot guarantee impunity to his conquests, our lawyers will." We need to ignore niceties and get rid of Hussein.

12/7/90, "Saddam's First Card," *Wall Street Journal*—Critical
Saddam's decision to release hostages is a good sign. Saddam would stand no chance if it comes to war, and his best hope lies in American division over what should be done. "Americans will never be safe traveling the world or economically secure at home" if Saddam gets away with the invasion of Kuwait.

1/2/91, "Decks Cleared?" *Wall Street Journal*—Critical
Discusses Bush's declining political fortunes. "If the president succeeds in the Gulf he will be in a strong position to recoup." A short successful war or an anti-Saddam coup would "reinvigorate the prestige and morale of the administration."

1/3/91, "A Separate Peace," *Wall Street Journal*—Critical
Europe's attempts to solve the crisis will not succeed, and European countries cannot be the "leading player" in efforts to solve problems in the Gulf. Europe should get behind U.S. efforts to overthrow Hussein.

1/9/91, "Saddam's Reward," *Wall Street Journal*—Critical
While resolve of the Bush administration to stand up to Saddam is stronger than ever, the resolve of other Western countries and of Congress is questionable. The coalition is fragile, and a Middle East peace conference is a likely result of the crisis. Iraq is a "pirate nation" that will eventually turn on Israel, the Saudis, or Iran if it is appeased. Criticizes those that would make concessions to Saddam.

1/11/91, "Saddam's Protectors," *Wall Street Journal*—Critical
Criticizes the decision of many Congressional Democrats to vote against the use of force. Bush must be given the power to start the war if he decides to do so.

1/15/91, "If Not Now, When ?" *Wall Street Journal*—Critical
Reviews "why the impending war is necessary. In brief, because we have a monster on the loose in a crucial corner of the globe we share." Says "the future is at stake. . . . Saddam's ambitions extend far beyond Kuwait. . . . The reason for spending blood is to avoid even worse choices and even greater sacrifices in the future."

Notes

Chapter 1

1. The literature on international political crises is too vast to review here. An excellent introduction is still Glenn Snyder and Paul Diesing, *Conflict among Nations* (Princeton: Princeton University Press, 1977).

2. Most notably Bruce Bueno de Mesquita in various solo and coauthored works. See Bueno de Mesquita, *The War Trap* (New Haven, Conn.: Yale University Press, 1981); "The War Trap Revisited," *American Political Science Review* 79 (1985): 156–77; also Bueno de Mesquita and David Lalman, "Reason and War," *American Political Science Review* 80, no. 4 (1986): 1113–29; and *War and Reason* (New Haven, Conn.: Yale University Press, 1992). Bueno de Mesquita evaluates the expected utility associated with national choices prior to war, where the probability of victory is measured by a comparison of national capabilities and the utilities associated with potential outcomes are measured by a comparison of resulting alliance structures. Although critics dispute both the construction of the model and the interpretation of test results (see, e.g., R. Harrison Wagner, "War and Expected Utility Theory," *World Politics* 36, no. 3 [April 1984]: 407–23; and Michael Nicholson, "The Conceptual Bases of *The War Trap*," *Journal of Conflict Resolution* 31, no. 2 [June 1987]: 346–69), Bueno de Mesquita's work is clearly a landmark in terms of vision, method, and influence. To reverse and paraphrase Shakespeare's Marc Antony, I have come to praise Bueno de Mesquita, not bury him.

3. For example, Bueno de Mesquita claims: "My particular approach to the maximizing behavior of key leaders is shaped by two associated assumptions. First, I postulate that one nation's utility for another nation is a direct, positive function of the degree to which they share a common policy perspective" (*War Trap,* 29). The operationalization of these policy perspectives, however, depends entirely upon the set of military alliances each nation possesses, which in turn is assumed to determine that nation's level of security. To the degree that some nation does not possess that alliance portfolio that gives it the most security, that nation is assumed to be risk acceptant ("War Trap Revisited," 157). In an extension of this assumption regarding the maximization of security, see James Morrow, "On the Theoretical Basis of a Measure of National Risk Attitudes," *International Studies Quarterly* 31 (1987): 423–38.

4. As with several other concepts in this book, the literature on structural neorealism is too vast to cover adequately here. The foundations of modern realism are found in the writings of Hans Morgenthau and E. H. Carr, among others. Neorealism is often associated with Kenneth Waltz. For a good introduction to the tenets of structural neorealism

see Robert Keohane, ed., *Neorealism and Its Critics* (New York: Columbia University Press, 1986).

5. Interestingly, Bueno de Mesquita takes precisely this approach when he looks at domestic policy decisions. See *Forecasting Political Events: The Future of Hong Kong* (New Haven, Conn.: Yale University Press, 1985), coauthored with David Newman and Alvin Rabushka.

6. Robert C. North, *War, Peace, Survival: Global Politics and Conceptual Synthesis* (Boulder, Colo.: Westview Press, 1990), 154.

7. Karl W. Deutsch, "Mass Communications and the Loss of Freedom in National Decision-making: A Possible Research Approach to Interstate Conflicts," *Journal of Conflict Resolution* 1, no. 2 (1957): 200–211; Alexander George, *Propaganda Analysis: A Study of Inferences Made from Nazi Propaganda in World War II* (Evanston, Ill.: Row, Peterson, 1959).

8. I use the term *purely cooperative* loosely here, simply to get across the point that, even in a bargaining situation that can lead to mutual benefits, the incentive to hide intentions does not disappear or become counterproductive. As William Zartman puts it, all negotiations are "the controlled exchange of partial information" (*The Fifty-Percent Solution* [Garden City, N.Y.: Anchor Books, 1976], 14).

9. Deutsch, "Mass Communications," 201; my emphasis.

10. George himself owes an intellectual debt to Harold Lasswell, who pioneered the scientific study of regime communications in *Propaganda Technique in the World War* (New York: Knopf, 1927); and *World Revolutionary Propaganda* (New York: Knopf, 1939).

11. George, *Propaganda Analysis,* chap. 11: "Prediction of an Elite's Major Actions." As George points out, however, there were also prominent failures to predict German behavior on the basis of propaganda analysis. Chapter 2 speculates on the sources of success and failure for the intelligence agencies George examines.

12. "Monitoring the Integrative Complexity of American and Soviet Policy Rhetoric: What Can Be Learned?" *Journal of Social Issues* 44, no. 2 (1988): 101–31; "Integrative Complexity of American and Soviet Foreign Policy Rhetoric: A Time-Series Analysis," *Journal of Personality and Social Psychology* 49, no. 6 (1985): 1565–85; with Charles B. McGuire Jr., "Integrative Complexity of Soviet Rhetoric as a Predictor of Soviet Behavior," *International Journal of Group Tensions* 14, nos. 1–4 (1984): 113–28. Unfortunately, Tetlock is unable to demonstrate conclusively that his rhetoric measures are leading indicators of behavior. In "Monitoring" Tetlock simply announces that ARIMA and two-stage least squares regression analyses of his data support various conclusions without reporting the statistical test results.

Other researchers have had some success in using integrative complexity theory to find leading indicators of behaviors other than the decision for war. Michael Wallace and Peter Suedfeld employ the integrative complexity approach to generate an "early warning indicator of leadership performance in crisis" in "Leadership Performance in Crisis: The Longevity-Complexity Link," *International Studies Quarterly* 32, no. 4 (December 1988): 439–51. Their results are substantiated by Stephen Walker and George Watson ("Integrative Complexity and British Decisions during the Munich and Polish Crises," *Journal of Conflict Resolution* 38, no. 1 [March 1994]: 3–23).

Another research effort that shows public statements to be an effective predictive indicator, albeit on a relatively limited subject, is William Zimmerman and Glenn Palmer, "Words and Deed in Soviet Foreign Policy: The Case of Soviet Military Expenditures," *American Political Science Review* 77, no. 2 (June 1983): 358–67.

13. N. Bhaskara Rao, *Indo-Pak Conflict: Controlled Mass Communication in Inter-State Relations* (New Delhi: S. Chand, 1971).

14. As reported in the *Economist,* September 3, 1994, 47.

15. For simplicity's sake, I am condensing two of Richard Betts's forms of surprise, political and strategic, into one, strategic. By *strategic surprise* I mean a lack of warning for all events well prior to actual initiation. Betts's definition of *tactical surprise*—lack of warning for the imminent initiation of hostilities—is retained here. See Betts, *Surprise Attack* (Washington, D.C.: Brookings Institution, 1982), 4–5.

16. One might well ask, as does Zeev Maoz in *Paradoxes of War* (Boston: Unwin Hyman, 1990), why we persist in thinking of surprise as such an advantage when the historical record shows that most nations initiating a surprise attack end up losing the war. From the perspective of a national leader bent on war, however, this is not the real question, as the only pertinent issue is how to maximize the probability of success in war. If strategic surprise boosts a nation's chances, even if only in the short run, then a rational leader will seek to maintain such an advantage. In fact, Maoz's own resolution of the apparent paradox is that initiators are often much weaker than the countries they attack and that strategic surprise is the only way to have even a modest chance of success.

17. What's more, such states can rarely hide the deployment from each other, as U.S. and Russian interests in maintaining the status quo, combined with their far-reaching alliance portfolios, will usually move one or the other to reveal the information. This ability to use U.S. and Russian technology to prevent adversaries from managing the flow of information regarding capabilities would seem to be an important incentive for states to develop military alliances with superpowers.

18. Although the distinction between capabilities and intentions is conceptually clear, it is precisely in such attempts to operationalize intentions where the distinction loses focus. If we see Russian MRBM's positioned west of the Urals, that suggests completely different intentions than if we see those same missiles positioned just north of China, even though the position and number of these missiles is an issue of capabilities.

19. To be sure, one would expect that after a militarized crisis has developed more attention will be paid to indirect communications, since the higher stakes justify the higher costs of such an information collection effort. See John Arquilla, "Louder than Words: Tacit Communication in International Crises," *Political Communication* 9, no. 3 (July–September 1992): 155–72. Similarly, Russell Leng found that threatening words by American leaders were not a very effective tool for international bargaining with the Soviet Union during crises ("Reagan and the Russians: Crisis Bargaining Beliefs and the Historical Record," *American Political Science Review* 78, no. 2 [June 1984]: 338–52).

20. In information theory, direct communications as I have defined them are the equivalent of signals, indirect communications the equivalent of indices. See Robert Jervis, *The Logic of Images in International Relations* (Princeton: Princeton University Press, 1970), for a well-developed explication and application of the concepts. Chapter 2 of this book applies Jervis's "logic" to evaluate the potential for strategic interaction between countries on the basis of domestic media activity.

21. Claudio Cioffi-Revilla provides a detailed theoretical framework for differentiating types of international communications in "Diplomatic Communications Theory: Signals, Channels, Networks," *International Interactions* 6, no. 3 (1979): 209–65, although the ability of domestic communications to serve as an international signal is not discussed in detail.

22. In a face-to-face meeting on July 25 Saddam Hussein assured the U.S. ambassador that Iraq would not attack Kuwait to satisfy its claims; in the UN Security Council meeting of November 29 the United States claimed that its sole war aims were the removal of Iraqi troops from Kuwait; in a briefing for the foreign press corps in September the Iraqi government claimed that it had no intention of holding Westerners as hostages.

23. Just as the ability to tell a lie and be perceived as telling the truth is an advantage when seeking to manufacture surprise, the ability to tell the truth and be correctly perceived as telling the truth is an advantage in certain situations. For example, if a Russian cruiser sinks after striking an iceberg but the Russian government thinks it might have been an American torpedo, it is to the United States' advantage to be believed when it truthfully claims to have had nothing to do with the accident. A truthful reputation is key in both scenarios.

24. This is not to suggest that there are no advantages to having a reputation as a frequent bluffer. Opponents are likely to lose a greater than average amount of money when such a player truly has a strong hand, under the assumption that she is probably bluffing and that they should match her wagers. Such a process closely matches the information flow attempted by Anwar Sadat's Egyptian government, in which 1972 was consistently billed as the "year of decision," during which time Egypt would defeat Israel once and for all. The repeated bluffing helped lull Israel into believing the true threat in 1973 to be just another empty threat. The Sadat case is a negative image of the usual process, but the underlying logic is the same. In the usual process enough truthful statements are made to build credibility, and then a lie creates the divergence between expectations and reality. Here enough lies were made to lose all credibility, and then a truthful statement created the divergence between expectations and reality.

25. Exceptional politicians, from Augustus to Henri IV, have always possessed an innate feel for public opinion, regardless of the political system. And, to be fair, some exceptional political systems, notably Periclean Athens and Republican Rome, have rewarded domestic opinion management, regardless of the politician. Public opinion management was not even an accepted topic of academic study, however, until early in the twentieth century, and the notion of "propaganda" took even longer to enter the public consciousness. See J. Michael Sproule, "Propaganda Studies in American Social Science: The Rise and Fall of the Critical Paradigm," *Quarterly Journal of Speech* (February 1987): 60–77.

26. For a detailed look at why manipulating public opinion is particularly important to modern states, see Benjamin Ginsberg, *The Captive Public: How Mass Opinion Promotes State Power* (New York: Basic Books, 1986); see also Michael Leigh, *Mobilizing Consent* (Westport, Conn.: Greenwood Press, 1976).

27. The Weinberger Doctrine demands popular support for a winnable military action before troops may be sent into action.

28. For example, the U.S. Committee on Public Information was created after U.S. entry into World War I specifically to prevent foreign propaganda and to manipulate

domestic opinion according to official U.S. policy. For a description of its activities, including internal documents stating these goals, see James R. Mock and Cedric Larson, *Words That Won the War* (Princeton: Princeton University Press, 1939); and Stephen Vaughn, *Holding Fast the Inner Lines* (Chapel Hill: University of North Carolina Press, 1980). More recently, the Pentagon Papers confess to a similar attempt to control popular opinion concerning the Vietnam War.

29. During 1979 and 1980 the U.S. Air Force alone, through its public information outreach programs, put out 615,000 hometown news releases, 6,600 news media interviews, 3,200 news conferences, 500 news media orientation flights, 50 meetings with editorial boards, and 11,000 speeches (as reported in Edward S. Herman and Noam Chomsky, "Propaganda Mill," *Progressive* (June 1988): 16).

30. That governments try to influence foreign popular opinion seems clear. See, among others, S. D. Symms and E. D. Snow Jr., "Soviet Propaganda and the Neutron Bomb Decision," *Political Communication and Persuasion* 1 (1981): 257–68; and U.S. Arms Control and Disarmament Agency, *The Soviet Propaganda Campaign against the U.S. Strategic Defense Initiative* (Washington, D.C.: USGPO, 1986). Whether governments are ever successful in such attempts is another question. For an affirmative answer, see Mark J. DeHaven, "Internal and External Determinants of Foreign Policy: West Germany and Great Britain during the Two-Track Missile Controversy," *International Studies Quarterly* 35 (March 1991): 87–108.

31. One rationale for a New International Information Order is this imbalance in certain countries, with the claim that Western information is hopelessly biased. See Robert L. Stevenson and Donald L. Shaw, eds., *Foreign News and the New World Information Order* (Ames: Iowa State University Press, 1984).

32. For example, a *Washington Post* article of October 2, 1985, revealed that John Poindexter, Reagan's national security advisor, planted false stories in the *Wall Street Journal* concerning the administration's intentions toward Libya in an attempt to keep Libyan leader Gadhafi confused and frightened. Revelations regarding Pentagon dissemination of falsified SDI tests suggest a similar government-media relationship. Not that such story planting is limited to the Reagan/Bush years. John F. Kennedy was especially noted for calling editorial boards to get them to place a favorable opinion or squelch a piece. For two examples from his administration, see Peter H. Wyden, *Bay of Pigs: The Untold Story* (New York: Simon and Schuster, 1979); and Roger Hilsman, *To Move a Nation* (New York: Doubleday, 1967). For other examples in American politics, from opposite ends of the political spectrum, see Joseph Keeley, *The Left-Leaning Antenna: Political Bias in Television* (New Rochelle, N.Y.: Arlington House, 1971); and James Aronson, *The Press and the Cold War* (Indianapolis, Ind.: Bobbs-Merrill, 1974).

33. For recent examinations of this process, see W. Lance Bennett, "Toward a Theory of Press-State Relations," *Journal of Communications* 40, no. 2 (1990): 103–25; John Zaller, *The Nature and Origins of Mass Opinion* (New York: Cambridge University Press, 1992); Stephen Ansolabehere, Roy Behr, and Shanto Iyengar, *The Media Game: American Politics in the Television Age* (New York: Macmillan, 1993); and Simon Serfaty, ed., *The Media and Foreign Policy* (New York: St. Martin's Press, 1991).

34. Edward S. Herman and Noam Chomsky, *Manufacturing Consent: The Political Economy of the Mass Media* (New York: Pantheon Books, 1988), 18–19.

35. Richard Barnet, *The Rocket's Red Glare* (New York: Simon and Schuster, 1990), 335.

36. The emphasis here is on relations with the executive branch, primarily because in nonparliamentary governments with open media systems the executive generally takes the lead in foreign policy-making. In parliamentary systems we have no such concern, as the same party or coalition of parties will control both the executive and legislative branches.

37. Unlike the print media, broadcast media is subject to government licensing and is required to play by the rules set down by the government in order to maintain that license. For a discussion of the legal requirements placed on broadcasters in the United States, see Henry Geller, "Mass Communication Policy: Where We Are and Where We Should Be Going," in Judith Lichtenberg, ed., *Democracy and the Mass Media* (Cambridge: Cambridge University Press, 1990), 290–323.

38. The Reagan staff's attention to and manipulation of television media is legendary. See Mark Hertsgaard, *On Bended Knee: The Press and the Reagan Presidency* (New York: Farrar, Straus, and Giroux, 1988).

39. The assumption of a monolithic group of government decision makers is examined somewhat more closely in chapter 5's discussion of U.S. decision making leading to the Gulf War of 1990–91. The theoretical salience for this model of a strong opposition party is discussed in chapter 2.

40. As John Zaller puts it in *The Nature and Origins of Mass Opinion,* public opinion is not "dominated" by elites, as there is often disagreement between elites on proper policy as well as consensus among experts on the inherent merit of policy proposals despite ideological differences, but, certainly, elite opinion (as filtered through the largely independent incentives of mass media institutions) tends to drive mass opinion more than the other way around.

41. For an analysis of such differences between the United States, France, Japan, and West Germany, see Thomas Risse-Kappen, "Public Opinion, Domestic Structure, and Foreign Policy in Liberal Democracies," *World Politics* 43 (July 1991): 479–512.

42. The Spanish-American War is sometimes pointed to as just such an example, but, as the authors noted in chapter 5 show, McKinley projected an aura of reluctance more for political gain than because those feelings were genuine.

43. Although the Imperial Presidency following World War II was perhaps the high-water mark in relative executive control over foreign policy, the pendulum of power over foreign policy still seems to favor the executive. See Barbara Hinckley, *Less than Meets the Eye: Foreign Policy Making and the Myth of the Assertive Congress* (Chicago: University of Chicago Press, 1992).

44. Gabriel Almond, *The American People and Foreign Policy* (Westport, Conn.: Greenwood Press, 1950).

45. Under a bottom-up assumption we might expect media opinions regarding future conflict to appear earlier than under a top-down assumption. That is, it seems reasonable to expect that it would take longer for leaders to appreciate a groundswell of popular opinion *and* mount their own subsequent campaign to convince and reassure citizens than it would take for leaders simply to begin a media campaign. Also, with a bottom-up model we might expect the nature of the media complaints to be quite variable during the hypothesized percolation phase, as many independent voices attempt to define the

issue, and quite focused during the subsequent government phase, when a single voice largely takes over. With a top-down model we might expect a focused approach from the start.

46. Cited in Simon Collier, "The First Falklands War? Argentine Attitudes," *International Affairs* 57, no. 3 (Summer 1983) : 459.

47. General Assembly Resolution 1514, 15 UN GAOR Supplement (no. 16) at 66–67. UN doc. no. A/4684 (1961).

48. The UN chronology presented here is taken liberally from Raphael Perl, ed., *The Falkland Islands Dispute in International Law and Politics* (London: Oceana Publications, 1983), 82–84.

49. General Assembly Resolution 2065, 20 UN GAOR Supplement (no. 14) at 57. UN doc. no. A/6015 (1966). The year 1966 also saw a rather farcical military operation directed against British occupation of the islands, the Condor affair, in which a small band of lightly armed Argentines hijacked a DC4, landed at the Stanley airport, claimed the territory for Argentina, and were promptly arrested. It seems improbable that the Argentine government, then controlled by the Ongania junta, had any knowledge of the operation, as the hijackers were members of the antigovernment Montoneros guerrilla group.

50. General Assembly Resolution 3160, 28 UN GAOR Supplement (no. 30) at 108–9. UN doc. no. A/9030 (1974).

51. OEA Serie Q/IV.12.CJI-2, 17–22; as found in *Falkland Islands Dispute,* 83.

52. *Times of London,* February 6, 1976; as found in *Falkland Islands Dispute,* 83.

53. *Times of London,* July 14, December 13, 1977, and November 27, 1980; as found in the *Falkland Islands Dispute,* 83–84.

54. The South Georgias are not part of the Falklands per se but are another South Atlantic island group claimed by Britain. Along with the South Sandwich Islands these territories were the primary targets of the war.

55. *Operacion Rosario,* preface by Adm. Carlos Busser (Buenos Aires: Editorial Atlantida, 1984), 7; as found in Lawrence Freedman and Virginia Gamba-Stonehouse, *Signals of War: The Falklands Conflict of 1982* (Princeton: Princeton University Press, 1991), 12.

56. Paul Eddy and Magnus Linklater, *The Falklands War* (London: Andre Deutsch Ltd., 1982), 58.

57. Guillermo Makin, "Argentine Approaches to the Falklands/Malvinas: Was the Resort to Violence Foreseeable?" *International Affairs* (Summer 1983): 398.

58. Quoted from the *Operacion Rosario* report, in Freedman and Gamba-Stonehouse, *Signals of War,* 12.

59. The official British postmortem, *Falkland Islands Review: Report of a Committee of Privy Counselors,* Lord Franks, ed. (London: Her Majesty's Stationery Office, 1983); as well as an analysis of that report by R. Reginald and Jeffrey M. Elliot, *Tempest in a Teapot: The Falklands War* (San Bernardino, Calif.: Borgo Press, 1983) provide analyses of the evidence of Argentine intentions revealed after the fact. Even during the crisis leading up to the war the Argentine junta itself took steps to counter criticism that its aggressive Falklands policy stemmed from desires to limit domestic criticism or build public support. See the February 24 speech by undersecretary for foreign relations, Ambassador Enrique Ros, in *TELAM* (Buenos Aires), February 24, 1982; as reported and

translated by *Foreign Broadcast Information Service, South America* 6, February 25, 1982, B1.

60. Although not directly related to the trade-off between public support and strategic surprise, the rally-round-the-flag effect, or the tendency for public support of any regime to increase following the initiation of hostile action against another nation, is another fairly robust observation linking public support and conflict initiation. For examples of the phenomenon in recent U.S. diplomatic history, see John Mueller, "Presidential Popularity from Truman to Johnson," *American Political Science Review* 64 (1970): 18–34. Such an effect is usually significant but almost always short-lived. Since regimes can expect such an effect to occur, many analysts have suggested that unpopular regimes often initiate conflict to bolster their popularity and remain in power. Although any regime might well take advantage of this effect, such a temporary shot in the arm would seem to be primarily useful for desperate regimes in danger of collapsing. Since the strength of a regime is not necessarily related to its form, we cannot make as clear a distinction between democratic and authoritarian regimes on this criterion as we could on the basis of reliance on popular support for legitimacy. For example, a tottering authoritarian government would seem to have more cause to seek out the rally-round-the-flag effect than would a stable democracy.

61. See Christopher Dobson, John Miller, and Ronald Payne, *The Falklands Conflict* (London: Coronet Books, 1982), for a discussion of the failure of British intelligence to anticipate Argentine intentions prior to the April 2 invasion. For a more detailed look at what British intelligence knew and when they knew it, see Franks, *Falkland Islands Review;* and Reginald and Elliot, *Tempest in a Teapot.*

62. Don Lippencott and Gregory Treverton, "Negotiations Concerning the Falklands/ Malvinas Dispute," *Pew Case Studies in International Affairs* (case no. 406, 1988), pt. A, 14.

63. Lippencott and Treverton, "Negotiations," pt. B, 5.

64. See Dobson, *Falklands Conflict.*

65. Lippencott and Treverton, "Negotiations," pt. A, 12.

66. *Times of London,* April 31, 1982.

67. *Noticias Argentinas* (Buenos Aires), January 13, 1982; as reported and translated by *Foreign Broadcast Information Service, South America* 6, January 18, 1982, B3 (Washington, D.C.: USGPO, 1982). *TELAM,* January 15, 1982; as reported and translated by *Foreign Broadcast Information Service, South America* 6, January 19, 1982, B1.

68. *TELAM,* January 21, 1982; as reported and translated by *Foreign Broadcast Information Service, South America* 6, January 22, 1982, B1.

69. *TELAM,* January 22, 1982; as reported and translated by *Foreign Broadcast Information Service, South America* 6, January 25, 1982, B1.

70. Makin, "Argentine Approaches," 399.

71. *TELAM,* January 26, 1982; as reported and translated by *Foreign Broadcast Information Service, South America* 6, January 27, 1982, B1.

72. *Noticias Argentinas,* January 23, 1982; as reported and translated by *Foreign Broadcast Information Service, South America* 6, February 1, 1982, B1.

73. *La Nacion* and *La Prensa,* January 19, 1982.

74. Associated Press (AP) News Wire, 112 GMT, February 23, 1982; and *TELAM,* February 23, 1982; as reported and translated by *Foreign Broadcast Information Service, South America* 6, February 24, 1982, B1.

75. *Noticias Argentinas,* February 25, 1982; as reported and translated by *Foreign Broadcast Information Service, South America* 6, February 26, 1982, B1. Interestingly, Costa Mendez was in his second stint as foreign minister. His first, under the Ongania regime, saw the Falklands come to the fore as a salient Argentine foreign policy issue, with the ludicrous Condor operation and the more substantive presentation of Argentine grievances to the United Nations.

76. Again, the British were not the only foreign information consumers fooled by Argentina's careful management of direct communications, even in neighboring Latin American nations. Foreign reports concerning the increasing friction between Argentina and Chile were entirely managed by the Argentine regime and their spokesmen. For example, Brazil's *Jornal do Brasil* reported on January 17, "That a spokesman of the Argentine Foreign Ministry has confirmed that serious incidents took place in 1981 is clear-cut evidence that the Pope's mediation has been unable to do away with friction between Chileans and Argentineans and that a war could break out any time" (*Jornal do Brasil* [Rio de Janeiro], January 17, 1982; as reported and translated by *Foreign Broadcast Information Service, South America* 6, January 20, 1982, B1).

77. Freedman and Gamba-Stonehouse, *Signals of War,* 33–34.

78. Freedman and Gamba-Stonehouse, *Signals of War,* 33–34.

79. *Noticias Argentinas,* February 2, 1982; as reported and translated by *Foreign Broadcast Information Service, South America* 6, February 4, 1982, B2.

80. *TELAM,* February 16, 1982; as reported and translated by *Foreign Broadcast Information Service, South America* 6, February 17, 1982, B1.

81. "Observers close to the negotiations indicated today that the British delegates seem to be ready to try to avoid the subject [an Argentine declaration of sovereignty over the Falklands issued in July 1981] and to drag out the talks even more" (*TELAM,* February 26, 1982; as reported and translated by *Foreign Broadcast Information Service, South America* 6, February 24, 1982, B1).

82. *Reuter's Latin News Wire,* March 5, 1982; as reported and translated by *Foreign Broadcast Information Service, South America* 6, March 8, 1982, B3.

83. *Reuter's Latin News Wire.*

84. Franks, *Falkland Islands Review,* 42.

85. *Noticias Argentinas,* March 31, 1982; as reported and translated by *Foreign Broadcast Information Service, South America* 6, April 1, 1982, B1.

86. "Negotiations Concerning the Falklands/Malvinas Dispute," pt. A, 15.

87. *TELAM,* April 1, 1982; as reported and translated by *Foreign Broadcast Information Service, South America* 6, April 2, 1982, B1.

88. Eddy and Linklater, *Falklands War,* 58. More recent interviews cast into some doubt the precise role of Costa Mendes, although the general pattern of media influence is not denied. According to Freedman and Gamba-Stonehouse (*Signals of War,* 23–24): "Costa Mendes was unaware of the planning exercise [of the Joint Armed Forces committee] when he prepared his diplomatic initiative in January. He only knew that the Junta intended to increase tension if the British failed to offer serious concessions. . . .

When Costa Mendes was eventually informed in February of the military plans being drawn up to recover the Islands he responded cautiously."

89. *Falkland Islands Review,* 25.

90. *La Prensa,* January 24, 1982, 1, 5. As Guillermo Makin points out, Rouco's celebrity status as a political commentator in Argentina had no real parallel in the U.S. and European press. If one can imagine a combination of Bob Woodward (Rouco was one of two investigative reporters exposing rampant military corruption in Argentina) and the entire *New York Times* op-ed page, one might come close to putting Rouco in perspective. In any event he was uniquely positioned to disseminate information regarding government intentions to the domestic Argentine audience. Moreover, he was recognized as fulfilling that role by his Argentine readers.

91. As reported by Makin, "Argentine Approaches," 400.

92. As reported by Makin, "Argentine Approaches," 400.

93. By March 19 Costa Mendes was put in the position of having to deny these rumors (*Noticias Argentinas,* March 19, 1982; as reported and translated by *Foreign Broadcast Information Service, South America* 6, March 22, 1982, B1).

94. See chapter 4 for a full accounting of each editorial as well as a comparison to the muted media activity during previous Argentine crises that did *not* lead to war.

95. *Noticias Argentinas,* March 1, 1982; as reported and translated by *Foreign Broadcast Information Service, South America* 6, March 3, 1982, B1. These words are almost identical to those used by Israel one month before its air attacks began the Six Day War.

96. *Clarin,* March 2, 1982; cited by Makin, "Argentine Approaches," 400.

97. *Noticias Argentinas,* March 1, 1982; as reported and translated by *Foreign Broadcast Information Service, South America* 6, March 3, 1982, B1.

98. Freedman and Gamba-Stonehouse, *Signals of War,* 31.

99. Freedman and Gamba-Stonehouse, *Signals of War,* 25.

100. As early as January 25, some media commentaries were already making the argument that taking a firm stand with Chile about the Beagle Channel was analogous to taking a firmer stand with Britain about the Falklands. See the text of Ambassador Ortiz de Rosas's comments to Radio Mitre, in *Noticias Argentinas,* January 25, 1982; as reported and translated by *Foreign Broadcast Information Service, South America* 6, January 27, 1982, B1.

101. In fact, by late February the Argentine media was falling over itself to say kind, or at least neutral, things about Chile. Even immediately after the torpedo boat incident in the Beagle Channel an editorial in *La Nacion* read:

> Quite probably—and let us hope this will be the case—the Deceit Island incident will be no more than another episode of a very long and exhausting dispute which periodically provokes the tempers on both sides of the Andes.
>
> Let us hope the peaceful spirit the two countries promised the pope they would maintain will prevail because only thus will the mediation arrive at an honorable and durable solution. Without such a solution the Argentine community, as well as the Chilean community, will be exposed to the uncertainty of new incidents like the Deceit Island incident, or maybe even more serious and painful ones.

Clearly, these are not the words of saber rattlers (*La Nacion,* February 24, 1982, 6).

102. Continuing his January 24 opinion piece in *La Prensa,* "The Foreign Offensive."

Chapter 2

1. I have chosen to model this equilibrium in terms of utility maximization, following classical theory of the consumer, rather than in terms of expenditure minimization, even though the latter is an equally pertinent analogy. In any event the results are the same. As Hal Varian points out, "any demanded bundle can be expressed *either* as the solution to the utility maximization problem or the expenditure minimization problem" (*Microeconomic Analysis,* 2d ed. [New York: W. W. Norton, 1984], 126).

2. The terms *democracy, liberal state,* and *liberal democracy* are used interchangeably in this chapter to describe regimes that hold meaningfully contested elections for political office and that do not rely on police powers to maintain power (and the counterpart terms *nondemocracy, illiberal state,* and *authoritarian regime* to describe regimes that do). Of course, I realize that these terms are not perfectly equivalent and that there are important differences between regimes that may fall into one of these broad categories. Subsequent chapters will apply a more nuanced operationalization of regime type to the empirical tests suggested by this theoretical analysis. For the heuristic purposes of this preliminary discussion, however, a looser application of the terms seems more appropriate.

3. Other authors have looked at specific cases of this phenomenon. For example, Thomas Risse-Kappen, in "Public Opinion, Domestic Structure, and Foreign Policy in Liberal Democracies" (*World Politics* 43 [July 1991]: 479–512), looks at differences between American, French, Japanese, and West German attempts to "sell" Soviet policy to their domestic audiences.

4. Since utility is maximized at the point where the slope of the budget line equals the slope of the tangential utility curve, and since we are assuming convex indifference curves, a regime with a less steep budget line will find its tangent on an indifference curve at a point to the right (greater x_1) of a regime with a steeper budget line. Note that I am not assuming that the two budget lines being compared find a tangent on the same indifference curve, only that the indifference curves are generated by the same utility function. Depending on the x_2 intercept of the budget line, the total utility of the bundle may be greater or less. If we assume a tangent point on the same indifference curve, the equilibrium point for the regime faced with expensive acquisition of public support will have both greater x_1 and lower x_2 coordinates than the equilibrium point for a regime not faced with these problems.

5. This is a fairly standard claim by authors looking at foreign policy and democratic rule, either ruefully (e.g., George Kennan, *American Diplomacy,* expanded ed. [Chicago: University of Chicago Press, 1984]) or applaudingly (e.g., Bruce Russett, *Controlling the Sword* [Cambridge: Harvard University Press, 1990]; and Miroslav Nincic, *Democracy and Foreign Policy* [New York: Columbia University Press, 1992]).

6. There appears to be almost as much variation within the set of liberal democracies in the resources they expend on maintaining secrecy as between the set of democracies and nondemocracies, making it difficult to operationalize and test hypotheses derived

from these arguments empirically. See K. G. Robertson, *Public Secrets: A Study in the Development of Government Secrecy* (Hong Kong: Macmillan, 1982); and Itzak Galnoor, ed., *Government Secrecy in Democracies* (New York: New York University Press, 1977).

7. Equilibrium relationships exist between public support and goals of a regime other than international secrecy, relationships that in some cases may be more influential on behavior than the support/secrecy process discussed here. For example, demonstrating resolve in the international arena is clearly a goal of states and has some sort of relationship with efforts to build public support (see James Fearon, "Domestic Political Audiences and the Escalation of International Disputes," *American Political Science Review* 88, no. 3 [1994]: 577–92, for one approach to this puzzle). The support/secrecy relationship is one of several important equilibria between domestic and international behaviors; for cases of war, especially wars that are seen as bolts from the blue, I think it is the most relevant. See chapter 6 for further discussion of the relative merits of this particular equilibrium relationship.

8. ICPSR study no. 9044, *Wages of War, 1816–1980,: Augmented with Disputes and Civil War Data;* see also *The Wages of War, 1816–1965: A Statistical Handbook* (New York: John Wiley and Sons, 1972).

9. For this cursory examination I will equate *open media system* with *democracy.* The empirical examination in subsequent chapters will be more nuanced.

10. Although the set of bundles is represented as a contiguous area in subsequent diagrams illustrating this assumption and its corollaries, this is purely a heuristic device. Whether the set of bundles is a single point, a line of points, a set of disjointed points, or a solid area is immaterial to the conclusions derived here.

The decision makers clause of this assumption is included to reinforce the idea that I am working with a purely procedural conception of rationality, where the actual conception of the size of this set of bundles is a completely subjective calculation. Under identical circumstances the set may be immense to an Adolf Hitler and minuscule to a Caspar Milquetoast. My only claim is that these calculations are made, however imperfectly, that decision makers do indeed weigh domestic support and international secrecy when contemplating going to war.

11. One must be particularly careful with this sort of probabilistic reasoning. As Joseph Nye points out in *Nuclear Ethics* (New York: Free Press, 1986), this assumption is often erroneously used to claim that nuclear war is inevitable. I am not claiming that conflict is inevitable, or even probable, nor that the chances of conflict do not change over time and across nations. I am only claiming that at any given point in time, for any particular nation, there is a more or less independent probability of going to war with any of its potential targets. This argument is rather similar to John Mearsheimer's claim that, all other factors held constant, today's multipolar Europe will be inherently more conflict prone than the bipolar Europe of the Cold War. See "Back to the Future: Instability in Europe After the Cold War," *International Security* 15, no. 1 (Summer 1990): 5–56.

12. See, among others, Melvin Small and J. David Singer, "The War Proneness of Democratic Regimes," *Jerusalem Journal of International Relations* 1, no. 1 (1976): 41–64; Erich Weede, "Democracy and War Involvement," *Journal of Conflict Resolution* 28, no. 4 (1984): 649–64; Zeev Maoz and Nasrin Abdolali, "Regime Type and

International Conflict, 1816–1976," *Journal of Conflict Resolution* 33, no. 1 (1989): 3–35; Michael Doyle, "Liberalism and World Politics," *American Political Science Review* 80, no. 4 (1986): 1151–61; Steve Chan, "Mirror, mirror, on the wall . . . Are the freer countries more pacific?" *Journal of Conflict Resolution* 28, no. 4 (1984): 617–64; Rudolph Rummel, "Libertarianism and International Violence," *Journal of Conflict Resolution* 27, no. 1 (1985): 27–71.

For a critical view of democratic peace theory, see Christopher Layne, "Kant or Cant: The Myth of the Democratic Peace," *International Security* 19, no. 2 (Fall 1994): 5–49; see also David Spiro, "The Insignificance of the Liberal Peace," *International Security* 19, no. 2 (Fall 1994): 50–86.

13. Zeev Maoz and Bruce Russett, "Normative and Structural Causes of Democratic Peace, 1946–1986," *American Political Science Review* 87, no. 3 (September 1993): 624–38.

14. This exposition of signaling games follows Jeffrey S. Banks introduction to the subject almost word for word. For an excellent summary of the existing literature, see his book *Signaling Games in Political Science* (Chur, Switz.: Harwood Academic Publishers, 1991). Note that this discussion has no relationship to the "signaling problem" that I hypothesized to characterize different media systems.

15. To name a few authors and works, Thomas Gilligan and Keith Krehbiel, "Asymmetric Information and Legislative Rules with a Heterogeneous Committee," *American Journal of Political Science* 33 (1989): 459–90; Thomas Gilligan, *Information and Legislative Organization* (Ann Arbor: University of Michigan Press, 1994); Randall Calvert, "Reputation and Legislative Leadership," *Public Choice* 55 (1987): 81–119; Steven Matthews, "Veto Threats: Rhetoric in a Bargaining Game," *Quarterly Journal of Economics* 104 (1989): 347–69; David Austen-Smith and William Riker, "Asymmetric Information and the Coherence of Legislation," *American Political Science Review* 81 (1987): 897–918.

16. James Fearon develops a formal model of the process described here in "Domestic Political Audiences and the Escalation of International Disputes," *American Political Science Review* 83, no. 3 (1994): 577–92.

17. Michael Spence, *Market Signaling: Informational Transfer in Hiring and Related Screening Processes* (Cambridge: Harvard University Press, 1974), is perhaps the single most influential work in the literature on signaling games.

18. Robert Jervis, *The Logic of Images in International Relations* (Princeton: Princeton University Press, 1970).

19. Jervis, *Logic of Images,* 18.

20. Jervis, *Logic of Images,* 45–46; and works cited therein.

21. Alexander George, in *Propaganda Analysis,* points out that German propaganda was never a particularly reliable index of German military plans, despite great Allied efforts to identify such a linkage, precisely because Nazi propaganda strategy changed over time.

22. Jervis credits Thomas Schelling with this point (*Logic of Images,* 55–56).

23. Jervis, *Logic of Images,* 65; based on work of Irving Heymont, *Combat Intelligence in Modern Warfare* (Harrisburg: Stackpole, 1960).

24. Jervis is not the only one to make this point. See, for example, Alan Whiting's discussion of various indices that could have clued in American analysts that China was

indeed preparing to enter the Korean War in force (*China Crosses the Yalu* [New York: Macmillan, 1960]).

25. Robert Powell, in *Nuclear Deterrence Theory: The Search for Credibility* (New York: Cambridge University Press, 1990), sets forth a series of counterintuitive results concerning the role of resolve in international signaling games. For example, under certain conditions the state with *less* resolve is more likely to prevail in a crisis.

26. See Paul Bracken, *The Command and Control of Nuclear Forces* (New Haven: Yale University Press, 1983), esp. chap. 2; also Bruce Blair, *Strategic Command and Control: Redefining the Nuclear Threat* (Washington, D.C.: The Brookings Institution, 1985).

27. Spence models wage anticipation rather than war anticipation, but otherwise *Market Signaling* provides perfect templates for understanding these dynamics.

28. This same effect can be generated if the receiver is extremely risk averse. The greater the risk aversion of the signal receiver, the greater the assessment bias toward 1 and away from 2. See Spence, *Market Signaling,* app. C.

29. Although not a systematic study of the level of signal misperception in diplomatic relations (nor intended as such), many of the decision-making pathologies identified by Robert Jervis in parts 2 and 3 of *Perception and Misperception in International Politics* (Princeton: Princeton University Press, 1976) work precisely in ways that push receiving nations to downgrade the cost of signals.

30. If this book sells millions of copies, and it becomes accepted wisdom that domestic opinion building efforts are an incredibly reliable index of regime intentions, then we should expect to see more use of such efforts as a signal. Such a future would also make the predictions from this methodology less accurate, as occasional false signals would be mixed with truthful ones. Would that any academic author have such influence!

Chapter 3

1. Coders were graded on an identical sample of dates and newspapers before beginning their assignment to make sure they understood the instructions; in addition, all coders were spot-checked for accuracy. Instructions for coders are reproduced in appendix 2.1, as are results of intercoder reliability tests.

2. Ithiel de Sola Pool pioneered this sort of content analysis work in the early 1950s. My research effort is a direct intellectual descendent of her landmark study, *The "Prestige Papers": A Survey of Their Editorials* (Stanford: Stanford University Press, 1952). Since then a slew of authors have used her techniques to examine specific linkages between regimes and newspapers in a variety of contexts. For example, Madeleine Albright essentially used de Sola Pool's methods to look at the regime bias of Polish newspapers over time in *Poland: The Role of the Press in Political Change* (New York: Praeger, 1983).

Newspapers used here are listed in appendix 2.2. Reference sources include UNESCO, *World Communications* (New York: Gower Press, 1975); Eleanor Block, *Communication and the Mass Media: A Guide to the Reference Literature* (Englewood Cliffs, N.J.: Libraries Unlimited, 1991); John Lent, *Global Guide to Media and Communications* (New York: K. G. Saur, 1987); L. John Martin, ed., *Comparative Mass Media Systems* (New York: Longman, 1983); *World Media Handbook* (New York: UN Department of Public Information, 1990–92); Brian Jacobs, *The Leo Burnett Worldwide Advertising and Media Factbook* (Chicago: Triumph Books, 1994). For example, *World Media Handbook* gives ownership information on most newspapers in the world, including a history and assessment of regime relations with those owners.

3. For a detailed examination of the perils of aggregation, see John R. Freeman, "Systematic Sampling, Temporal Aggregation, and the Study of Political Relationships," in James Stimson, ed., *Political Analysis,* vol. 1 (Ann Arbor: University of Michigan Press, 1990).

4. Christopher Achen, *The Statistical Analysis of Quasi-Experiments* (Berkeley: University of California Press, 1986).

5. Bueno de Mesquita and Lalman, *War and Reason,* 283.

6. MS; private communication. For a good example of how medical statisticians work with logit analysis in this vein, see Joseph L. Fleiss, *Statistical Methods for Rates and Proportions* (New York: John Wiley and Sons, 1981), 64–67.

7. The initiator of the Second Kashmir War is not entirely clear, as both nations played escalatory roles prior to the acknowledged date of full hostilities, August 16, 1965. By most accounts, however, Pakistan is considered to be more of an initiator here than India.

8. See King, *Unifying Political Methodology,* chap. 9, for a detailed look at the effect of truncated data on parameter estimates.

9. ICPSR study no. 9044, *Wages of War, 1816–1980: Augmented with Disputes and Civil War Data;* see also *The Wages of War, 1816–1965: A Statistical Handbook* (New York: John Wiley and Sons, 1972). For a description of various research efforts connected with the COW project, see J. David Singer and Paul Diehl, eds., *Measuring the Correlates of War* (Ann Arbor: University of Michigan Press, 1990).

10. Codebook for ICPSR study no. 9044, *Wages of War, 1816–1980,* pt. 1.

11. See table 3.4 for my coding of another civil war turned interstate war—the Vietnam War—that Singer and Small do not place in the civil/colonial war category.

12. Rodger Yeager, *Tanzania: An African Experiment* (Boulder, Colo.: Westview Press, 1989), 135–37.

13. Loosely translated as "Cuban Solidarity with the African People Is Unwavering!" and "We Help the Ethiopian Revolution Today and Tomorrow!"

14. Andargachew Tiruneh, *The Ethiopian Revolution: 1974–1987* (London: Cambridge University Press, 1993), 378–83.

15. For a description of this database, see Edward E. Azar, "The Conflict and Peace Data Bank (COPDAB) Project," *Journal of Conflict Resolution* 24 (1980): 143–52; see also Claudio Cioffi-Revilla, "The Interstate Conflict Datasets Catalog: A Progress Report," *DDIR-Update* 3 (1988): 1–4; and Richard L. Merritt, Robert G. Muncaster, and Dina A. Zinnes, eds., *International Event-Data Developments: DDIR Phase II* (Ann Arbor: University of Michigan Press, 1993).

16. Certainly, COPDAB is not a perfect dataset. In particular, events are coded rather inconsistently across coders and across regions, especially with cooperative behaviors (see Francis Beer et al., "Ranking International Cooperation and Conflict Events," *International Interactions* 17, no. 4 [1992]: 321–48). Fortunately, this research program looks only at conflictual events, in which the inconsistency is not so pronounced. In fact, the findings reported here are robust and significant even when looking at only the high-

est coding levels of conflict, for which there is very little inconsistency or bias. For a detailed discussion of the strengths and weaknesses of event count data sets in general and COPDAB in particular, see Joshua Goldstein and John Freeman, *Three-Way Street: Strategic Reciprocity in World Politics* (Chicago: University of Chicago Press, 1990), 37–41. Since the COPDAB data ends in 1979, event counts for the warring and nonwarring cases in this data set after 1979 were generated by the same coding rules provided by Azar et al., using the *New York Times, Jerusalem Post,* and *Foreign Broadcast Information Service* as source material.

17. In fact, Alex Mintz and Philip A. Schrodt find that COPDAB events in particular are distributed according to an underlying Poisson distribution in "Distributional Patterns of Regional Interactions: A Test of the Poisson Process as a Null Model," in Claudio Cioffi-Revilla, Richard Merritt, and Dina Zinnes, eds., *Communication and Interaction in Global Politics* (Beverly Hills, Calif.: Sage Publications, 1987), 237–54.

18. Treating conflict as a contagious process is not new to this project. Randolph Siverson and Harvey Starr, for example, attempt to model both how participants in a conflict escalate their behaviors and how nations originally outside the conflict join the fight (*The Diffusion of War: A Study of Opportunity and Willingness* [Ann Arbor: University of Michigan Press, 1991]. Using a disease analogy, they look at both why nations get sicker over time and why the sickness spreads to other countries. I am looking at one form of contagion—the tendency of a nation to continue or increase directed events once begun—and modeling it explicitly in the regression analysis.

19. See Gary King, *Unifying Political Methodology: The Likelihood Theory of Statistical Inference* (Cambridge: Cambridge University Press, 1989), chap. 3.

20. Data from the Correlates of War project, as described in J. David Singer, Stuart Bremer, and John Stuckey, "Capability Distribution, Uncertainty, and Major Power War, 1820–1965," in Bruce Russett, ed., *Peace, War, and Numbers* (Beverly Hills, Calif.: Sage Publications, 1972). See also J. David Singer and Paul F. Diehl, eds., *Measuring the Correlates of War* (Ann Arbor: University of Michigan Press, 1990), esp. sec. 2.

21. The continued alliance of the United States and the United Kingdom throughout the late nineteenth and entire twentieth century would seem to be the clearest example of this phenomenon, although any such analysis depends in large part upon your definition of a hegemon as well as what nations are considered to be in the international system. See Robert Gilpin, *War and Change in World Politics* (Cambridge: Cambridge University Press, 1981), for the view that declining hegemons always go to war to protect their faltering position in the international system.

22. See chapter 1 note 2.

23. To calculate the predicted values of the COPDAB event count on the basis of the parameters generated by the negative binomial regression, one takes an exponential function of the sum of independent variables multiplied by their estimates; $E(Y_i) = \exp(\chi_i \beta)$. Thus, any particular predicted value of COPDAB count in table 3.11 equals $\exp(-1.553 + .462*\text{Editorial Count}_{t-1} + .384*\text{COPDAB 11-Count}_{t-1})$. Note that the contagion parameter is an estimate of the variance of the mean number of expected events within observations; it is not part of the functional form. The contagion estimate reported here is the natural logarithm of the actual contagion parameter.

24. Azar, "Conflict and Peace Data Bank," 36.

Scale Point	Weighted Value
15	102
14	65
13	50
12	44
11	29
10	16

25. Ted Robert Gurr, *Polity II: Political Structures and Regime Change, 1800–1986,* ICPSR no. 9263 (Ann Arbor: University of Michigan, 1989).

26. I chose this threshold point for influential dailies as it is both the median and the mode of this variable.

27. As with the statistical analysis of conflict, alternative methods exist to investigate the rate of editorial writing. Appendix 1.3 reports the full regression statistics for those alternative model specifications.

28. Of course, a regime may pay a political price by starting a war that it loses (see Bruce Bueno de Mesquita, Randolph Siverson, and Gary Woller, "War and the Fate of Regimes: A Comparative Analysis," *American Political Science Review* 86 [1992]: 638–46), but that is a different story entirely.

29. See "An Early Warning Model of International Hostilities," in Nazli Choucri and Thomas Robinson, eds., *Forecasting in International Relations,* 223–39 (New York: W. H. Freeman, 1978). Dina Zinnes and Robert Muncaster reach similar conclusions in "Hostile Activity and the Prediction of War," *Journal of Conflict Resolution* 28, no. 2 (June 1984): 187–230. Likewise, Michael Don Ward finds a high degree of foreign policy "reactivity" in his examination of COPDAB and WEIS, that if nation *i* hits nation *j,* nation *j* is very likely to hit *i* back ("Cooperation and Conflict in Foreign Policy Behavior," *International Studies Quarterly* 26, no. 1 [March 1982]: 87–126).

30. For example, are there predictable patterns of reciprocity in the ways nations react to policies directed toward them? With an affirmative answer, see Joshua Goldstein and John Freeman, *Three-Way Street: Strategic Reciprocity in World Politics* (Chicago: University of Chicago Press, 1990).

31. *Paths to Conflict: International Dispute Initiation, 1816–1976* (Boulder, Colo.: Westview Press, 1982), 72.

32. I do, as the model would expect, find an unusually large number of *Egyptian* editorials critical of Israel in the month prior to the initiation of war. A natural extension of this research would be to develop a long-term time series of Egyptian editorial activity to mirror that collected here for Israel.

Chapter 4

1. On first cut it might seem that critical editorials can simply be classified as aggressive and analytic editorials as reactive, but this characterization can be slightly misleading. That is, even the most aggressive editorial tries to couch the proposed escalatory action in terms of responding to some evil perpetrated by the opposing nation. Classification on the spectrum of inward or outward focus has a similar problem, since

an editorial advocating unilateral action generally mentions some foreign action as a casus belli. Relying solely on the implications of the editorial in question for the status quo can be difficult as well, primarily because calls for a return to the status quo ante can often be calls for extreme escalation depending on how long ago the status quo ante existed. For example, when an Argentine editorial calls for a return to the Malvinas status quo, they are perhaps trying to go back over 150 years. Although the coding is usually very clear, the coders were told to keep these caveats in mind.

2. Also, every U.S. editorial used for the analysis in chapter 5 is summarized and coded as analytic or critical in appendix 3. Although the entire text is not reprinted, readers may wish to examine these summaries to get a better feel for the difference in editorial type.

3. See Randolph Siverson and Ross Miller, "The Escalation of Disputes to War," *International Interactions* 19, nos. 1–2: 78, for a good discussion of the limitations of existing crisis data sets.

4. Michael Brecher and Jonathan Wilkenfeld, ICPSR study no. 9286 (Ann Arbor: University of Michigan, 1992).

5. As described by Thomas Princen, Divine Providence in the form of papal intercession just barely prevented a major war. See "Beagle Channel Negotiations," *Pew Case Studies in International Affairs,* case no. 401 (1988): pts. A, B, and C, 1988.

6. The efforts of both India and Pakistan to secure third-party support for this conflict is an interesting story in its own right and perhaps has implications for this model. Recall that direct power comparisons affect the degree of risk associated with initiating war. Should one of the combatants be able to anticipate this process and either bring an ally onboard during the prewar phase or prevent its adversary from doing the same, the power comparisons within the model might shift appreciably. Since India and Pakistan's potential allies, China and the Soviet Union, are two of the most powerful nations on earth, the Indo-Soviet Treaty signed in August makes sense in light of this dynamic, as does Pakistan's attempts to tie China to its side and drive a wedge between India and the Soviet Union.

7. Interestingly, a similar editorial pattern appears to exist for the Second Kashmir War, as found in the media examinations of Rao (see chap. 1 n. 13). Rao's coding of editorials prior to the August war initiation according to references to internal affairs and "trust-suspicion" dimensions suggests the occurrence of a similar pattern of analytic editorials followed by critical editorials immediately prior to the war.

8. Robert Jackson, *South Asian Crisis: India, Pakistan, and Bangladesh* (New York: Praeger, 1975). "The army and intelligence services were watching the development of the constitutional crisis in Pakistan with close attention. But their advice to the Cabinet at the end of March 1971 appears to have been that India was not ready for immediate intervention in East Bengal, and that any military action to help the Bengalis would have to wait until after the mid-year monsoon" (37–38).

9. Jackson, *South Asian Crisis,* 150–52.

10. *Jerusalem Post,* May 17, 1967.

11. *Jerusalem Post,* May 24, May 30, 1967.

12. Chaim Herzog, *The Arab-Israeli Wars: War and Peace in the Middle East from the War of Independence through Lebanon* (New York: Vintage Books, 1982), 234.

13. See William A. Rugh, *The Arab Press* (Syracuse: Syracuse University Press, 1979), 43–49.

14. *Jerusalem Post,* March 4, 1982. Keep in mind that the *Post* is not the Likud government's biggest fan. As we shall see when comparing this crisis to the Lebanese crisis of 1981, this sort of tone is about as virulent as the *Post* gets in the 1980s.

15. *Jerusalem Post,* May 17, 1982.

16. *Jerusalem Post,* February 24, 1982.

17. *Jerusalem Post,* May 14, 1982.

18. *Jerusalem Post,* April 29, 1981.

19. *Jerusalem Post,* May 17, 1981.

20. *Jerusalem Post,* May 3, May 8, May 13, May 21, June 4, 1981.

21. Jiri Valenta, *Soviet Intervention in Czechoslovakia, 1968: Anatomy of a Decision* (Baltimore: Johns Hopkins University Press, 1979), 36.

22. Valenta, *Soviet Intervention,* 35.

23. Valenta, *Soviet Intervention,* 145.

24. Richard Wich, *Sino-Soviet Crisis Politics: A Study of Political Change and Communication* (Cambridge, Mass: Council on East Asian Studies, 1980). To Wich the key to understanding the Chinese decision to test the USSR over the islands is the Soviet invasion of Czechoslovakia and the estrangement that intervention bred between the two countries.

25. February 2, criticizing the USSR for praising Nixon's Inaugural Address; February 4, criticizing the USSR for its oppressive domestic policies. Both editorials would be coded as analytic, not critical.

26. The closest media piece Wich can find that is critical of China is a December 3, 1968, *Izvestia* article by the commander of the Soviet Far East Military District, reporting how vigilant his troops are, given a possible Chinese threat (*Sino-Soviet Crisis Politics,* 99).

27. Wich is quite clear that he believes the March 15 clash was initiated by the Soviet Union as a signal to the Chinese leadership that the Soviets would not give in on this issue.

28. Wich, *Sino-Soviet Crisis Politics,* 105–6.

29. Franz Mogdis and Karen Tidwell, "Sino-Soviet Interaction 1950–1967: Project Triad," ICPSR study no. 5016 (Ann Arbor: University of Michigan, 1971).

30. Henry S. Bradsher, *Afghanistan and the Soviet Union* (Durham: Duke University Press, 1985).

31. My use of the term *crisis* glosses over differences between crises, militarized disputes, protracted disputes, and enduring rivalries. Although theoretically distinct, little is gained for the purposes of this project by belaboring the distinction. Randolph Siverson and Ross Miller ("The Escalation of Disputes to War," *International Interactions* 19, nos. 1–2: 77–97) provide a comprehensive differentiation between these concepts. Interestingly, their review article suggests that domestic level attributes are key to understanding how nations move from dispute to war—precisely the focus of this book.

32. John Herz, "Idealist Internationalism and the Security Dilemma," *World Politics* 2 (January 1950): 157–80; Arnold Wolfers, *Discord and Collaboration* (Baltimore:

278   *Notes to Pages 107–10*

Johns Hopkins Press, 1962); Robert Jervis, "Cooperation under the Security Dilemma," *World Politics* 30 (January 1978): 167–214.

33. Another way to think of this differentiation is to consider the three models that Zeev Maoz identifies as providing internal motivation for "the road to initiation": the Frustration model, the Threat model, and the Power Transition model. When what Maoz identifies as systemic constraints on this process—systemic tightness, power distribution, and peacefulness—are pressing, these models lead to behavior that I characterize as a security dilemma. When governments have relative freedom from these constraints, then these same internal models generate the decisions of what I call a unilateral road to war. See *Paths to Conflict: International Dispute Initiation, 1816–1976* (Boulder, Colo.: Westview Press, 1982), esp. chap. 4.

34. Dina A. Zinnes, "Research Frontiers in the Study of International Politics," in Fred Greenstein and Nelson Polsby, eds., *Handbook of Political Science,* vol. 8: *International Politics* (New York: Addison-Wesley, 1975); Dina A. Zinnes, "Expression and Perception of Hostility in Prewar Crisis: 1914," in J. D. Singer, ed., *Quantitative International Politics* (New York: Free Press, 1968); Ole Holsti, Robert North, and Richard Brody, "Perception and Action in the 1914 Crisis," in Singer, *Quantitative International Politics;* Robert C. North, "Perception and Action in the 1914 Crisis," *Journal of International Affairs* 21, no. 1 (1967): 103–22.

35. Scott Sagan, "1914 Revisited: Allies, Offense and Instability," *International Security* (Fall 1986): 151–77.

36. See, among other writings by Fritz Fischer, *War of Illusions: German Policies from 1911 to 1914* (New York: W. W. Norton, 1975).

37. See, among others, Kenneth Organski, *World Politics* (New York: Knopf, 1958); Kenneth Organski and Jacek Kugler, *The War Ledger* (Chicago: University of Chicago Press, 1980); Robert Gilpin, *War and Change in World Politics* (Cambridge: Cambridge University Press, 1981).

38. See, for example, Stephen Van Evera, "The Cult of the Offensive and the Origins of the First World War"; and Jack Snyder, "Civil-Military Relations and the Cult of the Offensive, 1914 and 1984," in Steven E. Miller, ed., *Military Strategy and the Origins of the First World War* (Princeton: Princeton University Press, 1985).

39. With randomization of strategies the frontier is some continuous function that includes the most optimal achievable settlements; without randomization we can think of the frontier as simply the set of those points. The illustrations here are highly stylized. For example, the set of possible settlements should almost certainly *not* include points with zero utility for either side; the line denoting the frontier should almost certainly *not* hit either axis.

40. I will not attempt even a partial list of such works here, as it would leave out too many necessary authors. Thomas Schelling was one of the first, if not the first, to write of international crises in such terms; *Strategy of Conflict* (Cambridge, Mass.: Harvard University Press, 1960) remains a vital piece of work 35 years after publication.

41. Mayer looks primarily at the determination and evolution of domestic factions' utility reservation curves, but the logic is the same for a unitary state actor in competition with another state ("Managing Domestic Differences in International Negotiations: The Strategic Use of Internal Side-payments," *International Organization* 46, no. 4 [Autumn 1992]: 793–818.

42. For an empirical examination of this process, see W. Ben Hunt, "International Crisis Escalation: Evidence for Event Horizons," MS, New York University Dept. of Politics, 1996; for a theoretical examination, see Fearon, op. cit.

43. Robert Jervis, "Cooperation under the Security Dilemma," *World Politics* 30 (January 1978): 167–214.

44. Robert Axelrod, *The Evolution of Cooperation* (New York: Basic Books, 1984).

45. Kenneth Oye, "The Sterling-Dollar-Franc Triangle: Monetary Diplomacy 1929–1937," in Kenneth Oye, ed., *Cooperation under Anarchy* (Princeton: Princeton University Press, 1986).

46. George W. Downs, David M. Rocke, and Randolph M. Siverson, "Arms Races and Cooperation," 118–45, in Oye, *Cooperation under Anarchy.*

47. Arthur Stein, "When Misperception Matters," *World Politics* 34, no. 4 (July 1982): 505–26.

48. To the degree that these punitive abilities cannot be used to mount or shield a first strike, I am making Jervis's argument on the benefits of defensive weapons and doctrine ("Cooperation under the Security Dilemma"; see also George Quester, *Offense and Defense in the International System* [New York: Wiley, 1977]). I am less sanguine than Jervis about the prospects of such offense-defense differentiation, however. See Richard Burt, "New Weapons Technologies: Debate and Directions," *Adelphi Paper 126* (London: International Institute for Strategic Studies, 1976).

49. Recall that a great deal of conflict can take place during the prewar period, although not with the frequency and intensity of all-out war.

50. The implications of linkage strategies for bargaining theory has long been a topic of interest, particularly in the arms control and disarmament literature. See, for example, Thomas Schelling and Morton Halperin, *Strategy and Arms Control* (New Haven, Conn.: Yale University Press, 1961).

51. For an early yet relevant illustration of linkage in terms of game theory, see Arthur Stein, "The Politics of Linkage," *World Politics* 33, no. 1 (October 1980): 62–81.

52. Alternative representations of a bargaining space with linked issues, such as Edgeworth boxes, are appropriate here as well; I find the three-dimensional representations intuitively more pleasing. For a theoretical discussion of the role and representation of linkage in crisis negotiations, see T. Clifton Morgan, *Untying the Knot of War: A Bargaining Theory of International Crises* (Ann Arbor: University of Michigan Press, 1994), esp. chap. 4.

53. In expected utility terms, behavioral choice is a function of the gains and losses associated with a behavior and the probabilities associated with the gains and losses given that behavior. In a choice between war and peace, nation i must weigh the gains and probability of continued cooperation against the gains and probability of success in war. A misguided negotiation linkage could well have the effect of magnifying the latter calculation relative to the former, even if the former is increasing, especially if the linkage involves military capabilities.

54. If weapons, deployments, and strategies could be categorized consistently in terms of their offensive or defensive capabilities, then a linkage between security issues could theoretically avoid the difficulties posed here. Again, I am moving back to Jervis's prescriptions for avoiding the security dilemma; again, I am not confident that any weapon is so clearly offensive or defensive. For example, submarine-based nuclear missiles

are often pointed to as essentially defensive weapons with guaranteed survivability and little first-strike capability. Yet technological advancements in guidance and propulsion, creating extremely accurate SLBM's with depressed trajectories, combine with the submarine's ability to get very close to the adversary's shore to make a highly effective first-strike offensive weapon.

55. This is the central argument of Joseph Grieco's realist critique of neoliberal theories of international cooperation in "Anarchy and the Limits of Cooperation" (*International Organization* 42 [1988]: 485–507) and *Cooperation among Nations* (Ithaca: Cornell University Press, 1990): that absolute gains through economic cooperation may eventually be reflected as a relative loss in security comparisons.

56. See, among other articles, Amos Tversky and Daniel Kahneman, "Judgment under Uncertainty: Heuristics and Biases," *Science* 185:1124–30. See also Daniel Kahneman, Paul Slovic, and Amos Tversky, eds., *Judgment under Uncertainty: Heuristics and Biases* (Cambridge: Cambridge University Press, 1982); and Jervis, "Political Implications of Loss Aversion." Kahneman and Tversky develop their own theory of decision making, prospect theory, to deal with what they see as the flaws in expected utility decision-making theories (Daniel Kahneman and Amos Tversky, "Prospect Theory: An Analysis of Decision under Risk," *Econometrica* 47, no. 2 [March 1979]: 263–92. (For an earlier incarnation of prospect theory, see John W. Pratt, "Risk Aversion in the Small and in the Large," *Econometrica* 32, nos. 1–2 [January–April 1964]: 122–36.) I am wary of prospect theory's assumption that, because decision makers are risk acceptant in monetary lotteries, they are risk acceptant when it comes to comparing all small losses and large gains. In support of the view that human utility functions for money are almost always nonlinear and are quite different depending on what commodity is at stake, see Milton Friedman and Donald Savage, "The Utility Analysis of Choices Involving Risk," *Journal of Political Economy* 56 (1948): 279–304.

57. For example, Richard Ned Lebow, *Between Peace and War* (Baltimore: Johns Hopkins University Press, 1981), 242–47.

58. For example, Kahneman and Tversky found that subjects presented with a hypothetical vaccination policy for which the accidental deaths sure to occur were emphasized were less likely to approve the policy than subjects presented with the same policy but for which the lives saved were emphasized, even though the projections of lives saved and lives lost were identical in each presentation.

59. In most game theoretic treatments of crises (or any bargaining situation) preference orderings are held constant for each player, and equilibria (if any) are sought; see, for example Steven Brams, *Superpower Games* (New Haven, Conn.: Yale University Press, 1985); and *Negotiation Games* (New York: Routledge, 1990). In treatments of crisis behavior that do not rely on formal theory, initiators are generally assumed to have some particular goal in mind, implying that preferences remain constant over the course of the crisis. See, for example, Richard Ned LeBow's list of desired objectives by brinkmanship crisis initiators (*Between Peace and War,* 59).

60. A variety of scholars have bemoaned microeconomic theory's assumption of exogenous preferences, usually at the same time they critique neorealism (e.g., Robert Jervis, "Realism, Game Theory, and Cooperation," *World Politics* 30, no. 3 [April 1988]: 324–29), but even these authors focus on long-term sources of preference change, not the short-term effects noted here.

61. Jervis hints at this research program in "Political Implications of Loss Aversion," writing, "we should try to see whether actors manipulate frames—i.e., an actor who knows what decision he wants to emerge should frame the question in a way that is more likely to elicit this answer" ("Realism, Game Theory, and Cooperation," 21).

62. Regime and media spin on information is the primary source of what Russell Neuman et al. call the "construction" of public opinion (W. Russell Neuman, Marion Just, and Ann Crigler, *Common Knowledge: News and the Construction of Political Meaning* [Chicago: University of Chicago Press, 1992]).

63. Chapter 5 examines how the United States got to the Gulf War in more detail. John Kirton ("National Mythology and Media Coverage: Mobilizing Consent for Canada's War in the Gulf," *Political Communication* 10, no. 4 [1993]: 425–41), finds precisely the same efforts at framing in the Canadian road to war, in which public support "depended on the presence, particularly in television network news, of a portrait of the conflict that cast it as a mythological replay of World War II, in which Canada went to war with Britain and France, without the United States, in support of its League of Nations obligations, to emerge victorious and thus rid the world of Hitlerian atrocities against defenseless British, European, and Jewish civilians" (425).

64. As Richard Brody put it, "how can we give a Taylor Manifest-Anxiety Scale to Khrushchev during the Hungarian revolt, a Semantic Differential to Chiang Kai-Shek while Quemoy is being shelled, or simply interview Kennedy during the Cuban missile crisis?" ("The Study of International Politics Qua Science," in Klaus Knorr and James N. Rosenau, eds., *Contending Approaches to International Politics* [Princeton: Princeton University Press, 1969]). Actually, we come pretty close to his last query with the ExCom tapes secretly recorded by Kennedy.

Chapter 5

1. For a good description of the prevalence of this practice, see Mel Laracey, "The Presidential Newspaper: The Forgotten Way of Going Public," MS, University of Michigan.

2. Dumas Malone, *Jefferson and His Time,* vol. 2 (Boston: Little, Brown, 1951) , 425. See also Richard Barnet, *The Rockets' Red Glare* (New York: Simon and Schuster, 1990), 36.

3. Barnet, *Rockets' Red Glare,* 79.

4. Barnet, *Rockets' Red Glare,* 82–91.

5. Walter Dean Burnham, *The Current Crisis in American Politics* (New York: Oxford University Press, 1982), 83.

6. Barnet, *Rockets' Red Glare,* 126.

7. See, for example, George Kennan, *American Diplomacy* (Chicago: University of Chicago Press, 1951), 11.

8. Robert Hilderbrand, *Power and the People: Executive Management of Public Opinion in Foreign Affairs, 1897–1921* (Chapel Hill: University of North Carolina Press, 1981), 28.

9. Hilderbrand, *Power and the People,* 23–26.

10. Hilderbrand, *Power and the People,* 26; italics mine.

11. David Green, *Shaping Political Consciousness: the Language of Politics in America from McKinley to Reagan* (Ithaca: Cornell University Press, 1987), 49.

12. For a good account of the events leading up to the Grenada invasion, see Reynold A. Burrowes, *Revolution and Rescue in Grenada* (Westport, Conn.: Greenwood Press, 1988).

13. Ronald Reagan, televised speech, March 23, 1983. In fact, Reagan had criticized Grenada publicly as early as April 1982 in a speech in Barbados, but, since this communication was not directed toward a U.S. audience, it does not meet my criteria for a domestic media effort (William Russell Nylen, "US-Grenada Relations, 1979–1983: American Foreign Policy towards a 'Backyard' Revolution," *Pew Case Study in International Affairs,* no. 306 [1988]: 23).

14. William McWhirter, *Time,* May 2, 1983, 38–39.

15. Jimmy Carter, *Keeping Faith: Memoirs of a President* (Toronto: Bantam Books, 1982), 440–47.

16. Carter, *Keeping Faith,* 451.

17. Carter, *Keeping Faith,* 456.

18. Bob Woodward, *The Commanders* (New York: Simon and Schuster, 1991), 224–26.

19. Carter's manic attention to detail comes out clearly in his description of Khomeini's threats. According to his diary entry of November 18, "There was some confusion about what Khomeini actually said—'if the Shah is not returned, the hostages could be tried' or 'will be tried.' We tried to get the Farsi or Persian-language version, to translate it ourselves for more accuracy" (Carter, *Keeping Faith,* 465). While Carter's willingness to look at media broadcasts is laudable (although this announcement was directed to the foreign press and, hence, highly suspect in the first place), one suspects that trying to ascertain whether Khomeini used the future or future conditional tense was largely a waste of time.

20. Carter, *Keeping Faith,* 467.

21. Carter, *Keeping Faith,* 485.

22. Cyrus Vance, *Hard Choices* (New York: Simon and Schuster, 1983), 405.

23. Carter, *Keeping Faith,* 498–99.

24. Although national security advisor Zbigniew Brzezinski was initially in favor of a punitive military action and continued to press for such a retributive action to be incorporated into the rescue attempt, the discussion quickly narrowed to the rescue option alone (Zbigniew Brzezinski, *Power and Principle* [New York: Farrar, Straus, and Giroux, 1983], 490–91).

25. For a detailed look at the negotiations following the abortive rescue attempt, see Russell Leigh Moses, "Mediation and Private Contacts in the Iran Hostage Crisis, April 1980–January 1981," *Pew Case Studies in International Affairs,* no. 316 (1989).

26. Brzezinski recalls suggesting that Carter convene the full National Security Council to tell members that he had decided *against* a military option, just in case there were any leaks in the Executive Branch. He also recalls holding his hand in front of his mouth when discussing the operation with Secretary Vance while standing in front of a window, just in case any lip-reading reporters with telescopes were watching from the White House Rose Garden (*Power and Principle,* 492–93).

27. Scott Sigmund Gartner identifies the rate of change of public opinion measures as a domestic-level leading indicator of presidential decisions, such as the rescue attempt ("Predicting the Timing of Carter's Decision to Initiate a Hostage Rescue Attempt: Modeling a Dynamic Information Environment," *International Interactions* 18, no. 4 [1993]: 365–86). The difficulty with using Gartner's approach for *ex ante* prediction is that we must have not only accurate public approval ratings but also knowledge of how presidential advisors will filter and relay that information in their policy briefings.

28. As the most recent of the cases examined here, I will go into the more detail concerning U.S. policy actions and decisions than with the other cases. Events and dates are taken from Bob Woodward, *The Commanders* (New York: Simon and Schuster, 1991); and Martin Staniland, "Getting to No—The Diplomacy of the Gulf Conflict, August 2, 1990–January 15, 1991," *Pew Case Studies in International Affairs,* no. 449 (1993): pts. 1–3. All statements concerning the U.S. decision-making process, unless otherwise noted, are from Woodward.

29. Woodward, *Commanders,* 212, 215.

30. Woodward, *Commanders,* 219, 223.

31. No pun intended, although Hussein did threaten to burn half of Israel.

32. Woodward, *Commanders,* 213.

33. Quoting from Pierre Salinger and Eric Laurent, *Secret Dossier: The Hidden Agenda behind the Gulf War* (New York: Penguin Books, 1991), 45.

34. Woodward, *Commanders,* 228–35.

35. Woodward, *Commanders,* 236–37.

36. Woodward, *Commanders,* 304.

37. This is not to suggest that Schwartzkopf was in favor of more men and an offensive strategy—quite the opposite. His and Powell's strategy seems to have been to ask for many more divisions than were actually necessary in order to dissuade the administration from pushing for the offensive option.

38. Woodward, *Commanders,* 310, 320.

39. Staniland provides a detailed discussion of the diplomacy leading up to UN Resolution 678. See Woodward, *Commanders,* 337–39, for reporting on U.S. congressional decision making.

40. Woodward, *Commanders,* 345.

41. Woodward, *Commanders,* 353–54.

42. *New York Times Sunday Magazine,* October 1, 1995.

43. Woodward, *Commanders,* 336–37.

44. *Washington Post,* October 6, 1. John Mueller, in *Policy and Opinion in the Gulf War* (Chicago: University of Chicago Press, 1994), has collected almost all of the U.S. public opinion polls surrounding the Gulf War and linked them to both external events and administration policy announcements. See also Lee Sigelman, James Lebovic, Clyde Wilcox, and Dee Allsop, "As Time Goes By: Daily Opinion Change during the Persian Gulf Crisis," *Political Communication* 10, no. 4 (1993): 353–67.

45. *Public Papers of the President, George Bush,* August 5 (Washington, D.C.: USGPO).

46. George Bush, televised speech, August 8, 1990.

47. Woodward, *Commanders,* 282.

48. Woodward, *Commanders,* 315–16.

49. Woodward, *Commanders,* 316.

50. Woodward, *Commanders,* 317–18.

51. Woodward, *Commanders,* 343–44.

52. A slew of articles document these efforts. In particular, see W. Lance Bennett and Jarol B. Manheim, "Taking the Public by Storm: Information, Cueing, and the Democratic Process in the Gulf Conflict," *Political Communication* 10, no. 4 (1993): 331–51. See also the individual chapters by John Zaller, Timothy Cook, Shanto Iyengar, and Adam Simon and Richard Brody in W. Lance Bennett and David L. Paletz, eds., *Taken by Storm: The Media, Public Opinion, and U.S. Foreign Policy in the Gulf War* (Chicago: University of Chicago Press, 1994).

53. In none of the cases examined in this chapter do we see the United States making as strong an effort to maintain international strategic surprise as to build public support. This is precisely the behavior we would expect, however, from a powerful nation that has little need for the force multiplier of strategic surprise (see chap. 2).

54. As reported in the *New York Times,* December 19, 1.

55. Both sets of newspaper editorials dealing with Iraq were examined independently by three coders. All three agreed on all *Journal* editorials; one coder disagreed on two *Times* editorials (one in August, one in October). The majority codings are presented here.

56. Interestingly, the role of the *New York Times* during the Gulf crisis closely resembles that played in Israel by the *Jerusalem Post* in the Lebanese crisis of 1981, one year prior to the Lebanese crisis leading to the 1982 invasion. In the spring and early summer of 1981 many Likud-oriented media sources advocated moving into Lebanon to silence the PLO and remove Syrian SAM systems; the Labor-oriented *Jerusalem Post,* like the *New York Times* in the Iraqi case, advocated collective security agreements and negotiated settlements.

57. Avi Shlaim, *The United States and the Berlin Blockade, 1948–1949* (Berkeley: University of California Press, 1983), 44.

58. According to Truman's memoirs, "On March 31 the deputy military governor of the Soviet Union, General Dratvin, notified our military government in Berlin that in two days, beginning April 1, the Russians would check all U.S. personnel passing through their zone for identification and would inspect all freight shipments and all except personal baggage" (*Memoirs of Harry S. Truman,* vol. 2 [New York: Da Capo Press, 1956], 122).

59. Shlaim, *United States and the Berlin Blockade,* 44.

60. Truman, *Memoirs,* 123.

61. Shlaim, *United States and the Berlin Blockade,* 172.

62. Shlaim, *United States and the Berlin Blockade,* 285.

63. Truman, *Memoirs,* 128–31.

64. Barnet, *Rockets' Red Glare,* 265.

65. Truman, *Memoirs,* 125–26. In fact, Truman went ahead with the airlift rather than a rail convoy, despite the very real danger that a Soviet attack on the transport planes would leave the American forces in Europe at grave risk if war developed, specifically because it was a less aggressive move.

66. Truman, *Memoirs,* 338–39. The announcement set a new U.S. policy course for all of Asia, not just Korea. New military assistance was ordered for the French in Indochina as well as new forces to be stationed in the Philippines. Most important for the immediate future, however, the Seventh Fleet was given increased latitude to support Chinese nationalist forces on Taiwan. In sharp contrast to MacArthur's eventual strategy, initial White House planning meetings were quite clear in the decision to limit Korean military options to territory south of the 38th parallel.

67. Truman, *Memoirs,* 348.

68. MacArthur favored an aggressive military stance to bring Chiang Kai-shek's forces back to the mainland.

69. Truman, *Memoirs,* 360.

70. Truman, *Memoirs,* 361–71.

71. Truman, *Memoirs,* 377.

72. With the exception that I focus specifically on newspaper editorials, this is precisely Alexander George's research program for understanding German strategy during World War II. See *Propaganda Analysis,* chap. 11: "Prediction of an Elite's Major Actions."

73. For a good summary of international law on this point and its impact on U.S. policy prior to World War I, see Charles Seymour, *American Diplomacy during the World War* (Baltimore: Johns Hopkins Press, 1934), chaps. 2 and 3: "Allied Interference with Neutral Trade" and "The Submarine."

74. According to Ernest R. May, the United States protested the German submarines more than the English mines because the mines were a theoretical rather than a practical invasion of American rights at sea, while the submarines were both (*World War and American Isolation* [Cambridge: Harvard University Press, 1959]). The British justified the mining of German harbors in part as a reprisal for German gas attacks on the Continent.

75. For the text of this note, see Ernest R. May, *The Coming of War, 1917* (Berkeley: Berkeley Series in American History, 1963), 3.

76. Fred W. Wellborn, *Diplomatic History of the United States* (Ottawa: Littlefield, Adams, 1966), 267.

77. For the text of Bryan's letter of protest, see May, *Coming of War,* 9–10.

78. Samuel Huntington, *Soldier and the State* (New York: Vintage, 1964), 144.

79. Hilderbrand, *Power and the People,* 96.

80. George Juergens, *News from the White House: The Presidential-Press Relationship in the Progressive Era* (Chicago: University of Chicago Press, 1981), 267.

81. Arthur S. Link, et al., eds., *The Papers of Woodrow Wilson* (Princeton: Princeton University Press, 1980), vol. 36, 466–71.

82. The diplomatic ineptitude of the Germans is well documented both in May's and Seymour's accounts. Combined with the Anglophile sentiments of people such as Wilson's close advisor Colonel House, the cards were well stacked against the German position from the start.

83. Wilson was not particularly concerned about the strategic implications of the telegram, as German agents had been actively funding Mexican groups hostile to the United States for a number of years. See Michael Lutzker, "President Wilson's German and

Mexican Policies: Two Crises, One War," paper presented at the 1991 annual meeting of the Society for Historians of American Foreign Relations, 3–4. Wilson was very concerned, however, with the domestic political implications of the telegram, as he had weathered substantial political pressure to launch a full-scale war against Mexico since Pancho Villa's raid on New Mexico in February 1916. For example, throughout 1916 the Hearst newspapers, with their relatively independent and inflammatory editorial stance, called adamantly for war with Mexico (but much less so for war with Germany). In fact, Wilson *did* invade Mexico, albeit a limited invasion without a formal declaration of war, sending Gen. Pershing and a "Punitive Expedition" of 7,000 men across the border.

84. Truman, *Memoirs,* 337.

Chapter 6

1. For a review on the political science side, see the authors in Alfred C. Maurer, Marion D. Tunstall, and James M. Keagle, eds., *Intelligence: Policy and Process* (Boulder, Colo.: Westview Press, 1985); see also Richard K. Betts, "Analysis, War, and Decision: Why Intelligence Failures Are Inevitable," *World Politics* 31, no. 1 (October 1978): 61–89. On the historical side, see the authors in Ernest R. May, ed., *Knowing Ones' Enemies: Intelligence Assessment before the Two World Wars* (Princeton: Princeton University Press, 1986).

2. One of only six Foreign Broadcast Information Service (FBIS) reports is devoted entirely to the former Soviet Union (the FBIS is a CIA-sponsored service that monitors radio and television broadcasts around the world). The employment of "Kremlinologists" adept at interpreting internal Russian media signals is well-known. For an internal analysis of CIA resource limitations and allocations with the end of the Cold War, particularly in regards to the collection of signals intelligence, see Jack Davis, "The Challenge of Opportunity Analysis," MS, Center for Study of Intelligence, July 1992.

3. For a similar defense of "mere prediction," see A. F. K. Organski and Samuel Eldersveld's concluding remarks in Bruce Bueno de Mesquita, ed., *European Community Decision Making: Models, Application and Comparisons* (New Haven, Conn.: Yale University Press, 1994), 215.

4. As James Lee Ray and Bruce Russett point out in "The Future as Arbiter of Theoretical Controversies: Predictions, Explanations, and the End of the Cold War" (MS), there is no shortage of scholars who deny even the potential of a self-consciously scientific study of politics to make meaningful predictions, despite good evidence to the contrary. Even social scientists sometimes claim that prediction is not a reasonable goal; see, for example, Ithiel de Sola Pool, in "The Art of the Social Science Soothsayer," in Nazli Choucri and Thomas Robinson, eds., *Forecasting in International Relations* (New York: W. H. Freeman, 1978), 23–34.

5. All quotations from "The Sound and the Fury: The Social Scientist versus War in History," in Stanley Hoffmann, *The State of War* (New York: Praeger, 1965), 254–76.

6. Kenneth Waltz, *Theory of International Politics* (Reading, Mass.: Addison-Wesley, 1979), esp. chap. 4, pts. 1–2.

7. Other recent work has also shown the weaknesses of systemic theory in accounting for the historical record and suggests broadly applied domestic or bargaining

variables that bridge the gap between systemic theory and case study. For example, Paul Huth, Christopher Gelpi, and Scott Bennett test hypotheses derived from structural realism against those derived from deterrence theory and find far more support for the latter, in "The Escalation of Great Power Militarized Disputes: Testing Rational Deterrence Theory and Structural Realism," *American Political Science Review* 87, no. 3 (September 1993): 609–23.

8. Like many others, I will take Waltz's book *Theory of International Politics* as the sacred text of "pure" neorealist theory.

9. To the degree this basic model more accurately predicts and explains war than Waltz's model, I suggest that looking rigorously at unit-level attributes makes more sense in this case than looking rigorously at systemic attributes despite the more parsimonious nature of systemic theory.

10. See, among others, Nazli Choucri and Robert C. North, *Nations in Conflict: National Growth and International Violence* (San Francisco: W. H. Freeman, 1975); Robert C. North and Richard Lagerstrom, *War and Domination: A Theory of Lateral Pressure* (New York: General Learning Press, 1971).

11. Thucydides was the first in this long line of theorists. Somewhat more recently Kenneth Organski and Robert Gilpin have written in this vein.

12. See, among others, George Modelski, "The Long Cycle of Global Politics and the Nation-State," *Comparative Studies in Society and History* 20 (1978): 214–38; Raimo Vayrynen, "Economic Cycles, Power Transitions, Political Management and Wars between Major Powers," *International Studies Quarterly* 27 (1983): 389–418; Joshua Goldstein, "Kondratieff Waves as War Cycles," *International Studies Quarterly* 29 (1985): 411–44.

Bibliography

Achen, Christopher. 1986. *The Statistical Analysis of Quasi-Experiments*. Berkeley: University of California Press.

Albright, Madeleine. 1983. *Poland: The Role of the Press in Political Change*. New York: Praeger.

Almond, Gabriel. 1950. *The American People and Foreign Policy*. Westport, Conn.: Greenwood Press.

Ansolabehere, Stephen, Roy Behr, and Shanto Iyengar. 1993. *The Media Game: American Politics in the Television Age*. New York: Macmillan.

Aronson, James. 1974. *The Press and the Cold War*. Indianapolis: Bobbs-Merrill.

Arquilla, John. 1992. "Louder than Words: Tacit Communication in International Crises." *Political Communication* 9, no. 3 (July–September): 155–72.

Austen-Smith, David, and William Riker. 1987. "Asymmetric Information and the Coherence of Legislation." *American Political Science Review* 81:897–918.

Axelrod, Robert. 1984. *The Evolution of Cooperation*. New York: Basic Books.

Azar, Edward E. 1978. "An Early Warning Model of International Hostilities." In Nazli Choucri and Thomas Robinson, eds., *Forecasting in International Relations*. New York: W. H. Freeman.

———. 1980. "The Conflict and Peace Data Bank (COPDAB) Project." *Journal of Conflict Resolution* 24:143–52.

Banks, Jeffrey S. 1991. *Signaling Games in Political Science*. Chur, Switz.: Harwood Academic Publishers.

Barnet, Richard. 1990. *The Rocket's Red Glare*. New York: Simon and Schuster.

Bennett, W. Lance. 1990. "Toward a Theory of Press-State Relations." *Journal of Communications* 40, no. 2: 103–25.

Bennett, W. Lance, and Jarol B. Manheim. 1993. "Taking the Public by Storm: Information, Cueing, and the Democratic Process in the Gulf Conflict." *Political Communication* 10, no. 4: 331–51.

Bennett, W. Lance, and David L. Paletz, eds. 1994. *Taken by Storm: The Media, Public Opinion, and U.S. Foreign Policy in the Gulf War*. Chicago: University of Chicago Press.

Betts, Richard K. 1978. "Analysis, War, and Decision: Why Intelligence Failures Are Inevitable." *World Politics* 31, no. 1 (October): 61–89.

———. 1982. *Surprise Attack*. Washington. D.C.: Brookings Institution.

Blair, Bruce. 1985. *Strategic Command and Control: Redefining the Nuclear Threat*. Washington, D.C.: The Brookings Institution.

Block, Eleanor. 1991. *Communication and the Mass Media: A Guide to the Reference Literature.* Englewood Cliffs, N.J.: Libraries Unlimited.

Bracken, Paul. 1983. *The Command and Control of Nuclear Forces.* New Haven: Yale University Press.

Bradsher, Henry S. 1985. *Afghanistan and the Soviet Union.* Durham: Duke University Press.

Brams, Steven. 1985. *Superpower Games.* New Haven, Conn.: Yale University Press.

———. 1990. *Negotiation Games.* New York: Routledge.

———. 1994. *Theory of Moves.* New York: Cambridge University Press.

Brecher, Michael, and Jonathan Wilkenfeld. 1992. *International Crisis Behavior Project, 1918–1988.* ICPSR study no. 9286. Ann Arbor: University of Michigan.

Brody, Richard. 1969. "The Study of International Politics Qua Science." In Klaus Knorr and James N. Rosenau, eds., *Contending Approaches to International Politics.* Princeton: Princeton University Press.

Brzezinski, Zbigniew. 1983. *Power and Principle.* New York: Farrar, Straus, and Giroux.

Bueno de Mesquita, Bruce. 1981. *The War Trap.* New Haven, Conn.: Yale University Press.

———. 1985. "The War Trap Revisited." *American Political Science Review* 79:156–77.

Bueno de Mesquita, Bruce, and David Lalman. 1986. "Reason and War." *American Political Science Review* 80, no. 4: 1113–29.

———. 1992. *War and Reason.* New Haven, Conn.: Yale University Press.

Bueno de Mesquita, Bruce, David Newman, and Alvin Rabushka. 1985. *Forecasting Political Events: The Future of Hong Kong.* New Haven, Conn.: Yale University Press.

Bueno de Mesquita, Bruce, Randolph Siverson, and Gary Woller, 1992. "War and the Fate of Regimes: A Comparative Analysis." *American Political Science Review* 86:638–46.

Burnham, Walter Dean. 1982.*The Current Crisis in American Politics.* New York: Oxford University Press.

Burrowes, Reynold A. 1988. *Revolution and Rescue in Grenada.* Westport, Conn.: Greenwood Press.

Burt, Richard. 1976. "New Weapons Technologies: Debate and Directions." Adelphi Paper no. 126. London: International Institute for Strategic Studies.

Calvert, Randall. 1987. "Reputation and Legislative Leadership." *Public Choice* 55:81–119.

Carter, James E. 1982. *Keeping Faith: Memoirs of a President.* Toronto: Bantam Books.

Chan, Steve. 1984. "Mirror, mirror, on the wall . . . Are the freer countries more pacific?" *Journal of Conflict Resolution* 28, no. 4: 617–64.

Choucri, Nazli, and Robert North. 1975. *Nations in Conflict: National Growth and International Violence.* San Francisco: W. H. Freeman.

Cioffi-Revilla, Claudio. 1979. "Diplomatic Communications Theory: Signals, Channels, Networks." *International Interactions* 6, no. 3: 209–65.

———. 1988. "The Interstate Conflict Datasets Catalog: A Progress Report." *DDIR-Update* 3:1–4.

Collier, Simon. 1983 . "The First Falklands War? Argentine Attitudes." *International Affairs* 57, no. 3 (Summer): 459–64.

Davis, Jack. 1992. "The Challenge of Opportunity Analysis." MS. Center for the Study of Intelligence, July.

de Sola Pool, Ithiel. 1952. *The "Prestige Papers": A Survey of Their Editorials.* Stanford: Stanford University Press.

———. 1978. "The Art of the Social Science Soothsayer." In Nazli Choucri and Thomas Robinson, eds., *Forecasting in International Relations.* New York: W. H. Freeman.

DeHaven, Mark J. 1991. "Internal and External Determinants of Foreign Policy: West Germany and Great Britain during the Two-Track Missile Controversy." *International Studies Quarterly* 35 (March): 87–108.

Deutsch, Karl W. 1954. *Political Community at the International Level: Problems of Definition and Measurement.* Garden City, N.Y.: Doubleday.

———. 1957. "Mass Communications and the Loss of Freedom in National Decisionmaking: A Possible Research Approach to Interstate Conflicts." *Journal of Conflict Resolution* 1, no. 2: 200–211.

Dobson, Christopher, John Miller, and Ronald Payne. 1982. *The Falklands Conflict.* London: Coronet Books.

Downs, George W., David M. Rocke, and Randolph M. Silverson. 1986. "Arms Races and Cooperation." In Kenneth Oye, ed., *Cooperation Under Anarchy.* Princeton: Princeton University Press.

Doyle, Michael. 1986. "Liberalism and World Politics." *American Political Science Review* 80, no. 4: 1151–61.

Eddy, Paul, and Magnus Linklater. 1982. *The Falklands War.* London: Andre Deutsch Ltd.

Fearon, James. 1994. "Domestic Political Audiences and the Escalation of International Disputes." *American Political Science Review* 88, no. 3: 577–92.

Fein, Helen, ed. 1992. *Genocide Watch.* New Haven, Conn.: Yale University Press.

Fischer, Fritz. 1975. *War of Illusions: German Policies from 1911 to 1914.* New York: W. W. Norton.

Fleiss, Joseph L. 1981. *Statistical Methods for Rates and Proportions.* New York: John Wiley and Sons.

Franks, Lord, ed. 1983. *Falkland Islands Review: Report of a Committee of Privy Counselors.* London: Her Majesty's Stationery Office.

Freedman, Lawrence, and Virginia Gamba-Stonehouse. 1991. *Signals of War: The Falklands Conflict of 1982.* Princeton: Princeton University Press.

Freeman, John R. 1990. "Systematic Sampling, Temporal Aggregation, and the Study of Political Relationships." In James Stimson, ed., *Political Analysis,* vol. 1. Ann Arbor: University of Michigan Press.

Friedman, Milton, and Donald Savage. 1948. "The Utility Analysis of Choices Involving Risk." *Journal of Political Economy* 56:279–304.

Galnoor, Itzak, ed. 1977. *Government Secrecy in Democracies.* New York: New York University Press.

Gartner, Scott Sigmund. 1993. "Predicting the Timing of Carter's Decision to Initiate a Hostage Rescue Attempt: Modeling a Dynamic Information Environment." *International Interactions* 18, no. 4: 365–86.

Geller, Henry. 1990. "Mass Communication Policy: Where We Are and Where We Should Be Going." In Judith Lichtenberg, ed., *Democracy and the Mass Media.* Cambridge: Cambridge University Press.

George, Alexander. 1959. *Propaganda Analysis: A Study of Inferences Made from Nazi Propaganda in World War II.* Evanston, Ill.: Row, Peterson.

Gilligan, Thomas. 1994. *Information and Legislative Organization.* Ann Arbor: University of Michigan Press.

Gilligan, Thomas, and Keith Krehbiel. 1989. "Asymmetric Information and Legislative Rules with a Heterogeneous Committee." *American Journal of Political Science* 33:459–90.

Gilpin, Robert. 1981.*War and Change in World Politics.* Cambridge: Cambridge University Press.

Ginsberg, Benjamin. 1986. *The Captive Public: How Mass Opinion Promotes State Power.* New York: Basic Books.

Goldstein, Joshua. 1985. "Kondratieff Waves as War Cycles." *International Studies Quarterly* 29:411–44.

Goldstein, Joshua, and John Freeman. 1990. *Three-Way Street: Strategic Reciprocity in World Politics.* Chicago: University of Chicago Press.

Graber, Doris A. 1968. *Public Opinion, the President, and Foreign Policy: Four Case Studies from the Formative Years.* New York: Holt, Rinehart and Winston.

Green, David. 1987. *Shaping Political Consciousness: The Language of Politics in America from McKinley to Reagan.* Ithaca: Cornell University Press.

Grieco, Joseph. 1988. "Anarchy and the Limits of Cooperation." *International Organization* 42:485–507.

———. 1990. *Cooperation among Nations.* Ithaca: Cornell University Press.

Herman, Edward S., and Noam Chomsky. 1988. *Manufacturing Consent: The Political Economy of the Mass Media.* New York: Pantheon Books.

———. 1988. "Propaganda Mill." *Progressive* (June): 16.

Hertsgaard, Mark. 1988. *On Bended Knee: The Press and the Reagan Presidency.* New York: Farrar, Straus, and Giroux.

Herz, John. 1950. "Idealist Internationalism and the Security Dilemma." *World Politics* 2 (January): 157–80.

Herzog, Chaim. 1982. *The Arab-Israeli Wars: War and Peace in the Middle East from the War of Independence through Lebanon.* New York: Vintage Books.

Hilderbrand, Robert. 1981. *Power and the People: Executive Management of Public Opinion in Foreign Affairs, 1897–1921.* Chapel Hill: University of North Carolina Press.

Hilsman, Roger. 1967. *To Move a Nation.* New York: Doubleday.

Hinckley, Barbara. 1992. *Less than Meets the Eye: Foreign Policy Making and the Myth of the Assertive Congress.* Chicago: University of Chicago Press.

Hoffmann, Stanley. 1965. "The Sound and the Fury: The Social Scientist Versus War in History." *The State of War,* 254–76. New York: Praeger.

Holsti, Ole, Robert North, and Richard Brody. 1968. "Perception and Action in the 1914 Crisis." In J. D. Singer, ed., *Quantitative International Politics.* New York: Free Press.

Hunt, W. Ben. 1996. "International Crisis Escalation: Evidence for Event Horizons." MS. Department of Politics, New York University.

Huntington, Samuel. 1964. *Soldier and the State.* New York: Vintage.

Huth, Paul, Christopher Gelpi, and Scott Bennett. 1993. "The Escalation of Great Power Militarized Disputes: Testing Rational Deterrence Theory and Structural Realism." *American Political Science Review* 87, no. 3 (September): 609–23.

Jackson, Robert. 1975. *South Asian Crisis: India, Pakistan, and Bangladesh.* New York: Praeger.

Jacobs, Brian. 1994. *The Leo Burnett Worldwide Advertising and Media Factbook.* Chicago: Triumph Books.

Jervis, Robert. 1970. *The Logic of Images in International Relations.* Princeton: Princeton University Press.

———. 1976. *Perception and Misperception in International Politics.* Princeton: Princeton University Press.

———. 1978. "Cooperation under the Security Dilemma."*World Politics* 30 (January): 167–214.

———. 1988. "Realism, Game Theory, and Cooperation." *World Politics* 30, no. 3 (April): 324–29.

Juergens, George. 1981. *News from the White House: The Presidential-Press Relationship in the Progressive Era.* Chicago: University of Chicago Press.

Kahneman, Daniel, and Amos Tversky. 1979. "Prospect Theory: An Analysis of Decision under Risk." *Econometrica* 47, no. 2 (March): 263–92.

Kahneman, Daniel, Paul Slovic, and Amos Tversky, eds. 1982. *Judgment under Uncertainty: Heuristics and Biases.* Cambridge: Cambridge University Press.

Keeley, Joseph. 1971. *The Left-Leaning Antenna: Political Bias in Television.* New Rochelle, N.Y.: Arlington House.

Kennan, George. 1984. *American Diplomacy.* Expanded ed. Chicago: University of Chicago Press.

King, Gary. 1989. *Unifying Political Methodology: The Likelihood Theory of Statistical Inference.* Cambridge: Cambridge University Press.

Kirton, John. 1993. "National Mythology and Media Coverage: Mobilizing Consent for Canada's War in the Gulf." *Political Communication* 10, no. 4: 425–41.

Laracey, Mel. "The Presidential Newspaper: The Forgotten Way of Going Public." Paper presented at the 1994 Annual Meeting of the American Political Science Association.

Lasswell, Harold. 1927. *Propaganda Technique in the World War.* New York: Knopf.

———. 1939. *World Revolutionary Propaganda.* New York: Knopf.

Layne, Christopher. 1994. "Kant or Cant: The Myth of the Democratic Peace." *International Security* 19, no. 2 (Fall): 5–49.

Lebow, Richard Ned. 1981. *Between Peace and War.* Baltimore: Johns Hopkins University Press.

Leigh, Michael. 1976. *Mobilizing Consent.* Westport, Conn.: Greenwood Press.

Leng, Russell. 1984. "Reagan and the Russians: Crisis Bargaining Beliefs and the Historical Record." *American Political Science Review* 78, no. 2 (June): 338–52.

Lent, John. 1987. *Global Guide to Media and Communications.* New York: K. G. Saur.

Link, Arthur S. et al., eds. 1980. *The Papers of Woodrow Wilson.* Princeton: Princeton University Press.

Lippencott, Don, and Gregory Treverton. 1988. "Negotiations Concerning the Falklands/Malvinas Dispute." *Pew Case Studies in International Affairs* (no. 406), pt. A.

Lutzker, Michael. 1991. "President Wilson's German and Mexican Policies: Two Crises, One War." Paper presented at the annual meeting of the Society for Historians of American Foreign Relations.

Makin, Guillermo. 1983. "Argentine Approaches to the Falklands/Malvinas: Was the Resort to Violence Foreseeable?" *International Affairs* (Summer): 391–403.

Malone, Dumas. 1951. *Jefferson and His Time.* Vol. 2. Boston: Little, Brown.

Maoz, Zeev. 1982. *Paths to Conflict: International Dispute Initiation, 1816–1976.* Boulder: Westview Press.

———. 1990. *Paradoxes of War.* Boston: Unwin Hyman.

Maoz, Zeev, and Nasrin Abdolali. 1989. "Regime Type and International Conflict, 1816–1976." *Journal of Conflict Resolution* 33, no. 1: 3–35.

Maoz, Zeev, and Bruce Russett. 1993. "Normative and Structural Causes of Democratic Peace, 1946–1986." *American Political Science Review* 87, no. 3 (September): 624–38.

Margolis, Michael, and Gary Mauser, eds. 1989. *Manipulating Public Opinion: Essays on Public Opinion as a Dependent Variable.* Pacific Grove, Calif.: Brooks/Cole Pub. Co.

Martin, L. John, ed. 1983. *Comparative Mass Media Systems.* New York: Longman.

Matthews, Steven. 1989. "Veto Threats: Rhetoric in a Bargaining Game." *Quarterly Journal of Economics* 104: 347–69.

Maurer, Alfred C., Marion D. Tunstall, and James M. Keagle, eds. 1985. *Intelligence: Policy and Process.* Boulder: Westview Press.

May, Ernest R. 1959. *World War and American Isolation.* Cambridge, Mass.: Harvard University Press.

———. 1963. *The Coming of War, 1917.* Berkeley: Berkeley Series in American History.

———. 1986. *Knowing Ones' Enemies: Intelligence Assessment before the Two World Wars.* Princeton: Princeton University Press.

Mayer, Frederick. 1992. "Managing Domestic Differences in International Negotiations: The Strategic Use of Internal Side-payments." *International Organization* 46, no. 4 (Autumn): 793–818.

Mearsheimer, John J. 1990. "Back to the Future: Instability in Europe After the Cold War." *International Security* 15, no. 1: 5–56.

Merritt, Richard L., Robert G. Muncaster, and Dina A. Zinnes, eds. 1993. *International Event-Data Developments: DDIR Phase II.* Ann Arbor: University of Michigan Press.

Mintz, Alex, and Philip A. Schrodt. 1987. "Distributional Patterns of Regional Interactions: A Test of the Poisson Process as a Null Model." In Claudio Cioffi-Revilla, Richard Merritt, and Dina Zinnes, eds., *Communication and Interaction in Global Politics,* 237–54. Beverly Hills, Calif.: Sage Publications.

Mock, James R., and Cedric Larson. 1939. *Words That Won the War.* Princeton: Princeton University Press.

Modelski, George. 1978. "The Long Cycle of Global Politics and the Nation-State." *Comparative Studies in Society and History* 20:214–38.

Mogdis, Franz, and Karen Tidwell. 1971. "Sino-Soviet Interaction 1950–1967: Project Triad." MS. (ICPSR) 5016. University of Michigan.

Morgan, T. Clifton. 1993. "Democracy and War: Reflections of the Literature." *International Interactions* 18, no. 3: 197–203.

———. 1994. *Untying the Knot of War: A Bargaining Theory of International Crises.* Ann Arbor: University of Michigan Press.

Morgan, T. Clifton, and Sally H. Campbell. 1991. "Domestic Structure, Decisional Constraints and War: So Why Kant Democracies Fight?" *Journal of Conflict Resolution* 35:187–211.

Morrow, James. 1987. "On the Theoretical Basis of a Measure of National Risk Attitudes." *International Studies Quarterly,* no. 31: 423–38.

Moses, Russell Leigh. 1989. "Mediation and Private Contacts in the Iran Hostage Crisis, April 1980–January 1981." *Pew Case Studies in International Affairs,* no. 316.

Mueller, John. 1970. "Presidential Popularity from Truman to Johnson." *American Political Science Review* 64: 18–34.

———. 1994. *Policy and Opinion in the Gulf War.* Chicago: University of Chicago Press.

Neuman, W. Russell, Marion Just, and Ann Crigler. 1992. *Common Knowledge: News and the Construction of Political Meaning.* Chicago: University of Chicago Press.

Nicholson, Michael. 1987. "The Conceptual Bases of *The War Trap.*" *Journal of Conflict Resolution* 31, no. 2 (June): 346–69.

Nincic, Miroslav. 1992. *Democracy and Foreign Policy.* New York: Columbia University Press.

North, Robert C. 1967. "Perception and Action in the 1914 Crisis." *Journal of International Affairs* 21, no. 1: 103–22.

———. 1990. *War, Peace, Survival: Global Politics and Conceptual Synthesis.* Boulder, Colo.: Westview Press.

North, Robert C., and Richard Lagerstrom. 1971. *War and Domination: A Theory of Lateral Pressure.* New York: General Learning Press.

Nye, Joseph. 1986. *Nuclear Ethics.* New York: Free Press.

Nylen, William Russell. 1988. "US-Grenada Relations, 1979–1983: American Foreign Policy towards a 'Backyard' Revolution." *Pew Case Study in International Affairs,* no. 306.

Oren, Ido. 1994. "Perceptions of Germany in Early American Political Science: A Parable of the Democratic Peace." MS. Paper presented at the annual meeting of the American Political Science Association.

Organski, A. F. K. 1958. *World Politics.* New York: Knopf.

Organski, A. F. K., and Samuel Eldersveld. 1994. *European Community Decision Making: Models, Application and Comparisons.* Ed. Bruce Bueno de Mesquita. New Haven, Conn.: Yale University Press.

Organski, A. F. K., and Jacek Kugler. 1980. *The War Ledger.* Chicago: University of Chicago Press.

Oye, Kenneth. 1986. "The Sterling-Dollar-Franc Triangle: Monetary Diplomacy 1929–1937." In Kenneth Oye, ed., *Cooperation under Anarchy,* 173–99. Princeton: Princeton University Press.

Perl, Raphael, ed. 1983. *The Falklands Island Dispute in International Law and Politics: A Documentary Sourcebook.* London: Oceana Publications.

Powell, Robert. 1990. *Nuclear Deterrence Theory: The Search for Credibility.* New York: Cambridge University Press.

Pratt, John W. 1964. "Risk Aversion in the Small and in the Large." *Econometrica* 32, nos. 1–2 (January–April): 122–36.

Princen, Thomas. 1988. "Beagle Channel Negotiations." *Pew Case Studies in International Affairs,* no. 401, pts. A, B, and C.

Quester, George. 1977. *Offense and Defense in the International System.* New York: Wiley.

Rao, N. Bhaskara. 1971. *Indo-Pak Conflict: Controlled Mass Communication in Inter-State Relations.* New Delhi: S. Chand.

Rapoport, Anatol, and Melvin Guyer. 1966. "A Taxonomy of 2X2 Games." *General Systems* 11:203–14.

Ray, James Lee, and Bruce Russett. "The Future as Arbiter of Theoretical Controversies: Predictions, Explanations, and the End of the Cold War." MS.

Reginald, R., and Jeffrey M. Elliot. 1983. *Tempest in a Teapot: The Falklands War.* San Bernardino, Calif.: Borgo Press.

Risse-Kappen, Thomas. 1991. "Public Opinion, Domestic Structure, and Foreign Policy in Liberal Democracies." *World Politics* 43 (July): 479–512.

Robertson, K. G. 1982. *Public Secrets: A Study in the Development of Government Secrecy.* Hong Kong: Macmillan.

Rugh, William A. 1979. *The Arab Press.* Syracuse: Syracuse University Press.

Rummel, Rudolph. 1983. "Libertarianism and International Violence." *Journal of Conflict Resolution* 27, no. 1: 27–71.

Russett, Bruce. 1990. *Controlling the Sword.* Cambridge, Mass.: Harvard University Press.

Sagan, Scott. 1986. "1914 Revisited: Allies, Offense and Instability." *International Security* (Fall): 151–77.

Salinger, Pierre, and Eric Laurent. 1991. *Secret Dossier: The Hidden Agenda behind the Gulf War.* New York: Penguin Books.

Schelling, Thomas. 1960. *Strategy of Conflict.* Cambridge, Mass.: Harvard University Press.

Schelling, Thomas, and Morton Halperin. 1961. *Strategy and Arms Control.* New Haven, Conn.: Yale University Press.

Serfaty, Simon, ed. 1991.*The Media and Foreign Policy.* New York: St. Martin's Press.

Seymour, Charles. 1934. *American Diplomacy during the World War.* Baltimore: Johns Hopkins Press.

Shlaim, Avi. 1983. *The United States and the Berlin Blockade, 1948–1949.* Berkeley: University of California Press.

Sigelman, Lee, James Lebovic, Clyde Wilcox, and Dee Allsop. 1993. "As Time Goes By: Daily Opinion Change during the Persian Gulf Crisis." *Political Communication* 10, no. 4: 353–67.

Singer, J. David, and Melvin Small. 1972. *The Wages of War 1816–1965: A Statistical Handbook.* New York: John Wiley and Sons.

————. *Wages of War, 1816–1980,: Augmented with Disputes and Civil War Data.* University of Michigan, ICPSR study no. 9044.

Singer, J. David, and Paul F. Diehl, eds. 1990. *Measuring the Correlates of War.* Ann Arbor: University of Michigan Press.

Singer, J. David, Stuart Bremer, and John Stuckey. 1972. "Capability Distribution, Uncertainty, and Major Power War, 1820–1965." In Bruce Russett, ed., *Peace, War, and Numbers.* Beverly Hills, Calif.: Sage Publications.

Siverson, Randolph, and Ross Miller. "The Escalation of Disputes to War." *International Interactions* 19, nos. 1–2: 77–97.

Siverson, Randolph, and Harvey Starr. 1991. *The Diffusion of War: A Study of Opportunity and Willingness.* Ann Arbor: University of Michigan Press.

Small, Melvin, and J. David Singer. 1976. "The War Proneness of Democratic Regimes." *Jerusalem Journal of International Relations* 1, no.1: 41–64.

Snyder, Glenn, and Paul Diesing. 1977. *Conflict among Nations.* Princeton: Princeton University Press.

Snyder, Jack. 1985. "Civil-Military Relations and the Cult of the Offensive, 1914 and 1984." In Steven E. Miller, ed., *Military Strategy and the Origins of the First World War.* Princeton: Princeton University Press.

Spence, Michael. 1974. *Market Signaling: Informational Transfer in Hiring and Related Screening Processes.* Cambridge, Mass.: Harvard University Press.

Spiro, David. 1994. "The Insignificance of the Liberal Peace." *International Security* 19, no. 2 (Fall): 50–86.

Sproule, J. Michael. 1987. "Propaganda Studies in American Social Science: The Rise and Fall of the Critical Paradigm." *Quarterly Journal of Speech* (February): 60–77.

Staniland, Martin. 1993. "Getting to No—the Diplomacy of the Gulf Conflict, August 2, 1990–January 15, 1991." *Pew Case Studies in International Affairs,* no. 449, pts 1–3.

Stein, Arthur. 1980. "The Politics of Linkage." *World Politics* 33, no. 1 (October): 62–81.

————. 1982. "When Misperception Matters." *World Politics* 34, no. 4 (July): 505–26.

Stevenson, Robert L., and Donald L. Shaw, eds. 1984. *Foreign News and the New World Information Order.* Ames: Iowa State University Press.

Symms, S. D., and E. D. Snow Jr. 1981. "Soviet Propaganda and the Neutron Bomb Decision." *Political Communication and Persuasion* 1:257–68.

Tetlock, Philip. 1985. "Integrative Complexity of American and Soviet Foreign Policy Rhetoric: A Time-Series Analysis." *Journal of Personality and Social Psychology* 49, no. 6: 1565–85.

————. 1988. "Monitoring the Integrative Complexity of American and Soviet Policy Rhetoric: What Can Be Learned?" *Journal of Social Issues* 44, no. 2: 101–31.

Tetlock, Philip, and Charles B. McGuire Jr. 1984. "Integrative Complexity of Soviet Rhetoric as a Predictor of Soviet Behavior." *International Journal of Group Tensions* 14, nos. 1–4: 113–28.

Tiruneh, Andargachew. 1993. *The Ethiopian Revolution: 1974–1987.* London: Cambridge University Press.

Truman, Harry S. 1956. *Memoirs of Harry S. Truman.* Vol. 2. New York: Da Capo Press.

U.S. Arms Control and Disarmament Agency. 1986. *The Soviet Propaganda Campaign against the U.S. Strategic Defense Initiative.* Washington, D.C.: USGPO.

United Nations Educational, Scientific, and Cultural Organization (UNESCO). 1975. *World Communications.* New York: Gower Press.

United Nations (UN). 1992. *World Media Handbook.* New York: UN Department of Public Information.

Valenta, Jiri. 1979. *Soviet Intervention in Czechoslovakia, 1968: Anatomy of a Decision.* Baltimore: Johns Hopkins University Press.

Van Evera, Stephen. 1985. "The Cult of the Offensive and the Origins of the First World War." In Steven E. Miller, ed., *Military Strategy and the Origins of the First World War.* Princeton: Princeton University Press.

Vance, Cyrus. 1983. *Hard Choices.* New York: Simon and Schuster.

Varian, Hal. 1984. *Microeconomic Analysis.* 2d ed. New York: W. W. Norton.

Vaughn, Stephen. 1980. *Holding Fast the Inner Lines.* Chapel Hill: University of North Carolina Press.

Vayrynen, Raimo. 1983. "Economic Cycles, Power Transitions, Political Management and Wars between Major Powers." *International Studies Quarterly* 27:389–418.

Wagner, R. Harrison. 1984. "War and Expected Utility Theory." *World Politics* 36, no. 3 (April): 407–23.

Walker, Stephen, and George Watson. 1994. "Integrative Complexity and British Decisions during the Munich and Polish Crises." *Journal of Conflict Resolution* 38, no. 1 (March): 3–23.

Wallace, Michael, and Peter Suedfeld. 1988. "Leadership Performance in Crisis: The Longevity-Complexity Link." *International Studies Quarterly* 32, no. 4 (December): 439–51.

Waltz, Kenneth. 1979. *Theory of International Politics.* Reading, Mass.: Addison-Wesley.

Ward, Michael Don. 1982. "Cooperation and Conflict in Foreign Policy Behavior." *International Studies Quarterly* 26, no. 1 (March): 87–126.

Weede, Erich. 1984. "Democracy and War Involvement." *Journal of Conflict Resolution* 28, no. 4: 649–64.

Wellborn, Fred W. 1966. *Diplomatic History of the United States.* Ottawa: Littlefield, Adams.

Whiting, Alan. 1960. *China Crosses the Yalu.* New York: Macmillan.

Wich, Richard. 1980. *Sino-Soviet Crisis Politics: A Study of Political Change and Communication.* Cambridge, Mass: Council on East Asian Studies.

Wolfers, Arnold. 1962. *Discord and Collaboration.* Baltimore: Johns Hopkins Press.

Woodward, Bob. 1991. *The Commanders.* New York: Simon and Schuster.

Wyden, Peter H. 1979. *Bay of Pigs: The Untold Story.* New York: Simon and Schuster.

Yeager, Rodger. 1989. *Tanzania: An African Experiment.* Boulder, Colo.: Westview Press.

Zaller, John. 1992. *The Nature and Origins of Mass Opinion.* New York: Cambridge University Press.

Zartman, William. 1976. *The Fifty-Percent Solution.* Garden City, N.Y.: Anchor Books.

Zimmerman, William, and Glenn Palmer. 1983. "Words and Deed in Soviet Foreign Policy: The Case of Soviet Military Expenditures." *American Political Science Review* 77, no. 2 (June): 358–67.

Zinnes, Dina A. 1968. "Expression and Perception of Hostility in Prewar Crisis: 1914." In J. D. Singer, ed., *Quantitative International Politics,* 85–119. New York: Free Press.

———. 1975. "Research Frontiers in the Study of International Politics." In Fred Greenstein and Nelson Polsby, eds., *Handbook of Political Science,* vol. 8: *International Politics.* New York: Addison-Wesley.

———. 1984. "Hostile Activity and the Prediction of War." *Journal of Conflict Resolution* 28, no. 2 (June): 187–230.

Zinnes, Dina A., and Robert Muncaster. 1987. "Transaction Flows and Integrative Processes." In Claudio Cioffi-Revilla, Richard Merritt, and Dina Zinnes, eds., *Communication and Interaction in Global Politics,* 23–48. Beverly Hills, Calif.: Sage Publications.

Index

DATE DUE

APR 2 3 1999			
MAY 0 9 2003			
DEC 1 9 2003			
GAYLORD			PRINTED IN U.S.A